TOTAL READING

GRADE 4

AMERICAN EDUCATION PUBLISHING™

Columbus, Ohio

Copyright © 2005 School Specialty Publishing. Published by American Education Publishing™, an imprint of School Specialty Publishing, a member of the School Specialty Family.

Send all inquiries to:
School Specialty Publishing
8720 Orion Place
Columbus, OH 43240-2111

ISBN 0-7696-3884-8

5 6 7 8 9 10 WAL 09 08 07

Table of Contents

Phonics and Vocabulary

Reading Skills and Comprehension

Name _____

Short Vowels

Vowels are the letters **a, e, i, o, u**, and sometimes **y**. There are five short vowels: **ă** as in **a**pple, **ĕ** as in **e**gg and br**ea**th, **ĭ** as in **i**gloo, **ŏ** as in t**o**p, and **ŭ** as in **u**p.

Directions: Complete the exercises using words from the box.

blend	insist	health	pump	crop
fact	pinch	pond	hatch	plug

1. Write each word below its vowel sound.

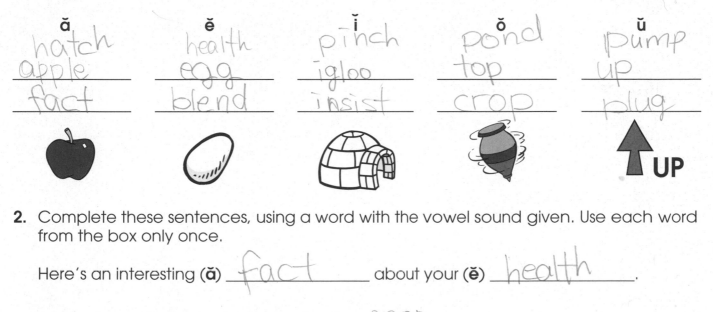

ă	**ĕ**	**ĭ**	**ŏ**	**ŭ**
hatch	health	pinch	pond	pump
apple	egg	igloo	top	up
fact	blend	insist	crop	plug

2. Complete these sentences, using a word with the vowel sound given. Use each word from the box only once.

Here's an interesting (**ă**) _fact_ about your (**ĕ**) _health_.

Henry was very pleased with his corn (**ŏ**) _crop_.

The boys enjoyed fishing in the (**ŏ**) _pond_.

They (**ĭ**) _insist_ on watching the egg (**ă**) _hatch_.

(**ĕ**) _Blend_ in a (**ĭ**) _pinch_ of salt.

The farmer had to (**ŭ**) _pump_ water from the lake for his cows to drink.

Did you put the (**ŭ**) _plug_ in the bathtub this time?

Name __Jung Min__

Short Vowels

Directions: Read the words. After each, write the correct vowel sound. Underline the letter or letters that spell the sound in the word. The first one has been done for you.

	Word	Vowel			Word	Vowel
1.	str__u__ck	U	9.	br__ea__th	ea
2.	scr__a__mble	a	10.	__e__dge	e
3.	str__o__ng	o	11.	k__i__ck	i
4.	ch__i__ll	i	12.	st__o__p	o
5.	th__u__d	u	13.	qu__i__z	أون
6.	dr__ea__d	eَa	14.	br__u__sh	u
7.	pl__u__nge	u	15.	cr__a__sh	a
8.	m__a__sk	a	16.	d__o__dge	o

Directions: List four words (nouns and verbs) with short vowel sounds. Then, write two sentences using the words.

Example: Ann, can, hand, Pam
        Ann can give Pam a hand.

__breath, sister, can, Tom__

_____

_____

_____

1. __Tom's sister can breath all the time.__

_____

2. _____

_____

I. Reading
A. Directions
B. Sequencing
C. Main Idea
II. Writing
A. Capitalization
B. Proofreading

Name _Jung Min_

Listening for Vowels

Directions: Circle the word in each row with the same vowel sound as the first word. The first one has been done for you.

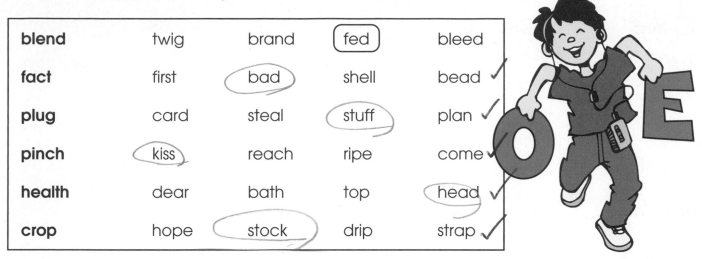

blend	twig	brand	(fed)	bleed
fact	first	(bad)	shell	bead ✓
plug	card	steal	(stuff)	plan ✓
pinch	(kiss)	reach	ripe	come ✓
health	dear	bath	top	(head) ✓
crop	hope	(stock)	drip	strap ✓

Directions: Write the words from the box that answer the questions.

(blend) (insist) (health) (pump) (crop) fact (pinch) (fond) (hatch) (plug)

1. Which two words have the same vowel sound as the first vowel in **bundle**?

   pump ✓ , _plug_ ✓

2. Which two words have the same vowel sound as the first vowel in **bottle**?

   crop ✓ , _fond_ ✓

3. Which two words have the same vowel sound as the first vowel in **wilderness**?

   insist ✓ , _pinch_ ✓

4. Which two words have the same vowel sound as the first vowel in **manner**?

   fact ✓ , _hatch_ ✓

5. Which two words have the same vowel sound as the first vowel in **measure**?

   health ✓ , _blend_ ✓

GRADE 4

I. Reading
  A. Directions
  B. Sequencing
  C. Main Idea
II. Writing
  A. Capitalization
  B. Proofreading

Name _____

Long e and a

Long ē can be spelled **ea** as in **real** or **ee** as in **deer**. Long ā can be spelled **a** as in **apron**, **ai** as in **pail**, **ay** as in **pay**, or **a-e** as in **lake**.

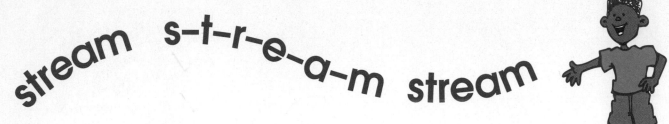

stream   s–t–r–e–a–m   stream

Directions: Complete the exercises with words from the box.

deal	clay	grade	weave	stream
pain	tape	sneeze	claim	treat

1. Write each word in the row with the matching vowel sound.

   ā   _____ _____ _____ _____ _____

   ē   _____ _____ _____ _____ _____

2. Complete each sentence, using a word with the vowel sound given. Use each word from the word box only once.

   Everyone in (ā) _____ four ate an ice-cream (ē) _____.

   Every time I (ē) _____, I feel (ā) _____ in my chest.

   When I (ē) _____ with yarn, I put a piece of (ā) _____ on the loose ends so they won't come undone.

   You (ā) _____ you got a good (ē) _____ on your new bike, but I still think you paid too much.

   We camped beside a (ē) _____.

   We forgot to wrap up our (ā) _____ and it dried out.

Long e and a

When a vowel is long, it sounds the same as its letter name.

Examples: Long ē as in **treat**, **eel**, **complete**.
Long ā as in **ape**, **trail**, **say**, **apron**.

Directions: Read the words. After each word, write the correct vowel sound. Underline the letter or letters that spell the sound in the word. The first one has been done for you.

Word	Vowel	Word	Vowel
1. sp<u>ee</u>ch	e	9. plate	_____
2. grain	_____	10. breeze	_____
3. deal	_____	11. whale	_____
4. baste	_____	12. clay	_____
5. teach	_____	13. veal	_____
6. waiting	_____	14. apron	_____
7. cleaning	_____	15. raining	_____
8. crane	_____	16. freezer	_____

Directions: Choose one long vowel sound. On another sheet of paper, list six words (nouns and verbs) that have that sound. Below, write two sentences using the words.

Example: freeze, teaches, breeze, speech, keep, Eve

Eve teaches speech in the breeze.

_____

_____

Name _____

Vowel Sounds

Directions: Follow the instructions below.

1. Circle the word in each row with the same vowel sound as the first word. The first one has been done for you.

deal	pail	church	(greet)	stove
pain	free	frame	twice	whole
weave	grape	stripe	least	thrill
grade	teach	case	joke	leave
treat	greed	throw	tent	truck

2. Write a word from the box that rhymes with each word below.

deal	clay	grade	weave	stream	pain	tape	sneeze	claim	treat

lame _____   shape _____

may _____   feel _____

cream _____   leave _____

laid _____   drain _____

feet _____   trees _____

3. The words below are written the way they are pronounced. Write the word from the box that sounds like:

klā _____   klām _____

wēv _____   trēt _____

dēl _____   grād _____

strēm _____   pān _____

tāp _____   snēz _____

Making New Words

Directions: Unscramble these letters to spell the ā and ē words you have been practicing. If you need help with spelling, look at the box on page 8. The first one has been done for you.

ay + lc   = ___clay___   ee + zsne = _____

ea + mtrs = _____   a-e + pt   = _____

ea + vew = _____   a-e + drg = _____

ea + rtt = _____   ai + np   = _____

ea + ld   = _____   ai + mlc = _____

Directions: Circle the spelling mistakes and write the words correctly. The first one has been done for you.

1. We made statues out of (cley).   ___clay___

2. Do you ever fish in that streem?   _____

3. Jason sneesed really loudly in class.   _____

4. Running gives me a pane in my side.   _____

5. We are tapeing the show for you.   _____

6. She klaims she won, but I came in first. _____

7. Would you share your treet with me?   _____

8. He is gradeing our papers right now.   _____

9. She is weeving a placemat of ribbons.   _____

10. What is the big deel, anyway?   _____

Name _____

Long i and o

Long ī can be spelled **i** as in **wild**, **igh** as in **night**, **i-e** as in **wipe**, or **y** as in **try**. Long ō can be spelled **o** as in **most**, **oa** as in **toast**, **ow** as in **throw**, or **o-e** as in **hope**.

| stripe | groan | glow | toast | grind | fry | sight | stove | toads | flight |

Directions: Complete the exercises with words from the box.

1. Write each word from the box with its vowel sound.

ī _____

ō _____

2. Complete these sentences, using a word with the given vowel sound. Use each word from the box only once.

We will (ī) _____ potatoes on the (ō) _____.

I thought I heard a low (ō) _____, but when I looked, there was nothing

in (ī) _____.

The airplane for our (ī) _____ had a (ī) _____ painted on its side.

I saw a strange (ō) _____ coming from the toaster while

making (ō) _____.

Do (ō) _____ live in the water like frogs?

We need to (ī) _____ up the nuts before we put them in the cookie dough.

Name _____

Long i and o

Directions: Read the words. After each word, write the correct long vowel sound. Underline the letter or letters that spell the sound. The first one has been done for you.

Word	Vowel		Word	Vowel
1. br<u>i</u>ght	i		9. white	_____
2. globe	_____		10. roast	_____
3. plywood	_____		11. light	_____
4. mankind	_____		12. shallow	_____
5. coaching	_____		13. myself	_____
6. prize	_____		14. throne	_____
7. grind	_____		15. cold	_____
8. withhold	_____		16. snow	_____

Directions: Below are words written as they are pronounced. Write the words that sound like:

1. thrōn _____ 5. brīt _____

2. skōld _____ 6. grīnd _____

3. prīz _____ 7. plīwood _____

4. rōst _____ 8. mīself _____

GRADE 4

I. Reading
   A. Directions
   B. Sequencing
   C. Main Idea
II. Writing
   A. Capitalization
   B. Proofreading

Name _____

Long u

Long **ū** can be spelled, **u-e** as in **cube** or **ew** as in **few**. Some sounds are similar in sound to **u** but are not true **u** sounds, such as the **oo** in **tooth**, the **o-e** in **move**, and the **ue** in **blue**.

Directions: Complete each sentence using a word from the box. Do not use the same word more than once.

blew
tune
flute
cute
stew
June
glue

1. Yesterday, the wind _____ so hard it knocked down a tree on our street.

2. My favorite instrument is the _____.

3. The little puppy in the window is so _____.

4. I love _____ because it's so warm, and we get out of school.

5. For that project, you will need scissors, construction paper, and _____.

6. I recognize that song because it has a familiar _____.

7. My grandmother's beef _____ is the best I've ever tasted.

GRADE
4

I. Reading
  A. Directions
  B. Sequencing
  C. Main Idea
II. Writing
  A. Capitalization
  B. Proofreading

Name _____

The Long and Short of It

Directions: Fill in the circle next to the word that has the same vowel sound as the first word in the row.

1. **shop**	○ lot	○ should	○ show	○ load
2. **huge**	○ bug	○ team	○ bib	○ suit
3. **seal**	○ mice	○ meet	○ whole	○ side
4. **pin**	○ pine	○ pan	○ till	○ slide
5. **lock**	○ luck	○ pot	○ cloak	○ load
6. **peg**	○ sale	○ bead	○ bed	○ raid
7. **ran**	○ rain	○ sit	○ pat	○ race
8. **mile**	○ bee	○ mean	○ moan	○ mine
9. **fox**	○ rock	○ duck	○ axe	○ toad
10. **dime**	○ dim	○ tile	○ dip	○ deep
11. **doe**	○ wave	○ hot	○ low	○ dot
12. **us**	○ bun	○ use	○ fuse	○ box
13. **ride**	○ rain	○ road	○ pie	○ rip
14. **sit**	○ map	○ find	○ ties	○ fill
15. **bone**	○ time	○ soap	○ band	○ bond
16. **nuts**	○ bus	○ let	○ sand	○ tune
17. **jet**	○ jeans	○ bean	○ red	○ jut
18. **paid**	○ pad	○ main	○ lad	○ lied
19. **bell**	○ tall	○ ball	○ bead	○ test
20. **ape**	○ pay	○ cap	○ tap	○ tie

Name _____

The k Sound

The **k** sound can be spelled with **k** as in **peek**, **c** as in **cousin**, **ck** as in **sick**, **ch** as in **Chris**, and **cc** as in **accuse**. In some words, however, one **c** may be pronounced **k** and the other **s** as in **accident**.

Directions: Answer the questions with words from the box.

ache	freckles	command	cork	jacket
accused	castle	stomach	rake	accident

1. Which two words spell **k** with a **k**?

   _____   _____

2. Which two words spell **k** with **ck**?

   _____   _____

3. Which two words spell **k** with **ch**?

   _____   _____

4. Which five words spell **k** with **c** or **cc**? _____

   _____   _____

   _____   _____

5. Complete these sentences, using a word with **k** spelled as shown. Use each word from the box only once.

   The wooden (**k**) _____ made my hands (**ch**) _____.

   There are (**ck**) _____ on my face and (**ch**) _____.

   The people (**cc**) _____ her of taking a (**ck**) _____.

   The police took (**c**) _____ after the (**cc**) _____.

   The model of the (**c**) _____ was made out of

   (**c and k**) _____.

Name _____

The f Sound

The **f** sound can be spelled with **f** as in **fun**, **gh** as in **laugh**, or **ph** as in **phone**.

Directions: Answer the questions with words from the box.

fuss	paragraph	phone	friendship	freedom
defend	flood	alphabet	rough	laughter

1. Which three words spell **f** with **ph**?

   _____ _____ _____

2. Which two words spell **f** with **gh**?

   _____ _____

3. Which five words spell **f** with an **f**?

   _____ _____ _____

   _____ _____

4. Complete these sentences, using a word with **f** spelled as shown. Use each word from the box only once.

   I don't know why my teacher makes so much (**f**) _____ over writing

   a (**ph**) _____.

   A (**f**) _____ can help you through (**gh**) _____ times.

   The soldiers will (**f**) _____ our (**f**) _____.

   Can you say the (**ph**) _____ backwards?

   When I answered the (**ph**) _____, all I could

   hear was (**gh**) _____.

   If it keeps raining, we'll have a (**f**) _____.

Name _____

The s Sound

The **s** sound can be spelled with **s** as in **super** or **ss** as in **assign**, **c** as in **city**, **ce** as in **fence**, or **sc** as in **scene**. In some words, though, **sc** is pronounced **sk**, as in **scare**.

Directions: Answer the questions using words from the box.

exciting	medicine	lettuce	peace	scissors
slice	scientist	sauce	bracelet	distance

1. Which five words spell **s** with just an **s** or **ss**?

_____ _____ _____

_____ _____

2. Which two words spell **s** with just a **c**?

_____ _____

3. Which six words spell **s** with a **ce**?

_____ _____ _____

_____ _____ _____

4. Which two words spell **s** with **sc**?

_____ _____

5. Complete these sentences, using a word with **s** spelled as shown. Use each word from the box only once.

My (**ce**) _____ fell off my wrist into the tomato

_____ (**s** and **ce**).

My salad was just a (**s** and **ce**) _____ of (**ce**) _____.

It was (**c**) _____ to see the lions, even though they were a long

(**s** and **ce**) _____ away.

The (**sc** and **s**) _____ invented a new (**c**) _____.

If I lend you my (**sc**) _____ , will you leave me in

(**ce**) _____ ?

Name _____

Syllables

A **syllable** is a word—or part of a word—with only one vowel sound. Some words have just one syllable, such as **cat**, **dog**, and **house**. Some words have two syllables, such as **in-sist** and **be-fore**. Some words have three syllables, such as **re-mem-ber**; four syllables, such as **un-der-stand-ing**; or more. Often words are easier to spell if you know how many syllables they have.

Directions: Write the number of syllables in each word below.

Word	Syllables	Word	Syllables
1. amphibian	_____	11. want	_____
2. liter	_____	12. communication	_____
3. guild	_____	13. pedestrian	_____
4. chili	_____	14. kilo	_____
5. vegetarian	_____	15. autumn	_____
6. comedian	_____	16. dinosaur	_____
7. warm	_____	17. grammar	_____
8. piano	_____	18. dry	_____
9. barbarian	_____	19. solar	_____
10. chef	_____	20. wild	_____

Directions: Next to each number, write words with the same number of syllables.

1 _____ _____ _____ _____

2 _____ _____ _____

3 _____ _____ _____

4 _____ _____ _____

5 _____ _____

Name _____

Syllables

Directions: Write each word from the box next to the number that shows how many syllables it has.

fuss	paragraph	phone	friendship	freedom
defend	flood	alphabet	rough	laughter

One: _____ _____ _____ _____

Two: _____ _____ _____ _____

Three: _____ _____

> How many syllables are there in the word *friendship*?

Directions: Circle the two words in each row that have the same number of syllables as the first word.

Example: fact (clay) happy (phone) command

rough	freckle	pump	accuse	ghost
jacket	flood	laughter	defend	photograph
accident	paragraph	carpenter	stomach	castle
~~comfort~~	agree	friend	friendship	health
	collect	blend	freedom	hatch
	thankful	notebook	enemy	unhappy
	midnight	defending	grading	telephone

Sweet Syllables

Directions: Write the number of syllables you hear in each word.

pear	Africa	magnify	feast
Olympic	cheese	supper	flash
Samantha	lemonade	husband	skate
peanut	expected	dress	pineapple
magic	sesame	pizza	hamburger

Name _____

Syllables

Directions: Color the spaces for each word:

green if the word has **4 syllables**

blue if the word has **3 syllables**

brown if the word has **2 syllables**

red if the word has **1 syllable**

What is it? _____

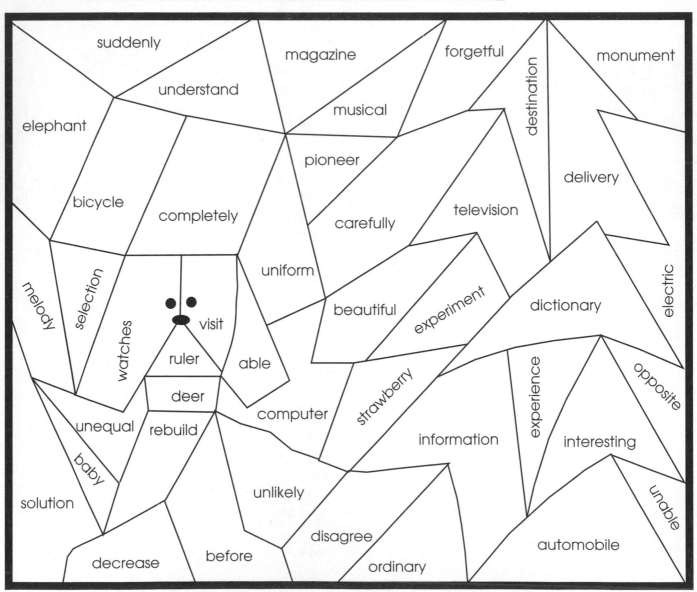

Name _____

Synonyms

Synonyms are words that mean the **same** thing.
> **Big** and **huge** are **synonyms**.
> **Tiny** and **small** are **synonyms**.

Directions: Circle the synonym for each word.

ugly	humbly	hasty	homely	hosiery
mean	vicious	vigorous	various	valiant
kind	generate	generous	genius	general
beautiful	eloquent	elevate	element	elegant

Write a paragraph using the four words you circled.

_____

_____

_____

_____

_____

_____

_____

GRADE 4

I. Reading
A. Directions
B. Sequencing
C. Main Idea
II. Writing
A. Capitalization
B. Proofreading

Name _____

Synonyms

Directions: Write a synonym for each word from the word box.

1 timid
_____

2 large
_____

3 rush
_____

4 ill
_____

yell	under	small
smile	sick	big
close	help	start
stay	shy	talk
stop	hurry	fix

7 scream
_____

8 begin
_____

5 tiny
_____

6 repair
_____

12 below
_____

9 grin
_____

10 aid
_____

11 remain
_____

13 halt
_____

14 speak
_____

15 shut
_____

Name _____

Antonyms

Antonyms are words that mean the **opposite**.
    Big and **small** are **antonyms**.
    Hot and **cold** are **antonyms**.

Directions: Look at the picture and read the sentence. Circle the word that does **not** make sense. Then, write the word that would make the sentence true.

I. Pam is surprised because there is something in the box.

_____

nothing   everything

2. The plane will leave at one o'clock.

_____

runway   arrive

3. Tim doesn't know that there is a bee on the front of his shirt.

_____

sleeve   back

4. When you set the table, place the fork on the right side of the plate.

_____

left   same

5. Kim is sad because she found the missing bunny.

_____

tired   happy

6. He stayed in bed because he was well.

_____

sick   young

I. Reading
   A. Directions
   B. Sequencing
   C. Main Idea
II. Writing
   A. Capitalization
   B. Proofreading

Name _____

Antonyms

Directions: Circle the pair of antonyms in each box. Complete each sentence with one of the circled words.

sweet	quiet	noisy	fast

1. The blowing horns were _____.

2. It was _____ in the library.

rough	empty	smooth	straight

3. The cat's fur felt _____.

4. The sandpaper was _____.

close	wrong	near	right

5. Never drive the _____ way on a one-way street.

6. Jan has the _____ answer.

bought	decorated	sent	sold

7. I _____ my old bike when I outgrew it.

8. Mom _____ me a warmer jacket.

laugh	sleepy	lose	find

9. Did you _____ the key I lost?

10. In a strange place, it's easy to _____ your way.

break	own	hurt	repair

11. A flying ball might _____ a window.

12. He needed tools to _____ the car.

Name _____

Homophones

Homophones are two words that sound the same, have different meanings, and are usually spelled differently.

Example: **write** and **right**

Directions: Write the correct homophone in each sentence below.

weight — how heavy something is
wait — to be patient

threw — tossed
through — passing between

steal — to take something that doesn't belong to you
steel — a heavy metal

1. The bands marched _____ the streets lined with many cheering people.

2. _____ for me by the flagpole.

3. One of our strict rules at school is: Never _____ from another person.

4. Could you estimate the _____ of this bowling ball?

5. The bleachers have _____ rods on both ends and in the middle.

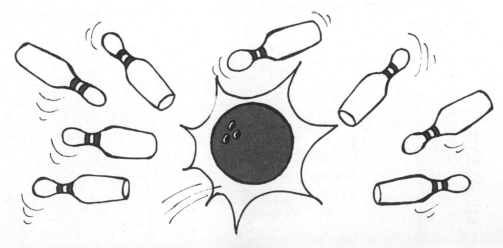

Name _____

Homophones

Directions: Write the correct homophone in each sentence below.

cent — a coin having the value of one penny
scent — odor or aroma

chews — grinds with the teeth
choose — to select

course — the path along which something moves
coarse — rough in texture

heard — received sounds in the ear
herd — a group of animals

1. My uncle Mike always _____

   each bite of his food 20 times!

2. As we walked through her garden, we detected

   the _____ of roses.

3. It was very peaceful sitting on the hillside watching

   the _____ of cattle grazing.

4. Which flavor of ice cream did you _____ ?

5. The friendly clerk let me buy the jacket even though I was one _____ short.

6. You will need _____ sandpaper to make the wood smoother.

Name _____

Homophone Hype

= **b**

```
G S B R I D L E W O J M
E H R Q M N S L H G V A
G N I L A X H E A R W N
D R D W I C R N F A S E
R M A I N E Q I S Z K R
V G L Y W N F S C E N T
N D I N S T L L K H N S
R U U O N P W E I G H T
D E W S P C H D L V E Y
O F A I S L E I L B R L
R L Y O M S Y E R G T   A
```

Directions: For each word given below, list the homophones in the spaces provided. Find and circle the homophone in the word search. Then, write a sentence using the given word and at least one homophone.

1. here _____

   Sentence: _____

2. bridle _____

   Sentence: _____

3. I'll _____ _____

   Sentence: _____

4. graze (Hint: plural form of a color) _____ _____

   Sentence: _____

5. main _____ _____

   Sentence: _____

6. whey _____ _____

   Sentence: _____

7. dew _____ _____

   Sentence: _____

8. scent _____ _____

   Sentence: _____

Name _____

Stop for Directions

Directions: Follow the directions to draw a picture in the rectangle.

1. Draw a yellow house in the middle of the rectangle.

2. On the right side of the house, draw a tree.

3. Draw seven red apples growing on the tree.

4. Draw a big yellow sun shining in the upper right-hand corner.

5. Draw two red birds flying in the sky over the house.

6. Draw a black cat sitting in front of the house.

7. Underneath the apple tree, draw a patch of green grass and three purple tulips.

8. To the left of the house, draw a boy wearing a green baseball cap.

Making a Flag

Directions: Read about the fourth-grade's flag.

Miss Freed's fourth-grade class just finished studying flags. They learned that countries, states, and even some cities and towns have flags. So, they decided to design a class flag.

They chose blue felt for the background and agreed to use other felt and fabric scraps to make objects for the flag.

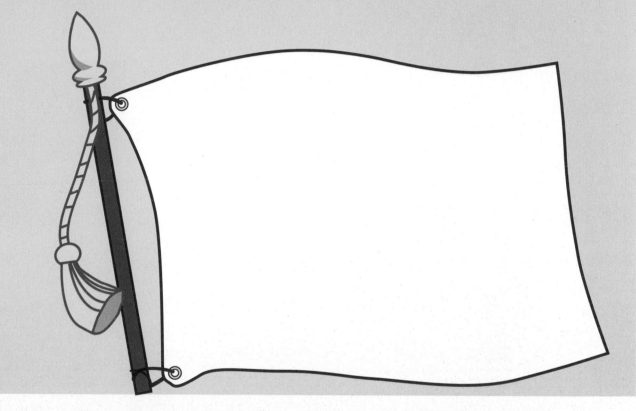

Directions: Now, follow the numbered directions to draw what the flag looks like.

1. They put the school mascot, a duck, in the bottom left corner.

2. They put the class pet, a bunny, in the middle of the flag.

3. The fourth grade had won second place for its bubble-gum ice cream at the ice-cream social. So, they put a second-place ribbon and an ice-cream cone in the top right corner.

4. The boys won the basketball tournament this year, and the girls won the volleyball tournament. They put a big trophy and two balls in the upper left-hand corner.

5. Since everyone enjoys reading, they put a book in the lower right corner.

Name _____

Directions Dilemma

Mark invited a new friend to his house. Since he couldn't remember the street names, Mark used landmarks to give his friend directions.

Directions: Follow Mark's directions. Draw a route on the map for Mark's friend to follow.

1. Starting at school, head down the street that runs past Sam's Supermarket.

2. Then, turn left just past City Hall.

3. Next, turn right on the street that runs in between the park and the mall.

4. Go straight until you come to the baseball fields, park, and ponds. Then, turn left.

5. After you pass the first pond, my house is the first house on the left.

6. Draw a star on Mark's house.

7. Draw a swimming pool in Mark's backyard. Draw a fence around it.

GRADE
4

I. Reading
   A. Directions
   B. Sequencing
   C. Main Idea
II. Writing
   A. Capitalization
   B. Proofreading

Name _____

Following Directions: Maps

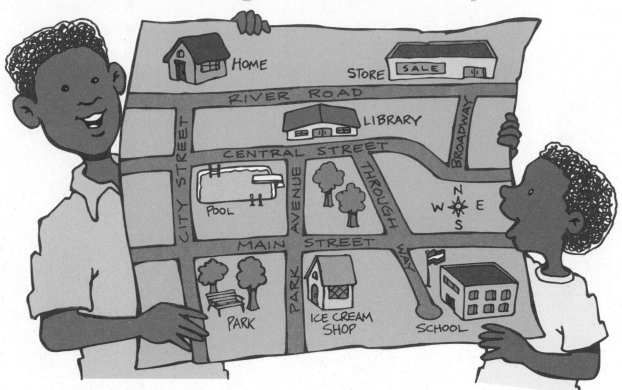

Directions: Follow the directions below to reach a "mystery" location on the map.

1. Begin at home.
2. Drive east on River Road.
3. Turn south on Broadway.
4. Drive to Central Street and turn west.
5. When you get to City Street, turn south.
6. Turn east on Main Street and drive one block to Park Avenue; turn north.
7. At Central Street turn east, then turn southeast on Through Way.
8. Drive to the end of Through Way. Your "mystery" location is to the east.

You are at the _____ .

Can you write an easier way to get back home?

_____

_____

_____

Name _____

Following Directions: Recipes

Sequencing is putting items or events in logical order.

Directions: Read the recipe. Then, number the steps in order for making brownies.

Preheat the oven to 350 degrees. Grease an 8-inch square baking dish.

In a mixing bowl, place two squares (2 ounces) of unsweetened chocolate and ⅓ cup butter. Place the bowl in a pan of hot water and heat it to melt the chocolate and the butter.

When the chocolate is melted, remove the pan from the heat. Add 1 cup sugar and two eggs to the melted chocolate and beat it. Next, stir in ¾ cup sifted flour, ½ teaspoon baking powder, and ½ teaspoon salt. Finally, mix in ½ cup chopped nuts.

Spread the mixture in the greased baking dish. Bake for 30 to 35 minutes. The brownies are done when a toothpick stuck in the center comes out clean. Let the brownies cool. Cut them into squares.

_____ Stick a toothpick in the center of the brownies to make sure they are done.

_____ Mix in chopped nuts.

_____ Melt chocolate and butter in a mixing bowl over a pan of hot water.

_____ Cool brownies and cut into squares.

_____ Beat in sugar and eggs.

_____ Spread mixture in a baking dish.

_____ Stir in flour, baking powder, and salt.

_____ Bake for 30 to 35 minutes.

_____ Turn oven to 350 degrees and grease pan.

Name _____

Finding the Gold

Can you find the gold?

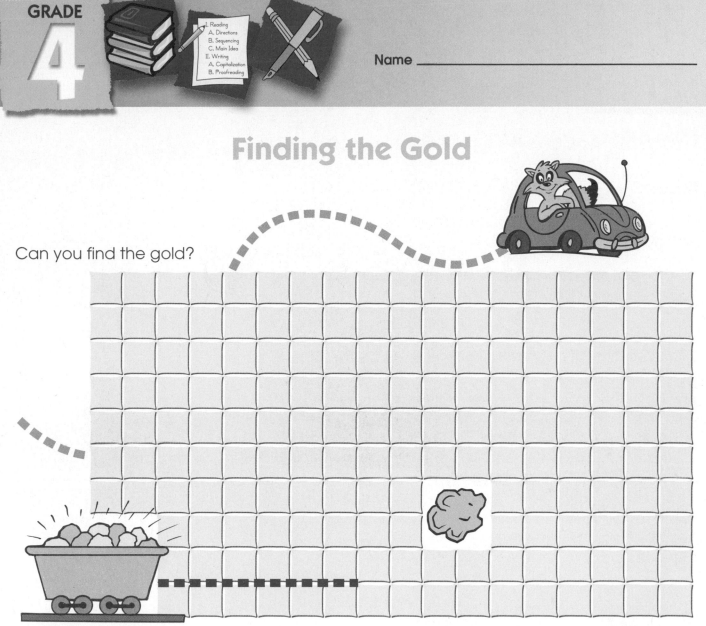

Mine Entrance

Directions: Follow the directions to draw a line to the gold.

1. Start at the mine entrance.
2. Follow the dashed line east 7 spaces.
3. Next, go north 5 spaces.
4. Then, go east 3 spaces.
5. Now, go north 3 spaces.
6. Turn and go east 3 spaces.
7. Turn again and go south 6 spaces.
8. Now, go west 2 spaces. You have found it!
9. Color that space yellow.

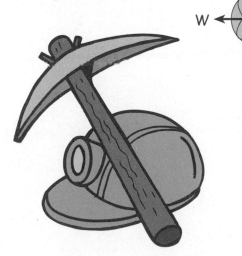

Name _____

First Things First

Sequence is the order in which things happen. It can also be the steps that you follow when doing something. Sometimes clue words like **first**, **after**, **then**, **next**, **later**, or **last** will help you find the order of events.

Example: Beth saw flames coming from the vacant house. **Next**, she ran home to call the Fire Department. **Then**, the firemen arrived to put out the fire. The fire was extinguished **after** three hours.

What happened first? <u>Beth saw flames.</u>

What happened last? <u>The fire was extinguished.</u>

Directions: Underline the clue words and write the answers.

1. To wash your hair, first wet your hair with warm water. Next, pour some shampoo in your hair and rub. Then, rinse all of the shampoo from your hair. Finally, dry your hair with a big, fluffy towel.

   What happens second?

   _____

2. Rosa and her mom arrived at the ballet at 2:00. They gave the usher their tickets. Then, they found seats. The dancers performed for an hour and a half. Afterwards, the audience gave the dancers a standing ovation.

   What happened third?

   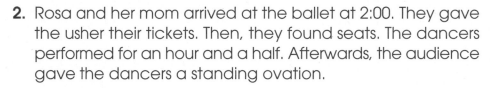

   _____

3. After Michael and Tony walked to the library, they turned in the books they had finished reading. Next, the boys looked for new books to read. Finally, they each checked out four books.

   What happened first?

   _____

GRADE 4

I. Reading
A. Directions
B. Sequencing
C. Main Idea
II. Writing
A. Capitalization
B. Proofreading

Name _____

A Series of Wishes

Directions: Read all the sentences. Write the numbers 1–8 in the circles to put the sentences in order. Then, rewrite the sentences in the correct order at the bottom.

◯ The traveler began to rub the sand off the lantern.

◯ Second, he wished that he could find his family again.

◯ The genie said that he would grant the traveler three wishes.

◯ A traveler had lost his way as he crossed the desert.

◯ His third wish was that he could have three more wishes.

◯ As he rubbed the lantern, a genie appeared in a cloud of smoke.

◯ The lost traveler found an old lantern lying in the sand.

◯ First, the traveler wished that he would find his way out of the desert.

1. _____

2. _____

3. _____

4. _____

5. _____

6. _____

7. _____

8. _____

GRADE
4
I. Reading
   A. Directions
   B. Sequencing
   C. Main Idea
II. Writing
   A. Capitalization
   B. Proofreading

Name _____

Sentence Shift

Some events may not be written in the same order as they actually occurred. Use clue words like **before** or **after** to find out what happened first.

Example: Before Dad ate breakfast, <u>he ran three miles in the park</u>.

Directions: Underline the event in each sentence that happened first. Then, write the numbers 1–2 or 2–1 to tell the order of the events in the sentence.

1. _____ _____ Shortly after the tennis match began, the star player fell and broke his arm.

2. _____ _____ The speaker finished his speech just after the clock struck 3:00.

3. _____ _____ The detective searched for clues before questioning suspects.

4. _____ _____ Kelly bought a bouquet of flowers before she visited her grandparents.

5. _____ _____ Before the land was settled, it was covered with evergreen forests.

6. _____ _____ The class saw a film about space travel before it visited the planetarium.

7. _____ _____ Before going to the ball game, Mike and Paul stopped for hamburgers.

Name _Jung Min_

An Orderly Trip

As you read, it often helps to picture the events as they occur in the story.

Directions: Read the story. Then, write the numbers 1–7 to show the sequence of events.

Emily awoke early. She and her family would be visiting the zoo today. For the past month at school, her class had been studying about animals. Although Emily had seen pictures and videos of animals, she was anxious to see what these animals looked like in real life.

Emily burst through the zoo gates at 10:00 A.M., just as the zoo opened. First, she saw the Siberian tigers and the leopards. Emily loved the size of those cats. Next, she watched the zookeeper feed three elephants. Then, just before stopping at the Snack Shack for lunch, Emily and her family went in the petting zoo where they fed and petted a variety of barnyard animals.

In the afternoon, Emily saw monkeys, zebras, and giraffes. It was one of the best days Emily could ever remember! That night, she wrote in her journal about all the animals she saw that day.

_3_ Emily visited the tigers and leopards.

_5_ She visited the petting zoo.

_2_ Emily's family arrived at the zoo at 10:00 A.M.

_4_ The zookeeper fed the elephants.

_1_ Emily awoke early.

_7_ Emily wrote in her journal.

_6_ They had lunch at the Snack Shack.

Name ___Jung Min___

A Visit to the Shedd Aquarium

Directions: Read each paragraph and answer the questions.

Before going to the Shedd Aquarium, Janie and her brother Jim planned their trip. First, they looked at maps of Chicago to see where the aquarium was located. Then, they checked the bus routes to see which bus to take. Next, Janie and Jim discussed which exhibits they wanted to view.

1. What did Janie and Jim do first in planning their trip? _they looked at maps of Chicago to see where the aquarium was located_

2. What did they do after that? _they checked the bus routes to see which bus to take._

3. What did Janie and Jim do last? _They discussed which exhibits they wanted to view._

The next morning, the two children boarded the bus for the aquarium. They paid the fare and found seats together. When the bus stopped at the Field Museum, Janie and Jim got off and walked a block to the aquarium. They waited in line an hour to buy tickets.

4. What did the children do after they got on the bus? _they paid the fare and found seats together._

5. What did Janie and Jim do right after they got off the bus? _they walked a block to the aquarium._

6. What did they do before they bought tickets? _they waited in line an hour_

Name _Jung Min_

Jung Min

Mindy Gets the Main Idea!

The **main idea** is what a story is about.

Directions: Help Mindy figure out the main idea of the passages below. Write a check mark next to each main idea.

Sammy spends much of his free time at homeless shelters and soup kitchens. He also gives time to many local charities.

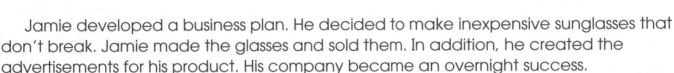

What is the main idea?

_____ Sammy is a hard worker.

_____ Sammy is busy.   ✓ Sammy is unselfish.

Jamie developed a business plan. He decided to make inexpensive sunglasses that don't break. Jamie made the glasses and sold them. In addition, he created the advertisements for his product. His company became an overnight success.

What is the main idea?

_____ Jamie must be tired.   _____ Jamie is a popular person.

✓ Jamie is an intelligent businessman.

Mr. Waterford loves the taste of fast food! He enjoys the smell of the greasy grill, and he certainly loves sinking his teeth into a tasty cheeseburger.

What is the main idea?

_____ Mr. Waterford must have high cholesterol.

✓ Mr. Waterford enjoys visiting fast-food places.

_____ Mr. Waterford loves french fries.

GRADE 4

I. Reading
   A. Directions
   B. Sequencing
   C. Main Idea
II. Writing
   A. Capitalization
   B. Proofreading

Name _Jung Min_

The Heart

Have you ever imagined that your heart looked like a valentine? Your heart is really about the size and shape of your fist. Every time your heart beats it pumps blood to your body. Your heart never rests. It beats 100,000 times a day.

One part of your heart sends blood to all parts of your body. The blood carries the oxygen that your body needs to live. Another part of the heart takes in the blood coming back from your body and sends it to your lungs for more oxygen. Then, the fresh blood is pumped back to your body again.

Directions: Circle the letter that answers each question the best.

1. Which sentence best summarizes the main idea of this passage?

   A. Your heart does not look like a valentine.

   B. Your heart is constantly working to pump blood in your body.

   C. Your heart sends blood to the lungs for more oxygen.

   D. Your heart beats 100,000 times a day.

2. The heart does all of the following except—

   A. rest.

   B. send blood to parts of the body.

   C. beat.

   D. send blood to the lungs.

3. Which of the following statements is true?

   A. Your heart is shaped like a valentine.

   B. Your heart beats 96 times a day.

   C. The heart has one part.

   D. The lungs add oxygen to the blood.

4. Which of the following would be the best title for this passage?

   A. A Valentine Surprise

   B. Life-Giving Oxygen

   C. Your Amazing Heart

   D. Have a Heart

Name __Sung Min__

Hibernation

Have you ever wondered why some animals hibernate? Hibernation is a long sleep that some animals take for the winter.

Animals get their warmth and energy from food. Some animals cannot find enough food in the winter. They must eat large amounts of food in the fall. Their bodies store this food as fat. Then, in winter, they hibernate. Their bodies live on the stored fat. Since their bodies need much less food during hibernation, they can stay alive without eating new food during the winter.

Some animals that hibernate are bats, chipmunks, bears, snakes, and turtles.

Directions: Circle the letter that answers each question the best.

1. The best title for this passage is—

    A. Sleepy Snakes.

    B. The Long Sleep.

    C. Winter Wonders.

    D. Bears and Their Habitats.

2. Which of the following statements is not true?

    A. Animals get their warmth and energy from food.

    B. Some animals cannot find enough food in the winter.

    C. Animals hibernate because they are lazy.

    D. Animals need less food while they are hibernating.

3. The main idea of this passage can best be summarized by which sentence?

    A. Hibernation is necessary for all animals in the winter.

    B. Hibernation is a time for bats, chipmunks, bears, snakes, and turtles to gather food.

    C. Hibernation is a long sleep that helps animals stay alive during winter.

    D. Hibernation means to store food as fat.

GRADE
4

I. Reading
   A. Directions
   B. Sequencing
   C. Main Idea
II. Writing
   A. Capitalization
   B. Proofreading

Name _____

Ice Cream

Almost everyone loves to eat ice cream. In fact, ice cream has been a favorite treat for thousands of years. Long ago, Roman rulers enjoyed eating mountain snow. In Europe, people flavored ice for a special dish. Later, cream was used to make ice cream much like we enjoy today.

Until 1851, ice cream was made most often at home. Today, most ice cream is produced in ice-cream plants. These plants use machines to mix milk, sugar, and water. The mixture is pumped into a cooler. After it is chilled, it is put into storage tanks. Special flavors and colors are added to make many different kinds of ice cream. The mixtures are then frozen at a temperature of -22°F. Then, fan-like blades slice through the frozen mixture and whip air into it. This fluffy ice cream is placed in a hardening room for 12 hours. Then, it is delivered to stores.

Directions: Circle the letter that answers each question the best.

1. Which sentence best states the main idea of the first paragraph?

    A. Ice cream has been a favorite treat for thousands of years.

    B. In Europe, people flavored ice for a special dish.

    C. Later, cream was used to make ice cream.

    D. Roman rulers ate the mountain snow.

2. Which sentence best states the main idea of the second paragraph?

    A. Until 1851, ice cream was made most often at home.

    B. After it is chilled, the mixture is put into storage tanks.

    C. Today, most ice cream is made in plants.

    D. After the hardening room, off to the stores it goes!

GRADE 4

I. Reading
   A. Directions
   B. Sequencing
   C. Main Idea
II. Writing
   A. Capitalization
   B. Proofreading

Name _____

Let's Compromise

Sarah needed new clothes because she grew a lot in the past year. She and Mom went shopping at the Dukwilma Mall. They went into the children's department at J.Z. Lenny's. Mom went to the rack with dresses hanging in neat rows. She picked out two of them and then picked out a pair of black patent leather shoes. Mom asked Sarah to try them on.

Sarah really wanted new jeans and T-shirts. She tried on one dress and the black patent leather shoes. She wiggled and squirmed and made nasty faces. She especially disliked the black patent leather shoes and would rather buy a comfortable pair of tennis shoes.

Well, Mom wouldn't let Sarah have her way, so Sarah and Mom compromised. They bought one of the dresses, a pair of blue jeans, a T-shirt, and the tennis shoes.

Directions: Fill in a circle for each correct answer.

1. This story is about how Mom and Sarah compromised about . . .

○ where they went shopping.

○ what they bought at J.Z. Lenny's.

What did Mom want to buy? What did Sarah want to buy?

Sarah	Mom	
2. ○	○	black patent leather shoes
3. ○	○	jeans and T-shirts
4. ○	○	pretty dresses
5. ○	○	tennis shoes

Name _____

Mainly About . . .

The **topic** tells what a paragraph or story is about in one or two words.
The **main idea** is the most important idea about the topic.

Directions: Read each paragraph. Then, write the topic and main idea about each paragraph.

The ancient Mayan Indians lived in Central America and southern Mexico. During the peak of their civilization, from 250 to 900 A.D., they lived in the tropical rainforests of the lowlands. Today, descendants of the Mayan people still live there.

1. What is the topic? _____

_____

2. What is the main idea? _____

_____

_____

The Mayas developed the first advanced form of writing called *hieroglyphics*. Written records of dates and important events were written on pottery, monuments, and palace walls. The Mayan people lived and wrote until the 16th century when the Spanish invaded and overcame the Mayas of Mexico and Central America.

1. What is the topic? _____

_____

2. What is the main idea? _____

_____

GRADE 4

I. Reading
A. Directions
B. Sequencing
C. Main Idea
II. Writing
A. Capitalization
B. Proofreading

Name _____

Origin of the Moon

Directions: Look for facts and details as you read these paragraphs.

The Moon is over four billion years old. How the Moon formed remains a mystery. Here are four theories that scientists use to explain the Moon's origin.

The "Escape" Theory

Some scientists believe that Earth and the Moon were once a single body. Earth was spinning much faster than it does today. The Sun's gravitational pull caused a bulge on one side of the rapidly spinning Earth. As the lopsided Earth spun, the bulge eventually broke away to form the Moon.

The "Capture" Theory

Possibly, the Moon was once a planet that traveled around the Sun, just as Earth does. The Moon and Earth had similar orbits. Every few years, Earth and the Moon would come close to each other. One time, their orbits brought them so close that the Moon was captured by the pull of Earth's gravity. The Moon became a satellite of Earth.

The "Formation" Theory

This theory says that the Moon and Earth formed at about the same time. The two bodies were formed from huge whirlpools of gas and dust left over from when the Sun was formed. Earth and the Moon started out as two separate bodies that stayed near each other, similar to a double planet.

The "Collision" Theory

A fourth theory is that a huge body from space smashed into Earth. The impact was so great that pieces of Earth broke off. These pieces began orbiting Earth. Eventually the material grouped together, forming a single body known as the Moon.

GRADE 4

I. Reading
A. Directions
B. Sequencing
C. Main Idea
II. Writing
A. Capitalization
B. Proofreading

Name _____

Moon Facts

Directions: Write a word from "Origin of the Moon" on page 47 that matches each given detail.

1. _____ A theory that says the Moon originally had an orbit that was much like Earth's orbit.

2. _____ A theory that says Earth and the Moon were formed from gas and dust left by the Sun.

3. _____ A theory that says the Moon was pulled out of Earth by the pull from the Sun's gravity.

4. _____ A theory that says a piece of Earth broke off when a body from space smashed into it.

5. _____ The escape theory explains that the Sun's gravity created this on one side of Earth.

6. _____ This word for a collision may have caused pieces of Earth to break off.

7. _____ Earth and the Moon were double planets in this theory.

8. _____ This word describes what the Moon became after it was captured by Earth.

I. Reading
  A. Directions
  B. Sequencing
  C. Main Idea
II. Writing
  A. Capitalization
  B. Proofreading

Name _____

Recognizing Details: Blind Bats

Directions: Read about bats. Then, answer the questions.

Bats sleep all day because they cannot see well in the bright sunlight. They hang upside down in dark places such as barns, caves, or hollow trees. As soon as darkness begins to fall, bats wake up. They fly around easily and quickly at night.

Bats make sounds that help them fly, since they cannot see well. People cannot hear these sounds. When bats make sounds, the sounds hit objects in front of them and bounce back at them. Bats can tell if something is in their way because there is an echo. Some people say this is like a radar system!

There are many different kinds of bats. Some bats fly all night, while others fly only in the evening or the early morning.

Most bats eat mosquitoes and moths, but there are some bats that will catch fish swimming in water and eat them. Still other kinds of bats eat birds or mice. Bats that live in very hot areas eat only some parts of flowers.

Bats that live in cold areas of the country sometimes sleep all winter. That means they *hibernate*. Other bats that live in cold areas fly to warmer places for the winter. We call this *migration*.

1. Who cannot hear the sounds bats make? _____

2. Why do bats sleep all day? _____

3. When do bats eat? _____

4. Where do bats that eat only parts of flowers live? _____

5. Why do bats make sounds? _____

6. What does *hibernate* mean? _____

7. What is the main idea of this selection? _____

_____

8. Do you think a bat would make a good pet? Why or why not? _____

_____

_____

Name _____

Recognizing Details: "Why Bear Has a Short Tail"

Some stories try to explain the reasons why certain things occur in nature.

Directions: Read the legend "Why Bear Has a Short Tail." Then, answer the questions.

Long ago, Bear had a long tail like Fox. One winter day, Bear met Fox coming out of the woods. Fox was carrying a long string of fish. He had stolen the fish, but that is not what he told Bear.

"Where did you get those fish?" asked Bear, rubbing his paws together. Bear loved fish. It was his favorite food.

"I was out fishing and caught them," replied Fox.

Bear did not know how to fish. He had only tasted fish that others gave him. He was eager to learn to catch his own.

"Please Fox, will you tell me how to fish?" asked Bear.

So, the mean old Fox said to Bear, "Cut a hole in the ice and stick your tail in the hole. It will get cold, but soon the fish will begin to bite. When you can stand it no longer, pull your tail out. It will be covered with fish!"

"Will it hurt?" asked Bear, patting his tail.

"It will hurt some," admitted Fox. "But the longer you leave your tail in the water, the more fish you will catch."

Bear did as Fox told him. He loved fish, so he left his tail in the icy water a very, very long time. The ice froze around Bear's tail. When he pulled free, his tail remained stuck in the ice. That is why bears today have short tails.

1. How does Fox get his string of fish? _____

2. What does he tell Bear to do? _____

_____

3. Why does Bear do as Fox told him? _____

_____

4. How many fish does Bear catch?_____

5. What happens when Bear tries to pull his tail out? _____

_____

GRADE
4

I. Reading
  A. Directions
  B. Sequencing
  C. Main Idea
II. Writing
  A. Capitalization
  B. Proofreading

Name _____

Recognizing Details: "Why Bear Has a Short Tail"

Directions: Review the legend "Why Bear Has a Short Tail." Then, answer the questions.

1. When Bear asks Fox where he got his fish, is Fox truthful in his response? Why or why not?

_____

_____

2. Why does Bear want to know how to fish? _____

_____

3. In reality, are bears able to catch their own fish? How? _____

_____

4. Is Bear very smart to believe Fox? Why or why not? _____

_____

5. How would you have told Bear to catch his own fish? _____

_____

6. What is one word you would use to describe Fox? _____

Explain your answer. _____

_____

7. What is one word you would use to describe Bear? _____

Explain your answer. _____

_____

8. Is this story realistic? _____

9. Could it have really happened? Explain your answer. _____

_____

I. Reading
  A. Directions
  B. Sequencing
  C. Main Idea
II. Writing
  A. Capitalization
  B. Proofreading

Name _____

What Is Precycling?

Directions: Draw your own conclusions as you read these paragraphs.

Most of us have heard of recycling. Some families recycle cans, glass jars and bottles, newspapers, and plastic containers. There may be a recycling bin at your school or in the parking lot of a nearby store. But what does it mean to precycle?

We think about recycling after we've bought something. *Precycling* means to think ahead, before buying. One can even precycle while shopping. Try to buy only foods that are packaged in materials that can be recycled. By making careful choices, consumers can reduce the amount of garbage headed for landfills.

Used packaging materials present a serious disposal problem. Almost everything on grocery store shelves is either packed in a container or wrapped in paper or plastic. Much of that packaging is unnecessary. Here are some precycling tips for shoppers:

- Buy products that have a recycle label or are made from recycled materials.
- Buy things in bulk. Buying one large container means less packaging to throw away.
- Try using cloth shopping bags instead of paper or plastic. Bring your own bags along when you shop.
- Choose products with the least packaging. Try to think of packaging as cleverly designed garbage.

Do you buy a product for its pretty packaging? Manufacturers think you do. Think twice before you buy. Precycling is for people who want to conserve natural resources and make our planet a better place for the future!

Name _____

Conclusions About Precycling

Directions: Read each sentence. Write **true** or **false** on the line.

1. Precycling is something you do before riding a bicycle. _____

2. You have to think ahead to precycle. _____

3. Buying in bulk means buying fattening food. _____

4. Packaging materials can be wasteful. _____

Directions: Make conclusions and write your answers in complete sentences.

1. What does the phrase "cleverly designed garbage" mean?_____

_____

2. List some ways you can precycle._____

_____

_____

3. Explain why using cloth shopping bags is a way to help save the earth.

_____

_____

4. "Precycle," is a made-up word. Tell why you think it is a good word to use.

_____

_____

5. Tell how you think precycling will help save the earth. _____

_____

_____

GRADE 4

I. Reading
A. Directions
B. Sequencing
C. Main Idea
II. Writing
A. Capitalization
B. Proofreading

Name _____

A Picture Is Worth . . .

Directions: Look at the first picture. Put a check mark in the box by each sentence which seems sensible. Look at the second picture. Write six sentences that tell your conclusions about the picture.

☐ It is a very hot day.

☐ The beach is a popular place to go.

☐ The beach is a quiet place to study.

☐ Some people picnic at the beach.

☐ A lifeguard helps protect swimmers.

☐ It is hard to nap at a noisy beach.

☐ Sailing is just for kids.

☐ Sailing and swimming are fun water sports.

☐ Every town has a beach.

Write your own conclusions.

1. _____

2. _____

3. _____

4. _____

5. _____

6. _____

I. Reading
   A. Directions
   B. Sequencing
   C. Main Idea
II. Writing
   A. Capitalization
   B. Proofreading

Name _____

Reading Skills: Bus Schedules

Schedules are important to our daily lives. Your parents' jobs, school, even watching television—all are based on schedules. When you travel, you probably follow a schedule, too. Most forms of public transportation, such as subways, buses, and trains, run on schedules. These "timetables" tell passengers when they will leave each stop or station.

Directions: Use the following city bus schedule to answer the questions.

No. 2 Cross-Town Bus Schedule

State St. at Park Way	Oak St. at Green Ave.	Fourth St. at Ninth Ave.	Buyall Shopping Center
5:00 A.M.	5:14 A.M.	5:23 A.M.	5:30 A.M.
6:38	6:52	7:01	7:08
7:50	8:05	8:14	8:21
9:04	9:18	9:27	9:34
10:15	10:29	10:38	10:47
12:20 P.M.	12:34 P.M.	12:43 P.M.	12:50 P.M.
1:46	2:00	2:09	2:16
3:30	3:44	3:53	4:00
5:20	5:34	5:43	5:50
6:02	6:16	6:25	6:32

1. The first bus of the day leaves the State St./Park Way stop at 5 A.M. What time does the last bus of the day leave this stop? _____

2. The bus that leaves the Oak St./Green Ave. stop at 8:05 A.M. leaves the Buyall Shopping Center at what time? _____

3. What time does the first afternoon bus leave the Fourth St./Ninth Ave. stop? _____

4. How many buses each day run between the State St./Park Way stop and the Buyall Shopping Center? _____

Reading Skills: Labels

Directions: You should never take any medicine without your parents' permission, but it is good to know how to read the label of a medicine bottle. Read the label to answer the questions.

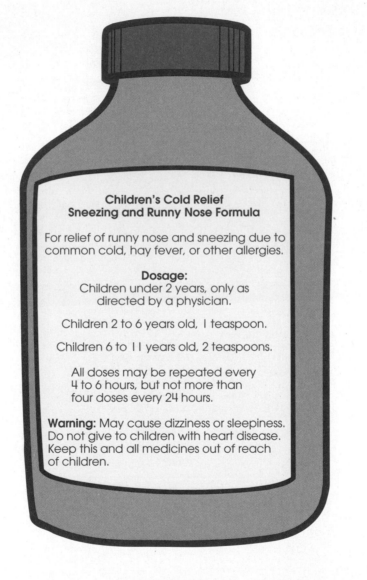

**Children's Cold Relief
Sneezing and Runny Nose Formula**

For relief of runny nose and sneezing due to common cold, hay fever, or other allergies.

Dosage:
Children under 2 years, only as directed by a physician.

Children 2 to 6 years old, 1 teaspoon.

Children 6 to 11 years old, 2 teaspoons.

All doses may be repeated every 4 to 6 hours, but not more than four doses every 24 hours.

Warning: May cause dizziness or sleepiness. Do not give to children with heart disease. Keep this and all medicines out of reach of children.

1. How much medicine should a 5-year-old take? _____

2. How often can this medicine be taken? _____

3. How do you know how much medicine to give a 1-year-old? _____

4. Who should not take this medicine? _____

I. Reading
A. Directions
B. Sequencing
C. Main Idea
II. Writing
A. Capitalization
B. Proofreading

Name _____

A Class of Its Own

Classifying means putting things that are similar or related to each other into groups. Words that belong together can be sorted into a certain class or category.

Directions: In each list, cross out the word that does not belong. Then, write the name of the category on the line. The first one is done for you.

Birds	_____	_____	_____
duck	math	apple	Maryland
pelican	movie	corn	Florida
~~snake~~	science	pear	Chicago
turkey	spelling	watermelon	California
parrot	history	peach	Indiana

_____	_____	_____	_____
boxer	friend	tulip	Pete
poodle	brother	rose	George
dachshund	sister	violet	Ted
collie	mother	purple	Mark
lion	father	daisy	Lisa

Directions: Write your own words that belong in each category below.

Sports Teams	Languages	Hobbies	Colors
_____	_____	_____	_____
_____	_____	_____	_____
_____	_____	_____	_____
_____	_____	_____	_____

Name _____

Categorizing Books

Directions: Write the letter of the shelf on which each book belongs.

Shelf A—Mystery	Shelf B—Sports
Shelf C—Science	Shelf D—Cooking
Shelf E—Riddles and Jokes	Shelf F—Famous People

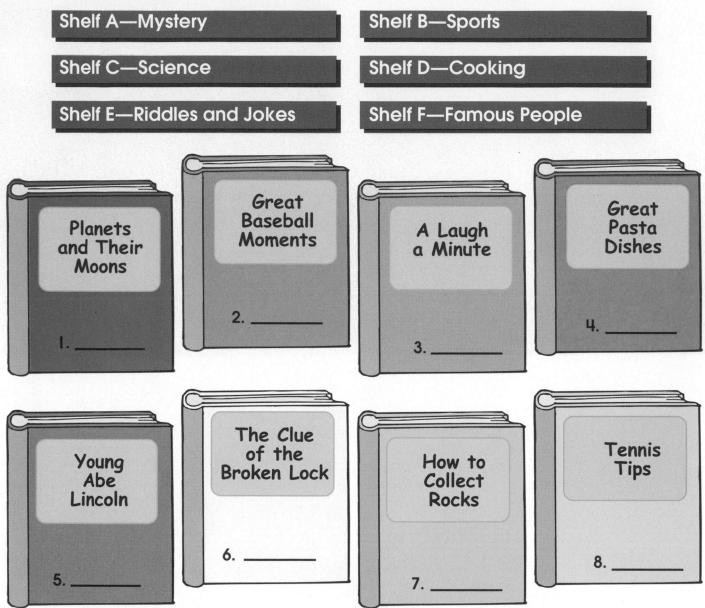

Planets and Their Moons

1. _____

Great Baseball Moments

2. _____

A Laugh a Minute

3. _____

Great Pasta Dishes

4. _____

Young Abe Lincoln

5. _____

The Clue of the Broken Lock

6. _____

How to Collect Rocks

7. _____

Tennis Tips

8. _____

Directions: Write the letter of the shelf where you might find this information.

1. _____ How do you prepare a spaghetti dinner?

2. _____ How long does the Moon take to orbit Earth?

3. _____ Where does a five-hundred pound angry elephant sit?

4. _____ Which presidents once served as members of Congress?

Name _____

"Bee"-lieve It or Not!

Directions: Circle the bee in the correct column to tell whether the sentence is fact or fantasy.

Fact   **Fantasy**

1. Every year except leap year has 365 days.

2. Zebras' stripes can be washed off by rain.

3. Baseball and tennis are both sports.

4. December is the twelfth month of the year.

5. Some kinds of dogs can speak like people.

6. A supermarket sells many kinds of food.

7. Paul Bunyan carved the Grand Canyon.

8. The letters **a**, **e**, **i**, **o**, and **u** are called *vowels*.

9. The Moon is made of green cheese.

10. Beavers use wood to build their homes.

Directions: Write the correct letter from above on each line.

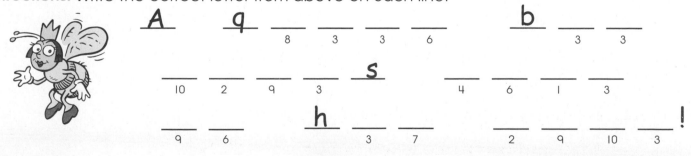

A q ___ ___ ___ ___   b ___ ___
       8   3   3   6   3   3

___ ___ ___ ___ s ___ ___ ___ ___
10 2   9   3   4   6   1   3

___ h ___ ___   ___ ___ ___ ___!
9   6   3   7   2   9   10 3

I. Reading
  A. Directions
  B. Sequencing
  C. Main Idea
II. Writing
  A. Capitalization
  B. Proofreading

Name _____

Person to Person

Directions: Write a category heading for each list. Then, add an appropriate third word to each list.

Category Headings		
Royalty	Musicians	Doctors
Baseball Players	Relatives	Officers

1. _____

    catcher

    batter

    _____

2. _____

    princess

    duke

    _____

3. _____

    nephew

    uncle

    _____

4. _____

    violinist

    composer

    _____

5. _____

    veterinarian

    surgeon

    _____

6. _____

    class president

    sergeant

    _____

GRADE 4

I. Reading
  A. Directions
  B. Sequencing
  C. Main Idea
II. Writing
  A. Capitalization
  B. Proofreading

Name _____

Camping Supplies

Donald's class is going on an overnight camping trip. Right now, Miss Reed is helping the class decide what to bring. Some items are important, and students will <u>need</u> to bring them. Other items are not necessary, but students may <u>want</u> to bring them.

Directions: Look at the list of supplies below. In the first column, write the items you think students will need for an overnight camping trip. In the second column, write the items you would think they might want to bring. You may add other items to the list that are not listed.

What they <u>need</u> to take	What they may <u>want</u> to take

food

water

sunglasses

cell phone

marshmallows

radio

first-aid kit

book

tent

flashlight

popcorn

camera

Analogies

An **analogy** indicates how different items go together or are similar in some way.

Examples: **Petal** is to **flower** as **leaf** is to **tree**.
Book is to **library** as **food** is to **grocery store**.

If you study the examples, you will see how the second set of objects is related to the first set. A petal is part of a flower, and a leaf is part of a tree. A book can be found in a library, and food can be found in a grocery store.

Directions: Fill in the blanks to complete the analogies. The first one has been done for you.

1. Cup is to saucer as glass is to _____coaster_____ .

2. Paris is to France as London is to _____ .

3. Clothes are to hangers as _____ are to boxes.

4. California is to _____ as Ohio is to Lake Erie.

5. _____ is to table as blanket is to bed.

6. Pencil is to paper as _____ is to canvas.

7. Cow is to _____ as child is to house.

8. State is to country as _____ is to state.

9. Governor is to state as _____ is to country.

10. _____ is to ocean as sand is to desert.

11. Engine is to car as hard drive is to _____ .

12. Beginning is to _____ as stop is to end.

Directions: Write three analogies of your own.

_____

_____

_____

Name _____

Analogies

Directions: Write a word from the box to complete the following analogies.

fence	club	glove	saw	father
blanket	dish	rug	snow	ten
compass	hat	brake	finger	blue

1. Racket is to tennis as _____ is to golf.

2. Glass is to drink as _____ is to eat.

3. Wheel is to steer as _____ is to stop.

4. Roof is to house as _____ is to floor.

5. Rain is to storm as _____ is to blizzard.

6. Clock is to time as _____ is to directions.

7. Lid is to pan as _____ is to head.

8. Hammer is to pound as _____ is to cut.

9. Mother is to daughter as _____ is to son.

10. Shoe is to foot as _____ is to hand.

11. Five is to ten as _____ is to twenty.

12. Shade is to lamp as _____ is to bed.

13. Toe is to foot as _____ is to hand.

14. Frame is to picture as _____ is to yard.

15. Green is to grass as _____ is to sky.

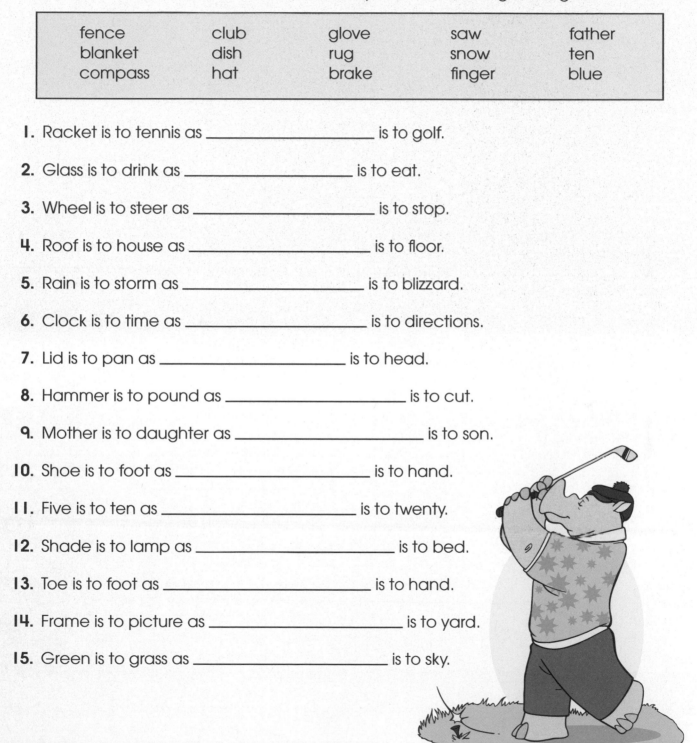

Name _____

Figures of Speech

A **figure of speech** can make a sentence more interesting.
Here are four popular kinds of figures of speech:

Personification—gives human characteristics to things.
Example: The Sun touched us with its warm fingers.

Hyperbole—a great exaggeration.
Example: She's the happiest person in the universe.

Simile—compares two unlike things, using **like** or **as**.
Example: He is hungry as a horse.

Metaphor—suggests a comparison of two unlike things.
Example: The vacant field was a desert.

Directions: Underline each figure of speech. Write the type on each line.

1. The wind howled as the storm grew closer. _____

2. The little lady nibbled at her lunch like a bird. _____

3. Sarah's little sister was a doll in her new clothes. _____

4. The camp leader said he would never sleep again. _____

5. The banana cream pie was heaven. _____

6. We were as busy as bees all day long. _____

7. His patience just flew out the window. _____

8. He said that his life was an open book. _____

9. The heavy fog crept slowly into shore. _____

10. The champion wrestler is as strong as an ox. _____

11. I am so full that I never want to eat again. _____

12. Sometimes my memory is a blank tape. _____

Directions: Write four sentences that contain a figure of speech.

1. (personification) _____

2. (hyperbole) _____

3. (simile) _____

4. (metaphor) _____

I. Reading
  A. Directions
  B. Sequencing
  C. Main Idea
II. Writing
  A. Capitalization
  B. Proofreading

Name _____

Like . . . a Simile

Directions: In the sentences below, underline the two things or persons being compared. In the blank, write **simile** or **metaphor**. Remember, a simile uses **like** or **as**; metaphors do not.

1. Angel was as mean as a wild bull. _____

2. Toni and Mattie were like toast and jam. _____

3. Mr. Ashby expected the students to be as busy as beavers.

   _____

4. The pin was a masterpiece in Mattie's mind. _____

5. The park's peacefulness was a friend to Mattie. _____

6. The words came as slow as molasses into Mattie's mind. _____

7. Mrs. Stamp's apartment was like a museum. _____

8. Mrs. Benson was as happy as a lark when Mattie won

   the contest. _____

9. Mr. Phillip's smile was a glowing beam to Mattie and Mrs. Benson.

   _____

10. Mattie ran as fast as the wind to get her money. _____

11. Angel's mean words cut through Charlene like glass. _____

12. Mr. Bacon was a fairy godmother to Mattie. _____

13. The gingko tree's leaves were shaped like fans. _____

Directions: Complete the following sentences using similes.

1. Matt was as artistic as _____.

2. Hannibal's teeth were like _____.

3. Toni's mind worked fast like _____.

4. Mattie was as sad as _____.

5. Mrs. Stamp was like _____.

Knight in Training

Directions: Read this letter.

March 15, 1405

Dear Father,

I miss you and the family, but I am happy to be living here and serving Sir Stephen. Castle life is exciting while I learn the skills and behavior expected of a knight.

Many things are required of pages like me. My duties include serving Sir Stephen and caring for his horses. I am also learning to fight with a sword and hunt with a falcon. I often play chess and other games that require great skill and strategy.

I can hardly wait seven years until I am sixteen. Then, I can become a squire. A squire serves his master as a valet and is trained to become a mounted soldier. He also rides in battle with his master. The most exciting thing squires do is test their skill in a contest, called *jousting*. In this, one squire tries to knock another squire off his horse with a long blunt lance.

My friend, Squire Robert, helps Sir Stephen put on his armor for contests and before a battle. Almost all of Sir Stephen□s body is covered with this metal suit. When he is covered in armor, we cannot recognize him; however, his coat of arms, a cross, is on his shield and his cloak.

I remain your faithful son,

Arthur

Name _____

Knight in Training

Remember that a **statement of fact** can be proven true or false. An **opinion** is what you believe or think. Use the information in the letter on page 66 to help you complete this activity.

Directions: Write **F** if the sentence is a statement of fact or **O** if it is an opinion.

_____ 1. Pages are young boys who serve knights.

_____ 2. Being a page is a hard job.

_____ 3. Some knights hunt with falcons.

_____ 4. A squire is a young man sixteen or older.

_____ 5. Being a squire is better than being a page.

_____ 6. A squire goes to battle with his knight.

_____ 7. Jousting is cruel to horses.

_____ 8. Jousting is the best kind of contest.

_____ 9. In jousting, a knight uses a lance to knock another knight off his horse.

_____ 10. All suits of armor are hot and ugly.

_____ 11. A knight wears armor to protect his body.

_____ 12. A knight's coat of arms is very beautiful.

_____ 13. A coat of arms helps spectators recognize the knights in armor.

_____ 14. Pages learn to hunt with falcons.

_____ 15. All squires are brave.

Name _____

Facts and Opinions

Facts are statements or events that have happened and can be proven to be true.

Example: George Washington was the first president of the United States.
This statement is a fact. It can be proven to be true by researching the history of our country.

Opinions are statements that express how someone thinks or feels.

Example: George Washington was the greatest president the United States has ever had.
This statement is an opinion. Many people agree that George Washington was a great president, but not everyone agrees he was the greatest president. In some people's opinion, Abraham Lincoln was our greatest president.

Directions: Read each sentence. Write **F** for fact or **O** for opinion.

_____ **1.** There is three feet of snow on the ground.

_____ **2.** A lot of snow makes the winter enjoyable.

_____ **3.** Chris has a better swing set than Mary.

_____ **4.** Both Chris and Mary have swing sets.

_____ **5.** California is a state.

_____ **6.** California is the best state in the West.

Directions: Write three facts and three opinions.

Facts:

1. _____

2. _____

3. _____

Opinions:

1. _____

2. _____

3. _____

GRADE 4

I. Reading
A. Directions
B. Sequencing
C. Main Idea
II. Writing
A. Capitalization
B. Proofreading

Name _____

Facts and Opinions

Directions: Write **F** before the facts and **O** before the opinions.

_____ **1.** Our school football team had a winning season this year.

_____ **2.** Mom's spaghetti is the best in the world!

_____ **3.** Autumn is the nicest season of the year.

_____ **4.** Mrs. Burns took her class on a field trip last Thursday.

_____ **5.** The library always puts 30 books in our classroom book collection.

_____ **6.** They should put only books about horses in the collection.

_____ **7.** Our new art teacher is very strict.

_____ **8.** Everyone should keep take-home papers in a folder so they don't have to look for them when it is time to go home.

_____ **9.** The bus to the mall goes right by Jane's house at 7:45 A.M.

_____**10.** Our new superintendent, Mr. Willeke, is very nice.

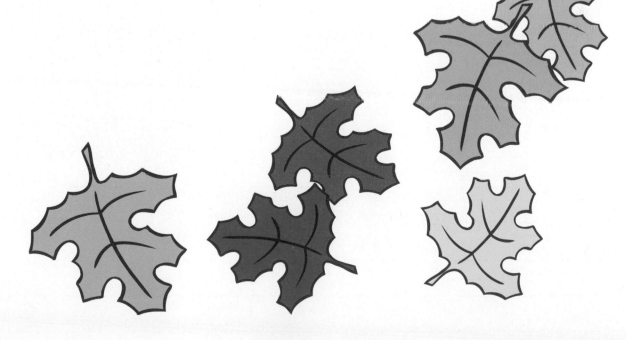

Name _____

Crater Lake

When you come to a word you don't know, look for clues to its meaning in the words around it. These nearby words are called **context clues** and can help you figure out a new word.

Example: Mount Mazama, an <u>ancient</u> volcano, collapsed thousands of years ago, leaving a huge bowl, or crater.

Context Clues: thousands, years ago
Meaning: very old

Directions: Fill in the circle next to the correct meaning of the underlined word.

1. Crater Lake, in the Cascade Mountains of southern Oregon, rests in an inactive volcano at an <u>altitude</u> of about 6,200 feet above sea level.

   ○ height   ○ average

2. No streams or rivers <u>supply</u> the lake with water. Precipitation, in the form of snow and rain, has filled the crater.

   ○ fill   ○ save

3. Crater Lake is the deepest lake in the United States. It is 1,932 feet at its greatest <u>depth</u>.

   ○ far   ○ measurement downward

4. Years ago, a mining <u>prospector</u> was looking for minerals and oil. He saw the lake and called it *Deep Blue Lake* because of its beautiful color.

   ○ explorer   ○ beautiful

5. Crater Lake and the area around it are now part of a National Park. The Park Service will <u>ensure</u> people do not pollute the lake.

   ○ protect   ○ make certain

6. There were no fish in Crater Lake until it was <u>stocked</u> with trout in 1888. People who fish are happy that more fish are still added each year.

   ○ stored   ○ filled

GRADE
4

I. Reading
   A. Directions
   B. Sequencing
   C. Main Idea
II. Writing
   A. Capitalization
   B. Proofreading

Name _____

What's My Career?

Directions: Read each career description. Write the name of the career. Use context clues and the words in the box to help you.

Now Showing!

Careers

banker	veterinarian
artist	carpenter
actor	salesperson

1. Angela's mom likes to build houses for people. When she was young, she enjoyed building things with wood. Her wooden birdhouses and toy boxes were good enough to sell at stores.

   Angela's mom is a _____ .

2. Donald draws and paints well. He always wins the best picture contests in class.

   Donald could be an _____ when he grows up.

3. Maria likes animals. She is good at taking care of her dog and cat when they are sick.

   Maria could be a _____ when she grows up.

4. Lydia is good with numbers. She gets A's in math. She always checks her answers to make sure they are right.

   Lydia could be a _____ when she grows up.

5. Dominic's mom works at the mall. She sells rugs and furniture. When she was young, she was the top cookie seller for her Girl Scout troop.

   Dominic's mom works in a store as a _____ .

6. Antonio makes people smile and laugh. He likes to sing and dance. He is always in the school plays.

   Antonio could be an _____ when he grows up.

I. Reading
A. Directions
B. Sequencing
C. Main Idea
II. Writing
A. Capitalization
B. Proofreading

Name _____

Money Changers

Directions: Read the selection. Use context clues to help you find the meaning of the underlined words. Then, fill in the circle next to the correct meaning of each underlined word.

If you have ever traded something with a friend, then you already know something about the <u>origin</u> of money. Before people used coins and paper money, they did just what you have done—traded goods with each other. Animal hides, cattle, cloth, salt, and articles of gold or silver were traded, much as we trade money today.

Finding someone to make just the right trade wasn't always easy! Can you imagine taking a cow along with you every time you went to the store? Trading like this was rather <u>impractical</u>. Many historians believe that coins were first made around 600 B.C. in what is now Turkey. As early as 1100 B.C., the Chinese used <u>miniature</u> bronze tools for trade. In time, the little tools were developed into coins.

Marco Polo, the Italian trader, traveled to China in the 1200s and was amazed to see the Chinese using paper money instead of coins. When he returned to Europe in 1295, he told people what he'd <u>encountered</u>, but Europe was slow to catch on to the idea of using paper money. They didn't understand how paper could be valuable. It was several hundred years later before European banks <u>issued</u> paper notes that could be traded for gold or silver coins.

In the United States, only the Department of the Treasury and the Federal Reserve System may issue money. Coins come in six <u>denominations</u>: penny, nickel, dime, quarter, half dollar, and dollar. Paper money is issued in seven values.

1. <u>origin</u>
   - ○ purpose
   - ○ beginning

2. <u>impractical</u>
   - ○ unrealistic
   - ○ confusing

3. <u>miniature</u>
   - ○ little
   - ○ unique

4. <u>encountered</u>
   - ○ amazed
   - ○ discovered

5. <u>issued</u>
   - ○ imagined
   - ○ delivered

6. <u>denominations</u>
   - ○ values
   - ○ positions

I. Reading
  A. Directions
  B. Sequencing
  C. Main Idea
II. Writing
  A. Capitalization
  B. Proofreading

Name _____

Claudio's Context Clues

When you read, it's important to look for context clues. **Context clues** can help you figure out the meaning of a word, or a missing word, just by looking at the **other words** in the sentence.

Directions: Read each sentence below. Circle the context clues or other words in the sentence that give you hints. Then, choose a word from the word list to replace the **boldfaced** word. Write it on the line.

Word List		
walking	announced	fun
grow	sprinting	touch

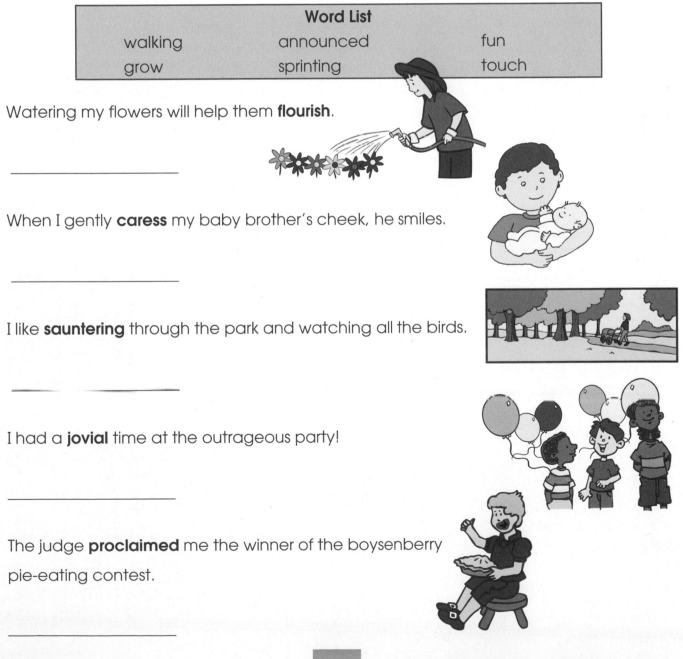

Watering my flowers will help them **flourish**.

_____

When I gently **caress** my baby brother's cheek, he smiles.

_____

I like **sauntering** through the park and watching all the birds.

_____

I had a **jovial** time at the outrageous party!

_____

The judge **proclaimed** me the winner of the boysenberry pie-eating contest.

_____

What Do You Mean?

Directions: Choose a word from the word list to replace the **boldfaced** word in each sentence. Write the word on the line. Use a dictionary to help you with any new words.

Word List		
fat	awful	strutting
shouting	skinny	empty

The **obese** elephant must have weighed 10 tons!

_____

The **clamor** from the lion's den frightened me.

_____

The skunk emitted a **repugnant** odor when a predator drew near him.

_____

Swaggering off the stage and holding a trophy, the boy smirked at everybody and shouted, "I am the best!"

_____

The island remained **desolate** for 100 years.

_____

I. Reading
  A. Directions
  B. Sequencing
  C. Main Idea
II. Writing
  A. Capitalization
  B. Proofreading

Name _____

Pick Another Word!

Directions: Choose a word from the word list to replace the **boldfaced** word in each sentence. Write it on the line. Use a dictionary to help you with any new words. One word may be used more than once.

Word List		
improve	limped	escape
douse	serious	

The wounded soldier **staggered** back from the battlefield.

_____

The special effects will **enhance** the quality of the movie and make it even more exciting to watch.

_____

The firefighter prepared to **extinguish** the fire by getting the hose ready.

_____

In order to **hone** my jumpshot, I need to practice on the basketball court every day.

_____

The robbers tried to **flee** from the police, but they were caught.

_____

A funeral is a **solemn** event.

_____

GRADE
4

I. Reading
  A. Directions
  B. Sequencing
  C. Main Idea
II. Writing
  A. Capitalization
  B. Proofreading

Name _____

Cause and Effect

Cause: An action or act that makes something happen.

Effect: Something that happens because of an action or cause.

Look at the following example of cause and effect.

Cause: We left our hot dogs on the grill too long.

Effect: Our hot dogs were burnt!

Directions: Read the story below. Then, write the missing effect.

Walter went to the art gallery to see the Picasso exhibit. He examined many of the paintings and felt inspired to paint himself. He visited the library and read about Picasso. He found out that many of Picasso's paintings had been influenced by African art and masks. Walter was now extremely excited to learn more about Picasso's art.

Cause: Walter did research about African art.

Effect: _____

How Did It Happen?

Directions: Read the stories below. Then, write the missing cause or effect.

James traveled on a long plane ride. When he arrived at his destination, he had to change his watch back 6 hours. When his friend asked him to go to dinner at 6 P.M., James said, "I am sorry, but not now."

Cause: _____

Effect: James could not make it to dinner.

Kevin's back ached because he had lifted heavy boxes all day long. Kevin set up an appointment at the yoga studio to work on stretching his muscles. Kevin learned new techniques and practiced them every day.

Cause: _____

Effect: Kevin learned yoga.

GRADE 4

I. Reading
   A. Directions
   B. Sequencing
   C. Main Idea
II. Writing
   A. Capitalization
   B. Proofreading

Name _____

Bonnie Blair

Speed skater Bonnie Blair is the only American woman to have won five Olympic gold medals. She is known as one of the best speed skaters in the world.

Born on March 18, 1964, Bonnie was the youngest in a speed skating family. Her five older brothers and sisters were champion skaters who encouraged her. They put a pair of skates over Bonnie's shoes when she was two years old because there weren't any skates small enough for her tiny feet.

As Bonnie grew, she trained hard six days a week, always pushing to improve her time. Bonnie kept this up until she was the world's best female speed skater. She won her first Olympic gold medal in the 500-meter race in 1988. In 1992, she won both the 500-meter and the 1,000-meter Olympic races in Albertville, France. She repeated her victories in 1994 in Lillehammer, Norway.

Bonnie's Olympic successes made her famous all over the world. Bonnie retired from speed skating in 1995 to focus on other competitions.

Directions: Answer the questions in complete sentences.

1. What was the effect of Bonnie being born into a speed skating family?

_____

2. What caused Bonnie's brothers and sisters to place skates over her shoes?

_____

3. What was the effect of Bonnie's practice and hard work?

_____

GRADE 4

I. Reading
   A. Directions
   B. Sequencing
   C. Main Idea
II. Writing
   A. Capitalization
   B. Proofreading

Name _____

Who Invented the Ice-Cream Cone?

Directions: Read the story below. Then, answer the questions.

"Dad, who invented the ice-cream cone?" asked Cody.

"What a good question! Lots of people claim to have invented the ice-cream cone, but the two most famous stories about how the ice-cream cone was invented include Italo Marchiony and Ernest Hamwi."

"Marchiony immigrated to New York City from Italy and sold ice cream from a cart. He wanted people to stop walking off with his cups that held the ice cream. So in 1896, he invented the ice-cream cone. In December 1903, he was granted a patent for it," he explained.

"What is a patent?" asked Cody.

"A patent helps protect your idea or invention if you don't want it to be copied. The other popular story about the invention of the ice-cream cone was in 1904 at the St. Louis World's Fair."

"The story says that there was an ice-cream booth at the fair, and the ice-cream vendor ran out of bowls to serve his ice cream. It was still early in the day. Desperately, he looked at the booth next to him and saw Ernest Hamwi selling a waffle-type pastry called a *Zalabia*. Mr. Hamwi said he had an idea

Name _____

Who Invented the Ice-Cream Cone? cont.

to solve the ice-cream vendor's problem. He then rolled one of his waffle Zalabias into a cone. When the cone cooled, the ice-cream vendor filled it with ice cream. The rest is ice-cream history!"

Use the information from the story to fill in the missing cause or effect below.

Cause	Effect
People kept walking off with Italo's ice-cream bowls.	_____
Italo wanted to protect his ice-cream cone idea.	_____
_____	The ice-cream vendor was desperate.
The ice-cream vendor looked at the booth next to him.	_____
Mr. Hamwi rolled one of his waffle-like pastries into a cone and let it cool.	_____

Name _____

Seashell Driveway!

There is something very strange about the driveways on the island of Nantucket in Massachusetts. Most of the driveways are made of seashells! Many people on this small island do not have black asphalt driveways or even dirt driveways. Their driveways are made entirely of real seashells.

Directions: Read the story on the following pages. Then, answer the questions.

One day, Kristin was visiting her friend Kari on Nantucket Island. Kari's mom said, "Girls, I need your help. Our driveway is a mess! All the shells have washed away over the winter, and we must make a new driveway for the summer. I will pay you girls a bag of candy for every large bucket of shells you collect."

Kristin and Kari smiled from ear to ear. Kari's driveway was long. They would need at least 8 huge buckets of shells to cover the driveway. That was a lot of candy! Kristin and Kari grabbed the biggest buckets they could find and headed towards the beach.

The ocean always washed up large deposits of shells on a sandbank a few feet from the shore. "Look, over there!" said Kristin. Beautiful white-and-pink scalloped shells glistened under the clear-blue water. The girls could not swim with their heavy buckets, so they lined them up on the beach.

I. Reading
   A. Directions
   B. Sequencing
   C. Main Idea
II. Writing
   A. Capitalization
   B. Proofreading

Name _____

Seashell Driveway! cont.

"Let's go!" said Kari. The girls swam out to the large shell deposit and dove down to the ocean bottom. Hundreds of shells were lying on the velvety, wet sand. They could not carry many shells in their hands. They had to swim back and forth all day to collect enough shells to fill the buckets. Finally, all 8 buckets were full with broken shells, beautiful pink shells, gray-striped shells, and smooth, white shells.

Kari's mom came and loaded the buckets of shells into the back of their old station wagon. "Wow! You girls did a great job and found the most beautiful shells! I think I have to double my offer of candy!" said Kari's mom.

When they got home, Kristin and Kari saved 12 beautiful shells that were too smooth and shapely to be used for the driveway. They would use them instead to hold barrettes or knick-knacks in their bedrooms.

Kari, Kristin, and Kari's mom then dumped all 8 buckets onto the driveway and spread the shells all over. "This looks great, girls! Now I need to crush them. Kari and Kristin stood back. Kari's mom drove the station wagon back and forth on the driveway, crushing the shells so they broke into tiny pieces. The shells made a pretty, hard driveway that would last all summer. Kristin, Kari, and Kari's mom looked at the beautiful white driveway and thought they must have made the most beautiful driveway on the whole island of Nantucket!

Name _____

Seashell Driveway! cont.

Directions: Use the information from the story to fill in the missing cause or effect below.

Cause	Effect
The winter snow washed away the shell driveway.	_____
_____	Kari's mom would pay them with candy.
Kari's driveway was long.	_____
The ocean washed the shells towards the shore.	_____
_____	They lined up 8 large buckets on the beach.
The girls did a great job collecting the shells.	_____
_____	The girls saved 12 shells for themselves.
Kari's mom drove the car over the shells.	_____

I. Reading
A. Directions
B. Sequencing
C. Main Idea
II. Writing
A. Capitalization
B. Proofreading

Name _____

500 Apples

Directions: Read the story below. Then, answer the question.

One day, a rickety old pickup truck stopped outside of my house. It was full of hundreds of red apples. The driver of the truck waved and called out the window, "Good morning, folks! You are the lucky winners of 500 red apples! Where would you like them?"

Use your imagination and tell what you think happens next in the story.

_____

_____

_____

_____

_____

_____

_____

_____

What Happens Next?

Directions: Read each paragraph below. Predict what will happen next in the story by placing an **X** in front of the best answer.

Jonathan met the old master chess player in the park for the sixth week in a row. Each week, the old master beat him at chess. Even still, Jonathan knew that he was getting better at chess. "Jonathan, you have a natural talent for playing chess. Every five years I take on one new pupil if I think he or she can handle my training."

_____ Jonathan gives up the game of chess.

_____ Jonathan accepts but soon finds he cannot handle the training.

_____ Jonathan accepts and one day beats the old master at a game.

_____ Jonathan says that he is content to just meet the master in the park.

Martha loves to bake cookies. Each day after school, she experiments with a new recipe. Oftentimes, she sells her most delicious recipes to stores and gives away samples to her friends.

_____ Martha will open her own cookie store one day.

_____ Martha will soon tire of baking cookies.

_____ Martha decides she wants to make more difficult desserts.

I. Reading
A. Directions
B. Sequencing
C. Main Idea
II. Writing
A. Capitalization
B. Proofreading

Name _____

A New Technique

Directions: Read the story on pages 87 and 88. Then, underline the best answers.

1. What statement best summarizes the story?

   Two best friends talk about video games while Megan's dad shops.

   While playing video games, the friends talk about Jim's sister.

   Two 4th-grade video game players can't wait to become older.

2. Why does Megan feel proud?

   Jim played well using the technique she had taught him.

   Megan's technique helped her hit with accuracy.

   They could play two more games with money Jim found.

3. What makes the new technique different from other playing methods?

   It is hard to learn.

   It is played with the left hand.

   It gave Megan confidence.

4. What statement best summarizes Jim and Megan's discussion?

   It will be fun to work on a summer work crew.

   Jim's sister will do something unusual this summer.

   Jim's dad lost his cool.

5. Why does Jim's dad lose his cool about the summer plans?

   He is surprised and worried.

   He is jealous and angry.

   He is delighted and happy.

6. How does Jim feel in the end about his sister's summer plans?

   He is proud.   He is frustrated.   He understands.

I. Reading
  A. Directions
  B. Sequencing
  C. Main Idea
II. Writing
  A. Capitalization
  B. Proofreading

Name _____

page 5

page 4

Megan felt proud as she watched Jim's score. Jim was using the left-handed technique she'd perfected and then passed on to him. She had discovered that her nondominant hand gave her that perfect balance of control and out-of-control movement required for tremendous accuracy!

Megan and Jim had each been given two dollars to play in the video arcade. As usual, they'd spent it long before Megan's dad finished grocery shopping.

Luckily, Jim had found a machine where someone had forgotten to pick up his change. They could play two more games.

Line C

Cut-and-Fold Story

Directions:

1. Tear page out of book.

2. Cut off small bottom strip along Line A.

3. Fold page along Line B so that the top meets the bottom. Make sure Line B is on the inside of the fold.

4. Cut along Line B.

5. Hold the two pieces together. Fold along Line C to make the book.

page 8

A New Technique

Line A

I. Reading
  A. Directions
  B. Sequencing
  C. Main Idea
II. Writing
  A. Capitalization
  B. Proofreading

Name _____

page 5

page 6

Having a fast-learning student confirmed her confidence in this technique. Jim's last statement distracted her from his game. "What's so wrong with being on a summer work crew?" she asked.

She'll spend five weeks back country camping in a national park," he replied. Jim whirled and yanked the joystick one last time to the right. "Your turn."

— Line B —

"I can't believe what my sister's doing. She's crazy!" Jim exclaimed to his best friend, Megan.

"What did she do this time?" Megan asked disinterestedly, as she tried, without being noticed, to see their neighbor's score. Megan had been watching his progress and taking pleasure in his low scores.

Frantically jamming the lever back and forth with just enough stop-action control for his score to continue its climb, Jim replied, "She volunteered for a summer work crew. Dad nearly lost his cool when he found out."

"Wow!" Megan said, as she turned her attention to the screen with her left hand on the joystick. Her body was bent slighty, ready for action. "Do you mean no toilet, showers, or video games for over a month? You're right, she is crazy!"

"Yeah," Jim reflected, "and no parents telling you what to do, either. I can't wait until I'm old enough to do it!"

page 2

page 7

Name _____

The Recycler

Hi there!

A **character** is the person, animal, or object that a story is about. You cannot have a story without a character.

Characters are usually people, but sometimes they can be animals, aliens (!), or even objects that come to life. You can have many characters in a story.

Directions: Read the story below. Then, answer the questions about character on the next page.

Sasha is president of the Recycling Club at her school. She meets with the 40 members in the club every week. At the meetings, she says, "We need to brainstorm ways to protect our environment! We need to stop adding unnecessary waste to landfills!"

Sasha came up with the idea of placing blue recycling bins next to every wastebasket in the school to recycle soda cans. She also put a recycling bin next to the teachers' copy machine that says, "Please, recycle." Sasha is very passionate about recycling.

At home, she organized and labeled her family's three trash cans. One is for paper waste, one is for aluminum cans and glass, and one is for regular waste. Her parents call her "The Recycler"! Sasha knows how important it is to protect the earth, and recycling is a big part of doing that.

Name _____

More About the Recycler

First, authors must decide who the main character is going to be in their story. Then, they reveal the character's personality by:

what the character does
what the character says
what other people say about the character

Directions: Answer the following questions about character.

Give two examples of what Sasha **does** to show that she is passionate about recycling.

1. _____

2. _____

Give an example of what Sasha **says** to reveal that she is passionate about recycling.

_____

Give an example of what **other people say** about Sasha and her recycling efforts.

_____

If Sasha drank a soda at a park and there was no recycling bin for the can, what do you think she would do? What would you do? Write your answers on the lines below.

_____

_____

Name _____

Conducting an Interview

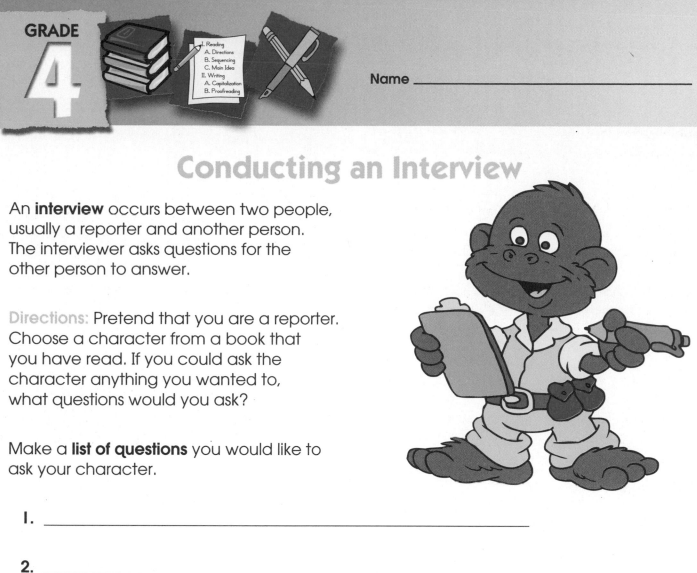

An **interview** occurs between two people, usually a reporter and another person. The interviewer asks questions for the other person to answer.

Directions: Pretend that you are a reporter. Choose a character from a book that you have read. If you could ask the character anything you wanted to, what questions would you ask?

Make a **list of questions** you would like to ask your character.

1. _____

2. _____

3. _____

4. _____

Now, pretend that your character has come to life and could **answer your questions**. Write what you think your character would say.

1. _____

2. _____

3. _____

4. _____

Setting—Place

Every story has a setting. The **setting** is the **place** where the story happens. Think of a place that you know well. It could be your bedroom, your kitchen, your backyard, your classroom, or an imaginary place.

Brainstorm some words and ideas about that place. Think about what you see, hear, smell, taste, or feel in that place.

Directions: Now, write down your ideas for a setting below.

_____

_____

_____

_____

see   hear   smell

taste   touch

_____

_____

_____

_____

_____

_____

_____

Where are you? _____

I. Reading
   A. Directions
   B. Sequencing
   C. Main Idea
II. Writing
   A. Capitalization
   B. Proofreading

Name _____

Amundsen-Scott Station

Directions: Read the story below and then answer the questions about the setting.

There is a place on Earth that is very cold and very icy. The few planes that travel there must have skis attached to their undersides so that they can land! This place is the continent of Antarctica, the coldest place on Earth. In fact, the coldest temperature on the entire planet was recorded in Antarctica in July of 1983. It was more than 100 degrees below zero! Actually, it was –128.6° Fahrenheit, to be exact.

Ninety percent of the world's ice is in Antarctica. It is a continent over 5,000,000 square miles in area and is owned by no country. A small number of scientific research stations set up by a few countries that have claimed territory in Antarctica fill the continent. The Amundsen-Scott station is an American scientific research station in Antarctica named after Roald Amundsen and Robert Scott. Amundsen was the first person to ever reach the South Pole. He did so in December of 1911. Scott, from the United Kingdom, reached the South Pole a month later in January of 1912.

I. Reading
A. Directions
B. Sequencing
C. Main Idea
II. Writing
A. Capitalization
B. Proofreading

Name _____

Amundsen-Scott Station, cont.

Scientists who stay at the station today have to be very careful because of the dangerous climate. There are only six months of sunlight followed by six months of darkness. In the summer months, the scientists must be careful to protect their eyes from the constant sunlight reflecting off the snow and ice. All of that sunlight can actually burn their eyes and cause blindness. At times, the wind can be fierce, and it howls over the ice. This makes it even colder and more difficult to see.

Antarctica has one of the harshest climates on Earth. Even so, many scientists who visit it say that all of the pure, white ice makes it one of the most beautiful places on Earth.

Directions: Write about what you would see, hear, and feel.

What would you **see** if you visited the Amundsen-Scott station in Antarctica?

_____

_____

_____

What might you **hear** living at the station? _____

_____

_____

What would you **feel** living at the station? _____

_____

_____

I. Reading
  A. Directions
  B. Sequencing
  C. Main Idea
II. Writing
  A. Capitalization
  B. Proofreading

Name _____

Happy Kwanzaa!

The **setting** is the **place** where the story happens. The setting is also the **time** in which the story takes place. A reader needs to know **when** the story is happening. Does it take place at night? On a sunny day? In the future? During the winter?

Time can be: time of day
                 a holiday
                 a season of the year
                 a time in history
                 a time in the future

Directions: Read the following story. Then, answer the questions below.

Kwanzaa is the name of an African-American holiday. It is named after the Swahili phrase, "Matunda ya kwanzaa," which means "first fruits." This holiday starts on December 26 and lasts through January 1. It commemorates African tribes coming together to sing, eat, dance, and celebrate the bounty of their fruit and vegetable harvests. Aisha celebrates Kwanzaa with her family. On December 31, there is a big feast. All of Aisha's relatives come over in the evening to share food, gifts, and song. If you ever celebrate Kwanzaa, make sure you can say, "Kwanzaa Yenu iwe na heri," which means, of course, "Happy Kwanzaa!"

When does the holiday of Kwanzaa take place?

_____

At **what time** and on **what day** do Aisha's relatives come over to celebrate the Kwanzaa feast?

_____

I. Reading
  A. Directions
  B. Sequencing
  C. Main Idea
II. Writing
  A. Capitalization
  B. Proofreading

Name _____

When and Where?

The **setting** tells **when** and **where** a story takes place.

Directions: Read the story settings below. Then, describe where and when each story takes place.

The balmy night air of San Juan feels nice against my skin. I often visit my Aunt Sylvia, who lives in San Juan, the capital of Puerto Rico. She says Puerto Rico has the best weather in the world. Other people say that during the winter months, only in Puerto Rico can you feel such warm, soft air.

When did this story take place? _____

Where did this story take place? _____

Last June, Regan traveled to an exotic destination. After working hard all year, she wanted to swim, read books, and relax. She found the vacation spot she was looking for when she visited the beautiful beaches of Costa Rica!

When did this story take place? _____

Where did this story take place? _____

The snowflakes fell hard on my face. My mittens were covered with snow. Even so, there was no way I was going to leave the November Championship Game at Rigby Field! I came here to root for my favorite team!

When did this story take place? _____

Where did this story take place? _____

GRADE 4

I. Reading
   A. Directions
   B. Sequencing
   C. Main Idea
II. Writing
   A. Capitalization
   B. Proofreading

Name _____

Make a Map

Think about a story or book you have read. Did the character take a journey or walk around his or her town? In your imagination, what does your character's home look like? Where did the main events in the story take place?

Directions: Keeping your story in mind and following the directions below, create a detailed map showing the place where the characters lived.

1. Draw the outline of your map on a sheet of paper.

2. Be sure to write the title and the author of the book at the top of the map.

3. Think about what places you want to include on your map, and then draw them.

4. Label the important places, adding a brief phrase or sentence about what happened there.

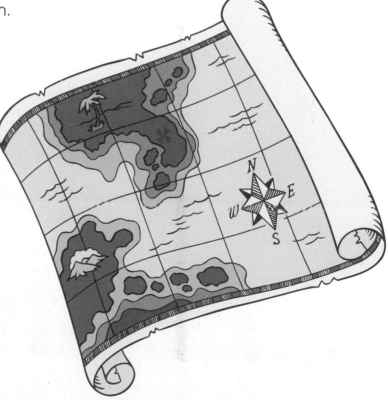

5. Add color and details.

6. Share your map with friends and tell them about the story you read.

Name _____

Travel Brochure

A **travel brochure** gives information about interesting places to visit. Travel brochures usually include beautiful colored pictures and descriptive sentences that make people want to visit that place. They also give useful facts about a place.

Directions: Plan a travel brochure for the **setting** of a book you have read.

1. First, brainstorm the things you would like to include in your travel brochure. You might include interesting places to visit, restaurants, what people eat there, or other interesting activities people do in this place.

2. Next, take a piece of paper and fold it into three sections. You can write on both the front and back sides of the paper.

3. Use crayons or markers to color your brochure.

4. Share your brochure with friends and tell them about the setting of your book.

I. Reading
  A. Directions
  B. Sequencing
  C. Main Idea
II. Writing
  A. Capitalization
  B. Proofreading

Name _____

The Princess and the Pea

Fairy tales are short stories written for children involving magical characters.

Directions: Read the story "The Princess and the Pea." Then, answer the questions.

Once there was a prince who wanted to get married. The catch was, he had to marry a real princess. The Prince knew that real princesses were few and far between. When they heard he was looking for a bride, many young women came to the palace. All claimed to be real princesses.

"Hmmm," thought the Prince. "I must think of a way to sort out the real princesses from the fake ones. I will ask the Queen for advice."

Luckily, since he was a prince, the Queen was also his mother. So of course she had her son's best interests at heart. "A real princess is very delicate," said the Queen. "She must sleep on a mattress as soft as a cloud. If there is even a small lump, she will not be able to sleep."

"Why not?" asked the Prince. He was a nice man but not as smart as his mother.

"Because she is so delicate!" said the Queen impatiently. "Let's figure out a way to test her. Better still, let me figure out a test. You go down and pick a girl to try out my plan."

The Prince went down to the lobby of the castle. A very pretty but humble-looking girl caught his eye. He brought her back to his mother, who welcomed her.

"Please be our guest at the castle tonight," said the Queen. "Tomorrow, we will talk with you about whether you are a real princess."

The pretty but humble-looking girl was shown to her room. In it was a pile of five mattresses, all fluffy and clean. "A princess is delicate," said the Queen. "Sweet dreams!"

The girl climbed to the top of the pile and laid down, but she could not sleep. She tossed and turned and was quite cross the next morning.

"I found this under the fourth mattress when I got up this morning," she said. She handed a small green pea to the Queen. "No wonder I couldn't sleep!"

The Queen clapped her hands. The Prince looked confused. "A real princess is delicate. If this pea I put under the mattress kept you awake, you are definitely a princess."

"Of course I am," said the Princess. "Now, may I please take a nap?"

I. Why does the Prince worry about finding a bride? _____

_____

2. According to the Queen, how can the Prince tell who is a real princess? _____

_____

3. Who hides something under the girl's mattress? _____

Name _____

Reviewing "The Princess and the Pea"

Directions: Review the story "The Princess and the Pea." Then, answer the questions.

1. Why does the Prince need a test to see who is a real princess?

_____

_____

2. Why does the Princess have trouble sleeping? _____

_____

3. In this story, the Queen puts a small pea under a pile of mattresses to see if the girl is delicate. What else could be done to test a princess for delicacy?_____

_____

_____

_____

The story does not tell whether or not the Prince and Princess get married and live happily ever after, only that the Princess wants to take a nap.

Directions: Write a new ending to the story.

What do you think happens after the Princess wakes up?

_____

_____

_____

_____

_____

_____

_____

GRADE
4

I. Reading
A. Directions
B. Sequencing
C. Main Idea
II. Writing
A. Capitalization
B. Proofreading

Name _____

The Frog Prince

Directions: Read the story "The Frog Prince." Then, answer the questions.

Once upon a time, there lived a beautiful princess who liked to play alone in the woods. One day, as she was playing with her golden ball, it rolled into a lake. The water was so deep she could not see the ball. The Princess was very sad. She cried out, "I would give anything to have my golden ball back!"

Suddenly, a large ugly frog popped out of the water. "Anything?" he croaked. The Princess looked at him with distaste. "Yes," she said, "I would give anything."

"I will get your golden ball," said the frog. "In return, you must take me back to the castle. You must let me live with you and eat from your golden plate."

"Whatever you want," said the Princess. She thought the frog was very ugly, but she wanted her golden ball.

The frog dove down and brought the ball to the Princess. She put the frog in her pocket and took him home. "He is ugly," the Princess said. "But a promise is a promise. And a princess always keeps her word."

The Princess changed her clothes and forgot all about the frog. That evening, she heard a tapping at her door. She ran to the door to open it and a handsome prince stepped in.

"Who are you?" asked the Princess, already half in love.

"I am the prince you rescued at the lake," said the handsome Prince. "I was turned into a frog one hundred years ago today by a wicked lady. Because she always keeps her promises, only a beautiful princess could break the spell. You are a little forgetful, but you did keep your word!"

Can you guess what happened next? Of course, they were married and lived happily ever after.

1. What does the frog ask the Princess to promise? _____

_____

2. Where does the Princess put the frog when she leaves the lake? _____

_____

3. Why could only a princess break the spell? _____

_____

_____

GRADE 4

I. Reading
  A. Directions
  B. Sequencing
  C. Main Idea
II. Writing
  A. Capitalization
  B. Proofreading

Name _____

Reviewing "The Frog Prince"

Directions: Review the story "The Frog Prince." Then, answer the questions.

1. What does the Princess lose in the lake? _____

2. How does she get it back? _____

_____

_____

3. How does the frog turn back into a prince? _____

_____

4. What phrases are used to begin and end this story? _____

_____

5. Are these words used frequently to begin and end fairy tales? _____

There is more than one version of most fairy tales. In another version of this story, the Princess has to kiss the frog in order for him to change back into a prince.

Directions: Write your answers.

1. What do you think would happen in a story where the Princess kisses the frog, but he remains a frog?

_____

_____

2. What kinds of problems would a princess have with a bossy frog in the castle? Brainstorm ideas and write them here.

_____

_____

3. Rewrite the ending to "The Frog Prince" so that the frog remains a frog and does not turn into a handsome prince. Continue your story on another sheet of paper.

_____

GRADE 4

I. Reading
  A. Directions
  B. Sequencing
  C. Main Idea
II. Writing
  A. Capitalization
  B. Proofreading

Name _____

Fairy Tales

Directions: Think of fairy tales you know from books or videos, like "Cinderella," "Snow White," "Sleeping Beauty," "Rapunzel," and "Beauty and the Beast." Then, answer the questions.

1. What are some common elements in all fairy tales? _____

_____

2. How do fairy tales usually begin? _____

_____

3. How do fairy tales usually end? _____

_____

Directions: Locate and read several different versions of the same fairy tale. For example, "Princess Furball," "Cinderlad," and "Yah Shen." Then, answer the questions.

1. How are the stories alike? _____

_____

_____

_____

2. How are they different? _____

_____

_____

3. Which story is best developed by the author? _____

4. Which story did you like best? Why? _____

_____

Name _____

The Hare and the Tortoise

"The Hare and the Tortoise" is called a **fable**. Fables are usually short stories. As you read this story and the other fables on the next few pages, look for two characteristics the fables have in common.

Directions: Read the fable "The Hare and the Tortoise." Then, answer the questions.

One day, the hare and the tortoise were talking. Or rather, the hare was bragging and the tortoise was listening.

"I am faster than the wind," bragged the hare. "I feel sorry for you because you are so slow! Why, you are the slowest fellow I have ever seen."

"Do you think so?" asked the tortoise with a smile. "I will race you to that big tree across the field."

Slowly, he lifted a leg. Slowly, he pointed toward the tree.

"Ha!" scoffed the hare. "You must be kidding! You will most certainly be the loser! But, if you insist, we will race."

The tortoise nodded politely. "I'll be off," he said. Slowly and steadily, the tortoise moved across the field.

The hare stood back and laughed. "How sad that he should compete with me!" he said. His chest puffed up with pride. "I will take a little nap while the poor old tortoise lumbers along. When I wake up, he will still be only halfway across the field."

The tortoise kept on, slow and steady, across the field. Some time later, the hare awoke. He discovered that while he slept, the tortoise had won the race.

1. What is the main idea? (Check one.)

_____ Tortoises are faster than hares.

_____ Hares need more sleep than tortoises.

_____ Slow and steady wins the race.

2. The hare brags that he is faster than what? (Check one.)

_____ a bullet

_____ a greyhound

_____ the wind

3. Who is modest, the tortoise or the hare? _____

Name _____

Reviewing "The Hare and the Tortoise"

Another important skill in reading is recognizing cause and effect. The **cause** is the reason something happens. The **effect** is what happens or the situation that results from the cause. In the story, the hare falling asleep is a cause. It causes the hare to lose the race. Losing the race is the effect.

Directions: Identify the underlined words or phrases by writing **cause** or **effect** in the blanks.

1. The hare and tortoise had a race because the hare bragged about being faster.

_____

2. The tortoise won the race because he continued on, slowly, but steadily.

_____

Directions: Review the fable "The Hare and the Tortoise." Then, answer the questions.

1. Who are the two main characters? _____

2. Where does the story take place? _____

3. What lessons can be learned from this story? _____

_____

4. The lesson that is learned at the end of a fable has a special name. What is that special name?

_____

5. Why did the tortoise want to race the hare? _____

_____

6. How do you think the hare felt at the end of the story? _____

_____

7. How do you think the tortoise felt at the end of the story? _____

_____

_____

Name _____

The Fox and the Crow

Directions: Read the fable "The Fox and the Crow." Then, number the events in order to show the **sequence** of the story.

Once upon a time, a crow found a piece of cheese on the ground. "Aha!" he said to himself. "This dropped from a workman's sandwich. It will make a fine lunch for me."

The crow picked up the cheese in his beak. He flew to a tree to eat it. Just as he began to chew it, a fox trotted by.

"Hello, crow!" he said slyly, for he wanted the cheese. The fox knew if the crow answered, the cheese would fall from its mouth. Then, the fox would have cheese for lunch!

The crow just nodded.

"It's a wonderful day, isn't it?" asked the fox.

The crow nodded again and held onto the cheese.

"You are the most beautiful bird I have ever seen," added the fox.

The crow spread his feathers. Everyone likes a compliment. Still, the crow held firmly to the cheese.

"There is something I have heard," said the fox, "and I wonder if it is true. I heard that you sing more sweetly than any of the other birds."

The crow was eager to show off his talents. He opened his beak to sing. The cheese dropped to the ground.

"I said you were beautiful," said the fox as he ran away with the cheese. "I did not say you were smart!"

_____ The crow drops the cheese.

_____ The crow flies to a tree with the cheese.

_____ The fox tells the crow he is beautiful.

_____ The fox runs off with the cheese.

_____ A workman loses the cheese from his sandwich.

_____ The fox comes along.

_____ The fox tells the crow he has heard that crows sing beautifully.

_____ The crow picks up the cheese.

GRADE
4

I. Reading
   A. Directions
   B. Sequencing
   C. Main Idea
II. Writing
   A. Capitalization
   B. Proofreading

Name _____

Reviewing "The Fox and the Crow"

Directions: Review the fable "The Fox and the Crow." Then, answer the questions.

1. With what words does the story begin? _____

2. What other type of story often begins with these same words? _____

3. Although it is not stated, where do you think the story takes place?

_____

4. How does the fox get what he wants from the crow? _____

_____

_____

5. How is the crow in this story like the hare in the last fable? _____

_____

_____

Predicting is telling or guessing what you think might happen in a story or situation based on what you already know.

Directions: Write predictions to answer these questions.

1. Based on what you read, what do you think the crow will do the next time he finds a piece of cheese?

_____

_____

2. What do you think the fox will do the next time he wants to trick the crow? _____

_____

_____

_____

_____

Name _____

The Boy Who Cried Wolf

Directions: Read the fable "The Boy Who Cried Wolf." Then, complete the puzzle.

Once, there was a shepherd boy who tended his sheep alone. The sheep were gentle animals. They were easy to take care of. The boy grew bored.

"I can't stand another minute alone with these sheep," he said crossly. He knew only one thing would bring people quickly to him. If he cried, "Wolf!" the men in the village would run up the mountain. They would come to help save the sheep from the wolf.

"Wolf!" he yelled loudly, and he blew on his horn.

Quick as a wink, a dozen men came running. When they realized it was a joke, they were very angry. The boy promised never to do it again. But a week later, he grew bored and cried, "Wolf!" again. Again, the men ran to him. This time they were very, very angry.

Soon afterwards, a wolf really came. The boy was scared. "Wolf!" he cried. "Wolf! Wolf! Wolf!"

He blew his horn, but no one came, and the wolf ate all his sheep.

Across:

2. This is where the boy tends sheep.

4. When no one came, the wolf _____ all the sheep.

5. Sheep are _____ and easy to take care of.

Down:

1. The people who come are from here.

2. At first, when the boy cries, "Wolf!" the _____ come running.

3. When a wolf really comes, this is how the boy feels.

Reviewing "The Boy Who Cried Wolf"

Directions: Identify the underlined words as a **cause** or an **effect**.

1. <u>The boy cries wolf</u> because he is bored. _____

2. <u>The boy blows his horn</u> and the men come running. _____

3. No one comes, and <u>the wolf eats all the sheep</u>. _____

Directions: Answer the questions.

1. What lesson can be learned from this story? _____

_____

_____

2. How is this story like the two other fables you read? _____

_____

_____

_____

3. Is the boy in the story more like the fox or the hare? How so? _____

_____

_____

_____

_____

_____

_____

_____

GRADE
4

I. Reading
A. Directions
B. Sequencing
C. Main Idea
II. Writing
A. Capitalization
B. Proofreading

Name _____

The City Mouse and the Country Mouse

Directions: Read the fable "The City Mouse and the Country Mouse." Then, answer the questions.

Once there were two mice, a city mouse and a country mouse. They were cousins. The country mouse was always begging his cousin to visit him. Finally, the city mouse agreed.

When he arrived, the city mouse was not very polite. "How do you stand it here?" he asked, wrinkling his nose. "All you have to eat is corn and barley. All you have to wear is old, tattered work clothes. And all you have to listen to are the other animals. Why don't you come and visit me? Then, you will see what it's like to really live!"

The country mouse liked corn and barley. He liked the sounds of the other animals. And he liked his old work clothes fine. Secretly, he thought his cousin was silly to wear fancy clothes. Still, the city sounded exciting. Why not give it a try?

Since he had no clothes to pack, the country mouse was ready in no time. His cousin told him stories about the city as they traveled. The buildings were so high! The food was so good! The girl mice were so beautiful!

The home of the city mouse was nice. He lived in a hole in the wall in an old castle. "It is only a hole in the wall," said the city mouse, "but it is a very nice wall, indeed!"

That night, the mice crept out of the wall. Everyone had eaten, but the maid had not cleaned up. The table was still loaded with good food. The mice ate and ate. The country mouse was not used to rich food. He began to feel sick to his stomach.

Just then, they heard loud barking. Two huge dogs ran into the room. They nearly bit off the country mouse's tail! He barely made it to the hole in the wall in time. That did it!

"Thank you for showing me the city," said the country mouse, "but it is too exciting for me. I am going home where it is peaceful. I can't wait to settle my stomach with some corn and barley."

1. What are three things the city mouse says are wrong with the country? _____

_____

2. Why doesn't it take the country mouse long to get ready to leave with the city mouse?

_____

3. Why does the country mouse secretly think his cousin is silly? _____

_____

Name _____

Reviewing "The City Mouse and the Country Mouse"

Directions: Review the fable "The City Mouse and the Country Mouse." Use the Venn diagram to compare and contrast the lifestyles of the city mouse and the country mouse.

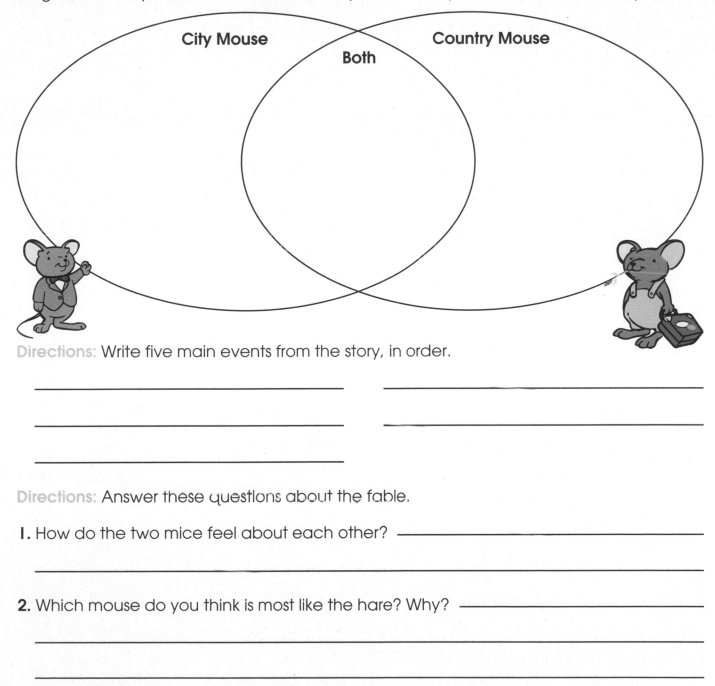

City Mouse   Both   Country Mouse

Directions: Write five main events from the story, in order.

_____   _____

_____   _____

_____

Directions: Answer these questions about the fable.

1. How do the two mice feel about each other? _____

_____

2. Which mouse do you think is most like the hare? Why? _____

_____

_____

GRADE
4

I. Reading
A. Directions
B. Sequencing
C. Main Idea
II. Writing
A. Capitalization
B. Proofreading

Name _____

Paul Bunyan

There is a certain kind of fable called a **tall tale**. In these stories, each storyteller tries to "top" the other. The stories get more and more unbelievable. A popular hero of American tall tales is Paul Bunyan, a giant of a man. Here are some of the stories that have been told about him.

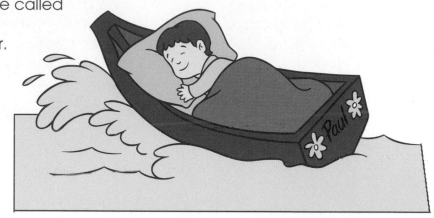

Even as a baby, Paul was very big. One night, he rolled over in his sleep and knocked down a mile of trees. Of course, Paul's father wanted to find some way to keep Paul from getting hurt in his sleep and to keep him from knocking down all the forests. So, he cut down some tall trees and made a boat for Paul to use as a cradle. He tied a long rope to the boat and let it drift out a little way into the sea to rock Paul to sleep.

One night, Paul had trouble sleeping. He kept turning over in his bed. Each time he turned, the cradle rocked. And each time the cradle rocked, it sent up waves as big as buildings. The waves got bigger and bigger until the people on the land were afraid they would all be drowned. They told Paul's parents that Paul was a danger to the whole state! So, Paul and his parents had to move away.

After that, Paul didn't get into much trouble when he was growing up. His father taught him some very important lessons, such as, "If there are any towns or farms in your way, be sure to step around them!"

Directions: Answer these questions about Paul Bunyan.

1. What kind of fable is the story of Paul Bunyan? _____

2. What did Paul's father make for Paul to use as a cradle? _____

3. What happened when Paul rolled over in his cradle? _____

_____

4. What did Paul's father tell Paul to do to towns and farms that were in his way?

_____

GRADE 4

I. Reading
   A. Directions
   B. Sequencing
   C. Main Idea
II. Writing
   A. Capitalization
   B. Proofreading

Name _____

More Paul Bunyan

When Paul Bunyan grew up, he was taller than other men—by about 50 feet or so! Because of his size, he could do almost anything. One of the things he did best was to cut down trees and turn them into lumber. With only four strokes of his axe, he could cut off all the branches and bark. After he turned all the trees for miles into these tall square posts, he tied a long rope to an axe head. Then, he yelled, "T-I-M-B-E-R-R-R!" and swung the rope around in a huge circle. With every swing, 100 trees fell to the ground.

One cold winter day, Paul found a huge blue ox stuck in the snow. It was nearly frozen. Although it was only a baby, even Paul could hardly lift it. Paul took the ox home and cared for it. He named it Babe, and they became best friends. Babe was a big help to Paul when he was cutting down trees.

When Babe was full grown, it was hard to tell how big he was. There were no scales big enough to weigh him. Paul once measured the distance between Babe's eyes. It was the length of 42 axe handles!

Once, Paul and Babe were working with other men to cut lumber. The job was very hard because the road was so long and winding. It was said that the road was so crooked that men starting home for camp would meet themselves coming back! Well, Paul hitched Babe to the end of that crooked road. Babe pulled and pulled. He pulled so hard that his eyes nearly turned pink. There was a loud snap. The first curve came out of the road and Babe pulled harder. Finally, the whole road started to move. Babe pulled it completely straight!

Directions: Answer these questions about Paul Bunyan and Babe.

1. What was Paul Bunyan particularly good at doing? _____

2. What did Paul find in the snow? _____

3. How big was the distance between Babe's eyes? _____

4. What did Babe do to the crooked road? _____

GRADE 4

I. Reading
A. Directions
B. Sequencing
C. Main Idea
II. Writing
A. Capitalization
B. Proofreading

Name _____

Mr. Nobody

Directions: After reading the poem "Mr. Nobody," number in order the things people blame him for.

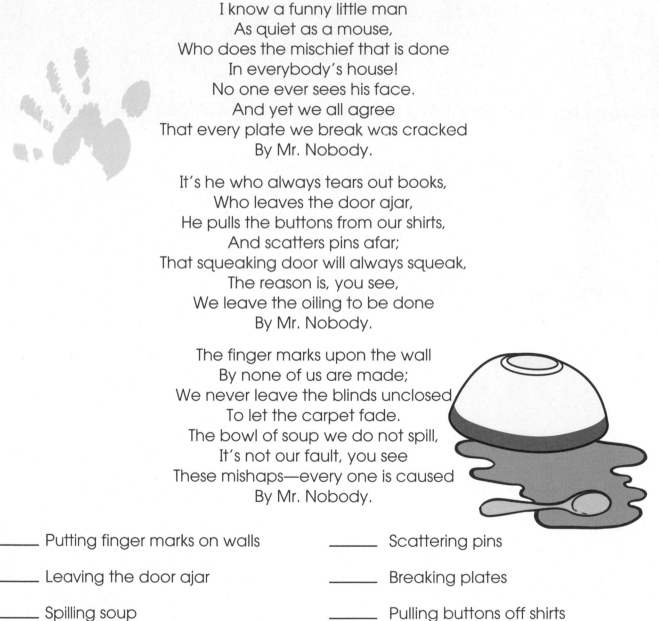

I know a funny little man
As quiet as a mouse,
Who does the mischief that is done
In everybody's house!
No one ever sees his face.
And yet we all agree
That every plate we break was cracked
By Mr. Nobody.

It's he who always tears out books,
Who leaves the door ajar,
He pulls the buttons from our shirts,
And scatters pins afar;
That squeaking door will always squeak,
The reason is, you see,
We leave the oiling to be done
By Mr. Nobody.

The finger marks upon the wall
By none of us are made;
We never leave the blinds unclosed
To let the carpet fade.
The bowl of soup we do not spill,
It's not our fault, you see
These mishaps—every one is caused
By Mr. Nobody.

_____ Putting finger marks on walls   _____ Scattering pins

_____ Leaving the door ajar   _____ Breaking plates

_____ Spilling soup   _____ Pulling buttons off shirts

_____ Tearing out books   _____ Squeaking doors

_____ Leaving the blinds open

I. Reading
A. Directions
B. Sequencing
C. Main Idea
II. Writing
A. Capitalization
B. Proofreading

Name _____

The Chickens

Directions: Read the poem "The Chickens." Then, answer the questions.

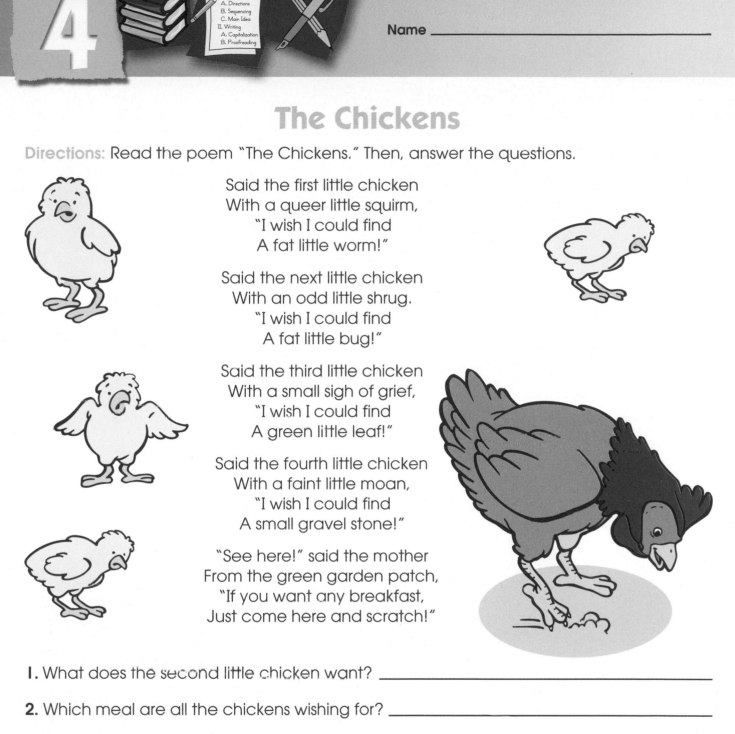

Said the first little chicken
With a queer little squirm,
"I wish I could find
A fat little worm!"

Said the next little chicken
With an odd little shrug.
"I wish I could find
A fat little bug!"

Said the third little chicken
With a small sigh of grief,
"I wish I could find
A green little leaf!"

Said the fourth little chicken
With a faint little moan,
"I wish I could find
A small gravel stone!"

"See here!" said the mother
From the green garden patch,
"If you want any breakfast,
Just come here and scratch!"

1. What does the second little chicken want? _____

2. Which meal are all the chickens wishing for? _____

3. Where is the mother hen? _____

4. Which of the following do the chickens not want?

_____ leaf   _____ corn   _____ worm   _____ bug   _____ stone

5. What does the mother hen tell her chicks to do if they want breakfast?

_____

Name _____

I'm Glad

Directions: Read the poem "I'm Glad." Then, work the puzzle.

I'm glad the sky is painted blue
And the Earth is painted green,
With such a lot of nice fresh air
All sandwiched in between.

Across:

3. The sky is painted this color.

4. How what we breathe is placed between the Earth and sky

6. This is what we breathe, and it's between the Earth and sky.

Down:

1. The color of the Earth in the poem

2. How the speaker feels

4. Painted blue

5. Painted green

I. Reading
  A. Directions
  B. Sequencing
  C. Main Idea
II. Writing
  A. Capitalization
  B. Proofreading

Name _____

Over the Hills and Far Away

Directions: Read the poem "Over the Hills and Far Away." Then, answer the questions.

Tom, Tom the piper's son,
Learned to play when he was one,
But the only tune that he could play
Was "Over the Hills and Far Away."

Now Tom with his pipe made such a noise
That he pleased the girls and he pleased the boys,
And they all danced when they heard him play
"Over the Hills and Far Away."

Tom played his pipe with such great skill,
Even pigs and dogs could not keep still.
The dogs would wag their tails and dance,
The pigs would oink and grunt and prance.

Yes, Tom could play, his music soared—
But soon the pigs and dogs got bored.
The children, too, thought it was wrong,
For Tom to play just one dull song.

I. How old is Tom when he learns to play? _____

2. What tune does Tom play? _____

_____

3. What do the dogs do when Tom plays? _____

_____

4. Why does everyone get tired of Tom's music? _____

_____

5. What do the pigs do when Tom plays? _____

_____

6. What instrument does Tom play? _____

I. Reading
  A. Directions
  B. Sequencing
  C. Main Idea
II. Writing
  A. Capitalization
  B. Proofreading

Name _____

The Spider and the Fly

Directions: Read the poem "The Spider and the Fly." Then, number the events in order.

"Won't you come into my parlor?" said the spider to the fly.
"It's the nicest little parlor that you will ever spy.
The way into my parlor is up a winding stair.
I have so many pretty things to show you inside there."

The little fly said, "No! No! No! To do so is not sane.
For those who travel up your stair do not come down again."

The spider turned himself around and went back in his den—
He knew for sure the silly fly would visit him again.
The spider wove a tiny web, for he was very sly.
He was making preparations to trap the silly fly.

Then out his door the spider came and merrily did sing,
"Oh, fly, oh lovely, lovely fly with pearl and silver wings."

Alas! How quickly did the fly come buzzing back to hear
The spider's words of flattery, which drew the fly quite near.

The fly was trapped within the web, the spider's winding stair,
Then the spider jumped upon him, and ate the fly right there!

_____ The spider sings a song about how beautiful the fly is.

_____ The spider jumps on the fly.

_____ The spider invites the fly into his parlor.

_____ The spider spins a tiny new web to catch the fly.

_____ The fly becomes caught in the spider's web.

_____ The fly says he knows it's dangerous to go into the spider's parlor.

_____ The spider eats the fly.

_____ The fly comes near the web to hear the song.

GRADE
4

I. Reading
   A. Directions
   B. Sequencing
   C. Main Idea
II. Writing
   A. Capitalization
   B. Proofreading

Name _____

Grasshopper Green

Directions: Read the poem "Grasshopper Green." Then, answer the questions.

Grasshopper Green is a comical guy,
He lives on the best of fare.
Bright little trousers, jacket, and cap,
These are his summer wear.

Out in the meadow he loves to go,
Playing away in the sun.
It's hopperty, skipperty, high and low,
Summer's the time for fun.

Grasshopper Green has a cute little house,
He stays near it every day.
It's under the hedge where he is safe,
Out of the gardener's way.

Gladly he's calling the children to play
Out in the beautiful sun
It's hopperty, skipperty, high and low,
Summer's the time for fun.

I. What does **comical** mean in this poem?_____

2. What are three things Grasshopper Green wears in the summer?

_____

3. Where does he love to go and play?_____

4. Whom does Grasshopper Green call to play?_____

5. What is summer the time for?_____

6. Use a dictionary. What does **fare** mean in this poem?_____

7. You won't find the words **hopperty** and **skipperty** in a dictionary. Based on the poem, write your own definitions of these words.

_____

_____

Name _____

Little Robin Redbreast

Directions: Read the poem "Little Robin Redbreast." Then, answer the questions.

Little Robin Redbreast
Sat up in a tree,
Up went the kitty cat
Down went he.

Down came the kitty cat—
Away Robin ran,
Said little Robin Redbreast,
"Catch me if you can."

Then Little Robin Redbreast
Hopped upon a wall,
Kitty cat jumped after him,
And almost had a fall.

Little Robin chirped and sang,
And what did kitty say?
Kitty cat said, "Meow!" quite loud,
And Robin flew away.

1. What is the main idea? (Check one.)

_____ The robin is smarter than the cat and a lot faster, too.

_____ When people see a robin, it means spring is near.

_____ The robin is scared away.

2. What nearly happens when the cat jumps on the wall?

_____

3. Where is the robin when the cat first goes after him? _____

4. Where does the robin go after the cat climbs the tree? _____

5. What does the robin say to the cat? _____

GRADE 4

I. Reading
A. Directions
B. Sequencing
C. Main Idea
II. Writing
A. Capitalization
B. Proofreading

Name _____

Hickory, Dickory, Dock

Directions: Read the poem "Hickory, Dickory, Dock." Then, answer the questions.

Hickory, dickory, dock,
The mouse ran up the clock.
The clock struck one,
And down he run,
Hickory, dickory, dock.

Dickory, dickory, dare,
The pig flew in the air.
The man in brown
Soon brought him down,
Dickory, dickory, dare.

Hickory
Dickory
Dock

1. What is the main idea? (Check one.)

_____ Mice and pigs can cause a lot of problems to clocks and men in brown suits.

_____ There is no main idea. This poem is just for fun.

_____ Beware of mice in your clocks and flying pigs.

2. Why do you think the mouse runs down the clock? _____

_____

Directions: Number these events in order.

_____ The clock strikes one.

_____ The mouse runs back down the clock.

_____ The mouse runs up the clock.

_____ The man in brown brings the pig down.

_____ The pig flies in the air.

Name _____

Camp Rules

Directions: Read the story and answer the questions that follow.
A made-up story is called **fiction**.

Donald, Arnold, and Jack are at Camp Explore-It-All this week. They think camp is a lot of fun. They have also learned from their instructors that there are some very important rules all campers must obey so that everyone has a good time.

All campers must take swimming tests to see what depth of water they can swim in safely. Donald and Jack pass the advanced test and can swim in the deep water. Arnold, however, only passes the intermediate test. He is supposed to stay in the area where the water is waist deep. When it is time to swim, Arnold decides to sneak into the advanced area with Donald and Jack. After all, he has been swimming in deep water for three years. No way is he going to stay in the shallow water with the babies.

Donald and Jack don't think Arnold should come into the deep water, but they can't tell him anything. So the boys jump into the water and start swimming and playing. Fifteen minutes later, Arnold is yelling, "Help!" He swims out too far and is too tired to make it back in. The lifeguard jumps in and pulls him out. Everyone stops to see what is happening. Arnold feels very foolish.

Check:
The main idea of this story is
☐ Arnold ends up feeling foolish.　　☐ Camp is fun.
☐ All campers take swimming tests.　　☐ Rules are made for good reasons.
☐ You can learn a lot from instructors.　☐ Rules are made to be broken.

Underline:
Arnold got himself into a(n) _____ situation.
　　　　　amusing　　funny　　dangerous　　ambiguous

Circle:
Arnold thought the guys in the shallow area were (bullies/babies). However, he should have (stayed with them/gone to the advanced area).

Write:
What lesson do you think Arnold learned? _____

_____

What do you think the other campers learned? _____

_____

GRADE 4

I. Reading
  A. Directions
  B. Sequencing
  C. Main Idea
II. Writing
  A. Capitalization
  B. Proofreading

Name _____

Dudley's Doing It Again!

Directions: Read the story and answer the questions that follow.

Dudley is up to his old tricks again. He just finished dog school six weeks ago, and he had really been doing so well. He fetched when he was told to fetch. He heeled when Donald said, "heel." He sat when he was supposed to sit. He would even do tricks like roll over, play dead, and speak to impress Donald's friends, if Donald gave him a doggy treat. But lately, Dudley hasn't been doing any of the things he was taught.

For the past several days, Dudley has been digging in the yard. This makes Donald's dad really mad. Dudley has also been chewing up the newspapers instead of bringing them to Donald's mom. One day, he chewed up all her grocery coupons. Boy, was she angry! And, Dudley won't sit or heel when Donald tells him to. Two days ago, Dudley knocked down Donald's friend Lee. Something has to be done about Dudley!

Circle:
Dudley seems to have forgotten . . .
    how to chew newspapers.
    everything he learned at dog school.
    everything Donald taught him.
    how to learn new tricks.

Check:

	Good Dog	Bad Dog
Dudley is up to his old tricks.	☐	☐
Dudley finished dog school.	☐	☐
Lee was knocked down by Dudley.	☐	☐
Dudley did tricks for treats.	☐	☐
Dudley has been digging in the yard.	☐	☐

Write:
What has Dudley forgotten that he learned at dog school?

_____

_____

What do you think Donald should do about Dudley? _____

_____

GRADE
4

I. Reading
A. Directions
B. Sequencing
C. Main Idea
II. Writing
A. Capitalization
B. Proofreading

Name _____

Lucky Beth or Lucky Kim?

Directions: Read the story and answer the questions that follow.

Kim thinks Beth is so lucky. Almost every day, Beth comes to school with something new. One day, she might be wearing a new outfit her mom bought her at the department store where her mom works. The next day, Beth may have something really unique from her father, like a watch that has the days of the week in a foreign language. He brings her gifts when he comes home from traveling on business.

Beth, however, does not think she is so lucky. Beth's mom works until 7 P.M. every night and also has to work every Saturday. Her father travels so much with his job, that Beth is lucky if she gets to see him one week a month. Beth loves her parents, but she wishes they were both home every night and every weekend like Kim's parents so they could do special things together. She also wishes she had a little brother like Kim does so she wouldn't be so lonely.

Check:

Kim thinks Beth is lucky because Beth . . .

☐ gets lots of neat gifts.

☐ doesn't have a brother or sister.

☐ has a father who travels a lot.

Circle:

Beth thinks Kim is lucky because . . .

Kim has a little brother.

Kim doesn't get a lot of new clothes.

Kim's parents are home at night and on the weekends.

Underline:

When something is unique, it is . . .

ugly   special   small   unusual   different

Write:

Who do you think is luckier, Kim or Beth? Why? _____

_____

_____

Name _____

The Day of the Game

Directions: Read the story. Then, fill in the circle next to the word or words that best complete each sentence.

Beth feels hot when she wakes up. She has a cough and a fever. Mom tells her she will have to stay in bed today. Beth is mad because she will miss the big baseball game between the Spiders and Gators. She's the best hitter on the Spiders. Without her, the team will lose for sure. Who wants to stay in bed eating chicken soup on the day of a big game? Would you?

After the game, Maria comes over to see how Beth feels. When Beth hears that the Spiders won without her, she feels hurt. Then, she remembers what Mr. Bryan said about each member of the team being important. Beth tells Maria she is happy that the team won without her.

I. Beth is ___ because she will miss the baseball game today.

   ○ happy   ○ mad

2. At the beginning of the story, Beth thinks the Spiders

   ○ will lose without her.   ○ will win without her.

3. At the end of the story, Beth remembers

   ○ she is the most important player.   ○ each team member is important.

Directions: Write a sentence telling how you felt when you missed something important.

_____

_____

The Spelling Bee

Directions: Read the story. Then, write a complete sentence to answer each question.

Lizzie and Erika are in the school spelling bee. Both girls work very hard. They write the spelling words over and over. They quiz each other after school for a week.

At the spelling bee, Lizzie and Erika are the last two spellers in all of the grades. Everyone else has missed a word. They both spell five words in a row without any mistakes. Then, Lizzie misses the word *submarine*. Erika spells it correctly. Then, Erika spells the next word correctly and wins the spelling bee.

Lizzie is disappointed but is happy that her friend won. Erika is pleased with herself but wishes that Lizzie could have won, too.

1. Why is Lizzie disappointed? _____

_____

2. When have you felt disappointed like Lizzie? _____

_____

3. How does Erika feel about winning the spelling bee? _____

_____

4. When have you felt pleased with yourself like Erika? _____

_____

_____

I. Reading
   A. Directions
   B. Sequencing
   C. Main Idea
II. Writing
   A. Capitalization
   B. Proofreading

Name _____

Jessie's Jobs

Directions: Read the story. Then, write an **X** next to the words that best complete each sentence.

Evan's little sister, Jessie, tries to do everything Evan does. She especially likes to help him do chores.

Evan has to take out the trash every Tuesday. He also has to vacuum every Saturday morning. On Mondays, it's his turn to wash the dishes.

Since Jessie is only five, her parents think she can't do any chores. As a result, she always tries to help Evan. Instead of helping, though, she usually causes more work for Evan. He has to pick up trash Jessie has dropped, change the vacuum bag after Jessie sweeps up an entire box of cereal, and rewash dishes Jessie thought she got clean. When Evan yells at her, she cries because she was really trying to help, and then he feels bad.

Evan finally decides to sit down with his parents to see what little tasks Jessie could do around the house to feel important. They appreciate Evan's thoughtfulness toward Jessie and agree to find something for her to do.

1. Evan doesn't want ___, but Jessie makes him mad and he yells.

   _____ to be helpful   _____ to be mean   _____ to make Jessie work

2. Evan is ___ his sister and asks his parents to find chores for her to do.

   _____ bigger than   _____ jealous of   _____ concerned about

3. Jessie needs chores to

   _____ feel important.   _____ feel tired.   _____ make Evan mad.

4. Evan's parents feel that he is very ___ toward Jessie.

   _____ rude   _____ mean   _____ thoughtful

GRADE 4

I. Reading
A. Directions
B. Sequencing
C. Main Idea
II. Writing
A. Capitalization
B. Proofreading

Name _____

Minnie the Mole

Directions: Read the story and complete the exercise on the next page.

Minnie the Mole and her five children lived in a burrow under Mr. Smith's garden. Minnie worked hard gathering treats of insects and worms. It wasn't easy, since moles eat their weight in food each day.

Mr. Smith didn't like the raised roofs of Minnie's tunnels in his garden. One summer day, as Minnie was digging with her sharp claws, she heard Mr. Smith pounding a trap into position at the front entrance!

Minnie hurried home to gather her children. "We are in danger! We must move quickly," demanded Minnie. The little moles with their short, stocky bodies followed her.

Minnie started digging as fast as she could. "We're going to Uncle Moody's burrow. We'll be safer there," Minnie said. After working for two hours, they were far from Mr. Smith's garden. Tired, but safe, the little group rested in the comfort of Uncle Moody's living room.

"You were as busy as beavers today," said Uncle Moody.

"I'd say we were more like a mole machine!" laughed Minnie.

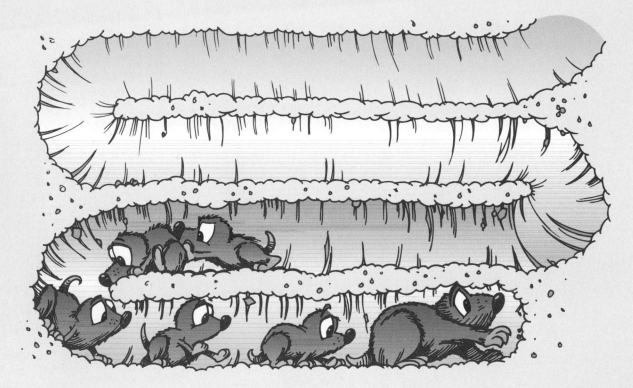

I. Reading
  A. Directions
  B. Sequencing
  C. Main Idea
II. Writing
  A. Capitalization
  B. Proofreading

Name _____

Minnie the Mole, cont.

Directions: Write the story elements to complete each sentence.

1. The main character is _____

2. She and her five children live in _____

   _____

3. Mr. Smith didn't like having moles in his garden because _____

   _____

4. Minnie's problem was that Mr. Smith _____

   _____

5. First, she told her children, _____

6. They dug for _____

7. The problem was solved when _____

   _____

8. Uncle Moody said Minnie and her children had worked like _____

   _____

9. Minnie said they had worked more like a _____

I. Reading
  A. Directions
  B. Sequencing
  C. Main Idea
II. Writing
  A. Capitalization
  B. Proofreading

Name _____

Magic Alphabet

Directions: Write the letter of the phrase that completes each statement about the magic trick below.

Hannah can make any letter of the alphabet appear on Rachel's hand. First, she asks Rachel to pick her favorite letter of the alphabet. Then, Hannah writes that letter on a sugar cube with a pencil. Next, she drops the sugar cube into a cup of water. Then, she asks Rachel to hold her hand over the glass and says, "Hocus-Pocus." The letter floats up onto Rachel's hand by magic!

What is Hannah's secret? After she writes the letter on the sugar cube, she presses her finger on it, and the letter rubs off. When Rachel holds her hand over the glass, Hannah touches it with her finger and the letter rubs off.

A. pressing hard on the sugar cube.

C. she can transfer the letter to her own hand.

B. she thinks it happens by magic.

D. the letter rubs off on Rachel's hand.

1. Hannah writes the letter on the sugar cube so that . . . _____

2. Hannah transfers the letter to her finger by . . . _____

3. When Hannah touches Rachel's hand with her finger, . . . _____

4. Since the letter appears to float onto Rachel's hand, . . . _____

Salt and Pepper

Directions: Read the story. Then, write a complete sentence to answer each question.

Salt and Pepper lived in the window at Peterson's Pet Shop. Salt was a little white kitten, whose cage sat in the front window beside a black dog named Pepper. As neighbors, the two became best friends.

One day, Manuel and his father came into the pet shop for a kitten. Manuel chose Salt because she was so playful. When Mr. Peterson lifted Salt out of her cage, Salt mewed sadly at Pepper who said bravely, "I'm sure we'll meet again someday."

Several days later, Lorinda and her mother stopped by the pet shop to look at the puppies. "Oh, Mama," said Lorinda. "This little black dog has such beautiful eyes."

"He seems to be just what we've been looking for," said her mother. "I hope he gets along with our neighbor Manuel's new white kitten."

"Oh, I think they'll be best friends," Lorinda replied. "Won't they be cute together? Just like salt and pepper!"

1. What was the effect of Salt and Pepper living near each other in the

   pet shop window? _____

2. What caused Manuel to come to the pet shop?

   _____

3. What caused Salt to feel sad?

   _____

4. What caused Lorinda and her mother to pick out Pepper?

   _____

Name _____

Arnold and Annie

Directions: Write an **X** next to each item that answers the question. You could have more than one answer for each question.

Arnold's sister Annie is watching TV. Arnold walks in and changes the channel to watch his favorite show, *Super Hero*. Annie says it's not fair because she was watching her movie first. Arnold tells Annie that she knows *Super Hero* is his favorite show and that she should just have expected him to turn the channel when it came on. He says she shouldn't have even started watching the movie.

Annie and Arnold continue to argue and fight over the TV. Finally, their mom comes in to see what's going on. When they tell her, she tells Arnold that Annie was there first and that he'll only miss one half of *Super Hero* because the movie will be over when the second half starts. But Arnold insists that he should get to watch all of his favorite show. He throws down the remote control and storms out of the room calling his sister a brat. Arnold's mom decides Arnold's TV watching is over for the rest of the day.

1. How would you describe Arnold's behavior?

☐ sympathetic ☐ mean ☐ rude

☐ understanding ☐ caring ☐ inconsiderate

2. What rude behavior did Arnold show?

☐ pulled his sister's hair ☐ called Annie a brat

☐ threw down the remote control ☐ kicked the TV

☐ insisted on having his way ☐ yelled at his mom

3. What might be Arnold's reasons for wanting to switch to *Super Hero*?

☐ his favorite show ☐ dislikes movies ☐ his daily habit

☐ enjoys fighting ☐ loves the heroes

Directions: On another sheet of paper, answer the following question.

Do you think Arnold's mom was unfair to him? Why or why not?

I. Reading
  A. Directions
  B. Sequencing
  C. Main Idea
II. Writing
  A. Capitalization
  B. Proofreading

Name _____

Kim's New Baby Brother

Directions: Write a word from the box to complete each sentence.

Kim is disappointed about her new baby brother. He screams and yells too much! Mom spends all of her time taking care of him. Kim is tired of being ignored.

Kim stuffs her backpack with her favorite toys and a peanut butter sandwich. She'll spend the day at a friend's house. She has had enough!

At her friend's house, Kim talks to Mrs. Sweetly. Mrs. Sweetly says that she understands how Kim feels, but that Kim should tell her mother.

When they talk, Mom tells Kim that she loves her just as much as ever and that baby brother loves her, too. Mom teaches Kim how to comfort the baby. Then, she takes Kim out for lunch, just the two of them. Now, Kim likes her baby brother and isn't jealous anymore.

angry	wise	love	jealous	better

1. Kim is _____ of her new baby brother.

2. Kim feels _____ while she is packing her backpack.

3. Mrs. Sweetly gives Kim _____ advice.

4. Kim feels _____ about the baby after talking to her mom.

5. Kim's mom gives Kim the _____ and attention she needs.

Name _____

A Black Hole

Directions: A story about something true is called **nonfiction**. Read about the black hole and answer the questions that follow.

Have you ever heard of a mysterious black hole? Some scientists believe that a black hole is an invisible object somewhere in space. Scientists believe that it has such a strong pull toward it, called *gravity*, that nothing can escape from it!

These scientists believe that a black hole is a star that has collapsed. The collapse made its pull even stronger. It seems invisible because even its own starlight cannot escape! It is believed that anything in space that comes near the black hole will be pulled into it forever. Some scientists believe there are many black holes in our galaxy.

Check: Some scientists believe that:

☐ a black hole is an invisible object in space.

☐ a black hole is a collapsed star.

☐ a black hole will not let its own light escape.

Write:

| A - gravity | ____ To fall or cave in |
| B - collapse | ____ A strong pull toward an object in space |

Draw what you think the inside of a black hole would be like.

GRADE 4

I. Reading
  A. Directions
  B. Sequencing
  C. Main Idea
II. Writing
  A. Capitalization
  B. Proofreading

Name _____

A Funnel Cloud–Danger!

Directions: Read about tornados and answer the questions that follow.

Did you know that a tornado is the most violent windstorm on Earth? A *tornado* is a whirling, twisting storm that is shaped like a funnel.

A tornado usually occurs in the spring on a hot day. It begins with thunderclouds and thunder. A cloud becomes very dark. The bottom of the cloud begins to twist and form a funnel. Rain and lightning begin. The funnel cloud drops from the dark storm clouds. It moves down toward the ground.

A tornado is very dangerous. It can destroy almost everything in its path.

Circle:

A (thunder, tornado) is the most vicious windstorm on Earth.

Check:

Which words describe a tornado?

☐ whirling   ☐ twisting   ☐ icy   ☐ funnel-shaped   ☐ dangerous

Underline:

A funnel shape is: ◯   ▢   ⬭   ▽   〰

Write and Circle:

A tornado usually occurs in the _____ on a (hot, cool) day.

Write 1 - 2 - 3 below and in the picture above.

◯ The funnel cloud drops down to the ground.

◯ A tornado begins with dark thunder clouds.

◯ The dark clouds begin to twist and form a funnel.

I. Reading
  A. Directions
  B. Sequencing
  C. Main Idea
II. Writing
  A. Capitalization
  B. Proofreading

Name _____

Hummingbirds

Hummingbirds are very small birds. This tiny bird is quite an acrobat. Only a few birds, such as kingfishers and sunbirds, can hover, which means to stay in one place in the air. But no other bird can match the flying skills of the hummingbird. The hummingbird can hover, fly backward, and fly upside down!

Hummingbirds got their name because their wings move very quickly when they fly. This causes a humming sound. Their wings move so fast that you can't see them at all. This takes a lot of energy. These little birds must have food about every 20 minutes to have enough strength to fly. Their favorite foods are insects and nectar. Nectar is the sweet water deep inside a flower. Hummingbirds use their long, thin bills to drink from flowers. When a hummingbird sips nectar, it hovers in front of a flower. It never touches the flower with its wings or feet.

Besides being the best at flying, the hummingbird is also one of the prettiest birds. Of all the birds in the world, the hummingbird's colors are among the brightest. Some are bright green with red and white markings. Some are purple. One kind of hummingbird can change its color from reddish-brown to purple to red!

The hummingbird's nest is special, too. It looks like a tiny cup. The inside of the nest is very soft. This is because one of the things the mother bird uses to build the nest is the silk from a spider's web.

Directions: Answer these questions about hummingbirds.

1. How did hummingbirds get their name? _____

   _____

2. What does *hover* mean? _____

3. How often do hummingbirds need to eat? _____

4. Name two things that hummingbirds eat. _____

5. What is one of the things a mother hummingbird uses to build her nest?

   _____

GRADE 4

I. Reading
  A. Directions
  B. Sequencing
  C. Main Idea
II. Writing
  A. Capitalization
  B. Proofreading

Name _____

Bats

Bats are the only mammals that can fly. They have wings made of thin skin stretched between long fingers. Bats can fly amazing distances. Some small bats have been known to fly more than 25 miles in one night.

Most bats eat insects or fruit. But some eat only fish, others only blood, and still others the nectar and pollen of flowers that bloom at night. Bats are active only at night. They sleep during the day in caves or other dark places. At rest, they always hang with their heads down.

You may have heard the expression "blind as a bat." But bats are not blind. They don't, however, use their eyes to guide their flight or to find the insects they eat. A bat makes a high-pitched squeak, then waits for the echo to return to it. This echo tells it how far away an object is. This is often called the bat's *sonar system*. Using this system, a bat can fly through a dark cave without bumping into anything. Hundreds of bats can fly around in the dark without ever running into each other. They do not get confused by the squeaks of the other bats. They always recognize their own echoes.

Directions: Answer these questions about bats.

1. Bats are the only mammals that
   ☐ eat insects. ☐ fly. ☐ live in caves.

2. Most bats eat
   ☐ plants. ☐ other animals. ☐ fruits and insects.

3. Bats always sleep
   ☐ with their heads down. ☐ lying down. ☐ during the night.

4. Bats are blind. True False

5. Bats use a built-in sonar system to guide them. True False

6. Bats are confused by the squeaks of other bats. True False

I. Reading
A. Directions
B. Sequencing
C. Main Idea
II. Writing
A. Capitalization
B. Proofreading

Name _____

Oceans

If you looked at Earth from up in space, you would see a planet that is mostly blue. This is because more than two-thirds of Earth is covered with water. You already know that this is what makes our planet different from the others, and what makes life on Earth possible. Most of this water is in the four great oceans: Pacific, Atlantic, Indian, and Arctic. The Pacific is by far the largest and the deepest. It is more than twice as big as the Atlantic, the second largest ocean.

The water in the ocean is salty. This is because rivers are always pouring water into the oceans. Some of this water picks up salt from the rocks it flows over. It is not enough salt to make the rivers taste salty. But the salt in the oceans has been building up over millions of years. The oceans get more and more salty every century.

The ocean provides us with huge amounts of food, especially fish. There are many other things we get from the ocean, including sponges and pearls. The oceans are also great "highways" of the world. Ships are always crossing the oceans, transporting many goods from country to country.

The science of studying the ocean is called *oceanography*. Today, oceanographers have special equipment to help them learn about the oceans and seas. Electronic instruments can be sent deep below the surface to make measurements. The newest equipment uses sonar or echo-sounding systems that bounce sound waves off the sea bed and use the echoes to make pictures of the ocean floor.

Directions: Answer these questions about the oceans.

1. How much of the Earth is covered by water? _____

2. Which is the largest and deepest ocean? _____

3. What is the science of studying the ocean? _____

4. What new equipment do oceanographers use? _____

GRADE
4

I. Reading
    A. Directions
    B. Sequencing
    C. Main Idea
II. Writing
    A. Capitalization
    B. Proofreading

Name _____

Deep-Sea Diving

One part of the world is still largely unexplored. It is the deep sea. Over the years, many people have explored the sea. But the first deep-sea divers wanted to find sunken treasure. They weren't really interested in studying the creatures or life there. Only recently have they begun to learn some of the mysteries of the sea.

It's not easy to explore the deep sea. Divers must have a way of breathing under water. They must be able to protect themselves from the terrific pressure. The pressure of air is about 15 pounds on every square inch. But the pressure of water is about 1,300 pounds on every square inch!

The first diving suits were made of rubber. They had a helmet of brass with windows in it. The shoes were made of lead and weighed 20 pounds each! These suits let divers go down a few hundred feet, but they were no good for exploring very deep waters. With a metal diving suit, a diver could go down 700 feet. Metal suits were first used in the 1930s.

In 1937, a diver named William Beebe wanted to explore deeper than anyone had ever gone before. He was not interested in finding treasure. He wanted to study deep-sea creatures and plants. He invented a hollow metal ball called the *bathysphere*. It weighed more than 5,000 pounds, but in it Beebe went down 3,028 feet. He saw many things that had never been seen by humans before.

Directions: Answer these questions about early deep-sea diving.

1. What were the first deep-sea divers interested in? _____

2. What are two problems that must be overcome in deep-sea diving?

    a. _____

    b. _____

3. How deep could a diver go wearing a metal suit? _____

4. Who was the deep-sea explorer who invented the bathysphere?

_____

GRADE

4

I. Reading
  A. Directions
  B. Sequencing
  C. Main Idea
II. Writing
  A. Capitalization
  B. Proofreading

Name _____

Space Pioneer

Neil Armstrong is one of the great pioneers of space. On July 20, 1969, Armstrong was commander of *Apollo 11*, the first manned American spacecraft to land on the Moon. He was the first person to walk on the Moon.

Armstrong was born in Ohio in 1930. He took his first airplane ride when he was 6 years old. As he grew older, he did jobs to earn money to learn to fly. On his 16th birthday, he received his student pilot's license.

Armstrong served as a Navy fighter pilot during the Korean War. He received three medals. Later, he was a test pilot. He was known as one of the best pilots in the world. He was also an engineer. He contributed much to the development of new methods of flying. In 1962, he was accepted into an astronaut training program.

Armstrong had much experience when he was named to command the historic flight to the Moon. It took four days to fly to the Moon. As he climbed down the ladder to be the first person to step onto the Moon, he said these now-famous words: "That's one small step for man, one giant leap for mankind."

Directions: Answer these questions about Neil Armstrong.

1. What did Neil Armstrong do before any other person in the world?

_____

2. How old was Neil Armstrong when he got his student pilot's license?

_____

3. What did Armstrong do during the Korean War?

_____

4. On what date did a person first walk on the Moon?

_____

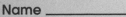

Name _____

Sally Ride, First Woman in Space

Directions: Read about Sally Ride. Then, answer the questions.

Sally Ride was the first American woman in space. She was only 31 years old when she went into space in 1982. Besides being the first American woman, she was also the youngest person ever to go into space!

Many people wanted to be astronauts. When Sally Ride was chosen, there were 8,000 people who wanted to be in the class. Only 35 were selected. Six of those people were women.

Sally Ride rode in the spaceship *Challenger*. She was called a *mission specialist*. Like any astronaut, Sally Ride had to study for several years before she went into space. She spent 6 days on her journey. She has even written a book for children about her adventure! It is called *To Space and Back*.

1. What was significant about Sally Ride's journey into space? _____

_____

2. How old was Sally ride when she went into space? _____

3. What was the name of her spaceship? _____

4. What was her title on the trip into space? _____

5. How long did Sally Ride's journey last? _____

6. What was the name of the book she wrote? _____

7. Why do you think many people want to be astronauts? _____

_____

_____

_____

_____

GRADE
4

I. Reading
A. Directions
B. Sequencing
C. Main Idea
II. Writing
A. Capitalization
B. Proofreading

Name _____

Clouds

Directions: Read about clouds. Then, answer the questions.

Have you ever wondered where clouds come from? Clouds are made from billions and billions of tiny water droplets in the air. The water droplets form into clouds when warm, moist air rises and is cooled.

Have you ever seen your breath when you were outside on a very cold day? Your breath is warm and moist. When it hits the cold air, it is cooled. A kind of small cloud is formed by your breath!

Clouds come in many sizes and shapes. On some days, clouds blanket the whole sky. Other times, clouds look like wispy puffs of smoke. There are other types of clouds as well.

Weather experts have named clouds. Big, fluffy clouds that look flat on the bottom are called *cumulus* clouds. *Stratocumulus* is the name for rounded clouds that are packed very close together. You can still see patches of sky, but stratocumulus clouds are thicker than cumulus ones.

If you spot *cumulonimbus* clouds, go inside. These clouds are wide at the bottom and have thin tops. The tops of these clouds are filled with ice crystals. On hot summer days, you may even have seen cumulonimbus clouds growing. They seem to boil and grow as though they are coming from a big pot. A violent thunderstorm usually occurs after you see these clouds. Often, there is hail.

Cumulus, stratocumulus, and cumulonimbus are only three of many types of clouds. If you listen closely, you will hear television weather forecasters talk about these and other clouds. Why? Because clouds are good indicators of weather.

1. How are clouds formed?_____

_____

2. How can you make your own cloud?_____

_____

3. What should you do when you spot cumulonimbus clouds?

_____

4. What often happens after you see cumulonimbus clouds? _____

_____

5. What kind of big fluffy clouds look flat on the bottom?_____

I. Reading
  A. Directions
  B. Sequencing
  C. Main Idea
II. Writing
  A. Capitalization
  B. Proofreading

Name _____

Thunderstorms

Directions: Read about thunderstorms. Then, answer the questions.

Thunderstorms can be scary! The sky darkens. The air feels heavy. Then, the thunder begins. Sometimes, the thunder sounds like a low rumble. Other times, thunder is very loud. Loud thunder can be heard 15 miles away.

Thunderstorms begin inside big cumulonimbus clouds. Remember, cumulonimbus are the summer clouds that seem to boil and grow. It is as though there is a big pot under the clouds.

Thunder is heard after lightning flashes across the sky. The noise of thunder happens when lightning heats the air as it cuts through it. Some people call this quick, sharp sound a *thunderclap.* Sometimes thunder sounds "rumbly." This rumble is the thunder's sound wave bouncing off hills and mountains.

Weather experts say there is an easy way to figure out how far away a storm is. First, look at your watch. Count the number of seconds between the flash of lightning and the sound of thunder. To find how far away the storm is, divide the number of seconds by five. This will give the number of miles the storm is from you.

How far away is the storm if you count 20 seconds between the flash of lightning and the sound of thunder? Twenty divided by five is four miles. What if you count only five seconds? One mile! Get inside quickly. The air is charged with electricity. You could be struck by lightning. It is not safe to be outside in a thunderstorm.

1. Where do thunderstorms begin? _____

2. When is thunder heard? _____

3. What causes thunder to sound "rumbly"?_____

_____

4. To find out how far away a storm is, count the seconds between the thunder and lightning and divide by what number?

_____

5. If you count 40 seconds between the lightning and thunder, how far away is the storm?

_____

6. What comes first, thunder or lightning? _____

I. Reading
  A. Directions
  B. Sequencing
  C. Main Idea
II. Writing
  A. Capitalization
  B. Proofreading

Name _____

Your Five Senses

Your senses are very important to you. You depend on them every day. They tell you where you are and what is going on around you. Your senses are sight, hearing, touch, smell, and taste.

Try to imagine for a minute that you were suddenly unable to use your senses. Imagine, for instance, that you are in a cave and your only source of light is a candle. Without warning, a gust of wind blows out the flame.

Your senses are always at work. Your eyes let you read this book. Your nose brings the scent of dinner cooking. Your tongue helps you taste dinner later. Your hand feels the softness as you stroke a puppy. Your ears tell you that a storm is approaching.

Your senses also help keep you from harm. They warn you if you touch something that will burn you. They keep you from looking at a light that is too bright, and they tell you if a car is coming up behind you. Each of your senses collects information and sends it as a message to your brain. The brain is like the control center for your body. It sorts out the messages sent by your senses and acts on them.

Directions: Answer these questions about the five senses.

1. Circle the main idea:

   Your senses keep you from harm.

   Your senses are important to you in many ways.

2. Name the five senses.

   a. _____

   b. _____

   c. _____

   d. _____

   e. _____

3. Which part of your body acts as the "control center"?

_____

GRADE 4

I. Reading
   A. Directions
   B. Sequencing
   C. Main Idea
II. Writing
   A. Capitalization
   B. Proofreading

Name _____

Touch

Unlike the other senses, which are located only in your head, your sense of touch is all over your body. Throughout your life, you receive an endless flow of information about the world and yourself from your sense of touch. It tells you if something is hot or cold, hard or soft. It sends messages of pain, such as a headache or sore throat, if there is a problem.

There are thousands of tiny sensors all over your body. They are all linked together. These sensors are also linked to your spinal cord and your brain to make up your central nervous system. Through this system, the various parts of your body can send messages to your brain. It is then the brain's job to decide what it is you are actually feeling. All this happens in just a split second.

Not all parts of your body have the same amount of feeling. Areas that have the most nerves, or sensors, have the greatest amount of feeling. For instance, the tips of your fingers have more feeling than parts of your arm.

Some sensors get used to the feeling of an object after a period of time. When you first put your shirt on in the morning, you can feel its pressure on your skin. However, some of the sensors stop responding during the day.

One feeling you cannot get used to is the feeling of pain. Pain is an important message, because it tells your brain that something harmful is happening to you. Your brain reacts by doing something right away to protect you.

Directions: Answer these questions about the sense of touch.

1. Circle the main idea:

   The sense of touch is all over your body.

   You cannot get used to the sense of pain.

2. The nerves, spinal cord, and brain are linked together to make the _____

   _____ .

3. One feeling you can never get used to is _____ .

4. All parts of your body have the same amount of feeling.   True   False

5. It is the brain's job to receive messages from the sensors
   on your body and decide what you are actually feeling.   True   False

GRADE 4

I. Reading
  A. Directions
  B. Sequencing
  C. Main Idea
II. Writing
  A. Capitalization
  B. Proofreading

Name _____

Smell

Your nose is your sense organ for smelling. Smells are mixed into the air around you. They enter your nose when you breathe.

In the upper part of your nose, there are special smell sensors. They pick up smells and send messages to your brain. The brain then decides what it is you are smelling.

Smelling can be a pleasant sense. Sometimes, smells can remind you of a person or place. For instance, have you ever smelled a particular scent and then suddenly thought about your grandmother's house? Smell also can make you feel hungry. In fact, your sense of smell is linked very closely to your sense of taste. Without your sense of smell, you would not taste food as strongly.

Smelling also can be quite unpleasant. But this, too, is important. By smelling food, you can tell if it is spoiled and not fit to eat. Your sense of smell also can sometimes warn you of danger, such as a fire.

The sense of smell tires out more quickly than your other senses. This is why you get used to some everyday smells and no longer notice them after a while.

Directions: Answer these questions about the sense of smell.

1. Smells are mixed in _____ .

2. The sense of smell is linked closely to the sense of _____ .

3. Give an example of why smelling bad smells can be important to you.

   _____

   _____

Name _____

Taste

The senses of taste and smell work very closely together. If you can't smell your food, it is difficult to recognize the taste. You may have noticed this when you've had a bad cold with a stuffed-up nose.

Tasting is the work of your tongue. All over your tongue are tiny taste sensors called *taste buds*. If you look at your tongue in a mirror, you can see small groups of taste buds. They are what give your tongue its rough appearance. Each taste bud has a small opening in it. Tiny pieces of food and drink enter this opening. There taste sensors gather information about the taste and send messages to your brain. Your brain decides what the taste is.

Taste buds located in different areas of your tongue recognize different tastes. There are only four tastes your tongue can recognize: sweet, sour, bitter, and salty. All other flavors are a mixture of taste and smell.

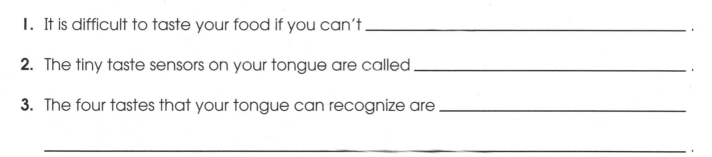

Directions: Answer these questions about the sense of taste.

1. It is difficult to taste your food if you can't _____ .

2. The tiny taste sensors on your tongue are called _____ .

3. The four tastes that your tongue can recognize are _____

_____ .

4. All other flavors are a mixture of _____ .

Name _____

Sight

You can see this page because of light. Without light, there would be no sight. In a dark room, you might see only a few large shapes. If it is pitch black, you can't see anything at all.

Light reflects, or bounces off, things and then travels to your eyes. The light enters your eye through the pupil. The pupil is the black circle in the middle of your eye. It gets bigger in low light to let in as much light as possible. In bright light, it shrinks so that too much light doesn't get in.

Light enters through the pupil and then passes through the lens. The lens bends the light so that it falls on the back of your eye on the retina. The retina has millions of tiny cells that are very sensitive to light. When an image is formed in the eye, it is upside down. This image is sent to your brain. The brain receives the message and turns the picture right side up again.

Some people are far-sighted. This means they can clearly see things that are far away, but things close by may be blurred. People who are near-sighted can clearly see things better if they are close by. Glasses or contact lenses can help correct these problems.

Some people can see only a little bit or perhaps not at all. This is called being blind. Blind people rely on their sense of touch to learn more about the world. They can even use their sense of touch to read. Some blind people read with a special printing system called *Braille*. The system is named for the man who invented it. Braille has small raised dots, instead of letters, on a page.

Directions: Answer these questions about the sense of sight.

1. Without _____ , there would be no sight.

2. *Reflect* means _____ .

3. The part of the eye that controls the amount of light entering your eye by getting

   bigger and smaller is called the _____ .

4. To correct near-sightedness or far-sightedness, you can wear _____

   _____ .

5. What is the name of the special printing system for blind people? _____

GRADE 4

I. Reading
A. Directions
B. Sequencing
C. Main Idea
II. Writing
A. Capitalization
B. Proofreading

Name _____

Sorting Nouns

Nouns are words that name a person, place, or thing.

Directions: Write each noun in the correct box.

Nouns

clouds	restaurant	grandpa	classroom
doctor	heart	desert	man
island	boy	bike	house
voice	planet	sunglasses	daughter
girl	hamster	teacher	museum

Person

_____

_____

_____

_____

_____

_____

_____

Place

_____

_____

_____

_____

_____

_____

Thing

_____

_____

_____

_____

_____

Let's sort the words.

Common and Proper Nouns

A **common noun** names a person, place, or thing. A common noun begins with a small, or lowercase, letter.

Examples: nurse   store   book

A **proper noun** names a particular person, place, or thing. Proper nouns begin with a capital, or uppercase, letter.

Examples: George Washington   Niagara Falls   Plymouth Rock

Directions: Write each noun on a jersey for the correct team. Remember to capitalize proper nouns.

Common Nouns

1. dentist
2. bear
3. tarzan
4. doctor
5. ohio
6. school
7. abe lincoln
8. pacific ocean
9. chief
10. peter pan
11. thanksgiving
12. computer

Proper Nouns

I. Reading
A. Directions
B. Sequencing
C. Main Idea
II. Writing
A. Capitalization
B. Proofreading

Name _____

All American

Directions: Color the spaces **red** that contain a common noun.
Color the spaces **blue** that contain a proper noun.

Directions: Unscramble the red letters to write the name of a famous American. Then, unscramble the blue letters to write another American's name.

_____

_____

GRADE
4

Name _____

All in a Name

Directions: Write a proper noun next to each common noun.

1. girl _____Susie_____
2. boy _____
3. teacher _____
4. pet _____
5. store _____
6. continent _____
7. state _____
8. lake _____
9. river _____
10. book _____

Directions: Write a common noun next to each proper noun.

1. the Chicago Bears _____team_____
2. Andover Middle School _____
3. *Newsweek* _____
4. April _____
5. Tuesday _____
6. Thanksgiving _____
7. Sue's Diner _____
8. Thomas Jefferson _____
9. San Francisco _____
10. Mt. Everest _____

Name _____

Common and Proper Nouns

Remember, a **common noun** names any person, place, or thing.
A **proper noun** names a specific person, place, or thing.
A proper noun always begins with a capital letter.

Example: boy, state (common nouns)
            Peter, Georgia (proper nouns)

Directions: Underline the nouns in the sentences.

1. Bobby was wondering what the weather would be on Friday.

2. The boys and girls from Lang School were planning a picnic.

3. Bobby asked his teacher, Mr. Lewis, how the class could find out.

4. The teacher suggested that the children call a local newspaper, *The Bugle*.

5. Ms. Canyon, the editor, read the forecast to Eddie.

6. Rain was predicted for the day of their picnic.

7. Their town, Grand Forks, also had a radio station.

8. When Rick called the number, he was disappointed.

9. The weatherman, George Lee, said that rain was possible.

10. The children were delighted when the sun came out on Friday.

Directions: Now, write each noun you have underlined in the correct category below.
Do not use any words more than once.

Common Nouns

1. _____   10. _____
2. _____   11. _____
3. _____   12. _____
4. _____   13. _____
5. _____   14. _____
6. _____   15. _____
7. _____   16. _____
8. _____   17. _____
9. _____

Proper Nouns

1. _____
2. _____
3. _____
4. _____
5. _____
6. _____
7. _____
8. _____
9. _____
10. _____

Name _____

Room for One More

A **singular noun** names one person, place, or thing. A **plural noun** names more than one person, place, or thing. Usually, to form the plural you just add **s**. Words that end in **s**, **sh**, **ch**, or **x** need **es** to form the plural.

Examples:

Singular Nouns	Plural Nouns
car	cars
bus	buses
lunch	lunches
fox	foxes

Directions: Write the correct singular or plural noun in parentheses to complete each sentence.

1. Mike was packing two (suitcase, suitcases) for a trip. _____

2. One (suitcase, suitcases) is a carry-on bag. _____

3. He decided to take three (shirt, shirts) along. _____

4. Mike will wear his favorite blue (shirt, shirts) on the plane. _____

5. He will leave the two tennis (shoe, shoes) at home. _____

6. Mike can't seem to find the one missing black (shoe, shoes)! _____

7. It's with the big (bunch, bunches) hiding under the bed. _____

8. Why do shoes hide in (bunch, bunches) like that? _____

9. Would one (sweater, sweaters) be enough? _____

10. (Sweater, Sweaters) seem to take up too much room. _____

11. Mike packs (box, boxes) of candy for his friends. _____

12. He will try to squeeze in one more (box, boxes). _____

Name _____

Forming Plural Nouns

Most **singular nouns** can be made into **plural nouns** by following one of these rules.

Rules	Examples
1. Add **s** to most nouns.	elephant, elephant**s**
2. If the noun ends in **s**, **sh**, **ch**, or **x**, add **es**.	box, box**es**
3. If the noun ends in **y** with a consonant before it, change the **y** to **i** and add **es**.	fly, fl**ies**
4. If the noun ends in **y** with a vowel before it, add **s**.	monkey, monkey**s**
5. To some nouns ending in **f**, add **s**.	chief, chief**s**
6. To some nouns ending in **f** or **fe**, change the **f** to **v** and add **es**.	knife, kni**ves** thief, thie**ves**
7. Some nouns stay the same for singular and plural.	sheep, **sheep**
8. Some nouns have an irregular plural.	goose, **geese**

Directions: Change each singular noun to plural. Write the number of the rule you used. Use a dictionary when needed.

Singular	Plural	Rule #	Singular	Plural	Rule #
1. chimney			11. woman		
2. class			12. bus		
3. wolf			13. judge		
4. deer			14. shelf		
5. story			15. chair		
6. elf			16. beach		
7. tooth			17. tax		
8. brush			18. lady		
9. attorney			19. roof		
10. mouse			20. penny		

Name _____

Totally Irregular!

Irregular nouns do not form the plural by adding **s** or **es**. You must memorize them. These nouns look the same whether singular or plural.

deer	salmon	trout	sheep	moose
tuna	cod	pike	bass	elk

These irregular nouns form their plurals using special spellings.

goose	geese
man	men
woman	women
tooth	teeth
ox	oxen
foot	feet
child	children
mouse	mice

Directions: Write singular or plural to identify the form of the underlined noun.

1. Many men, women, and <u>children</u> like fishing. _____

2. A child can easily catch a <u>bass</u> using live bait. _____

3. A salmon or a <u>cod</u> are not as easy for a child to catch. _____

4. Fly fishers can catch many <u>trout</u> without bait. _____

5. A fly rod can be six <u>feet</u> long. _____

6. Either a man or a <u>woman</u> can fish with a fly rod. _____

7. You might see an <u>elk</u> or a deer while fishing. _____

8. <u>Moose</u> are often found along the river also. _____

9. The cold river water can make your <u>teeth</u> chatter. _____

Name _____

I, We; Me, Us

I and **we** are **subject pronouns. Me** and **us** are **object pronouns.**

Examples:

Mark and **I** are on our way to the park.
  (subject pronoun)
We just love to launch rockets!
  (subject pronoun)
Will Sara come with **me**?
  (object pronoun)
Please feel welcome to join **us**.
  (object pronoun)

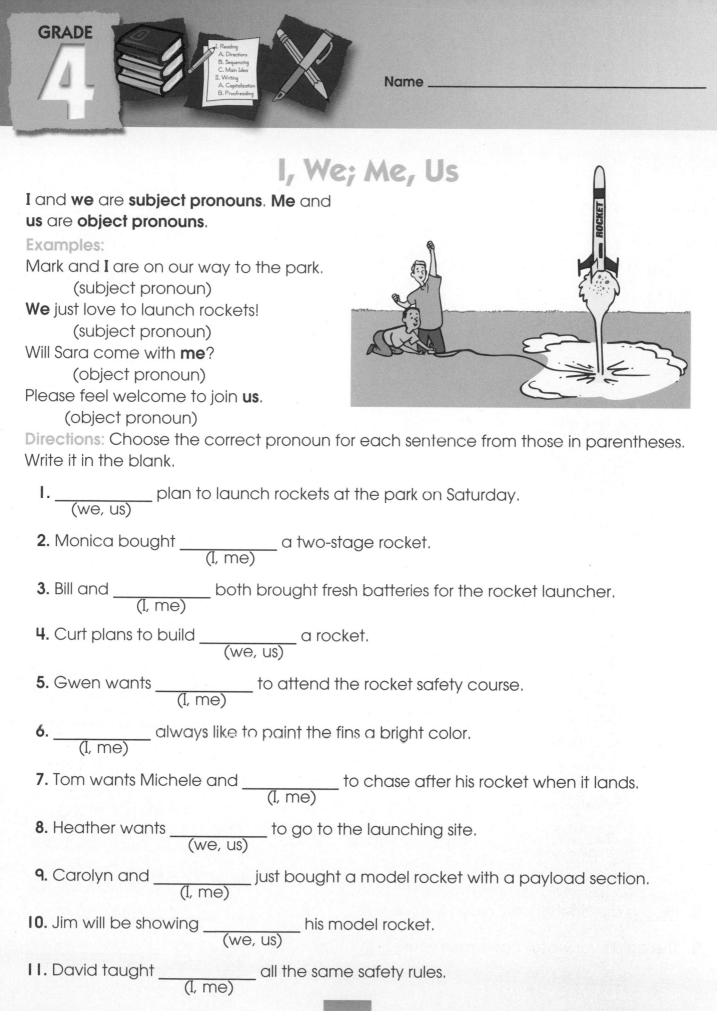

Directions: Choose the correct pronoun for each sentence from those in parentheses. Write it in the blank.

1. _____ plan to launch rockets at the park on Saturday.
   (we, us)

2. Monica bought _____ a two-stage rocket.
   (I, me)

3. Bill and _____ both brought fresh batteries for the rocket launcher.
   (I, me)

4. Curt plans to build _____ a rocket.
   (we, us)

5. Gwen wants _____ to attend the rocket safety course.
   (I, me)

6. _____ always like to paint the fins a bright color.
   (I, me)

7. Tom wants Michele and _____ to chase after his rocket when it lands.
   (I, me)

8. Heather wants _____ to go to the launching site.
   (we, us)

9. Carolyn and _____ just bought a model rocket with a payload section.
   (I, me)

10. Jim will be showing _____ his model rocket.
    (we, us)

11. David taught _____ all the same safety rules.
    (I, me)

Name _____

Pronoun Party

Pronouns are words that take the place of singular or plural nouns.

Singular	Plural	When Used
I, me	we, us	to talk about yourself
you	you	to talk to a person
he, she, it, him, her	they, them	to talk about other persons or things

Example: **Jeremy** brought a gift to the party.
He brought a gift to the party.

Directions: Write the pronoun that takes the place of the underlined noun or nouns.

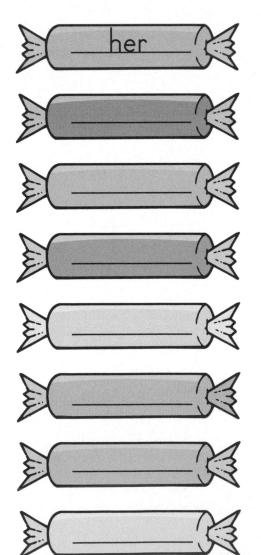

1. Nancy planned a party for <u>Pam</u>.

2. Is <u>Mom</u> going to take us?

3. <u>Tommy</u> is taking Pam a present.

4. <u>Todd and Neil</u> bought her a CD.

5. Dad gave <u>the boys</u> the money.

6. Pam will like <u>the music</u>.

7. Pam saw <u>Todd and me</u> yesterday.

8. <u>Todd and I</u> didn't talk about the party.

Name _____

Pick the Right Pronoun

Use **I**, **we**, **he**, or **she** when the pronoun is a subject.

Examples: **Craig** plays the violin.
He plays the violin.

Mindy plays the piano.
She plays the piano.

Use **me**, **us**, **her**, **him**, or **them** when the pronoun is not a subject.

Examples: Mom took **Connie** shopping.
Mom took **her** shopping.

Dad went fishing with **Alex**.
Dad went fishing with **him**.

Use **it** and **you** in any part of a sentence.

Examples: The **bicycle** is new.
It is new.

I waited for the **bus**.
I waited for **it**.

Directions: Write the correct pronoun that completes each sentence.

1. Danny and (me, I) went camping. _____

2. (We, Us) went to the baseball game. _____

3. The teacher took (we, us) to the library. _____

4. (Him, He) was a famous American. _____

5. Aunt Mary gave a dollar to (them, we). _____

6. (Her, You) and Greg are my best friends. _____

7. Please take this note to (he, him). _____

8. Charlie took Alan and (me, I) to the party. _____

Pronoun Progress

Remember that pronouns take the place of singular or plural nouns.

Directions: Underline each pronoun. Then, write the noun it stands for in the blue box below.

1. The children played baseball. <u>They</u> won 6 to 2.

2. John and Tim raked leaves. Mother thanked them.

3. The dog ran in the street. Sally ran after him.

4. The girls saw a movie. They like scary movies.

5. The boy picked apples. He baked apple pies.

6. Freddy, would you please clean the garage?

7. Sunshine is good for plants. It helps them grow.

8. Our class went on a trip. We had a picnic lunch.

me   her

us   him

    them

I   it
you   we
he   they
she

1. ___children___

2. _____

3. _____

4. _____

5. _____

6. _____

7. _____

8. _____

Name _____

That Belongs to Me!

A **possessive noun** shows ownership or possession. To make most nouns show possession, just add an **apostrophe** and **s**.

Examples: one eagle**'s** eggs
one child**'s** cap
two men**'s** trophy
the children**'s** school

When a plural noun ends in **s**, add an apostrophe <u>after</u> the **s** to show possession.

Examples: farmer**s'** rakes
sister**s'** report cards

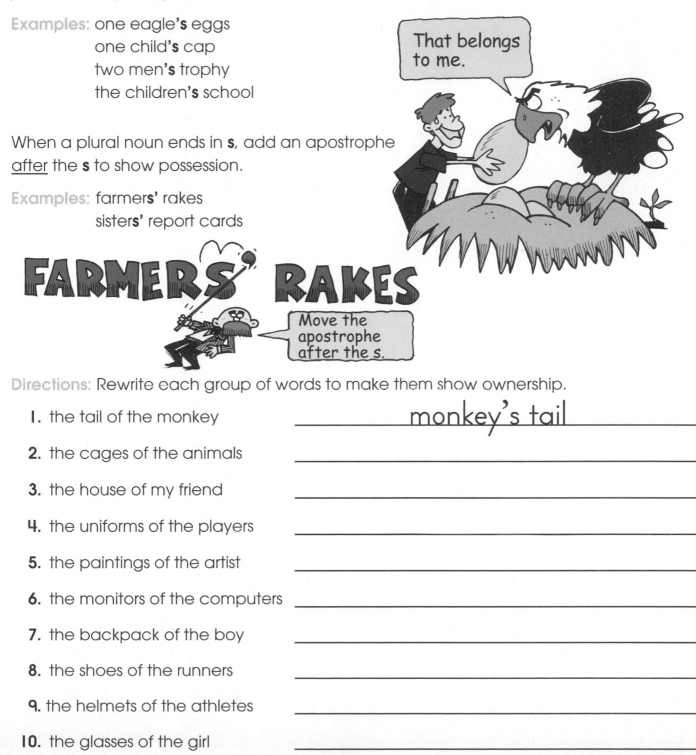

Directions: Rewrite each group of words to make them show ownership.

1. the tail of the monkey   monkey's tail

2. the cages of the animals _____

3. the house of my friend _____

4. the uniforms of the players _____

5. the paintings of the artist _____

6. the monitors of the computers _____

7. the backpack of the boy _____

8. the shoes of the runners _____

9. the helmets of the athletes _____

10. the glasses of the girl _____

Who Owns What?

Remember, a possessive noun shows ownership or possession. To make most nouns show possession, just add an **apostrophe** and **s**.

Examples: The display belongs to the store.
It is the store**'s** display.

The registers are assigned to the saleswomen.
They are the saleswomen**'s** registers.

When a plural noun ends in **s**, add an apostrophe <u>after</u> the **s** to show possession.

Example: The cashiers own the pencils.
They are the cashier**s'** pencils.

Directions: Rewrite each sentence using a phrase with a possessive noun.

1. The <u>parents of the children</u> were waiting in the parking lot.

_____

2. Motors were running in the <u>cars of all of the parents</u>.

_____

3. Everyone wondered why the <u>bell of the school</u> had not rung.

_____

4. The <u>students of the teachers</u> were getting restless.

_____

5. The <u>voice of the principal</u> suddenly announced, "Time to go!"

_____

6. In ten minutes, the <u>hallways of the building</u> were empty.

_____

Name _____

Possessive Nouns Review

Directions: Write the correct possessive form of the underlined noun.

1. The <u>balloon</u> string is long.   _____balloon's_____

2. <u>Mary</u> pencil was broken.   _____

3. Both <u>boys</u> grades were good.   _____

4. This house is <u>Cliff</u> house.   _____

5. <u>Tony</u> aunt came to visit.   _____

6. Some <u>flowers</u> leaves were large.   _____

7. We saw two <u>bears</u> tracks.   _____

8. The <u>children</u> room was messy.   _____

9. My <u>sister</u> birthday is today.   _____

10. The <u>clowns</u> acts made us laugh.   _____

11. Jonah filled <u>Pete</u> dish.   _____

12. Mark joined the two <u>boys</u> game.   _____

13. The baseball <u>players</u> uniforms are clean.   _____

14. The <u>dog</u> dish was empty.   _____

15. The three <u>cats</u> paws were wet.   _____

It's Mine!

GRADE 4

I. Reading
   A. Directions
   B. Sequencing
   C. Main Idea
II. Writing
   A. Capitalization
   B. Proofreading

Name _____

Possessive Pronouns

Possessive pronouns are pronouns that show ownership without using an apostrophe. Some possessive pronouns are used with nouns.

Examples:

Pronouns Used With a Noun

my house	**its** paws
your shoes	**our** pets
his dog	**their** names
her cat	

Directions: Write a possessive pronoun that completes the second sentence.

1. Chad, this book belongs to you. It is ___your___ book.

2. It came from the library we belong to. It came from _____ library.

3. I found it in the car that belongs to me. I found it in _____ car.

4. The cover of the book looked familiar. _____ cover looked familiar.

5. I thought it was Mary's book. I thought it was _____ book.

6. She said it was Jim Long's book. She said it was _____ book.

7. I went to the Long family's house. I went to _____ house.

8. Luckily, you were there to claim the book. You claimed _____ book.

9. I stayed to play with Jim's dog. I played with _____ dog.

10. The dog's collar is new. _____ collar is new.

GRADE 4

I. Reading
A. Directions
B. Sequencing
C. Main Idea
II. Writing
A. Capitalization
B. Proofreading

Name _____

Yours, Mine, and Ours

Possessive pronouns can show ownership with or without using the noun.

Examples:

The jacket is **my jacket**.
The jacket is **mine**.

The cap is **your cap**.
The cap is **yours**.

The shoes are **his shoes**.
The shoes are **his**.

The glove is **her glove**.
The glove is **hers**.

We have **our jackets**.
The jackets are **ours**.

The children have **their bats**.
The bats are **theirs**.

Directions: Write a possessive pronoun on the line that means the same as the words in parentheses.

1. The comb is _____. (your comb)

2. The bottle is _____. (the baby girl's bottle)

3. The books were _____. (Mark's books)

4. The computers are _____. (the sisters' computers)

5. The mailman brought _____. (our mail)

6. _____ are in bloom. (My flowers)

7. The blue bicycle is _____. (your bicycle)

8. _____ is today. (Sara's piano lesson)

Name _____

Pronoun Pro!

Remember, pronouns are words that take the place of singular or plural nouns. Possessive pronouns are a type of pronoun that shows ownership.

Directions: Write a pronoun from the box that can take the place of the underlined word or words.

we	she
he	his
yours	they
them	their
mine	ours

1. I forgot to bring <u>my lunch</u> today. _____

2. <u>Lisa</u> will share her lunch with me. _____

3. <u>Steve</u> has a soccer game on Friday. _____

4. <u>My game</u> is on Saturday. _____

5. <u>My friend and I</u> will ride bicycles to the game. _____

6. <u>Sam's bicycle</u> is a mountain bike. _____

7. What is <u>Sam's</u> chance of scoring a goal? _____

8. We plan to congratulate <u>the best players</u>. _____

9. Is <u>the Martin's</u> house on Main Street? _____

10. Their house looks just like <u>your house</u>. _____

11. <u>Purple and yellow pansies</u> grow in the flower bed. _____

12. I think <u>our pansies</u> are prettier than their pansies. _____

13. <u>Gina and Max</u> went grocery shopping. _____

14. Beth asked to go along with <u>Gina and Max</u>. _____

Verbs

A **verb** is a word that can show action. A verb can also tell what someone or something is or is like.

Examples: The boats **sail** on Lake Michigan.

We **eat** dinner at 6:00.

I **am** ten years old.

The clowns **were** funny.

Directions: Circle the verb in each sentence.

1. John sips milk.

2. They throw the football.

3. We hiked in the woods.

4. I enjoy music.

5. My friend smiles often.

6. A lion hunts for food.

7. We ate lunch at noon.

8. Fish swim in the ocean.

9. My team won the game.

10. They were last in line.

11. The wind howled during the night.

12. Kangaroos live in Australia.

13. The plane flew into the clouds.

14. We recorded the song.

15. They forgot the directions.

A **verb** is a word that can show action.

A verb can also tell what someone or something is or is like.

Name _____

What's the Action?

Verbs that tell what people or things do are called **action verbs**.

Examples: Birds **fly** over the water.
Laura **rakes** leaves.

Directions: Circle **yes** if the sentence tells about an action that could happen. Circle **no** if it tells about something that could not happen. Then, write the verb from each sentence on a line below.

1. Kevin threw a ball.	yes	no
2. An elephant sews clothes.	yes	no
3. My dog learned to read.	yes	no
4. Mom filled the tank with gas.	yes	no
5. Seatbelts protect passengers.	yes	no
6. Juanita searched for her necklace.	yes	no
7. Monkeys travel to Mars each year.	yes	no
8. It rained cats and dogs.	yes	no
9. Pedro read ten books in one month.	yes	no
10. Camels flew across the desert.	yes	no
11. We caught ten fish on Saturday.	yes	no
12. Apples grew on the cherry tree.	yes	no

_____   _____   _____

_____   _____   _____

_____   _____   _____

_____   _____   _____

GRADE
4

I. Reading
   A. Directions
   B. Sequencing
   C. Main Idea
II. Writing
   A. Capitalization
   B. Proofreading

Name _____

Helping Verbs

A **verb phrase** is a verb that has more than one word. It is made up of a **main verb** plus one or more **helping verbs**.

Example: verb phrase
          Tim **has practiced** hard.

          helping verb   main verb

These words are often used as helping verbs with the main verb.

am, **is**, **are**, **was**, **were**, **have**, **has**

Directions: Underline the helping verbs and circle the main verbs in the sentences below.

1. The instructor has taught science for several years.

2. The concert pianist was practicing before the performance.

3. Researchers are attempting to find a cure for the disease.

4. The architect has drawn detailed blueprints.

5. The scientist has researched the project carefully.

6. Several patients were waiting in the doctor's office.

7. During his lifetime, the artist has painted many beautiful pictures.

8. A touchdown was scored by the quarterback.

9. The ship's captain is giving orders to the first mate.

10. The clown has performed for many years.

11. The tailor was hemming the man's trousers.

12. The construction workers have finished with the project.

13. The secretary was typing the letters yesterday.

14. Lawyers have passed difficult state examinations.

15. A cab driver has transported many passengers by the end of the day.

Name _____

Verb Tenses

A **present-tense** verb shows action that is happening now. A **past-tense** verb shows action that happened earlier. A **future-tense** verb shows action that will take place in the future.

Examples: The clockmaker **repairs** the clock.   (present)
              The clockmaker **repaired** the clock.   (past)
              The clockmaker **will repair** the clock.   (future)

Directions: Write these verbs using the tenses shown in parentheses.

	try	**walk**	**work**
(present)	Tom _____	Karen _____	They _____
(past)	Tom _____	Karen _____	They _____
(future)	Tom _____	Karen _____	They _____

Directions: Write the correct verb in each blank below.

1. time (future)   **5.** tell (present)   **9.** help (past)

2. chart (present)   **6.** reset (future)   **10.** invent (past)

3. trickle (past)   **7.** dine (present)   **11.** operate (future)

4. use (past)   **8.** move (future)

1. John <u>will time</u> the runners in the race.

2. A calendar _____ the days of each month.

3. Sand _____ through the hourglass.

4. People _____ the hourglass before clocks were invented.

5. A pendulum _____ time by Earth's rotation.

6. John _____ his watch when changing time zones.

7. He _____ at 8:00 every evening during the week.

8. Martha _____ the hands of the clock.

9. In the distant past, the Sun and the Moon _____ man tell time.

10. The Egyptians _____ the solar calendar.

11. Timepieces 100 years from now _____ differently.

Name _____

Irregular Verbs

Verbs that do not add **ed** to form the past tense are called **irregular verbs**. The spelling of these verbs changes.

Examples:

present	past	present	past
begin, begins	**began**	do, does	**did**
break, breaks	**broke**	eat, eats	**ate**

Directions: Write the past tense of each irregular verb below.

1. Samuel almost _____ (fall) when he kicked a rock in the path.

2. Diana made sure she _____ (take) a canteen on her hike.

3. David _____ (run) over to a shady tree for a quick break.

4. Jimmy _____ (break) off a long piece of grass to put in his mouth while he was walking.

5. Eva _____ (know) the path along the river very well.

6. The clouds _____ (begin) to sprinkle raindrops on the hikers.

7. Kathy _____ (throw) a small piece of bread to the birds.

8. Everyone _____ (eat) a very nutritious meal after a long adventure.

9. We all _____ (sleep) very well that night.

Many irregular verbs have a different past-tense ending when the helping verbs **have** and **has** are used.

Examples: Steven **has worn** special hiking shoes today.
            Marlene and I **have known** about this trail for years.

Directions: Circle the correct irregular verb below.

1. Peter has (flew, flown) down to join us for the adventure.

2. Mark has (saw, seen) a lot of animals on the hike today.

3. Andy and Mike have (went, gone) on this trail before.

4. Bill has (took, taken) extra precautions to make sure no cacti prick his legs.

5. Heather has (ate, eaten) all the snacks her mom packed for her.

GRADE 4

I. Reading
   A. Directions
   B. Sequencing
   C. Main Idea
II. Writing
   A. Capitalization
   B. Proofreading

Name _____

Verb Search

Sometimes endings are added to verbs to tell about a past action. The **base word** is the verb without the ending.

Examples: Dad <u>washed</u> his new van.
(The base word is **wash**.)

We <u>walked</u> to the store.
(The base word is **walk**.)

Directions: Underline the verb in each sentence, and write the base word on the line.

1. She planned a trip to Colorado. _____

2. Nancy's dog followed her to the park. _____

3. My friends need help with their homework. _____

4. Can you carry the books for me? _____

5. Ethan explored the attic. _____

6. We painted our house white and green. _____

7. The whole class laughed at my jokes. _____

8. The chef baked delicious pies and cakes. _____

9. Judy slipped on the ice and broke her arm. _____

10. His family owns a large house. _____

11. Please read the second chapter by tomorrow. _____

12. We looked through the microscope. _____

13. She dreamed about sunny beaches. _____

14. Don't forget your socks! _____

Helping Verbs

A verb may be a single word or a group of words. A verb with more than one word has a **main verb** and one or more **helping verbs**. A helping verb comes before the main verb.

Example:

These words are <u>often</u> used as helping verbs:		These verbs are <u>always</u> used as helping verbs:	
am	have	can	may
is	has	could	might
are	had	will	shall
was	do	would	should
were	does		
did			

Directions: Underline the main verb once and the helping verb twice. The first one has been done for you.

1. Lori <u>should</u> <u>eat</u> her vegetables.

2. The flowers are growing tall.

3. Matt is playing the piano for the concert.

4. They were going to the movie.

5. Freddie should listen in class.

6. Maria might spend the night.

7. I will be twelve on my next birthday.

8. I can do my homework later.

I Need Help!

Always use helping verbs with **been**, **seen**, **done**, and **gone**.

Example: They <u>have</u> <u>been</u> ice skating.

Directions: Underline the main verb once and the helping verb twice.

1. I have seen your new clarinet.

2. Debbie has gone to the band meeting at school.

3. I have done my violin practicing.

4. Leon has been practicing the drum.

5. Pedro has gone to band camp before.

6. They have gone for more popcorn.

7. I have done a report on how much we sold.

8. Mary had been the top seller until this year.

9. Juanita had gone home early.

10. Aaron has been here since noon.

Directions: Write a helping verb that will complete each sentence.

1. Craig _____ been packing for the trip.

2. You _____ seen the rule about chewing gum on the bus.

3. Sara _____ done her homework in advance.

4. The children _____ seen buying snacks yesterday.

5. Elliott _____ gone to the concert hall once before.

6. Jill may _____ seen it already also.

7. Miguel _____ done a great job.

8. He _____ been one of three planners.

Let's Split!

Sometimes helping verbs and main verbs are separated by words that are not verbs.

Example: Jeff <u>can</u> usually <u>win</u> at word games.

Directions: Underline the main verb once and the helping verbs twice.

1. Carlos did not tell anyone his secret.

2. I am usually working on Saturday.

3. Frank will not get a new locker.

4. I might not finish the large pizza.

5. Does the basketball game start at noon?

6. Tim will not play baseball today.

7. Was your mother angry about the window?

8. I am often able to babysit on weekends.

9. Teaching school has always been my ambition.

10. Do not play the music loudly.

Directions: Write the correct helping verb to complete the sentence.

1. Joanie (are, is) going to the zoo.   _____

2. The policemen (is, are) directing traffic.   _____

3. I (was, is) eating pizza.   _____

4. I (is, am) doing a puzzle for my project.   _____

5. The birds (was, were) singing outside my window. _____

6. The frogs (was, were) croaking loudly.   _____

7. Max (is, are) sprinkling the lawn.   _____

8. We (was, were) jogging on the track.   _____

Name _____

Right Now

A verb is in the **present tense** when it tells what a noun does or is doing now. Generally, if the noun doing the action is singular, the present-tense verb will end in **s**.

Examples: Allison **walks** to school.

The girls **walk** to school.

Directions: Underline the correct present-tense verb in each sentence.

1. Stray dogs sometimes (bite, bites) strangers.

2. The warden (catch, catches) stray dogs.

3. She (tempt, tempts) them with dog treats.

4. My dog (knows, know) about this trick.

5. Other dogs (runs, run) away to safety.

Directions: Write the correct form of the present-tense verb to complete each sentence.

1. My father (shave, shaves) every day. _____

2. The chorus (sing, sings) beautifully. _____

3. The ice-cream cones (taste, tastes) delicious. _____

4. My neighbor (teach, teaches) French. _____

5. Meg (dash, dashes) to school every day. _____

6. The birds (fly, flies) from tree to tree. _____

7. Elm Street (cross, crosses) Main Street. _____

8. Michael and Keith (play, plays) tennis. _____

9. They (wait, waits) for the bus at the corner. _____

10. The clowns (make, makes) us laugh. _____

GRADE 4

I. Reading
A. Directions
B. Sequencing
C. Main Idea
II. Writing
A. Capitalization
B. Proofreading

Name _____

Done Deal

A verb is in the **past tense** when it tells what a noun already did or has done. Most verbs form their past tense by adding **ed** to the base word.

Example: walk   walked

Sometimes you must make spelling changes to form the past-tense verb.
When the verb ends in a silent **e**, drop the **e**, and add **ed**.

Example: hope   hoped

When the verb ends in **y** after a consonant, change the **y** to **i** and add **ed**.

Example: hurry   hurried

When the verb ends in a single consonant after a single short vowel, double the final consonant, then add **ed**.

Example: trap   trapped

Directions: Write each of the following verbs in the past tense.

1. study _____
2. bake _____
3. smell _____
4. wash _____
5. smile _____
6. grab _____
7. copy _____

8. name _____
9. spy _____
10. melt _____
11. clip _____
12. toast _____
13. pop _____
14. empty _____

Name _____

Irregular Verbs

Irregular verbs use special spellings to form their past tense in different ways.

Examples: Marge **breaks** a glass now.
(present tense)

Marge **broke** a glass earlier.
(past tense)

Marge **has broken** a glass before.
(past tense with helping verb)

You should memorize these common irregular verbs:

Present	Past (no helping verb)	Past (needs helping verb)
break	broke	broken
bring	brought	brought
come	came	come
drive	drove	driven
grow	grew	grown
run	ran	run
throw	threw	thrown

Directions: Write the correct form of the main verb for each sentence.

1. Julie has (came, come) to my piano recital. _____

2. Mom (drove, driven) me to my soccer game. _____

3. My sister (came, come) home from college. _____

4. My TV has been (broke, broken) all week. _____

5. Jimmy has (drove, driven) to Los Angeles. _____

6. I (broke, broken) my arm while skating. _____

7. Kaycie has (threw, thrown) a bone to the dog. _____

8. The dogs have (ran, run) away with the bone. _____

Name _____

Elephants Never Forget

Don't forget that every sentence has two parts. The **subject** tells who or what the sentence is about. The **predicate** tells what the subject does, did, is, or has.

Directions: Draw a line to connect each subject on the peanut to its predicate on the elephant.

The lions

The circus tent

Lots of children

The clowns

The circus

Big elephants

The smell of peanuts

The ringmaster

wore brightly colored makeup.

announced the circus acts.

enjoyed eating cotton candy.

paraded in a line.

growled at the crowd.

began at 7 P.M.

was filled with over 100 people.

filled the air.

Simple Subjects and Predicates

The **simple subject** is the most important word in the complete subject. It is a **noun** or **pronoun** that tells who or what the sentence is about.

The **simple predicate** is the most important word in the complete predicate. It is a **verb** that tells what the subject is or does.

Example: simple subject   simple predicate

Handmade pottery can be very beautiful.

complete subject   complete predicate

Directions: Underline the complete subject once and the complete predicate twice.

1. The science of pottery making is called *ceramics*.

2. Humans have been making pottery for thousands of years.

3. Early people made household utensils out of pottery.

4. Pottery has been made many different ways.

5. The earliest pottery making method was probably the hand-building method.

6. Clay coils were wound on top of one another.

7. Another method utilized the potter's wheel.

8. The Egyptians used the potter's wheel at least three thousand years ago.

9. The ancient Greeks used the potter's wheel when making pottery.

10. Their vases are excellent examples of simplicity of color and shape.

Directions: Write the simple subjects and the simple predicates from the sentences above.

Simple Subject	Simple Predicate		Simple Subject	Simple Predicate
1. _____	_____	6. _____	_____
2. _____	_____	7. _____	_____
3. _____	_____	8. _____	_____
4. _____	_____	9. _____	_____
5. _____	_____	10. _____	_____

Subjects and Predicates

Every sentence has two parts. The **subject** tells who or what the sentence is about. The **predicate** tells what the subject does, did, is, or has.

Example: <u>The snowman</u> <u>is melting</u>.

↑   ↑
subject   predicate

Directions: Draw one line under the subject and two lines under the predicate.

1. The horses are racing to the finish line.

2. Mrs. Porter went to see Jack's teacher.

3. Josh moved to Atlanta, Georgia.

4. Monica's birthday is July 15th.

5. The ball rolled into the street.

6. Tammy planned a surprise party.

7. The winning team received a trophy.

8. The fireworks displays were fantastic.

9. The heavy rain drove everyone inside.

10. Adam looked everywhere for his book.

11. You can hear the band outside.

12. My family has tickets for the football game.

13. Cats are furry and soft.

14. The police officer stopped the traffic.

15. All of the team played in the soccer tournament.

GRADE 4

I. Reading
   A. Directions
   B. Sequencing
   C. Main Idea
II. Writing
   A. Capitalization
   B. Proofreading

Name _____

Subjects and Predicates

Remember, the **subject** tells who or what the sentence is about. The **predicate** tells what the subject does, did, is doing, or will do. A complete sentence must have a subject and a predicate.

Examples:

Subject	Predicate
Sharon	writes to her grandmother every week.
The horse	ran around the track quickly.
My mom's car	is bright green.
Denise	will be here after lunch.

Directions: Circle the subject of each sentence. Underline the predicate.

1. My sister is a very happy person.

2. I wish we had more holidays in the year.

3. Laura is one of the nicest girls in our class.

4. John is fun to have as a friend.

5. The rain nearly ruined our picnic!

6. My birthday present was exactly what I wanted.

7. Your bicycle is parked beside my skateboard.

8. The printer will need to be filled with paper before you use it.

9. Six dogs chased my cat home yesterday!

10. Anthony likes to read anything he can get his hands on.

11. Twelve students signed up for the dance committee.

12. Your teacher seems to be a reasonable person.

Name _____

Subject and Predicate Review

Directions: Draw one line under the subject and two lines under the predicate.

1. The clever detective searched for hidden clues.

2. Many baseball fans lined up early to buy tickets.

3. Kelly and Eric will be the new class leaders.

4. The TV weatherman has predicted snowfall tonight.

5. The new restaurant serves many kinds of seafood.

Directions: Write a subject to complete each sentence.

1. _____ are my two favorite sports.

2. _____ floated high above the trees.

3. _____ discovered an Egyptian tomb.

4. _____ heard the sound of footsteps.

5. _____ left for a vacation this morning.

6. _____ is a famous national monument.

7. _____ entered the stadium to the roar of the crowd.

8. _____ was served steaming hot by the waiter.

Directions: Write a predicate to complete each sentence.

1. The tired hikers _____.

2. Each member of the team _____.

3. The curious sightseers _____.

4. Robin's horse _____.

5. The creaky old house _____.

6. Everyone in my class _____.

7. Four valuable paintings _____.

Name _____

Adjectives

Adjectives tell more about nouns. Adjectives are describing words.

Examples: **scary** animals   **bright** glow   **wet** frog

Directions: Add at least two adjectives to each sentence below. Use your own words or words from the box.

pale	soft	sticky	burning	furry	glistening	peaceful
faint	shivering	slippery	gleaming	gentle	foggy	tangled

Example: The stripe was blue.
The wide stripe was light blue.

1. The frog had eyes.

   _____

2. The house was a sight.

   _____

3. A boy heard a noise.

   _____

4. The girl tripped over a toad.

   _____

5. A tiger ran through the room.

   _____

6. They saw a glow in the window.

   _____

7. A pan was sitting on the stove.

   _____

8. The boys were eating french fries.

   _____

Name _____

Adjectives

Adjectives tell a noun's size, color, shape, texture, brightness, darkness, personality, sound, taste, and so on.

Examples: **color** — red, yellow, green, black
size — small, large, huge, tiny
shape — round, square, rectangular, oval
texture — rough, smooth, soft, scaly
brightness — glistening, shimmering, dull, pale
personality — gentle, grumpy, happy, sad

Directions: Follow the instructions below.

1. Get an apple, orange, or other piece of fruit. Look at it very carefully and write adjectives that describe its size, color, shape, and texture.

_____

_____

2. Take a bite of your fruit. Write adjectives that describe its taste, texture, smell, and so on.

_____

_____

3. Using all the adjectives from above, write a cinquain about your fruit. A *cinquain* is a five-line poem. See the form and sample poem below.

Form: Line 1 — noun   **Example:**   Apple

Line 2 — two adjectives   red, smooth

Line 3 — three sounds      crackling, smacking, slurping

Line 4 — four-word phrase   drippy, sticky, sour juice

Line 5 — noun   Apple

_____

_____ , _____

_____ , _____ , _____

_____

_____

Name _____

Adjectives That Add "er"

The suffix **er** is often added to adjectives to compare two things.

Example:

> My feet are **large**.
>
> Your feet are **larger** than my feet.

When a one-syllable adjective ends in a single consonant and the vowel is short, double the final consonant before adding **er**. When a word ends in two or more consonants, add **er**.

Examples:

> big — bigger (single consonant)
>
> bold — bolder (two consonants)

When an adjective ends in **y**, change the **y** to **i** before adding **er**.

Examples:

> easy — easier
>
> greasy — greasier
>
> breezy — breezier

Directions: Use the correct rule to add **er** to the words below. The first one has been done for you.

1. fast	faster	11. skinny	
2. thin		12. fat	
3. long		13. poor	
4. few		14. juicy	
5. ugly		15. early	
6. silly		16. clean	
7. busy		17. thick	
8. grand		18. creamy	
9. lean		19. deep	
10. young		20. lazy	

Name _____

Adjectives That Add "est"

The suffix **est** is often added to adjectives to compare more than two things.

Example:

My glass is **full**.

Your glass is **fuller**.

His glass is **fullest**.

When a one-syllable adjective ends in a single consonant and the vowel sound is short, you usually double the final consonant before adding **est**.

Examples:

big — biggest (short vowel)

steep — steepest (long vowel)

When an adjective ends in **y**, change the **y** to **i** before adding **est**.

Example:

easy — easiest

Directions: Use the correct rule to add **est** to the words below. The first one has been done for you.

1. thin _____thinnest_____   11. quick _____

2. skinny _____   12. trim _____

3. cheap _____   13. silly _____

4. busy _____   14. tall _____

5. loud _____   15. glum _____

6. kind _____   16. red _____

7. dreamy _____   17. happy _____

8. ugly _____   18. high _____

9. pretty _____   19. wet _____

10. early _____   20. clean _____

Name _____

How Adjectives Compare

There are certain spelling rules to follow when **adjectives** are used to compare people, places, or things.

1. To many adjectives, simply add **er** or **est** to the end.

    fast   fast**er**   fast**est**

2. When an adjective ends with a consonant preceded by a single vowel, double the final consonant and add **er** or **est**.

    fat   fat**ter**   fat**test**

3. When an adjective ends in an **e**, drop the final **e** and add **er** or **est**.

    brave   brav**er**   brav**est**

4. If an adjective ends in a **y** preceded by a consonant, change the **y** to **i** and add **er** or **est**.

    heavy   heav**ier**   heav**iest**

Directions: Complete the chart below using the spelling rules you have learned. Write the number of the rule you used.

Adjective	Add **er**	Add **est**	Rule
1. weak	weaker	weakest	1
2. kind			
3. easy			
4. clear			
5. close			
6. noisy			
7. large			
8. red			
9. pretty			
10. hungry			
11. big			
12. happy			
13. wet			
14. cute			
15. plain			
16. busy			
17. loud			
18. strong			
19. fresh			
20. hot			

Name _____

Adjectives Preceded by "More"

Most adjectives of two or more syllables are preceded by the word **more** as a way to show comparison between two things.

Examples:

    Correct: intelligent, more intelligent

    Incorrect: intelligenter

    Correct: famous, more famous

    Incorrect: famouser

Directions: Write **more** before the adjectives that fit the rule.
Draw an **X** in the blanks of the adjectives that do not fit the rule.
To test yourself, say the words aloud using **more** and adding **er** to
hear which way sounds correct. The first two have been done for you.

____X____ 1. cheap		_____ 11. awful
__more__ 2. beautiful		_____ 12. delicious
_____ 3. quick		_____ 13. embarrassing
_____ 4. terrible		_____ 14. nice
_____ 5. difficult		_____ 15. often
_____ 6. interesting		_____ 16. hard
_____ 7. polite		_____ 17. valuable
_____ 8. cute		_____ 18. close
_____ 9. dark		_____ 19. fast
_____ 10. sad		_____ 20. important

Name _____

Adverbs

Adverbs answer the questions **when**, **where**, and **how**. The adverbs in the sentences below answer **how**.

Directions: Underline the adverbs in each sentence. Then, circle the verb each adverb describes. The first one is done for you.

1. The two boys solemnly (shook) hands.

2. Chip looked down incredulously at the fallen shingle which landed softly at this feet.

3. "I don't salvage," remarked Rudy calmly when his counselor glared at him.

4. "Rudy," whispered Mike warningly. Chip was glaring in his direction.

5. The door opened and Mr. Warden emerged, smartly dressed in a white tennis outfit.

6. "Harold, you have no soul," explained Rudy pleasantly.

7. "Why do you immediately assume that I'm guilty?" asked Rudy in a hurt tone.

8. "I'd rather go back to arts and crafts," nodded Mike sheepishly.

9. "Tomorrow," Rudy said thoughtfully as they carefully daubed pale blue paint onto their creation, "we'll go earlier."

10. Arms flailing wildly, Chip rushed anxiously toward his cabin.

Directions: Write four sentences of your own containing adverbs. Underline the adverbs and circle the verbs that are described.

1. _____

_____

2. _____

_____

3. _____

_____

4. _____

_____

Name _____

Sorting Adverbs

Directions: Circle the 12 adverbs in the story. Then, write them in the correct box to show if they tell when, where, or how about the verb.

Don't Be Late!

Robert and Tom went inside to dress for the movies. They planned to watch *Sonic Man* today.

"Hurry, or we'll be late!" called Tom loudly.

They ran quickly to the bus stop and waited impatiently for the bus to arrive.

At the theater, the line wound outside. The boys worried they would have to return tomorrow.

The line moved slowly as the boys waited nervously. "I hope they have tickets left," moaned Robert quietly.

"Yes, we have seats left," said a ticket seller who stood nearby.

The movie began immediately as the boys settled in their seats.

HOW

1. _____ 2. _____ 3. _____

4. _____ 5. _____ 6. _____

WHEN

7. _____ 8. _____ 9. _____

WHERE

10. _____ 11. _____ 12. _____

Name _____

Missing Adverbs

Directions: Write a different adverb on each line to complete the sentence. Make sure your adverb tells what is shown in parentheses.

1. Our team played _____. (when)

2. Brian writes _____. (how)

3. The cows move _____. (how)

4. Melissa will dance _____. (when)

5. My dog went _____. (where)

6. We ran _____. (how)

7. The choir sang _____. (how)

8. The cat purred _____. (where)

9. Hilary spoke _____. (how)

10. We'll go on our vacation _____. (when)

11. The sign goes _____. (where)

12. Mother brought the groceries _____. (where)

13. David read the directions _____. (how)

14. We'll be leaving _____. (when)

15. We have three bedrooms _____. (where)

16. We will arrive _____. (when)

17. The mother bird leaves the nest _____. (when)

18. Don't let the cat _____. (where)

Where?

The monkeys are inside.

Adverbs

Adverbs are words that tell when, where, or how.

Adverbs of time tell when.

Example:

The train left yesterday.

Yesterday is an adverb of time. It tells when the train left.

Adverbs of place tell where.

Example:

The girl walked away.

Away is an adverb of place. It tells where the girl walked.

Adverbs of manner tell how.

Example:

The boy walked quickly.

Quickly is an adverb of manner. It tells how the boy walked.

Directions: Write the adverb for each sentence in the first blank. In the second blank, write whether it is an adverb of time, place, or manner. The first one has been done for you.

1. The family ate downstairs.   <u>downstairs</u>   <u>place</u>

2. The relatives laughed loudly.   _____   _____

3. We will finish tomorrow.   _____   _____

4. The snowstorm will stop soon.   _____   _____

5. She sings beautifully!   _____   _____

6. The baby slept soundly.   _____   _____

7. The elevator stopped suddenly. _____   _____

8. Does the plane leave today?   _____   _____

9. The phone call came yesterday. _____   _____

10. She ran outside.   _____   _____

GRADE 4

I. Reading
   A. Directions
   B. Sequencing
   C. Main Idea
II. Writing
   A. Capitalization
   B. Proofreading

Name _____

Adverb Review

Remember, adverbs tell when, where, or how about the verb in a sentence.

Directions: Circle the verb and underline the adverb in each sentence. Then, write the verb and adverb in the correct column. The first one has been done for you.

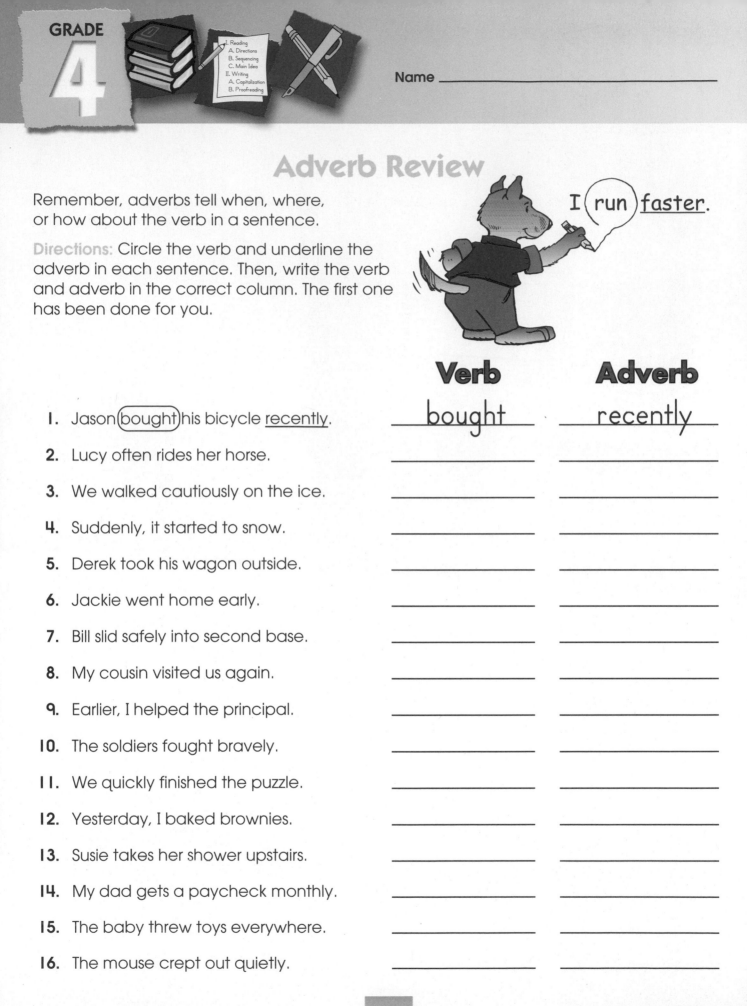

I (run) faster.

	Verb	**Adverb**
1. Jason (bought) his bicycle <u>recently</u>.	bought	recently
2. Lucy often rides her horse.	_____	_____
3. We walked cautiously on the ice.	_____	_____
4. Suddenly, it started to snow.	_____	_____
5. Derek took his wagon outside.	_____	_____
6. Jackie went home early.	_____	_____
7. Bill slid safely into second base.	_____	_____
8. My cousin visited us again.	_____	_____
9. Earlier, I helped the principal.	_____	_____
10. The soldiers fought bravely.	_____	_____
11. We quickly finished the puzzle.	_____	_____
12. Yesterday, I baked brownies.	_____	_____
13. Susie takes her shower upstairs.	_____	_____
14. My dad gets a paycheck monthly.	_____	_____
15. The baby threw toys everywhere.	_____	_____
16. The mouse crept out quietly.	_____	_____

Name _____

Misused Words

Sometimes, people have difficulty using **good**, **well**, **sure**, **surely**, **real**, and **really** correctly. This chart may help you.

Adjectives	Adverbs
Good is an adjective when it describes a noun. 　That was a **good** dinner.	**Good** is never used as an adverb.
Well is an adjective when it means in good health or having a good appearance. 　She looks **well**.	**Well** is an adverb when it is used to tell that something is done capably or effectively. 　She writes **well**.
Sure is an adjective when it modifies a noun. 　A robin is a **sure** sign of spring.	**Surely** is an adverb. 　He **surely** wants a job.
Real is an adjective that means genuine or true. 　That was a **real** diamond.	**Really** is an adverb. 　Mary **really** played a good game.

Directions: Use the chart to help you choose the correct word from those in parentheses. Write it in the blank.

I. You did a very _____ job of writing your book report. (good, well)

2. The detective in the story used his skills _____ . (good, well)

3. He _____ solved the case before anyone else did. (sure, surely)

4. I _____ want to read that book now. (real, really)

5. Did it take you long to decide who the _____ criminal was? (real, really)

6. Although the butler looked _____ and healthy, he died. (well, good)

7. Detective Rains read the clues _____ as he worked on the case. (good, well)

8. You will _____ get a good grade on that report. (surely, sure)

9. You had to _____ work hard to get those good grades. (real, really)

Name _____

Using Conjunctions

Conjunctions are joining words that can be used to combine sentences. Words such as **and**, **but**, **or**, **when**, and **after** are conjunctions.

Examples:

Sally went to the mall. She went to the movies.
Sally went to the mall, and she went to the movies.

We can have our vacation at home. We can vacation at the beach.
We can have our vacation at home, or we can vacation at the beach.

Mary fell on the playground. She did not hurt herself!
Mary fell on the playground, but she did not hurt herself!

Note: The conjunctions **after** or **when** are usually placed at the beginning of a sentence

Example: Marge went to the store. She went to the gas station.
          After Marge went to the store, she went tot the gas station.

Directions: Combine the following sentences using the conjunctions in parenthesis.

1. Peter fell down the steps. He broke his foot. (and)

_____

2. I visited New York. I would like to see Chicago. (but)

_____

3. Amy can edit books. She can write stories. (or)

_____

4. He played in the barn. John started to sneeze. (when)

_____

5. The team won the playoffs. They went to the championships. (after)

_____

Directions: Write three sentences of your own using the conjunctions **and, but, or, when, or after.**

_____

_____

_____

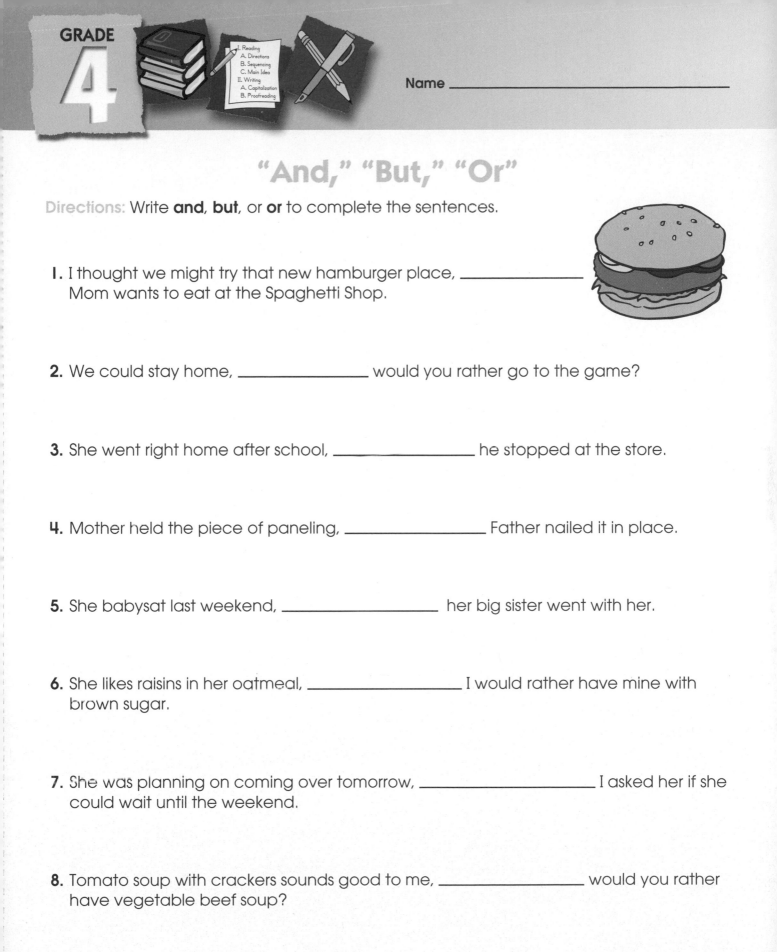

Name _____

"And," "But," "Or"

Directions: Write **and**, **but**, or **or** to complete the sentences.

1. I thought we might try that new hamburger place, _____
Mom wants to eat at the Spaghetti Shop.

2. We could stay home, _____ would you rather go to the game?

3. She went right home after school, _____ he stopped at the store.

4. Mother held the piece of paneling, _____ Father nailed it in place.

5. She babysat last weekend, _____ her big sister went with her.

6. She likes raisins in her oatmeal, _____ I would rather have mine with brown sugar.

7. She was planning on coming over tomorrow, _____ I asked her if she could wait until the weekend.

8. Tomato soup with crackers sounds good to me, _____ would you rather have vegetable beef soup?

I. Reading
A. Directions
B. Sequencing
C. Main Idea
II. Writing
A. Capitalization
B. Proofreading

Name _____

"Because" and "So"

Directions: Write **because** or **so** to complete the sentences.

1. She cleaned the paintbrushes _____ they would be ready in the morning.

2. Father called home complaining of a sore throat _____ Mom stopped by the pharmacy.

3. His bus will be running late _____ it has a flat tire.

4. We all worked together _____ we could get the job done sooner.

5. We took a variety of sandwiches on the picnic _____ we knew not everyone liked cheese and olives with mayonnaise.

6. All the school children were sent home _____ the electricity went off at school.

7. My brother wants us to meet his girlfriend _____ she will be coming to dinner with us on Friday.

8. He forgot to take his umbrella along this morning _____ now his clothes are very wet.

GRADE
4

I. Reading
  A. Directions
  B. Sequencing
  C. Main Idea
II. Writing
  A. Capitalization
  B. Proofreading

Name _____

"When" and "After"

Directions: Write **when** or **after** to complete the sentences.

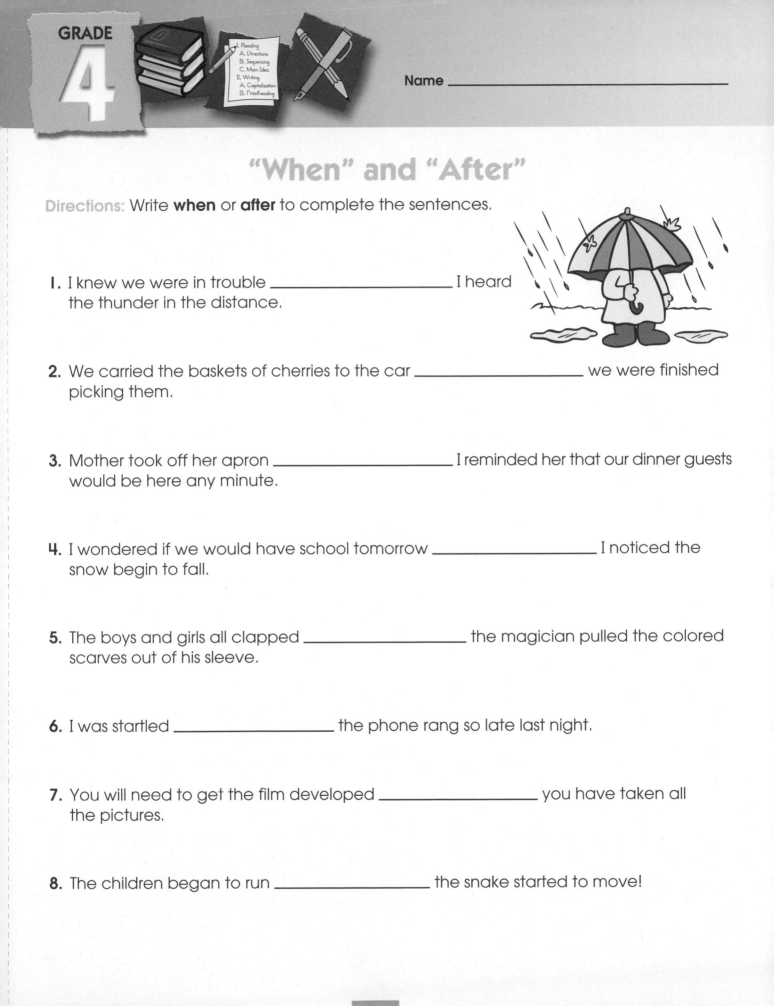

1. I knew we were in trouble _____ I heard
   the thunder in the distance.

2. We carried the baskets of cherries to the car _____ we were finished
   picking them.

3. Mother took off her apron _____ I reminded her that our dinner guests
   would be here any minute.

4. I wondered if we would have school tomorrow _____ I noticed the
   snow begin to fall.

5. The boys and girls all clapped _____ the magician pulled the colored
   scarves out of his sleeve.

6. I was startled _____ the phone rang so late last night.

7. You will need to get the film developed _____ you have taken all
   the pictures.

8. The children began to run _____ the snake started to move!

Name _____

Conjunctions

Directions: Choose the best conjunction from the box to combine the pairs of sentences. Then, rewrite the sentences.

and	but	or	because	when	after	so

1. I like Leah. I like Ben.

_____

2. Should I eat the orange? Should I eat the apple?

_____

3. You will get a reward. You turned in the lost item.

_____

4. I really mean what I say! You had better listen!

_____

5. I like you. You're nice, friendly, helpful, and kind.

_____

6. You can have dessert. You ate all your peas.

_____

7. I like your shirt better. You should decide for yourself.

_____

8. We walked out of the building. We heard the fire alarm.

_____

9. I like to sing folk songs. I like to play the guitar.

_____

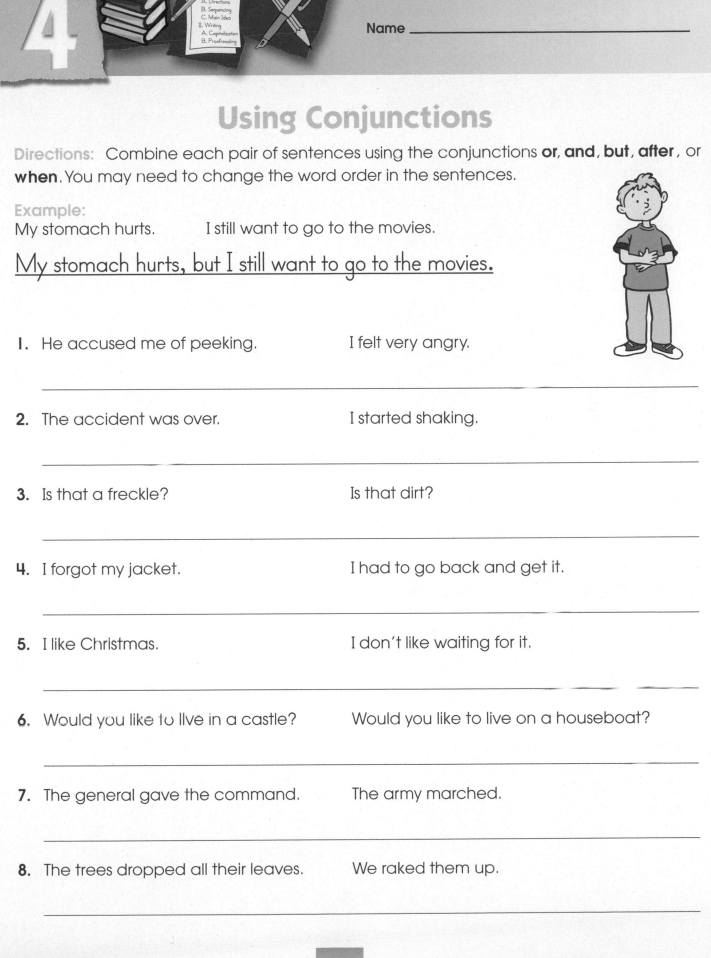

Using Conjunctions

Directions: Combine each pair of sentences using the conjunctions **or, and, but, after**, or **when**. You may need to change the word order in the sentences.

Example:
My stomach hurts.   I still want to go to the movies.

My stomach hurts, but I still want to go to the movies.

1. He accused me of peeking.   I felt very angry.

_____

2. The accident was over.   I started shaking.

_____

3. Is that a freckle?   Is that dirt?

_____

4. I forgot my jacket.   I had to go back and get it.

_____

5. I like Christmas.   I don't like waiting for it.

_____

6. Would you like to live in a castle?   Would you like to live on a houseboat?

_____

7. The general gave the command.   The army marched.

_____

8. The trees dropped all their leaves.   We raked them up.

_____

GRADE 4

I. Reading
A. Directions
B. Sequencing
C. Main Idea
II. Writing
A. Capitalization
B. Proofreading

Name _____

Abbreviations

An **abbreviation** is a shortened form of a longer word. Most abbreviations begin with a capital letter and end with a period.

Examples: February — Feb.
boulevard — Blvd.
inches — in.
meter — m
Monday — Mon.
Ohio — OH

Mr. Ronald Smith
85 Terrace Rd.
Charleston, WV 24512

Directions: Write the letter of the abbreviation that matches the word.

1. ____ street   **a.** oz.

2. ____ doctor   **b.** Ave.

3. ____ post office   **c.** lb.

4. ____ Mister   **d.** St.

5. ____ California   **e.** Wed.

6. ____ ounce   **f.** Mr.

7. ____ Junior   **g.** Mt.

8. ____ avenue   **h.** TN

9. ____ October   **i.** ft.

10. ____ foot   **j.** Dr.

11. ____ Wednesday   **k.** Oct.

12. ____ pound   **l.** Rd.

13. ____ mountain   **m.** Jr.

14. ____ centimeter   **n.** P.O.

15. ____ Tennessee   **o.** cm

16. ____ road   **p.** CA

Name _____

Short and to the Point

Directions: Write the abbreviation for each word. Then, connect each set of stars in the same order to spell out the answer to the question below.

1. President _____
2. Street _____
3. feet _____
4. gallon _____

5. Mister _____
6. inch _____
7. quart _____
8. Doctor _____
9. pound _____
10. General _____
11. Avenue _____

12. Professor _____
13. Road _____
14. Reverend _____
15. Company _____
16. Highway _____

Which country celebrates Independence Day on July 4? _____

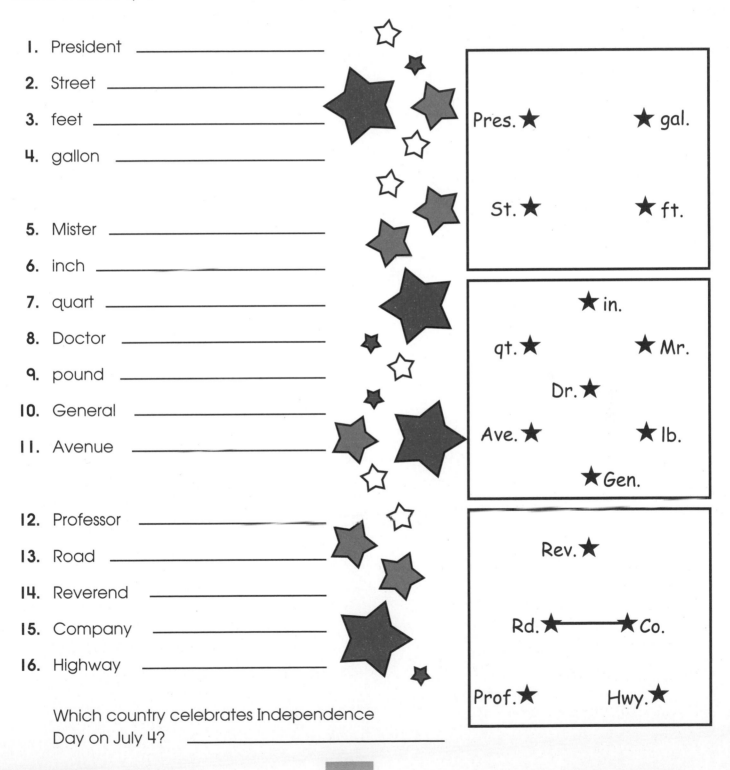

Pres. ★   ★ gal.

St. ★   ★ ft.

★ in.

qt. ★   ★ Mr.

Dr. ★

Ave. ★   ★ lb.

★ Gen.

Rev. ★

Rd. ★————★ Co.

Prof. ★   Hwy. ★

GRADE
4

I. Reading
A. Directions
B. Sequencing
C. Main Idea
II. Writing
A. Capitalization
B. Proofreading

Name _____

Captial Letters and Periods

The first letter of a person's first, last and middle name is always capitalized.

Example: **E**lizabeth **J**ane **M**arks is my best friend.

The first letter of a person's title is always capitalized.
If the title is abbreviated, the title is followed by a period.

Example: Her mother is **Dr**. Susan Jones Marks.
              Ms. Jessica Joseph was a visitor.

Directions: Write **C** if the sentence is punctuated and capitalized correctly. Draw an **X** if the sentence is not punctuated and capitalized correctly. The first one has been done for you.

_X_ **1.** I asked Elizabeth if I should call her mother Mrs. marks or dr. Marks.

_____ **2.** Mr. and Mrs. Francesco were friends of the DeVuonos.

_____ **3.** Dr. Daniel Long and Dr Holly Barrows both spoke with the patient.

_____ **4.** Did you get Mr. MacMillan for English next year?

_____ **5.** Mr. Sweet and Ms. Ellison were both at the concert.

_____ **6.** When did the doctor. tell you about this illness?

_____ **7.** Dr. Donovan is the doctor that Mr. Winham trusted.

_____ **8.** Why don't you ask Doctor. Williams her opinion?

_____ **9.** All three of the doctors diagnosed Ms. Twelp.

_____**10.** Will Ms. Davis and Ms Simpson be at school today?

_____**11.** Did Dr Samuels see your father last week?

_____**12.** Is Judy a medical doctor or another kind of specialist?

_____**13.** We are pleased to introduce Ms King and Mr. Graham.

Name _____

Capitalize I, Names, and Initials

The pronoun **I** is always capitalized. Each part of a person's or pet's name begins with a capital letter.

Examples: **I, M**ary **A**nn **S**mith, **L**assie

An initial (the first letter of a name) is always capitalized and is followed by a period.

Example: **M. A.** Smith

Directions: Rewrite each sentence using capital letters correctly.

1. Where did molly parsons get her dog, laddie?

_____

2. Her grandmother, louella cane, bought it for the family.

_____

3. The most unusual pet is tom simpson's parrot named showboat.

_____

4. I have heard showboat say words quite clearly.

_____

5. Tom says his parrot's full name is a. h. showboat.

_____

6. What do the initials a. h. stand for?

_____

7. tom told me that his parrot's first name is always and his middle name is hungry.

_____

8. i call my dog "m. m." instead of megan mae.

_____

Directions: Follow each direction carefully.

1. Write your full name.

_____

2. Write the full name and initials of one of your parents.

_____

3. Use the pronoun "I" to tell what you like to eat best.

_____

Name _____

Punctuation: Commas

Use a comma to separate the number of the day of a month and the year. Do not use a comma to separate the month and year if no day is given.

Examples:

June 14, 1999

June 1999

Use a comma after **yes** or **no** when it is the first word in a sentence.

Examples:

Yes, I will do it right now.

No, I don't want any.

Directions: Write **C** if the sentence is punctuated correctly. Draw an **X** if the sentence is not punctuated correctly. The first one has been done for you.

__C__ **1.** No, I don't plan to attend.

_____ **2.** I told them, oh yes, I would go.

_____ **3.** Her birthday is March 13, 1995.

_____ **4.** He was born in May, 1997.

_____ **5.** Yes, of course I like you!

_____ **6.** No I will not be there.

_____ **7.** They left for vacation on February, 14.

_____ **8.** No, today is Monday.

_____ **9.** The program was first shown on August 12, 1991.

_____ **10.** In September, 2007 how old will you be?

_____ **11.** He turned 12 years old on November, 13.

_____ **12.** I said no, I will not come no matter what!

_____ **13.** Yes, she is a friend of mine.

_____ **14.** His birthday is June 12, 1992, and mine is June 12, 1993.

_____ **15.** No I would not like more dessert.

Name _____

Punctuation: Commas

Use a comma to separate words in a series. A comma is used after each word in a series but is not needed before the last word. Both ways are correct. In your own writing, be consistent about which style you use.

Examples:

> We ate apples, oranges, and pears.
> We ate apples, oranges and pears.

Always use a comma between the name of a city and a state.

Example:

> She lives in Fresno, California.
> He lives in Wilmington, Delaware.

Directions: Write **C** if the sentence is punctuated correctly. Draw an **X** if the sentence is not punctuated correctly. The first one has been done for you.

__X__ 1. She ordered shoes, dresses, and shirts to be sent to her home in Oakland California.

_____ 2. No one knew her pets' names were Fido, Spot, and Tiger.

_____ 3. He likes green beans lima beans, and corn on the cob.

_____ 4. Typing paper, pens, and pencils are all needed for school.

_____ 5. Send your letters to her in College Park, Maryland.

_____ 6. Orlando Florida is the home of Disney World.

_____ 7. Mickey, Minnie, Goofy, and Daisy are all favorites of mine.

_____ 8. Send your letter to her in Reno, Nevada.

_____ 9. Before he lived in New York, City he lived in San Diego, California.

_____ 10. She mailed postcards, and letters to him in Lexington, Kentucky.

_____ 11. Teacups, saucers, napkins, and silverware were piled high.

_____ 12. Can someone give me a ride to Indianapolis, Indiana?

_____ 13. He took a train a car, then a boat to visit his old friend.

_____ 14. Why can't I go to Disney World to see Mickey, and Minnie?

Name _____

Punctuation: Quotation Marks

Use quotation marks (" ") before and after the exact words of a speaker.

Examples:

I asked Aunt Martha, "How do you feel?"

"I feel awful," Aunt Martha replied.

Do not put quotation marks around words that report what the speaker said.

Examples:

Aunt Martha said she felt awful.

I asked Aunt Martha how she felt.

Directions: Write **C** if the sentence is punctuated correctly. Draw an **X** if the sentence is not punctuated correctly. The first one has been done for you.

_C_ 1. "I want it right now!" she demanded angrily.

_____ 2. "Do you want it now? I asked."

_____ 3. She said "she felt better" now.

_____ 4. Her exact words were, "I feel much better now!"

_____ 5. "I am so thrilled to be here!" he shouted.

_____ 6. "Yes, I will attend," she replied.

_____ 7. Elizabeth said "she was unhappy."

_____ 8. "I'm unhappy," Elizabeth reported.

_____ 9. "Did you know her mother?" I asked.

_____ 10. I asked "whether you knew her mother."

_____ 11. I wondered, "What will dessert be?"

_____ 12. "Which will it be, salt or pepper?" the waiter asked.

_____ 13. "No, I don't know the answer!" he snapped.

_____ 14. He said "yes he'd take her on the trip.

_____ 15. Be patient, he said. "it will soon be over."

Name _____

Punctuation: Quotation Marks

Use quotation marks around the titles of songs and poems.

Examples:

Have you heard "Still Cruising" by the Beach Boys?

"Ode to a Nightingale" is a famous poem.

Directions: Write **C** if the sentence is punctuated correctly. Draw an **X** if the sentence is not punctuated correctly. The first one has been done for you.

_C_ 1. Do you know "My Bonnie Lies Over the Ocean"?

_____ 2. We sang The Stars and Stripes Forever" at school.

_____ 3. Her favorite song is "The Eensy Weensy Spider."

_____ 4. Turn the music up when "A Hard Day's "Night comes on!

_____ 5. "Yesterday" was one of Paul McCartney's most famous songs.

_____ 6. "Mary Had a Little Lamb" is a very silly poem!

_____ 7. A song everyone knows is "Happy Birthday."

_____ 8. "Swing Low, Sweet Chariot" was first sung by slaves.

_____ 9. Do you know the words to Home on "the Range"?

_____10. "Hiawatha" is a poem many older people had to memorize.

_____11. "Happy Days Are Here Again! is an upbeat tune.

_____12. Frankie Valli and the Four Seasons sang "Sherry."

_____13. The words to "Rain, Rain" Go Away are easy to learn.

_____14. A slow song I know is called "Summertime."

_____15. Little children like to hear "The Night Before Christmas."

Ask or Tell?

Remember, a question is a sentence that asks something. Questions end with a question mark.

Directions: Write a period at the end of each sentence that tells something and a question mark at the end of each sentence that asks something.

1. Would you like to go shopping ☐

2. We can go to the mall ☐

3. How long can you stay ☐

4. I want to go to the department store ☐

5. Where is the book store ☐

6. I'm getting hungry ☐

7. Would you like pizza or a hot dog ☐

8. Do you want another piece of pizza ☐

9. My sister wants me to buy a CD for her ☐

10. Where is the escalator ☐

11. The pet store is on the second level ☐

12. Are you going to buy new jeans ☐

13. Do you want to buy a toy for your brother ☐

14. It's already three o'clock ☐

15. Do you have to leave now ☐

16. When will the bus arrive ☐

17. Let's wrap the gifts tonight ☐

18. Is there time to play a video game ☐

I. Reading
A. Directions
B. Sequencing
C. Main Idea
II. Writing
A. Capitalization
B. Proofreading

Name _____

Perfectly Punctuated

A statement ends with a period. (.)
A question ends with a question mark. (?)
A command ends with a period. (.)
An exclamation ends with an exclamation mark. (!)

Directions: Write the correct punctuation mark in each box.

1. Every Saturday morning we help a senior citizen ☐

2. Would you like to help us this Saturday ☐

3. Be at my house at 8:00 ☐

4. You can help me gather the supplies we will need ☐

5. I won't be late ☐

6. Today we are raking Mrs. Ray's yard ☐

7. That elm tree is huge ☐

8. Take these lawn bags to Bob and Eric ☐

9. Tell Jan and Pat to mow the backyard ☐

10. Will you help them rake the backyard ☐

11. Don't mow too close to the flowers ☐

12. Look at that big gazebo ☐

13. Mrs. Ray has left lemonade there for us ☐

14. I will mow the front yard ☐

15. Will you sweep the front walks ☐

16. Go ask Mrs. Ray to come see her clean yard ☐

17. She thinks the yard looks super ☐

18. What will we do next Saturday ☐

GRADE
4

I. Reading
   A. Directions
   B. Sequencing
   C. Main Idea
II. Writing
   A. Capitalization
   B. Proofreading

Name _____

Writing: Punctuation

Directions: In the paragraphs below, use periods, question marks, or exclamation marks to show where one sentence ends and the next begins. Circle the first letter of each new sentence to show the capital.

Example: (m)y sister accused me of not helping her rake the leaves. (t)hat's silly! (i) helped at least a hundred times.

1. I always tie on my fishing line when it moves up and down, I know a fish is there after waiting a minute or two, I pull up the fish it's fun

2. I tried putting lemon juice on my freckles to make them go away did you ever do that it didn't work my skin just got sticky now, I'm slowly getting used to my freckles

3. once, I had an accident on my bike I was on my way home from school what do you think happened my wheel slipped in the loose dirt at the side of the road my bike slid into the road

4. one night, I dreamed I lived in a castle in my dream, I was the king or maybe the queen everyone listened to my commands then Mom woke me up for school I tried commanding her to let me sleep it didn't work

5. what's your favorite holiday Christmas is mine for months before Christmas, I save my money, so I can give a present to everyone in my family last year, I gave my big sister earrings they cost me five dollars

6. my dad does exercises every night to make his stomach flat he says he doesn't want to grow old I think it's too late don't tell him I said that

I. Reading
A. Directions
B. Sequencing
C. Main Idea
II. Writing
A. Capitalization
B. Proofreading

Name _____

Review

Directions: The following sentences have errors in punctuation, capitalization, or both. The number in parentheses **( )** at the end of each sentence tells you how many errors it contains. Correct the errors by rewriting each sentence.

1. I saw mr. Johnson reading War And Peace to his class. (3)

_____

2. Do you like to sing "Take me Out to The Ballgame"? (2)

_____

3. He recited Hiawatha to Miss. Simpson's class. (2)

_____

4. Bananas, and oranges are among Dr smith's favorite fruits. (3)

_____

5. "Daisy, daisy is a song about a bicycle built for two. (2)

_____

6. Good Morning, Granny Rose is about a woman and her dog. (1)

_____

7. Garfield goes to waist is a very funny book! (3)

_____

8. Peanut butter, jelly, and bread are Miss. Lee's favorite treats. (1)

_____

Proofreading

It is important to be able to **proofread** things that you write to correct any errors.

Directions: Read each paragraph. Proofread for these errors:

- indentation
- punctuation
- capitalization
- sentences which do not belong (mark out)
- spelling
- run-on sentences (rewrite as two sentences)

Then, rewrite each paragraph correctly on the lines.

1. my brother will graduate from college this week everyone is so excited for him Many of our relatives are coming from out of town for his graduation our town has a university. mom and Dad have planed a big surprise party

_____

_____

_____

2. riding in a hot air balloon is an incredible experience first, everyone climbs into the basket the pilot then starts the fuel which produces the hot air that makes the ballone rise. The road leads to an open field to lower the balloon, the pilot gradually releases air

_____

_____

_____

Directions: Rewrite this paragraph on another sheet of paper.

a caterpiller is a young butterfly the caterpillar originally hatches from an egg and later, it develops a hard case around its body inside the case, the caterpillow becomes a butterfly after a short time, the case opens and a beautiful butterfly flies out the tree has hndreds of blossoms

Proofreading

Proofreading means searching for and correcting errors by carefully reading and rereading what has been written. Use the proofreading marks below when correcting your writing or someone else's.

To insert a word or a punctuation mark that has been left out, use this mark: ∧. It is called a caret.

Example: We∧to the dance together.
(went inserted above)

To show that a letter should be capitalized, put three lines under it.

Example: Mrs. jones drove us to school.
(jones underlined three times)

To show that a capital letter should be a small or lower-case, draw a diagonal line through it.

Example: Mrs. Jones Drove us to school.
(diagonal line through D)

To show that a word is spelled incorrectly, draw a horizontal line through it and write the correct spelling above it.

Example: The ~~wolros~~ is an amazing animal.
(walrus written above)

Directions: Proofread the two paragraphs using the proofreading marks you learned. The author's last name, Towne, is spelled correctly.

The Modern ark

My book report is on the modern ark by Cecilia Fitzsimmons. The book tells abut 80 of worlds endangered animals. The book also an arc and animals inside for kids put together.

Their House

there house is a Great book! The arthur's name is Mary Towne. they're house tells about a girl name Molly. Molly's Family bys an old house from some people named warren. Then there big problems begin!

Name _____

Proofreading

Directions: Proofread the sentences. Write **C** if the sentence has no errors. Draw an **X** if the sentence contains missing words or other errors. The first one has been done for you.

__C__ 1. The new Ship Wreck Museum in Key West is exciting!

_____ 2. Another thing I liked was the litehouse.

_____ 3. Do you remember Hemingway's address in Key West?

_____ 4. The Key West semetery is on 21 acres of ground.

_____ 5. Ponce de eon discovered Key West.

_____ 6. The cemetery in Key West is on Francis Street.

_____ 7. My favorete tombstone was the sailor's.

_____ 8. His wife wrote the words on it. Remember?

_____ 9. The words said, "at least I know where to find him now!"

_____ 10. That sailor must have been away at sea all the time.

_____ 11. The troley ride around Key West is very interesting.

_____ 12. Do you why it is called Key West?

_____ 13. Can you imagine a lighthouse in the middle of your town?

_____ 14. It's interesting to no that Key West is our southernmost city.

_____ 15. Besides Harry Truman and Hemingway, did other famous people live there?

Name _____

Proofreading

Directions: Proofread the paragraphs, using the proofreading marks you learned. There are seven capitalization errors, three missing words, and eleven errors in spelling or word usage.

Key West

key West has been tropical paradise ever since Ponce de Leon first saw the set of islands called the keys in 1513. Two famus streets in Key West are named duval and whitehead. You will find the city semetery on Francis Street. The tombstones are funny!

The message on one is, "I told you I was sick!" On sailor's tombston is this mesage his widow: "At lease I no where to find him now."

The cemetery is on 21 akres in the midle of town. The most famous home in key west is that of the authur, Ernest Hemingway. Heminway's home was at 907 whitehead Street. He lived their for 30 years.

Name _____

Proofreading

Directions: Read more about Key West. Proofread and correct the errors. There are eight errors in capitalization, seven misspelled words, and three missing words.

More About Key West

a good way to lern more about key West is to ride the trolley. Key West has a great troley system. The trolley will take on a tour of the salt ponds. You can also three red brick forts. The troley tour goes by a 110-foot high lighthouse. It is rite in the middle of the city. Key west is the only city with a Lighthouse in the midle of it! It is also the southernmost city in the United States.

If you have time, the new Ship Wreck Museum. Key west was also the hom of former president Harry truman. During his presidency, Trueman spent many vacations on key west.

GRADE 4

I. Reading
A. Directions
B. Sequencing
C. Main Idea
II. Writing
A. Capitalization
B. Proofreading

Name _____

Run-On Sentences

A **run-on sentence** occurs when two or more sentences are joined together without punctuation.

Examples:

Run-on sentence: I lost my way once did you?
Two sentences with correct punctuation: I lost my way once. Did you?
Run-on sentence: I found the recipe it was not hard to follow.
Two sentences with correct punctuation: I found the recipe. It was not hard to follow.

Directions: Rewrite the run-on sentences correctly with periods, exclamation points, and question marks. The first one has been done for you.

1. Did you take my umbrella I can't find it anywhere!

Did you take my umbrella? I can't find it anywhere!

2. How can you stand that noise I can't!

_____

3. The cookies are gone I see only crumbs.

_____

4. The dogs were barking they were hungry.

_____

5. She is quite ill please call a doctor immediately!

_____

6. The clouds came up we knew the storm would hit soon.

_____

7. You weren't home he stopped by this morning.

_____

Two for One

You can combine two subjects with the word **and** to form one longer sentence. The new sentence will have a **compound subject**.

Example: **Dennis** painted the fence.
          Chuck painted the fence.
          Dennis and Chuck painted the fence.

Directions: Combine the subjects to write one longer sentence.

1. The quarter rolled under the sofa.
   The dime rolled under the sofa.

   _____

2. The sandwiches are in our picnic basket.
   The chips are in our picnic basket.

   _____

   _____

You can also combine two predicates with the word **and** to form one longer sentence. The new sentence will have a **compound predicate**.

Example: Our team won the tournament.
          Our team received a trophy.
          Our team won the tournament and received a trophy.

Directions: Combine the predicates to write one longer sentence.

1. The kids went to the library.
   The kids checked out books.

   _____

   _____

2. Katy folded her camp clothes.
   Katy packed them in her luggage.

   _____

   _____

Get Connected!

You can combine two shorter sentences into one longer sentence by using a connecting word. A combined sentence is usually more interesting.

Example: Barb doesn't like cooking.
She sees all the dirty dishes.
Barb doesn't like cooking **after** she sees all the dirty dishes.

Directions: Use the connecting word to write one longer sentence.

1. The picnic was lots of fun.   **until**
   It began to rain.

   _____

   _____

2. I talked to my friend on the phone.   **after**
   I finished my homework.

   _____

   _____

3. I read my book at the bus stop.   **while**
   I waited for the bus to arrive.

   _____

   _____

Directions: Write three long sentences of your own using each connecting word.

1. _____ until

   _____

2. _____ after

   _____

3. _____ while

   _____

Name _____

Combining Repeated Words

You can also combine two shorter sentences into one longer sentence by eliminating words that are repeated.

Example: <u>Dawn cleared leaves</u> from the front yard.
<u>Dawn cleared leaves</u> with a new rake.

Dawn cleared leaves from the front yard with a new rake.

Directions: Underline the repeated words and write a combined sentence.

1. I rode down the Grand Canyon trail.
   I rode on a donkey.

   _____

2. We are throwing a surprise birthday party for Jan.
   We are throwing a surprise birthday party next Saturday.

   _____

   _____

3. The chef served steaming hot pasta.
   The chef served pasta on a large platter.

   _____

4. I ran errands for my mom today.
   I ran errands because she was ill.

   _____

5. The detectives saw fresh footprints in the mud.
   They saw footprints under the window.

   _____

   _____

Name _____

Combining Sentences

Some simple sentences can be easily combined into one sentence.

Examples:

Simple sentences: The bird sang. The bird was tiny. The bird was in the tree.
Combined sentence: The tiny bird sang in the tree.

Directions: Combine each set of simple sentences into one sentence. The first one has been done for you.

1. The big girls laughed. They were friendly. They helped the little girls.

The big, friendly girls laughed as they helped the little girls.

2. The dog was hungry. The dog whimpered. The dog looked at its bowl.

_____

3. Be quiet now. I want you to listen. You listen to my joke!

_____

4. I lost my pencil. My pencil was stubby. I lost it on the bus.

_____

5. I see my mother. My mother is walking. My mother is walking down the street.

_____

6. Do you like ice cream? Do you like hot dogs? Do you like mustard?

_____

7. Tell me you'll do it! Tell me you will! Tell me right now!

_____

I. Reading
  A. Directions
  B. Sequencing
  C. Main Idea
II. Writing
  A. Capitalization
  B. Proofreading

Name _____

Combining Sentences

Two sentences can be written as one sentence by using **connecting words**.

Directions: Choose one of the words in the box to combine the two sentences into one sentence.

I am happy — when — I go to school.

1. We can eat now. We can eat after the game.

| while |
| or |
| because |

_____

_____

2. We stood on the cabin's deck. The sun rose over the deck.

| as |
| or |
| but |

_____

_____

3. Sarah wanted to watch TV. She had lots of homework to finish.

| because |
| when |
| but |

_____

_____

4. The concert did not begin on time. The conductor was late arriving.

| until |
| because |
| while |

_____

_____

5. The spectators cheered and applauded. The acrobats completed their performances.

| when |
| if |
| but |

_____

_____

6. The baseball teams waited in their dugouts. The rain ended and the field was uncovered.

| or |
| until |
| after |

_____

_____

GRADE 4

I. Reading
   A. Directions
   B. Sequencing
   C. Main Idea
II. Writing
   A. Capitalization
   B. Proofreading

Name _____

Writing: Putting Ideas Together

Directions: Make each pair of sentences into one sentence. (You may have to change the verbs for some sentences—from **is** to **are**, for example.)

Example: Our house was flooded. Our car was flooded.

Our house and car were flooded.

1. Kenny sees a glow.   Carrie sees a glow.

   _____

2. Our new stove came today.   Our new refrigerator came today.

   _____

3. The pond is full of toads.   The field is full of toads.

   _____

4. Stripes are on the flag.   Stars are on the flag.

   _____

5. The ducks took flight.   The geese took flight.

   _____

6. Joe reads stories.   Dana reads stories.

   _____

7. French fries will make you fat.   Milkshakes will make you fat.

   _____

8. Justine heard someone groan.   Kevin heard someone groan.

   _____

GRADE 4

I. Reading
A. Directions
B. Sequencing
C. Main Idea
II. Writing
A. Capitalization
B. Proofreading

Name _____

Writing: Putting Ideas Together

Directions: Write each pair of sentences as one sentence.

Example: Jim will deal the cards one at a time. Jim will give four cards to everyone.

Jim will deal the cards one at a time and give four cards to everyone.

1. Amy won the contest.   Amy claimed the prize.

   _____

2. We need to find the scissors.   We need to buy some tape.

   _____

3. The stream runs through the woods.   The stream empties into the East River.

   _____

   _____

4. Katie tripped on the steps.   Katie has a pain in her left foot.

   _____

   _____

5. Grandpa took me to the store.   Grandpa bought me a treat.

   _____

6. Charity ran 2 miles.   She walked 1 mile to cool down afterwards.

   _____

   _____

GRADE
4

I. Reading
A. Directions
B. Sequencing
C. Main Idea
II. Writing
A. Capitalization
B. Proofreading

Name _____

Writing: Using Fewer Words

Writing can be more interesting when fewer words are used. Combining sentences is easy when the subjects are the same. Notice how the comma is used.

Example: Sally woke up. Sally ate breakfast. Sally brushed her teeth.

Sally woke up, ate breakfast, and brushed her teeth.

Combining sentences with more than one subject is a little more complicated. Notice how commas are used to "set off" information.

Examples: Jane went to the store with Sally. Jane is Sally's sister.

Jane went to the store with Sally, her sister.

Eddie likes to play with cars. Eddie is my younger brother.

Eddie, my younger brother, likes to play with cars.

Directions: Write each pair of sentences as one sentence.

1. Jerry played soccer after school. He played with his best friend, Tom.

   _____

2. Spot likes to chase cats. Spot is my dog.

   _____

3. Lori and Janice both love ice cream. Janice is Lori's cousin.

   _____

4. Jayna is my cousin. Jayna helped me move into my new apartment.

   _____

5. Romeo is a big tomcat. Romeo loves to hunt mice.

   _____

Name _____

Combining Sentences in Paragraph Form

A **paragraph** is a group of sentences that share the same idea.

Directions: Rewrite the paragraph by combining the simple sentences into larger sentences.

    Jason awoke early. He threw off his covers. He ran to his window. He looked outside. He saw snow. It was white and fluffy. Jason thought of something. He thought of his sled. His sled was in the garage. He quickly ate breakfast. He dressed warmly. He got his sled. He went outside. He went to play in the snow.

_____

_____

_____

_____

_____

_____

_____

_____

_____

_____

_____

Paragraph Form

A **paragraph** is a group of sentences about one main idea.

When writing a paragraph:
1. **Indent** the first line.
2. **Capitalize** the first word of each sentence.
3. **Punctuate** each sentence.

There are many reasons to write a paragraph. A paragraph can describe something or tell a story. It can tell how something is made or give an opinion. Do you know other reasons to write a paragraph?

Directions: Read the paragraphs below. They contain errors. Rewrite the paragraphs correctly on the lines by following three basic rules:

    1. Indent   **2.** Capitalize   **3.** Punctuate

the number of teeth you have depends on your age a baby has no teeth at all gradually, milk teeth, or baby teeth, begin to grow later, these teeth fall out and permanent teeth appear by the age of twenty-five, you should have thirty-two permanent teeth

_____

_____

_____

_____

_____

my family is going to Disneyland tomorrow we plan to arrive early my dad will take my little sister to Fantasyland first meanwhile, my brother and I will visit Frontierland and Adventureland after lunch we will all meet to go to Tomorrowland

_____

_____

_____

_____

_____

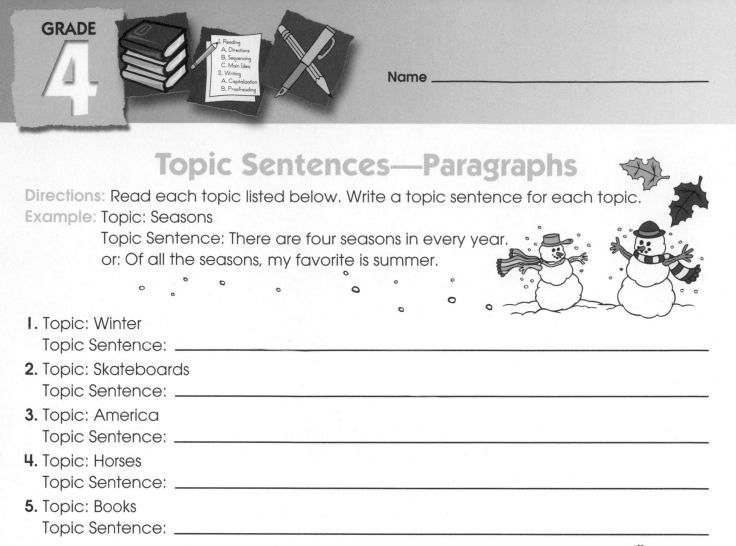

Topic Sentences—Paragraphs

Directions: Read each topic listed below. Write a topic sentence for each topic.

Example: Topic: Seasons

Topic Sentence: There are four seasons in every year.
or: Of all the seasons, my favorite is summer.

1. Topic: Winter
   Topic Sentence: _____

2. Topic: Skateboards
   Topic Sentence: _____

3. Topic: America
   Topic Sentence: _____

4. Topic: Horses
   Topic Sentence: _____

5. Topic: Books
   Topic Sentence: _____

Directions: Choose two of your best topic sentences from above.
Write each as the beginning sentence for the two paragraphs below.
Write at least four support sentences to go with each topic sentence to
make two complete paragraphs.

1. _____

_____

_____

_____

_____

2. _____

_____

_____

_____

_____

Name _____

Support Sentences

The **topic sentence** gives the main idea of a paragraph. The **support sentences** give the details about the main idea. Each sentence must relate to the main idea.

Directions: Read the paragraph below. Underline the topic sentence. Cross out the sentence that is not a support sentence. On the line, write a support sentence to go in its place.

Giving a surprise birthday party can be exciting but tricky. The honored person must not hear a word about the party! On the day of the party, everyone should arrive early. A snack may ruin your appetite.

_____

Directions: Write three support sentences to go with each topic sentence.

Giving a dog a bath can be a real challenge!

1. _____

2. _____

3. _____

I can still remember how embarrassed I was that day!

1. _____

2. _____

3. _____

Sometimes I like to imagine what our prehistoric world was like.

1. _____

2. _____

3. _____

A daily newspaper features many kinds of news.

1. _____

2. _____

3. _____

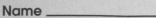

Name _____

Love a Llama

Directions: Read each paragraph. Underline the main idea. Then, write two supporting details.

The Indians of the South American Andes use llamas for a variety of purposes. The llama is best used as a pack animal because it is sure-footed, strong and gentle. As members of the camel family, llamas need little water and eat readily available plants. They may be raised for their meat or wool. The Indians use the llamas' wool for clothing and ropes and make sandals from their hides. Llamas are extremely important animals to these Indians.

Supporting Details

1. _____

_____

2. _____

_____

People find many reasons to like llamas. A llama is used to carrying a load on its back, so it doesn't mind giving rides to children. They are also hard-working and gentle when they are treated well. Because they are grazers, llamas could be used as "lawn mowers" on golf courses and large estates.

Supporting Details

1. _____

_____

2. _____

_____

Name _____

Main Ideas—Location

The **main idea** of a paragraph can be located anywhere in the paragraph. Although most main ideas are stated in the first sentence, many good paragraphs contain a topic sentence in the middle or even at the end.

Directions: Draw two lines under the topic sentence.
Draw one line under each support sentence.

We had a great time at the basketball game last Friday night. My dad took four of my friends and me to the gym at seven o'clock. We sat with other kids from our class. Our team was behind at the half but pulled ahead to win by eight points. After the game, we stopped for burgers before going home.

The alarm rang for a full minute before Jay heard it. Even then, he put his pillow over his head, rolled over, and moaned loudly. Getting up in the morning was always hard for Jay. As usual, his mom had to take the pillow off his head and make him get up for school.

Directions: On the lines below, write three paragraphs. Put the topic sentence in the correct place. Underline each topic sentence.

Paragraph 1 (Topic Sentence–Middle)

_____
_____
_____

Paragraph 2 (Topic Sentence–Beginning)

_____
_____
_____

Paragraph 3 (Topic Sentence–End)

_____
_____
_____

Name _____

That's a Mouthful!

Directions: Circle the word in each row that is first in A-B-C, or alphabetical, order. Then, write it on the lines.

1. hot   hen   the

2. swell   stick   watch

3. watch   taste   twist

4. stand   clock   glass

5. spider   monkey   babies

6. knife   plate   match

7. start   scarf   sharp

8. bat   box   bed

9. tub   tap   ten

10. under   shelf   scrub

Directions: Write the boxed letters with the same numbers below.

What is the world's biggest word?

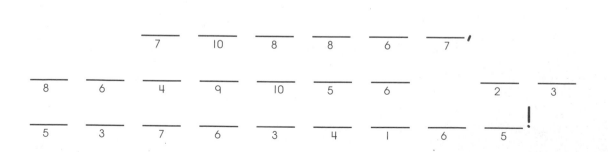

Johnny Appleseed

John Chapman, born in 1774, was better known as Johnny Appleseed. He planted a large number of apple trees along the early frontier.

Directions: Number the apple words in alphabetical order. Then, write the word on the line with the matching number to finish a ballad.

_____ blossoms   _____ nature   _____ near

_____ apple seeds   _____ crunchy   _____ Jonathan

_____ day   _____ brush   _____ name

_____ Winesap   _____ loved   _____ mother

_____ fame   _____ tasted   _____ wasted

_____ king   _____ fruit   _____ eat

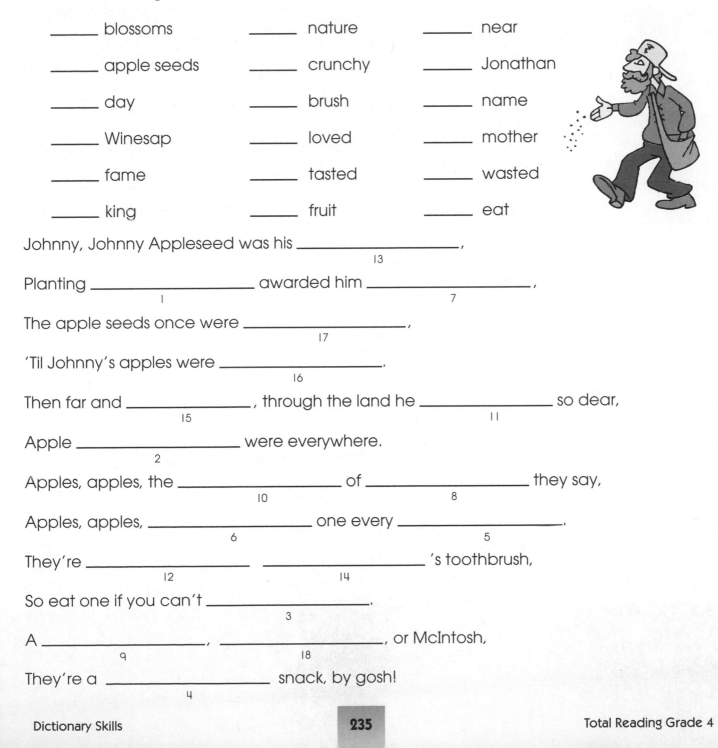

Johnny, Johnny Appleseed was his _____,
13

Planting _____ awarded him _____,
1   7

The apple seeds once were _____,
17

'Til Johnny's apples were _____.
16

Then far and _____, through the land he _____ so dear,
15   11

Apple _____ were everywhere.
2

Apples, apples, the _____ of _____ they say,
10   8

Apples, apples, _____ one every _____.
6   5

They're _____ _____ 's toothbrush,
12   14

So eat one if you can't _____.
3

A _____, _____, or McIntosh,
9   18

They're a _____ snack, by gosh!
4

GRADE 4

I. Reading
  A. Directions
  B. Sequencing
  C. Main Idea
II. Writing
  A. Capitalization
  B. Proofreading

Name _____

In Your Kitchen Cupboard

Directions: Write the names of the spices in alphabetical order.

paprika	chili pepper	black pepper	cardamom
cocoa	cinnamon	cloves	ginger
vanilla	allspice	turmeric	nutmeg
mace	cayenne		

1. _____
2. _____
3. _____
4. _____
5. _____
6. _____
7. _____

8. _____
9. _____
10. _____
11. _____
12. _____
13. _____
14. _____

Respellings in the dictionary can help you learn how to say a word correctly.

Directions: Draw a line to match the word to its pronunciation.

kī en´   pe´pər   kär´də məm   pə prē´ kə   tər´mər ik

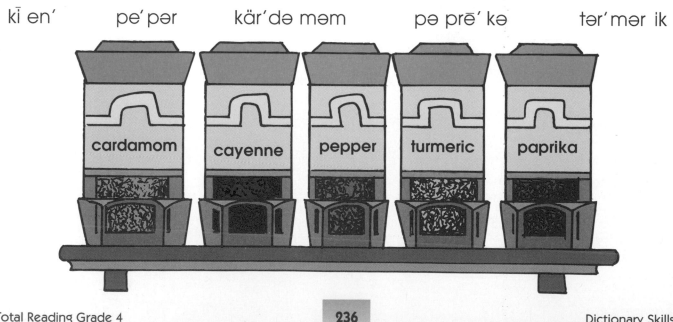

cardamom   cayenne   pepper   turmeric   paprika

A Word From Your Dictionary

A dictionary entry usually shows the following information:

Respelling — to help you say the word correctly

Part of speech — to help you use the word correctly

Syllables — to help you divide the word

Definition — to tell the meaning of the word

Sample sentence — to show how the word is used in context

rack•et[1] (rak′ət) *n.* also rac•quet, a light bat made of a frame laced with strong strings.

rack•et[2] (rak′ət) *n.* 1. a loud noise: *The fourth graders made a racket until the teacher asked them to work quietly.* 2. a fraudulent or dishonest business.

Directions: Use the dictionary entries above to help you write each answer.

1. Name the part of speech given for racket in both entries. _____

2. Write the sample sentence given for one definition. _____

_____

3. How many syllables are in *racket*? _____

4. Which syllable is accented, the first or the second? _____

Directions: Write the definition from above for each underlined word.

1. Who is making that terrible <u>racket</u> upstairs? _____

_____

2. Police officers arrested the men involved in a gambling <u>racket</u>.

_____

GRADE 4

I. Reading
  A. Directions
  B. Sequencing
  C. Main Idea
II. Writing
  A. Capitalization
  B. Proofreading

Name _____

Guide-Worthy Words

Directions: Use a pencil to write ten vocabulary words from the box under each of the guide words. Remember to put them in alphabetical order.

reflection	syllable

abrupt	authority

babyhood	crest

defense	exult

burrow	commerce	cordial	corporal	accustom
accidently	barracks	barometer	explosive	schoolmaster
stealth	allow	calamity	stance	defiant
epidemic	ancient	scowl	discard	ammunition
disturbance	subside	salute	reindeer	consternation
assign	demoralize	disposition	appoint	beneficial
resolute	enormous	ashamed	retort	entirely
earthenware	additional	commotion	almanac	surpass

GRADE
4

I. Reading
A. Directions
B. Sequencing
C. Main Idea
II. Writing
A. Capitalization
B. Proofreading

Name _____

Weird Words

Directions: Use a dictionary to help you answer the questions using complete sentences.

1. Which would you use to treat a sore throat: a **gargoyle** or a **gargle**?

   _____

2. Which might be used on a gravestone: an **epiphyte** or an **epitaph**?

   _____

3. Which is an instrument: **calligraphy** or a **calliope**?

   _____

4. Would a building have a **gargoyle** or an **argyle** on it?

   _____

5. If you trick someone, do you **bamboozle** him or **barcarole** him?

   _____

6. If you studied handwriting, would you learn **calligraphy** or **cajolery**?

   _____

7. What would a gondolier sing: a **barcarole** or an **argyle**?

   _____

8. If you tried to coax someone, would you be using **cajolery** or **calamity**?

   _____

9. Which might you wear: **argyles** or **calliopes**?

   _____

10. In Venice, Italy, would you travel in a **gondola** or a **calamity**?

   _____

GRADE
4

I. Reading
A. Directions
B. Sequencing
C. Main Idea
II. Writing
A. Capitalization
B. Proofreading

Name _____

Library Skills: Using the Library Catalog

Every book in a library is listed in the library's catalog. Videos, CD's, and other materials may also be included. Some library catalogs are drawers filled with file cards; some are computerized. Here is an example of a card from a card catalog:

970.2	
G84a	Indians
	Gridley, Marion E.
	American Indian Women
	Hawthorn Books, Inc., 1974

The catalog helps you find books and other materials. Library catalogs list items by titles, authors, and subjects. All three of these listings are in alphabetical order.

To find a book titled *Great Explorer: Christopher Columbus*, you would look under *G* in the card catalog. To find other books about Columbus, you would look under *C*. If you knew the name of an author who had written a book about Columbus, you could look in the card catalog under the author's last name.

Many libraries use computer catalogs instead of card catalogs. The computer catalog is also organized by titles, authors, and subjects. To find a book, type in the title, subject, or author's name.

Directions: Answer the questions about using a library catalog.

1. To find the book *American Indian Women*, would you look under the author, title, or subject? _____

2. To find a book about the Cherokee people, would you look under the author, title, or subject? _____

3. To find a book called *Animals of Long Ago*, would you look under the author, title, or subject? _____

4. Marion E. Gridley has written books about Native Americans. To find one of her books, would you look under the author, title, or subject? _____

5. To find books about the Moon, would you look under the author, title, or subject? _____

6. To find the book *Easy Microwave Cooking for Kids*, would you look under the author, title, or subject? _____

7. Diana Reische has written a book about the Pilgrims. Would you look under the author, title, or subject to find it? _____

Name _____

Library Skills: Using the Library Catalog

Authors are alphabetized by their last names first. In a library catalog, Blume, Judy would come before Viorst, Judith. Books are alphabetized by title. If a title begins with **The**, **A**, or **An**, ignore it, and use the second word of the title.

Directions: Look at the list of authors, subjects, and titles. Write **A** for author, **S** for subject, or **T** for title in the blanks. Then, write each on the card where it belongs in alphabetical order. Some have been done for you.

A Gallant, Roy A.

_____ Native Americans

T *Animals of Long Ago*

S gardens

_____ *The White House*

_____ Sandak, Cass R.

_____ *The Pony Express*

_____ Herbst, Judith

_____ Pilgrims

_____ *The Hobbit*

A Dicerto, Joseph J.

_____ planets

Author

Dicerto, Joseph J.
Gallant, Roy A.

Title

Animals of Long Ago

Subject

gardens

Name _____

Library Skills: Call Numbers

The **call number** of a book tells where it can be found among nonfiction books.

Information is presented differently on the title, subject, and author card for the same book. A computer listing for this book would look quite similar.

Author card

567.91	VanCleave, Janice
V278	Dinosaurs for Every Kid
	John Wiley & Sons, Inc., 1994

Subject card

567.91	DINOSAURS
V278	VanCleave, Janice
	Dinosaurs for Every Kid
	John Wiley & Sons, Inc., 1994

Title card

567.91	Dinosaurs for Every Kid
V278	VanCleave, Janice
	John Wiley & Sons, Inc., 1994

Directions: Answer the questions about what is shown on these cards.

1. What is written at the top of the subject card?

_____

2. What is written at the top of the title card?

_____

3. What is written at the top of the author card?

_____

4. Why do libraries have three different kinds of listings for the same book?

_____

5. What is the number listed at the top left of each card?_____

6. What other information is on the cards? _____

_____

Name _____

Library Skills: The Dewey Decimal System

Nonfiction books are books based on facts. **Biographies** are true books that tell about people's lives. **Autobiographies** are books that people write about their own lives. Using a library catalog helps you find the books you want. All nonfiction books—except biographies and autobiographies—are filed according to their call number.

The call numbers are part of the **Dewey Decimal System**. Each listing in a library catalog will include a book's call number.

Example:

918.8   Bringle, Mary
B85e   Eskimos
         F. Watts, 1973

All libraries using the **Dewey Decimal System** follow the same system for filing books. The system divides all nonfiction books into 10 main groups, each represented by numbers.

0–099	General works (libraries, computers, etc.)
100–199	Philosophy
200–299	Religion
300–399	Social Sciences
400–499	Language
500–599	Pure Science (math, astronomy, chemistry, etc.)
600–699	Applied Science (medicine, engineering, etc.)
700–799	Arts and Recreation
800–899	Literature
900–999	History

Each book is given a specific call number. A book about ghosts could be 133.1.

This is where some subjects fall in the Dewey Decimal System.

Pets	630	Maps	910	Cathedrals	236	Dinosaurs	560
Baseball	796	Monsters	791	Trees	580	Presidents	920
Butterflies	595	Mummies	390	Space	620	Cooking	640

Directions: Write the Dewey Decimal number for the following books.

_____ *Animals of Long Ago*   _____ *Our American Presidents*

_____ *City Leaves, City Trees*   _____ *Mummies Made in Egypt*

_____ *Easy Microwave Cooking for Kids* _____ *Real-Life Monsters*

_____ *To Space and Back*   _____ *Great Churches in Europe*

_____ *Amazing Baseball Teams*   _____ *The Children's Atlas*

Library Skills: The Dewey Decimal System

All libraries that use the Dewey Decimal System follow the same order. All books between 500 and 599 are related to science. All books between 900 and 999 are history.

Each library divides its system even further. For example, one library may have kites at 796.15, while another library may have kites at 791.13.

Directions: Look at the number on each book. Then, use the Dewey Decimal System directory at the bottom of the page to find out what the book is about. Write the subject on the line.

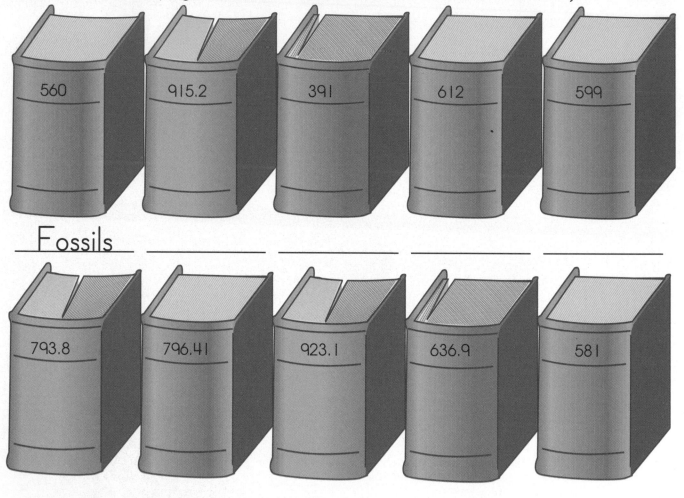

560 915.2 391 612 599

Fossils _____ _____ _____ _____

793.8 796.41 923.1 636.9 581

_____ _____ _____ _____ _____

Dewey Decimal System directory:

390–399 Costumes   590–599 Big Foot   790–795 Magic   920–929 Presidents
560–569 Fossils   610–619 Human Body 796–799 Gymnastics
580–589 Plants   630–639 Pets   910–919 Japan

Name _____

Encyclopedia Skills

Encyclopedias are sets of books that provide information about different subjects, If you want to know when cars were first made or who invented the phonograph, you could find the information in an encyclopedia.

Encyclopedias come in sets of books and on computer CD's. They contain many facts, illustrations, maps, graphs, and tables. Encyclopedias are **reference books** found in the reference section of the library.

Each subject listed in an encyclopedia is called an **entry**. Entries are organized alphabetically.

Some good encyclopedias for students are *World Book Encyclopedia, Compton's Encyclopedia*, and *Children's Britannica*.

Specialty encyclopedias, like the *McGraw-Hill Encyclopedia of Science and Technology*, contain information on one particular subject.

Directions: Number these encyclopedia entries in alphabetical order. The first one has been done for you.

_____ deep-sea diving

_____ deer

_____ Florida

_____ natural fiber

_____ Death Valley

_____ flour

_____ Gretzky, Wayne

_____ Little League

_____ Little Rock

_____ metric system

_____ United Nations

_____ poison oak

___1___ Air Force

_____ Carter, Jimmy

Name _____

Encyclopedia Skills: Using the Index

The **index** of an encyclopedia contains an alphabetical listing of all entries. To find information about a subject, decide on the best word to describe the subject. If you want to know about ducks, look up the word "duck" in the index. If you're really interested in learning about mallard ducks, then look under "mallard ducks." The index shows the page number and volume where the information is located.

Look at the index entry below about Neil Armstrong. Most index entries also tell you when a person lived and died and give a short description of the person.

ARMSTRONG, NEIL   United States astronaut, b. 1930
          Commander of *Gemini* 8, 1966; first man to walk on the Moon, July 1969
          References in
                Astronaut: illus. 2:56
                Space travel 17:214

Neil Armstrong is listed under "Astronaut" and "Space travel." You can find information about him in both articles. The first entry shows there is an illustration (illus.) of Neil Armstrong in volume 2 on page 56 (2:56).

If Neil Armstrong were listed in a separate article in the encyclopedia, the index would look something like this:

---
main article Armstrong, Neil
2:48

Directions: Answer these questions about using an encyclopedia index.

1. According to the index listing for Neil Armstrong, when was he born? _____

2. According to the index listing, who was Neil Armstrong? _____

_____

3. When did he walk on the Moon? _____

4. What are the titles of the two articles containing information about Neil Armstrong?

_____   _____

5. Where would you find the article on space travel?

     Volume number _____ , page number _____ .

I. Reading
   A. Directions
   B. Sequencing
   C. Main Idea
II. Writing
   A. Capitalization
   B. Proofreading

Name _____

Encyclopedia Skills

Each book in a set of encyclopedias has a volume number and lists the range of subjects included. Volume 10 shown below includes all articles that would fall alphabetically between *insect* and *leaf*. Note that Volume 30 in this set is the Index.

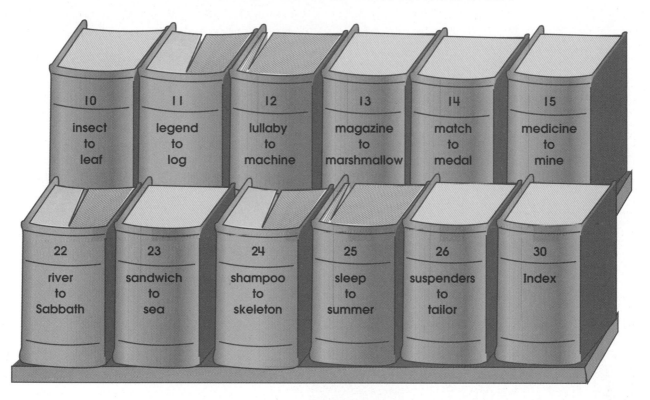

10	11	12	13	14	15
insect to leaf	legend to log	lullaby to machine	magazine to marshmallow	match to medal	medicine to mine

22	23	24	25	26	30
river to Sabbath	sandwich to sea	shampoo to skeleton	sleep to summer	suspenders to tailor	Index

Directions: Answer the questions.

_____ 1. In which volume would you look to find an article on lungs?

_____ 2. Which volume would contain an article on ladybugs?

_____ 3. In which volume would an article on Saturn be found?

_____ 4. Which volume would contain an article on swimming?

_____ 5. In which volume would you check for an article on John D. Rockefeller?

_____ 6. An article on soccer would be in which volume?

_____ 7. Which volume would contain an article on magic?

_____ 8. In which volume would you look to find an article on melons?

Name _____

Library Skills

Some books in a library are not filed by the Dewey Decimal System. Those books include biographies, autobiographies, and fiction. Biographies and autobiographies may be filed together in the 920s or be assigned a call number by subject.

Fiction books are stories that someone has made up. They are filed in alphabetical order by the author's last name in the fiction section of the library.

Directions: For each title, write **B** if it is a biography, **A** if it is an autobiography, or **F** if it is fiction. Then, circle the titles that would not be filed by the Dewey Decimal System.

_____ *Tales of a Fourth Grade Nothing*

_____ *The Real Tom Thumb*

_____ *Ramona the Pest*

_____ *Bill Peet: An Autobiography*

_____ *Abraham Lincoln*

_____ *Charlotte's Web*

_____ *The King and I*

_____ *My Life With Chimpanzees*

_____ *Sara Plain and Tall*

_____ *Michael Jordan, Basketball's Soaring Star*

_____ *The First Book of Presidents*

_____ *The Helen Keller Story*

Is It Fiction or Nonfiction?

Directions: Write on the blank **fiction** or **nonfiction**.

1. *The Chicken and the Dragon* by Arthur C. Feather. This is the story of a dragon who helps a chicken remember his way home.

    _____

2. *The Planets* by Peter Starlight. This book describes the planets in our solar system. Descriptions and pictures of each planet are included.

    _____

3. *Explorers Go to America* by James Boat. This book gives the routes the explorers took to America. Maps and illustrations are given.

    _____

4. *Pinky, the French Poodle* by James Poof-Poof. This is the story of a French poodle with pink fur.

    _____

5. *Dinosaurs of Long Ago* by Peter Tail. This book tells the types of dinosaurs that lived long ago.

    _____

6. *Dogs and Their Owners* by Roger Leash. This book describes the types of ways to train your dog.

    _____

7. *How to Start Your Aquarium* by Peter Fish. This book tells what to buy and how to put it together.

    _____

8. *Sports Legends* by Alvin Bat. This book tells us about famous sports stars.

    _____

9. *Flower Designs* by Hilda Vase. This book tells how to arrange flowers for special occasions.

    _____

10. *Hamsters! Hamsters! Hamsters!* by Roger Pellet. This book tells how to train and care for your hamster.

    _____

GRADE 4

I. Reading
   A. Directions
   B. Sequencing
   C. Main Idea
II. Writing
   A. Capitalization
   B. Proofreading

Name _____

Book Review

A **book review** is a good way to share a favorite book with others. Most good book reviews give facts about the book as well as the writer's opinions. There are many ways to write about a book, but it may be helpful to follow a basic plan.

1. Organize facts about the book.
2. Make notes of your opinions.
3. Write several paragraphs–combining facts and opinions.
4. End with a paragraph which tells why others should read the book.

Directions: Choose a favorite book. Use the plan to write a short book review.

FACTS

Title:_____

Author:_____Kind of book:_____

Setting:_____

Main characters:_____

Basic plot:_____

Special features:_____

OPINIONS

Which character did I like best and why?_____
_____

Was the plot interesting?_____

What was my favorite part?_____

Did the author use interesting language?_____

How would I change the book?_____

Other things I liked best about the book:_____
_____

Some things I did not like:_____
_____

WRITE REVIEW   SUMMARY

Directions: Use the information above to write a review of your book.

I have just read a fascinating book, _____

_____, by _____.

Finish writing your review on another sheet of paper.

Test Practice Table of Contents

About the Tests

What Are Standardized Achievement Tests?

Achievement tests measure what children know in particular subject areas such as reading, language arts, and mathematics. They do not measure your child's intelligence or ability to learn.

When tests are standardized, or *normed,* children's test results are compared with those of a specific group who have taken the test, usually at the same age or grade.

Standardized achievement tests measure what children around the country are learning. The test makers survey popular textbook series, as well as state curriculum frameworks and other professional sources, to determine what content is covered widely.

Because of variations in state frameworks and textbook series, as well as grade ranges on some test levels, the tests may cover some material that children have not yet learned. This is especially true if the test is offered early in the school year. However, test scores are compared to those of other children who take the test at the same time of year, so your child will not be at a disadvantage if his or her class has not covered specific material yet.

Different School Districts, Different Tests

There are many flexible options for districts when offering standardized tests. Many school districts choose not to give the full test battery, but select certain content and scoring options. For example, many schools may test only in the areas of reading and mathematics. Similarly, a state or district may use one test for certain grades and another test for other grades. These decisions are often based on

the amount of time and money a district wishes to spend on test administration. Some states choose to develop their own statewide assessment tests.

On pages 253-255 you will find information about these five widely used standardized achievement tests:

- California Achievement Tests (CAT)
- Terra Nova/CTBS
- Iowa Test of Basic Skills (ITBS)
- Stanford Achievement Test (SAT9)
- Metropolitan Achievement Test (MAT).

However, this book contains strategies and practice questions for use with a variety of tests. Even if your state does not give one of the five tests listed above, your child will benefit from doing the practice questions in this book. If you're unsure about which test your child takes, contact your local school district to find out which tests are given.

Types of Test Questions

Traditionally, standardized achievements tests have used only multiple choice questions. Today, many tests may include constructed response (short answer) and extended response (essay) questions as well.

In addition, many tests include questions that tap students' higher-order thinking skills. Instead of simple recall questions, such as identifying a date in history, questions may require students to make comparisons and contrasts or analyze results among other skills.

What the Tests Measure

These tests do not measure your child's level of intelligence, but they do show how well your child knows material that he or she has learned and that

is also covered on the tests. It's important to remember that some tests cover content that is not taught in your child's school or grade. In other instances, depending on when in the year the test is given, your child may not yet have covered the material.

If the test reports you receive show that your child needs improvement in one or more skill areas, you may want to seek help from your child's teacher and find out how you can work with your child to improve his or her skills.

California Achievement Test (CAT/5)

What Is the *California Achievement Test?*

The *California Achievement Test* is a standardized achievement test battery that is widely used with elementary through high school students.

Parts of the Test

The CAT includes tests in the following content areas:

Reading
- Word Analysis
- Vocabulary
- Comprehension

Spelling

Language Arts
- Language Mechanics
- Language Usage

Mathematics

Science

Social Studies

Your child may take some or all of these subtests if your district uses the *California Achievement Test.*

Terra Nova/CTBS (Comprehensive Tests of Basic Skills)

What Is the *Terra Nova/CTBS?*

The *Terra Nova/Comprehensive Tests of Basic Skills* is a standardized achievement test battery used in elementary through high school grades.

While many of the test questions on the *Terra Nova* are in the traditional multiple choice form, your child may take parts of the *Terra Nova* that include some open-ended questions (constructed-response items).

Parts of the Test

Your child may take some or all of the following subtests if your district uses the *Terra Nova/CTBS:*

Reading/Language Arts
Mathematics
Science
Social Studies
Supplementary tests include:
- Word Analysis
- Vocabulary
- Language Mechanics
- Spelling
- Mathematics Computation
Critical thinking skills may also be tested.

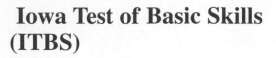

Iowa Test of Basic Skills (ITBS)

What Is the *ITBS?*

The *Iowa Test of Basic Skills* is a standardized achievement test battery used in elementary through high school grades.

Parts of the Test

Your child may take some or all of these subtests if your district uses the *ITBS*, also known as the *Iowa:*

Reading
- Vocabulary
- Reading Comprehension

Language Arts
- Spelling
- Capitalization
- Punctuation
- Usage and Expression

Math
- Concepts/Estimate
- Problems/Data Interpretation

Social Studies

Science

Sources of Information

Stanford Achievement Test (SAT9)

What Is the *Stanford Achievement Test?*

The *Stanford Achievement Test, Ninth Edition (SAT9)* is a standardized achievement test battery used in elementary through high school grades.

Note that the *Stanford Achievement Test (SAT9)* is a different test from the *SAT* used by high school students for college admissions.

While many of the test questions on the *SAT9* are in traditional multiple choice form, your child may take parts of the *SAT9* that include some open-ended questions (constructed-response items).

Parts of the Test

Your child may take some or all of these subtests if your district uses the *Stanford Achievement Test:*

Reading
- Vocabulary
- Reading Comprehension

Mathematics
- Problem Solving
- Procedures

Language Arts

Spelling

Study Skills

Listening

Critical thinking skills may also be tested.

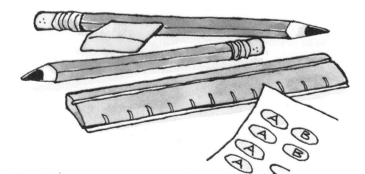

I. Reading
  A. Directions
  B. Sequencing
  C. Main Idea
II. Writing
  A. Capitalization
  B. Proofreading

Metropolitan Achievement Test (MAT7 and MAT8)

What Is the *Metropolitan Achievement Test*?

The *Metropolitan Achievement Test* is a standardized achievement test battery used in elementary through high school grades.

Parts of the Test

Your child may take some or all of these subtests if your district uses the *Metropolitan Achievement Test*.

Reading
- Vocabulary
- Reading Comprehension

Math
- Concepts and Problem Solving
- Computation

Language Arts
- Pre-writing
- Composing
- Editing

Science
Social Studies
Research Skills
Thinking Skills
Spelling

Statewide Assessments

Today, the majority of states give statewide assessments. In some cases, these tests are known as *high-stakes assessments*. This means that students must score at a certain level in order to be promoted. Some states use minimum competency or proficiency tests. Often, these tests measure more basic skills than other types of statewide assessments.

Statewide assessments are generally linked to state curriculum frameworks. Frameworks provide a blueprint, or outline, to ensure that teachers are covering the same curriculum topics as other teachers in the same grade level in the state. In some states, standardized achievement tests (such as the five described in this book) are used in connection with statewide assessments.

When Statewide Assessments Are Given

Statewide assessments may not be given at every grade level. Generally, they are offered at one or more grades in elementary school, middle school, and high school. Many states test at grades 4, 8, and 10.

State-by-State Information

You can find information about statewide assessments and curriculum frameworks at your state Department of Education Web site. To find the address for your individual state go to www.ed.gov, click on Topics A–Z, and then click on State Departments of Education. You will find a list of all the state departments of education, mailing addresses, and Web sites.

GRADE 4

I. Reading
   A. Directions
   B. Sequencing
   C. Main Idea
II. Writing
   A. Capitalization
   B. Proofreading

How to Help Your Child Prepare for Standardized Testing

Preparing All Year Round

Perhaps the most valuable way you can help your child prepare for standardized achievement tests is by providing enriching experiences. Keep in mind also, that test results for younger children are not as reliable as for older students. If a child is hungry, tired, or upset, this may result in a poor test score. Here are some tips on how you can help your child do his or her best on standardized tests.

Read aloud with your child. Reading aloud helps develop vocabulary and fosters a positive attitude toward reading. Reading together is one of the most effective ways you can help your child succeed in school.

Share experiences. Baking cookies together, planting a garden, or making a map of your neighborhood are examples of activities that help build skills that are measured on the tests such as sequencing and following directions.

Become informed about your state's testing procedures. Ask about or watch for announcements of meetings that explain about standardized tests and statewide assessments in your school district. Talk to your child's teacher about your child's individual performance on these state tests during a parent-teacher conference.

Help your child know what to expect. Read and discuss with your child the test-taking tips in this book. Your child can prepare by working through a couple of strategies a day so that no practice session takes too long.

Help your child with his or her regular school assignments. Set up a quiet study area for homework. Supply this area with pencils, paper, markers, a calculator, a ruler, a dictionary, scissors, glue, and so on. Check your child's homework and offer to help if he or she gets stuck. But remember, it's your child's homework, not yours. If you help too much, your child will not benefit from the activity.

Keep in regular contact with your child's teacher. Attend parent-teacher conferences, school functions, PTA or PTO meetings, and school board meetings. This will help you get to know the educators in your district and the families of your child's classmates.

Learn to use computers as an educational resource. If you do not have a computer and Internet access at home, try your local library.

Remember—simply getting your child comfortable with testing procedures and helping him or her know what to expect can improve test scores!

GRADE 4

I. Reading
 A. Directions
 B. Sequencing
 C. Main Idea
II. Writing
 A. Capitalization
 B. Proofreading

Getting Ready for the Big Day

There are lots of things you can do on or immediately before test day to improve your child's chances of testing success. What's more, these strategies will help your child prepare him, or herself for school tests, too, and promote general study skills that can last a lifetime.

Provide a good breakfast on test day.
Instead of sugar cereal, which provides immediate but not long-term energy, have your child eat a breakfast with protein or complex carbohydrates such as an egg, whole grain cereal or toast, or a banana-yogurt shake.

Promote a good night's sleep. A good night's sleep before the test is essential. Try not to overstress the importance of the test. This may cause your child to lose sleep because of anxiety. Doing some exercise after school and having a quiet evening routine will help your child sleep well the night before the test.

Assure your child that he or she is not expected to know all of the answers on the test. Explain that other children in higher grades may take the same test, and that the test may measure things your child has not yet learned in school. Help your child understand that you expect him or her to put forth a good effort—and that this is enough. Your child should not try to cram for these tests. Also avoid threats or bribes; these put undue pressure on children and may interfere with their best performance.

Keep the mood light and offer encouragement. To provide a break on test days, do something fun and special after school—take a walk around the neighborhood, play a game, read a favorite book, or prepare a special snack together. These activities keep your child's mood light—even if the testing sessions have been difficult—and show how much you appreciate your child's effort.

Taking Standardized Tests

No matter what grade you're in, this is information you can use to prepare for standardized tests. Here is what you'll find:

- Test-taking tips and strategies to use on test day and year-round.
- Important terms to know for Language Arts and Reading.
- General study/homework tips.

By opening this book, you've already taken your first step towards test success. The rest is easy—all you have to do is get started!

What You Need to Know

There are many things you can do to increase your test success. Here's a list of tips to keep in mind when you take standardized tests—and when you study for them, too.

Keep up with your school work. One way you can succeed in school and on tests is by studying and doing your homework regularly. Studies show that you remember only about one-fifth of what you memorize the night before a test. That's one good reason not to try to learn it all at once!

Keeping up with your work throughout the year will help you remember the material better. You also won't be as tired or nervous as if you try to learn everything at once.

Feel your best. One of the ways you can do your best on tests and in school is to make sure your body is ready. To do this, get a good night's sleep each night and eat a healthy breakfast (not sugary cereal that will leave you tired by the middle of the morning). An egg or a milkshake with yogurt and fresh fruit will give you lasting energy. Also, wear comfortable clothes, maybe your lucky shirt or your favorite color on test day. It can't hurt, and it may even help you relax.

Be prepared. Do practice questions and learn about how standardized tests are organized. Books like this one will help you know what to expect when you take a standardized test.

When you are taking the test, follow the directions. It is important to listen carefully to the directions your teacher gives and to read the written instructions carefully. Words like *not, none, rarely, never,* and *always* are very important in test directions and questions. You may want to circle words like these.

Look at each page carefully before you start answering. In school you usually read a passage and then answer questions about it. But when you take a test, it's helpful to follow a different order.

If you are taking a Reading test, first read the directions. Then read the questions before you read the passage. This way you will know exactly what kind of information to look for as you read. Next, read the passage carefully. Finally, answer the questions.

Manage your time. *Time management* means using your time wisely on a test so that you can finish as much of it as possible and do your best. Look over the test or the parts that you are allowed to do at one time. Sometimes you may want to do the easier parts first. This way, if you run out of time before you finish, you will have completed a good chunk of the work.

For tests that have a time limit, notice what time it is when the test begins and figure out when you need to stop. Check a few times as you work through the test to be sure you are making good progress and not spending too much time on any particular section.

You don't have to keep up with everyone else. You may notice other students in the class finishing before you do. Don't worry about this. Everyone works at a different pace. Just keep going, trying not to spend too long on any one question.

Fill in answer circles properly. Even if you know every answer on a test, you won't do well unless you fill in the circle next to the correct answer.

Fill in the entire circle, but don't spend too much time making it perfect. Make your mark dark, but not so dark that it goes through the paper! And be sure you only choose one answer for each question, even if you are not sure. If you choose two answers, both will be marked as wrong.

It's usually not a good idea to change your answers. Usually your first choice is the right one. Unless you realize that you misread the question, the directions, or some facts in a passage, it's usually safer to stay with your first answer. If you are pretty sure it's wrong, of course, go ahead and change it. Make sure you completely erase the first choice and neatly fill in your new choice.

Use context clues to figure out tough questions. If you come across a word or idea you don't understand, use context clues—the words in the sentences nearby— to help you figure out its meaning.

Sometimes it's good to guess. Should you guess when you don't know an answer on a test? That depends. If your teacher has made the test, usually you will score better if you answer as many questions as possible, even if you don't really know the answers.

On standardized tests, here's what to do to score your best. For each question, most of these tests let you choose from four or five answer choices. If you decide that a couple of answers are clearly wrong but you're still not sure about the answer, go ahead and make your best guess. If you can't narrow down the choices at all, then you may be better off skipping the question. Tests like these take away extra points for wrong answers, so it's better to leave them blank. Be sure you skip over the answer space for these questions on the answer sheet, though, so you don't fill in the wrong spaces.

Sometimes you should skip a question and come back to it. On many tests, you will score better if you answer more questions. This means that you should not spend too much time on any single question. Sometimes it gets tricky, though, keeping track of questions you skipped on your answer sheet.

If you want to skip a question because you don't know the answer, put a very light pencil mark next to the question in the test booklet. Try to choose an answer, even if you're not sure of it. Fill in the answer lightly on the answer sheet.

Check your work. On a standardized test, you can't go ahead or skip back to another section of the test. But you may go back and review your answers on the section you just worked on if you have extra time.

First, scan your answer sheet. Make sure that you answered every question you could. Also, if you are using a bubble-type answer sheet, make sure that you filled in only one bubble for each question. Erase any extra marks on the page.

Finally—avoid test anxiety! If you get nervous about tests, don't worry. *Test anxiety* happens to lots of good students. Being a little nervous actually sharpens your mind. But if you get very nervous about tests, take a few minutes to relax the night before or the day of the test. One good way to relax is to get some exercise, even if you just have time to stretch, shake out your fingers, and wiggle your toes. If you can't move around, it helps just to take a few slow, deep breaths and picture yourself doing a great job!

I. Reading
A. Directions
B. Sequencing
C. Main Idea
II. Writing
A. Capitalization
B. Proofreading

READING: VOCABULARY

● Lesson 1: Synonyms

Directions: Read each item. Choose the word that means the same or about the same as the underlined word.

Examples

A. fast vehicle
- Ⓐ runner
- Ⓑ animal
- Ⓒ car
- Ⓓ computer

B. To be healthy is to be —
- Ⓕ slow
- Ⓖ well
- Ⓗ active
- Ⓙ ill

Clue Make sure you look at the underlined word. Fill in the circle next to the synonym.

● Practice

1. attend a conference
- Ⓐ party
- Ⓑ game
- Ⓒ meeting
- Ⓓ race

2. beautiful painting
- Ⓕ pretty
- Ⓖ interesting
- Ⓗ colorful
- Ⓙ light

3. repair the car
- Ⓐ clean
- Ⓑ drive
- Ⓒ fix
- Ⓓ sell

4. thin slice
- Ⓕ short
- Ⓖ skinny
- Ⓗ long
- Ⓙ wide

5. To rush through your homework is to —
- Ⓐ relax
- Ⓑ slow
- Ⓒ finish
- Ⓓ hurry

6. Raw vegetables are —
- Ⓕ uncooked
- Ⓖ green
- Ⓗ smelly
- Ⓙ young

7. A dim light bulb is —
- Ⓐ dull
- Ⓑ bright
- Ⓒ unintelligent
- Ⓓ new

8. To walk quickly is to walk —
- Ⓕ confidently
- Ⓖ carefully
- Ⓗ rapidly
- Ⓙ happily

STOP

Name _____

READING: VOCABULARY

● **Lesson 2: Vocabulary Skills**

Directions: Read each item. Choose the word that means the same or about the same as the underlined word.

Examples

A. detect a clue

- (A) to find
- (B) to hide
- (C) to enjoy
- (D) to make up

B. She had to select the book for the next meeting. To select is to —

- (F) find
- (G) review
- (H) read
- (J) choose

Clue Make sure you look at the underlined word. Eliminate answer choices you know are wrong.

● **Practice**

1. venomous snake
   - (A) vicious
   - (B) poisonous
   - (C) sharp
   - (D) huge

2. encourage friends
   - (F) fascinate
   - (G) worry
   - (H) cheer up
   - (J) disappoint

3. mature person
   - (A) grown-up
   - (B) dying
   - (C) new
   - (D) green

4. The teacher was irritated. Irritated means —
   - (F) excited
   - (G) helpful
   - (H) annoyed
   - (J) boring

5. His pants were baggy. Baggy means —
   - (A) loose
   - (B) brown
   - (C) too small
   - (D) made of cotton

6. He was the first conductor of the train. A conductor is a —
   - (F) driver
   - (G) janitor
   - (H) owner
   - (J) rider

7. Sharon was elated when she won. Elated means —
   - (A) grim
   - (B) joyful
   - (C) outside
   - (D) unpleasant

STOP

Name _____

READING: VOCABULARY

● **Lesson 3: Antonyms**

Directions: Read each item. Choose the word that means the opposite of the underlined word.

Examples

A. The tortoise took a <u>leisurely</u> walk.
- (A) lovely
- (B) swift
- (C) leathery
- (D) delicious

B. <u>recall</u> information
- (F) forget
- (G) remember
- (H) write
- (J) find

Clue If you are not sure which answer is correct, take your best guess. Eliminate answer choices you know are incorrect.

● **Practice**

1. Leslie was <u>disappointed</u> when it rained.
   - (A) saddened
   - (B) pleased
   - (C) relieved
   - (D) entertained

2. The car was <u>fast</u>.
   - (F) shallow
   - (G) sluggish
   - (H) speedy
   - (J) rabbit

3. The dog's fur felt <u>silky</u>.
   - (A) soft
   - (B) smooth
   - (C) rough
   - (D) dirty

4. Banana slugs are <u>moist</u> to the touch.
   - (F) dry
   - (G) slimy
   - (H) rough
   - (J) rubbery

5. <u>rough</u> board
   - (A) large
   - (B) heavy
   - (C) smooth
   - (D) long

6. <u>docile</u> animal
   - (F) vicious
   - (G) gentle
   - (H) shy
   - (J) active

7. <u>active</u> child
   - (A) immobile
   - (B) exhausted
   - (C) bored
   - (D) thrilled

8. left <u>promptly</u>
   - (F) late
   - (G) recently
   - (H) quietly
   - (J) slowly

STOP

I. Reading
  A. Directions
  B. Sequencing
  C. Main Idea
II. Writing
  A. Capitalization
  B. Proofreading

Name _____

READING: VOCABULARY

● **Lesson 4: Multi-Meaning Words**

Example

For items A and 1–2, choose the answer in which the underlined word is used in the same way as the sentence in the box.

For items 3–5, read the two sentences with blanks. Choose the word that fits best in both sentences.

A. | **Please file these papers.**

Ⓐ The counselor pulled out her file on the Jones family.

Ⓑ Sally used a file to smooth her fingernails.

Ⓒ I put the file cards in order.

Ⓓ Jane asked her secretary to file the reports on water safety.

Clue If a question is too difficult, skip it and come back to it later if you have time.

● **Practice**

1. | **I used a lemon to make lemonade.**

   Ⓐ The color of the baby's room is lemon.
   Ⓑ That car was a lemon.
   Ⓒ This cleaner has a lovely lemon scent.
   Ⓓ Rachel bought a lemon at the store.

2. | **She could never reach the right note on the piano.**

   Ⓕ Please make a note of this change.
   Ⓖ I wrote a note so you will not forget.
   Ⓗ The musical note he asked us to play was C.
   Ⓙ Note the large size of the buildings.

3. Do you feel _____ ?
   We get our water from a _____ .

   Ⓐ well
   Ⓑ good
   Ⓒ pipe
   Ⓓ sick

4. Mrs. Johnson said Carrie was a _____ student.
   The light from the headlights was _____ .

   Ⓕ noisy
   Ⓖ red
   Ⓗ bright
   Ⓙ hard working

5. The surface of the car was _____ .
   Mr. Abed gave a _____ speech.

   Ⓐ dirty
   Ⓑ shiny
   Ⓒ painted
   Ⓓ dull

STOP

READING: VOCABULARY

● Lesson 5: Words in Context

Directions: Read the paragraph. Choose the word that fits best in each numbered blank.

Examples

In-line skating might be the fastest-growing _____(A) in America. Typical _____(B) follow roads, sidewalks, or bike paths. This sport is relatively new, but it is already enjoyed by people young and old.

A.
- (A) thing
- (B) people
- (C) town
- (D) sport

B.
- (F) skaters
- (G) vehicles
- (H) hikers
- (J) results

● Practice

Clue: Read the passage once. Then, read each sentence with a blank carefully. Use the meaning of the sentence to find the answer.

Glass is an amazing substance. Made by heating sand with a few other simple chemicals, glass is both _____(1) and beautiful. In the _____(2), you drink your juice in a glass. At your school, you may _____(3) the building through a glass door. The lights inside the school are made of glass, as is the _____(4) of the computer you will use. If you go to gym class, the basketball backboard might even be made of glass. Your family may have pieces of glass as decorations around the house, and if you go to a _____(5), you might see _____(6) glass from hundreds of years ago.

1.
- (A) ugly
- (B) useful
- (C) cloudy
- (D) thin

2.
- (F) evening
- (G) time
- (H) morning
- (J) mood

3.
- (A) open
- (B) see
- (C) like
- (D) enter

4.
- (F) inside
- (G) keyboard
- (H) screen
- (J) mouse

5.
- (A) aquarium
- (B) bus stop
- (C) gas station
- (D) museum

6.
- (F) new
- (G) antique
- (H) full
- (J) broken

STOP

Name _____

READING: VOCABULARY

● Lesson 6: Word Study

Directions: Read each item. Choose the answer you think is correct.

Examples

A. Which of these words probably comes from the Latin word *circui-tus*, meaning *a going around*?

- Ⓐ circus
- Ⓑ circuit
- Ⓒ cirrus
- Ⓓ circa

B. Let's _____ the ripe apples. Which word means to *gather* the ripe apples?

- Ⓕ eat
- Ⓖ collect
- Ⓗ check
- Ⓙ sell

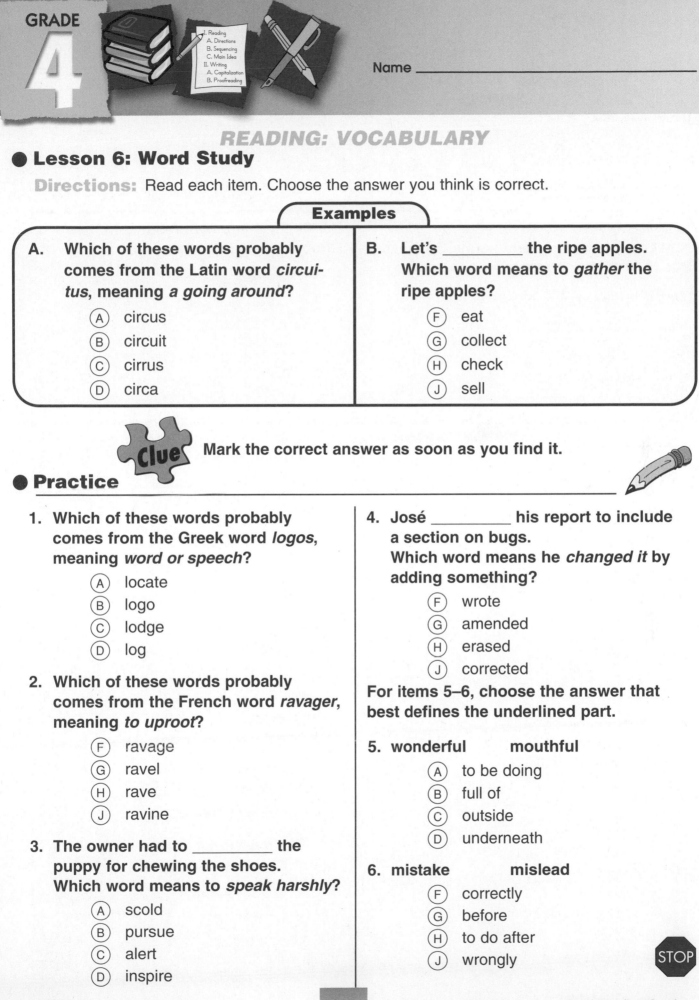

Clue Mark the correct answer as soon as you find it.

● Practice

1. Which of these words probably comes from the Greek word *logos*, meaning *word or speech*?

- Ⓐ locate
- Ⓑ logo
- Ⓒ lodge
- Ⓓ log

2. Which of these words probably comes from the French word *ravager*, meaning *to uproot*?

- Ⓕ ravage
- Ⓖ ravel
- Ⓗ rave
- Ⓙ ravine

3. The owner had to _____ the puppy for chewing the shoes. Which word means to *speak harshly*?

- Ⓐ scold
- Ⓑ pursue
- Ⓒ alert
- Ⓓ inspire

4. José _____ his report to include a section on bugs. Which word means he *changed it* by adding something?

- Ⓕ wrote
- Ⓖ amended
- Ⓗ erased
- Ⓙ corrected

For items 5–6, choose the answer that best defines the underlined part.

5. wonder**ful** mouth**ful**

- Ⓐ to be doing
- Ⓑ full of
- Ⓒ outside
- Ⓓ underneath

6. **mis**take **mis**lead

- Ⓕ correctly
- Ⓖ before
- Ⓗ to do after
- Ⓙ wrongly

STOP

GRADE 4

I. Reading
 A. Directions
 B. Sequencing
 C. Main Idea
II. Writing
 A. Capitalization
 B. Proofreading

Name _____

READING: VOCABULARY
SAMPLE TEST

Examples

For items A and 1–4, choose the word that means the same or about the same as the underlined word.

A.   calm ocean

- (A) water
- (B) sea
- (C) lake
- (D) body

For items B and 5–8, read each item. Choose the answer you think is correct.

B.   Infect means—

- (F) to act
- (G) to cheer up
- (H) to spread disease
- (J) to discover

---

1.   high fence

- (A) tall
- (B) happy
- (C) long
- (D) wide

2.   paste the paper

- (F) fold
- (G) attach
- (H) patch
- (J) glue

3.   fix the car

- (A) polish
- (B) repair
- (C) sell
- (D) buy

4.   chilly day

- (F) long
- (G) frozen
- (H) cold
- (J) unpleasant

5.   If something is moving swiftly, it is moving —

- (A) slowly
- (B) smoothly
- (C) quickly
- (D) on the land

6.   Shallow means —

- (F) not intelligent
- (G) deep
- (H) not deep
- (J) able to swim

7.   To remain is to —

- (A) stay
- (B) leave early
- (C) go to the middle
- (D) do over again

8.   That store was the nearest.

- (F) the most distant
- (G) biggest
- (H) best
- (J) the closest

GO ON

Name _____

READING: VOCABULARY
SAMPLE TEST (cont.)

For items 9–13, choose the meaning for each underlined word.

9. The wings of the butterflies were fluttering in the breeze.
   Fluttering means —
   - (A) waving
   - (B) colorful
   - (C) lovely
   - (D) flashing

10. Gazelles and impalas are prey to the cheetah.
    Prey means —
    - (F) food
    - (G) friends
    - (H) similar
    - (J) predators

11. David gave his sister a smirk.
    Smirk means —
    - (A) friendly smile
    - (B) scar
    - (C) smug expression
    - (D) facemask

12. We were exhausted after running.
    Exhausted means —
    - (F) very tired
    - (G) refreshed
    - (H) excited
    - (J) wide awake

13. I sprinted to the finish line.
    Sprinted means —
    - (A) skipped
    - (B) crawled
    - (C) ran very quickly
    - (D) tripped

For items 14–19, choose the word that means the opposite of the underlined word.

14. valuable painting
    - (F) strange
    - (G) expensive
    - (H) worthless
    - (J) humorous

15. loose tie
    - (A) tight
    - (B) lost
    - (C) plain
    - (D) ill fitting

16. narrow ledge
    - (F) thin
    - (G) cement
    - (H) skinny
    - (J) wide

17. We always use this road to go to school.
    - (A) never
    - (B) sometimes
    - (C) usually
    - (D) frequently

18. The workers wanted to unpack the truck.
    - (F) carry
    - (G) pack
    - (H) remove
    - (J) move

19. Tom was awake most of the night.
    - (A) up
    - (B) asleep
    - (C) restless
    - (D) watching TV

GO ON

Name _____

READING: VOCABULARY
SAMPLE TEST (cont.)

For items 20–23, read the two sentences with blanks. Choose the word that fits best in both sentences.

20. The sun _____ at 5:45.
    A _____ grew beside the steps.
    - (F) appeared
    - (G) rose
    - (H) flower
    - (J) set

21. It's not safe to _____ a boat.
    This _____ is too heavy to move.
    - (A) sink
    - (B) stone
    - (C) push
    - (D) rock

22. What _____ will you be on vacation?
    I enjoy eating _____ .
    - (F) days
    - (G) fruit
    - (H) weeks
    - (J) dates

23. The captain took _____ of the ship.
    The cavalry made a great _____.
    - (A) yell
    - (B) charge
    - (C) control
    - (D) run

24. | Follow the deer tracks. |

    In which sentence does the word tracks mean the same thing as in the sentence above?
    - (F) The train moved swiftly on the tracks.
    - (G) Gerald tracks satellites for the government.
    - (H) The dog made tracks in the snow.
    - (J) Never stop your car on the train tracks.

25. | Hand me that green plant. |

    In which sentence does the word plant mean the same thing as in the sentence above?
    - (A) The electric plant was a busy place to work.
    - (B) Plant those bushes here.
    - (C) They used Joe as a plant to spy on the kids.
    - (D) I gave Mom a plant for Mother's Day.

For items 26–27, choose the answer that best defines the underlined part.

26. motherless   painless
    - (F) with
    - (G) like
    - (H) more
    - (J) without

27. magnify   magnificent
    - (A) magnetic
    - (B) great
    - (C) smaller
    - (D) open

GO ON

READING: VOCABULARY
SAMPLE TEST (cont.)

28. Which of these words probably comes from the Latin word *lampein*, meaning *to shine*?

- (F) lampoon
- (G) lament
- (H) lamp
- (J) lamprey

29. Which of these words probably comes from the Middle English word *wose*, meaning *juice*?

- (A) ooze
- (B) worst
- (C) wowser
- (D) wound

30. _____, Mom had forgotten the can opener.
Which of these words means that it was *unlucky*?

- (F) Fortunately
- (G) Mournfully
- (H) Excitedly
- (J) Unfortunately

31. Dave _____ around the room.
Which of these words means that he *walked in a bragging manner*?

- (A) tiptoed
- (B) strutted
- (C) ran
- (D) skipped

Read the paragraph. Choose the word that fits best in each numbered blank.

Leslie is becoming _____(32). People know about her art and her athletics. She is _____(33) in the music department for her skills. I'm really _____(34) of what she's done.

32.
- (F) famous
- (G) released
- (H) exhausted
- (J) fragile

33.
- (A) disliked
- (B) prepared
- (C) respected
- (D) always

34.
- (F) confused
- (G) rejected
- (H) lessened
- (J) proud

STOP

READING: COMPREHENSION

● **Lesson 7: Main Idea**

Directions: Read the passage. Choose the best answer to the questions that follow.

Example

Mario walked back and forth at the end of the pool. He had been practicing his starts for months, and today he would have a chance to show off what he had learned. Just then Dave walked into the building. Mario felt a lump in his throat. Dave was the one person he would have a hard time beating.	**A. What is the main idea of this story?** (A) Mario has been practicing jumping into the pool. (B) Mario is nervous about beating Dave in the swimming race. (C) Dave is just as good at swimming as Mario. (D) Mario is a good swimmer.

Clue Skim the passage again after you have read it. Then, read the questions. You don't have to reread the story to answer each question.

● **Practice**

Thousands of immigrants arrived each day at Ellis Island in New York. This was one of the reception centers set up by the United States government. The immigrants arrived with high hopes. Many had a great deal to offer the United States. However, not all those who came through Ellis Island were allowed to stay in this country.

Immigrants had forms to fill out, questions to answer, and medical exams to face. They waited for many hours in the Great Hall to hear their names called. Many had spent months in poor conditions on ships to come to the United States to make a better life. They had spent their savings to make the trip. Even after this, some were turned away.

1. What is the main idea of paragraph 1?

(A) Thousands of immigrants arrived each day at Ellis Island.

(B) Many immigrants were not allowed to stay in the United States.

(C) Immigrants to the United States arrived at Ellis Island in New York.

(D) Many immigrants arrived in the United States at Ellis Island, but not all were allowed to stay.

2. What is the main idea of paragraph 2?

(F) Many immigrants had to go through a lot to get into the United States, and some did not make it.

(G) Immigrants had to stand in long lines.

(H) Many immigrants were poor.

(J) Immigrants stood in the Great Hall waiting for their names to be called.

STOP

READING: COMPREHENSION

● **Lesson 8: Recalling Details/Sequencing**

Directions: Read the passage. Choose the best answer to the questions that follow.

Example

A medal was given to Mrs. Garcia for bravery. While going shopping, Mrs. Garcia had seen a house on fire. She could hear someone screaming. Mrs. Garcia rushed into the house even though it was on fire and full of smoke. A few minutes later, she came out carrying a young boy.

A. How did Mrs. Garcia know there was someone inside the house?

- Ⓐ She knew he was always at home.
- Ⓑ Someone told her.
- Ⓒ She saw him.
- Ⓓ She could hear him screaming.

Clue

Read the question and all the answer choices. Once you have decided on the correct answer, ask yourself, "Does this really answer the question being asked?"

● **Practice**

People around the world use energy every day, and some forms of energy are being used up very quickly. But resources like energy from the sun, energy from ocean waves, and hydroelectric power do not get used up completely. These resources last and last. They are called *renewable resources*. *Hydropower* is a renewable resource that is very common. The beginning of this word, *hydro*, refers to water. So hydropower refers to power that comes from water.

What makes hydropower work? A dam, which looks like a tall cement wall built across a body of water, raises the level of water in an area by blocking it. This causes the water to fall over the side of the dam. The falling water pushes against a machine called a *turbine*. The force of the falling water makes the blades inside spin. A machine called a *generator* captures the power from the spinning turbines. This makes electrical energy and sends out electricity to people who need it.

1. Resources that last a long time are called —

- Ⓐ hydropower.
- Ⓑ energy.
- Ⓒ fossil fuels.
- Ⓓ renewable resources.

2. What happens after the water falls over the side of the dam?

- Ⓕ The dam blocks the water in.
- Ⓖ The force makes the blades spin.
- Ⓗ The water pushes against the turbine.
- Ⓙ A generator captures the power.

3. What produces the electrical energy from the water?

- Ⓐ generator
- Ⓑ turbine
- Ⓒ dam
- Ⓓ ocean waves

GRADE
4

I. Reading
  A. Directions
  B. Sequencing
  C. Main Idea
II. Writing
  A. Capitalization
  B. Proofreading

Name _____

READING: COMPREHENSION

● Lesson 9: Making Inferences/Drawing Conclusions

Directions: Read the passage. Choose the best answer to the questions that follow.

Example

Sometimes we see sand dunes near the water. These sand dunes do not always stay in the same place. The wind blows them along. Some sand dunes move only a few feet each year. Others move over 200 feet in a year.

A. Sand dunes move the most —

  (A) near the water.

  (B) where it is coldest.

  (C) where it is windiest.

  (D) where there are a lot of people.

Clue

After you read the story, think about why things happened and about what might happen after the end of the story.

● Practice

It's as black as ink out here in the pasture, and I'm as tired as an old shoe. But even if I were in my bed, I don't think I'd be sleeping like a baby tonight.

Last summer for my birthday, my parents gave me my dream horse. Her name is Goldie. She is a beautiful palomino. I love to watch her gallop around the pasture. She runs like the wind and looks so carefree. I hope I'll see her run that way again.

Yesterday, after I fed her, I forgot to close the door to the feed shed. She got into the grain and ate like a pig, which is very unhealthy for a horse. The veterinarian said I have to watch her like a hawk tonight to be sure she doesn't get colic. That's a very bad stomachache. Because he also said I should keep her moving, I have walked her around and around the pasture until I feel like we're on a merry-go-round.

Now the sun is finally beginning to peek over the horizon, and Goldie seems content. I think she's going to be as good as new.

1. **What will the narrator most likely do the next time she feeds the horse?**

  (A) She will feed the horse too much.

  (B) She will make sure she closes the feed shed door.

  (C) She will give the horse plenty of water.

  (D) She will leave the feed shed open.

2. **How much experience do you think the narrator has with horses?**

  (F) Lots. She's probably owned many horses before.

  (G) This is probably her first horse. She doesn't have a lot of experience.

  (H) She's probably owned a horse before this, but not many.

  (J) I can't tell from the story.

GRADE 4

I. Reading
 A. Directions
 B. Sequencing
 C. Main Idea
II. Writing
 A. Capitalization
 B. Proofreading

Name _____

READING: COMPREHENSION

● Lesson 10: Fact & Opinion/Cause & Effect

Directions: Read the passage. Choose the best answer to the questions that follow.

Example

The Hindenburg was an airship that was 804 feet (245 m) long. Airships are much more interesting than boats. Airships fly in the sky. In 1937 the Hindenburg was starting to land but blew up, killing and injuring many people.

A. Which states an opinion?

(A) Airships fly in the sky.

(B) The Hindenburg blew up, killing and injuring many people.

(C) The Hindenburg was an airship that was 804 feet (245 m) long.

(D) Airships are much more interesting than boats.

Clue Facts are pieces of information you can prove. Opinions are what people think about things. To see if something is a fact, think about whether or not you could prove it.

● Practice

During the 1770s, America worked to gain independence from the British. Many struggles happened as a result.

The British passed a law in 1765 that required legal papers and other items to have a tax stamp. It was called the Stamp Act. Colonists were forced to pay a fee for the stamp. Secret groups began to work against the requirement of the tax stamp. The law was finally taken away in 1766.

In 1767, the British passed the Townshend Acts. These acts forced people to pay fees for many items, such as tea, paper, glass, lead, and paint. This wasn't fair.

Colonists were furious. On December 16, 1773, they tossed 342 chests of tea over the sides of ships in Boston Harbor. This was later called the Boston Tea Party. Colonists had shown that they would not accept these laws.

1. **Which of the following sentences from the story states an opinion?**

(A) The British passed a law in 1765 that required legal papers and other items to have a tax stamp.

(B) The law was finally taken away in 1766.

(C) This was later called the Boston Tea Party.

(D) This wasn't fair.

2. **What caused the colonists to throw 342 chests of tea into Boston Harbor?**

(F) They were angry about the Townshend Acts.

(G) They wanted to make a big pot of tea.

(H) The tea was bad.

(J) They were angry because of the Stamp Act.

STOP

READING: COMPREHENSION

● **Lesson 11: Parts of a Story**

Directions: Read the passage. Choose the best answer to the question(s) that follows.

Example

Maggie and Isabel went to the park on Saturday. They both headed for the slides. But, they couldn't decide who should go first. Isabel said she should because she was older. Maggie said she should because Isabel always got to. Just then, Brett came over and said, "Why don't you each get on one slide and start down at the same time?"

And that's just what they did.

A. What is the turning point of this story?

(A) Maggie and Isabel argue over the slide.

(B) Brett comes up with a great solution.

(C) The girls go down the slides at the same time.

(D) The girls immediately head for the slides.

 **Clue** Look for the who, what, where, when, why, and how of the story.

● **Practice**

Joel's hockey team had been playing well all season, and this was their chance to win the tournament. He was their best player.

He glanced around at his teammates. "Guys," he said. "Let's skate really hard and show them how great we are!"

The team cheered and started to walk out to the ice. Joel turned around to grab his helmet, but it wasn't there. He looked under the benches and in the lockers, but his helmet wasn't anywhere. He sat down and felt his throat get tight. If he didn't have a helmet, he couldn't play.

Just then there was a knock on the door. Joel's mom peeked her head around the locker room door. "Thank goodness," she said. "I got here just in time with your helmet."

1. **This story takes place in —**

(A) a locker room.

(B) an ice center lobby.

(C) a sporting goods store.

(D) an outdoor playing field.

2. **Why does Joel become upset?**

(F) He can't find his hockey helmet.

(G) He missed his game.

(H) His mom will miss the game.

(J) His coach is counting on him.

3. **Joel's mom resolves the conflict by —**

(A) taking him out for pizza.

(B) finding his hockey stick.

(C) playing for him.

(D) bringing him his helmet.

GRADE 4

Name _____

READING: COMPREHENSION

● **Lesson 12: Fiction**

Directions: Read the passage. Choose the best answer to the questions that follow.

Example

Bobby saw Dad lying on the sofa. He looked peaceful with his eyes closed and his hands resting on his stomach. Bobby took his roller skates and quietly left the room. A few minutes later, Bobby's mother asked where Bobby was. His dad said that Bobby had gone roller skating.

A. How did Bobby's dad know where he was?

- (A) He has ESP.
- (B) He had set up a video camera to watch him.
- (C) He wasn't really asleep on the couch.
- (D) Bobby left a note for him.

Read carefully. Make sure you know all the characters and the main events. Skim or read again if necessary.

● **Practice**

Brian went zooming to the park to meet his buddies for an afternoon of hoops. It would have been a perfect day, but he had to drag his little brother Pete along.

"Wait for me, Brian," whined Pete.

Brian walked Pete over to a nearby tree, handed him his lunch, and said, "Sit here and eat. Don't move until I come back and get you." Brian ran off to meet his buddies.

As Pete began eating, he heard the pitter-patter of rain falling around him. When Pete saw lightning, he ran for shelter. Suddenly, a loud crack of lightning sounded. Looking behind him, Pete saw the top of the tree come crashing down right where he had been sitting. Brian saw it too, from the other side of the park.

"Pete!" Brian screamed as he ran. At the moment the lightning struck, Brian thought, "Pete's not the drag I always thought he was."

1. What is the main conflict in this story?

- (A) Brian has to drag his brother along to the park.
- (B) There is a lightning storm.
- (C) The tree crashes down.
- (D) Brian thinks Pete is hurt.

2. What is Brian going to the park to play?

- (F) baseball
- (G) tennis
- (H) basketball
- (J) soccer

3. Why does Brian realize that Pete is not such a drag?

- (A) They have fun together.
- (B) He didn't have to save him.
- (C) Pete turns out to be a great runner.
- (D) He realizes that he had been taking his little brother for granted.

I. Reading
  A. Directions
  B. Sequencing
  C. Main Idea
II. Writing
  A. Capitalization
  B. Proofreading

Name _____

READING: COMPREHENSION

● **Lesson 13: Fiction**

Directions: Read the passage. Choose the best answer to the questions that follow.

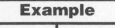
Example

"Please go to the store for me," said Mother. "I need a gallon of milk. Your aunt Jane is coming for supper, and I want to be sure to have enough of everything." Billy grabbed his umbrella and hurried to the store. He was glad to help because his aunt Jane was coming.

A. Why do you think Billy is glad to help?

- (A) He thinks his mother will give him money.
- (B) He loves to go to the store.
- (C) He likes his aunt Jane.
- (D) He likes to help his mother cook.

Clue Read carefully. Make sure you know all the characters and the main events. Skim or read again if necessary.

● **Practice**

"Cassie, you don't realize how grateful we are! We were afraid we wouldn't be able to get a babysitter. Here's a list of instructions. Bye, Bart," Mr. and Mrs. Bradford both said as they left.

Cassie read the note. She was supposed to feed Bart spaghetti, give him a bath, put on his pajamas, play a game with him, and then put him to bed.

But it wasn't that simple. When Bart didn't want to eat his spaghetti, he dumped it on her head. When she tried to give him a bath, he dumped the whole bottle of bubble bath in the tub. And when they tried to play a game, Bart threw blocks all over his room.

Just as Cassie was starting to relax after getting Bart in bed and cleaning up his messes, the Bradfords came home.

"The house looks great!" said Mrs. Bradford. "By the way, we would like to know if you can come back again tomorrow."

1. What is the main problem in this story?

- (A) Bart is misbehaving.
- (B) Cassie has to clean up a mess.
- (C) The Bradfords have gone out to dinner.
- (D) Cassie does not want to babysit again.

2. What do you think Cassie will do if the Bradfords ask her to babysit again?

- (F) She will do it.
- (G) She will find a way to get out of it.
- (H) She will volunteer eagerly.
- (J) She will offer to do it only if she doesn't have to feed Bart.

3. What did Bart do with his spaghetti?

- (A) He threw it in the tub.
- (B) He ate it.
- (C) He dumped it on Cassie's head.
- (D) He threw it around his room.

STOP

GRADE 4

I. Reading
  A. Directions
  B. Sequencing
  C. Main Idea
II. Writing
  A. Capitalization
  B. Proofreading

Name _____

READING: COMPREHENSION

● **Lesson 14: Fiction**

Directions: Read the passage. Choose the best answer to the questions that follow.

Example

Chandra was eating her lunch when she heard a desperate meow. She ran to the backyard to see what was wrong. Her white kitten, Darva, was up on a branch and couldn't get down. Chandra looked around the yard. She saw a ladder leaning against the shed.

A. What will Chandra most likely do?

(A) She will use the ladder to rescue the kitten.

(B) She will go back inside and finish her lunch.

(C) She will jump up to reach the kitten.

(D) She will lure the kitten down with a treat.

Clue

Skim the passage, then read the questions. Refer back to the passage to find the answers. You don't have to reread the story for each question.

● **Practice**

Waterland

"Hurray!" cried Meghan. "Today is the day we're going to Waterland!" It was a hot July day, and Meghan's mom was taking her to cool off on the water slides. Meghan's new friend, Jake, was going, too.

Just then, Meghan's mom came out of her bedroom. She did not look very happy. "What's the matter, Mom? Are you afraid to get wet?" Meghan teased. "I'll bet you'll melt, just like the Wicked Witch of the West!"

Mrs. Millett didn't laugh at the joke. Instead, she told the kids that she wasn't felling well. She was too tired to drive to the water park.

Meghan and Jake were disappointed. "My mom has chronic fatigue syndrome," Meghan explained. "Her illness makes her really tired. She's still a great mom."

"Thank you, dear," said Mrs. Millett. "I'm

too tired to drive, but I have an idea. You can make your own Waterland and I'll rest in the lawn chair."

Meghan and Jake set up three different sprinklers. They dragged the play slide over to the wading pool and aimed the sprinkler on the slide. Meghan and Jake got soaking wet. Mrs. Millett sat in a lawn chair and rested. The kids played all day.

"Thank you for being so understanding," Meghan's mom said. "Now I feel better, but I'm really hot! There's only one cure for that." She stood under the sprinkler with all her clothes on. She was drenched from head to toe.

Meghan laughed and said, "Now you have chronic wet syndrome." Mrs. Millett rewarded her daughter with a big, wet hug. It turned out to be a wonderful day after all, in the backyard waterland.

GO ON

READING: COMPREHENSION

● Lesson 14: Fiction (cont.)

1. **Which sentence best tells the main idea of this story?**

   Ⓐ Meghan's mom has chronic fatigue syndrome.

   Ⓑ Jake and Meghan miss out on Waterland, but they make their own water park and have fun anyway.

   Ⓒ Jake and Meghan cannot go to Waterland.

   Ⓓ Sprinklers make a great backyard water park.

2. **Which of the following happened after the kids dragged the slide over to the pool?**

   Ⓕ Jake arrived at Meghan's house.

   Ⓖ Meghan and Jake set up three sprinklers.

   Ⓗ Meghan's mom stood in the sprinkler with her clothes on.

   Ⓙ Meghan's mom was too tired to drive.

3. **How do you think Mrs. Millett feels about not being able to take the kids to Waterland?**

   Ⓐ She's glad that she won't have to spend her whole day with kids.

   Ⓑ She feels sorry for herself and is glad she got out of it.

   Ⓒ She's disappointed that she can't take them.

   Ⓓ She's hurt and confused.

4. **Why didn't Meghan and Jake go to Waterland?**

   Ⓕ They were too late.

   Ⓖ They wanted to play in the sprinklers instead.

   Ⓗ It was too hot outside.

   Ⓙ Mrs. Millett was too tired to drive them.

5. **What is the turning point of this story?**

   Ⓐ Meghan's mom feels better and gets wet in the sprinkler.

   Ⓑ Meghan and Jake can't go to Waterland.

   Ⓒ Meghan's mom gives her a wet hug.

   Ⓓ Jake arrives at the house early.

6. **Why did the author write this story?**

   Ⓕ to explain

   Ⓖ to persuade

   Ⓗ to entertain and inform

   Ⓙ to understand

STOP

READING: COMPREHENSION

● **Lesson 15: Fiction**

Directions: Read the passage. Choose the best answer to the questions that follow.

Example

Louis had a temperature of 101° F. He had a headache and an upset stomach. "You'd better go home," said Mr. Yeow. "You're too sick to stay in school. Don't worry about the math test. I'll give it to you when you're well enough to come back to school."

A. **Why did Louis have to leave school?**

- (A) He had been very bad.
- (B) He was too sick to stay.
- (C) He had a dentist appointment.
- (D) They had a half-day.

Skim the passage, then read the questions. Refer back to the passage to find the answers. You don't have to reread the story for each question.

● **Practice**

Home Alone

"Are you sure you're going to be all right at home alone?" Chun's mother asked. "Yes, Mom," Chun replied, trying not to roll her eyes. "I'm old enough to stay here alone for three hours."

Chun's mom and dad were going to a barbecue that afternoon. Since kids weren't invited, Chun was staying home alone. It was the first time her parents had left her home by herself. Chun was a little nervous, but she was sure she could handle it.

"Let me give you a last-minute quiz to make sure," her dad said. Chun's father was a teacher, and he was always giving her little tests. "What happens if somebody calls and asks for your mom or me?"

"I tell them that you are busy and can't come to the phone right now," Chun said. "Then I take a message."

"What if there is a knock on the door?" asked her dad.

"I don't answer it, because I can't let anyone in anyway."

"Okay, here's a tough one." Her father looked very serious. "What if you hear ghosts in the closets?"

"Dad!" Chun giggled. "Our house isn't haunted. I'll be fine. Look, I have the phone number of the house where you'll be, so I can call if I need to. I've got the numbers for the police, the fire department, and the poison control center. I won't turn on the stove or leave the house. And, I'll double lock the doors behind you when you leave."

Chun's parents were satisfied. They hugged her goodbye and left for the afternoon. Chun sat for a few minutes and enjoyed the quiet of the empty house. Then she went to the kitchen to fix herself a snack. She opened the cupboard door. Then she jumped back, startled. There was a ghost in the cupboard! Chun laughed and laughed. Her dad had taped up a picture of a ghost. It said, "BOO! We love you!"

GO ON

READING: COMPREHENSION

● **Lesson 15: Fiction (cont.)**

1. **Which answer shows the best summary of this story?**

   - (A) Chun is staying home by herself for the first time and must remember all the important safety rules.
   - (B) Chun cannot go to the barbecue with her mom and dad.
   - (C) Chun's parents play a trick on her by hiding a paper ghost in the cupboard.
   - (D) Chun enjoys a peaceful afternoon at home alone.

2. **What should Chun do if someone knocks at the door?**

   - (F) She should answer it.
   - (G) She should call her dad.
   - (H) She should not answer it and not let anyone in.
   - (J) She should see who it is before letting the person in.

3. **What do you think Chun will do if she spills drain cleaner and the dog accidentally licks some up?**

   - (A) She will call her friend Sam to tell him.
   - (B) She will call the fire department.
   - (C) She will do nothing.
   - (D) She will call the poison control center and then her parents.

4. **Because kids are not invited to the barbecue, —**

   - (F) they won't have any fun.
   - (G) the parents will not go.
   - (H) Chun must stay home alone.
   - (J) Chun will not get any dinner.

5. **Who are the main characters in this story?**

   - (A) Chun, her mom, and her dad
   - (B) Chun and her friend Sam
   - (C) Chun, her dad, and the dog
   - (D) Chun and her dad

6. **What is the main reason Chun's dad keeps asking her questions?**

   - (F) He wants to make sure she knows all the emergency phone numbers.
   - (G) He wants to make sure she will be safe while they are gone.
   - (H) He likes giving her quizzes.
   - (J) He played a trick on her.

READING: COMPREHENSION

● **Lesson 16: Nonfiction**

Directions: Read the passage. Choose the best answer to the questions that follow.

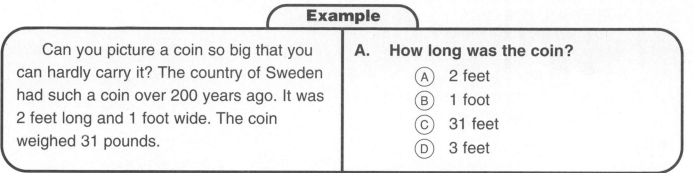

Example

Can you picture a coin so big that you can hardly carry it? The country of Sweden had such a coin over 200 years ago. It was 2 feet long and 1 foot wide. The coin weighed 31 pounds.

A. How long was the coin?

- (A) 2 feet
- (B) 1 foot
- (C) 31 feet
- (D) 3 feet

 **Clue** Skim the passage then read the questions. Refer back to the passage to find the answers. You don't have to reread the story for each question.

● **Practice**

Fossils are most often found in sedimentary rock. Suppose that a plant or animal died millions of years ago near a lake or an ocean. The mud and sand could cover it. Over many years, the mud and sand would harden and form sedimentary rock.

Two kinds of fossils in sedimentary rock are *cast* and *mold*. The mold fossil is a rock with an empty space left after the creature caught in the sediment wore away.

The cast fossil looks like a mold fossil that has been filled. Solid matter from the ground fills the empty space.

Suppose that a dinosaur stepped into soft ground and made a footprint. This would not be a cast or mold fossil. Those come from what is left of plants and creatures when they die. If a dinosaur made a footprint and walked away, the creature would not be there anymore. If the footprint hardened into rock and a scientist found it millions of years later, he would be looking at a *trace fossil*.

1. Why does a cast fossil look like a filled mold?

- (A) The animal leaves a footprint in the dirt.
- (B) Scientists fill the empty space with plaster after they find it.
- (C) Solid matter from the ground fills the empty space left by the animal.
- (D) The fossil was found in sedimentary rock.

2. In what kind of rock are most fossils found?

- (F) sedimentary
- (G) metamorphic
- (H) cast
- (J) mold

3. What is the best title for this passage?

- (A) Fossil Rocks
- (B) Trace Fossils
- (C) Cast Fossils
- (D) Dinosaur Footprints

STOP

READING: COMPREHENSION

● Lesson 17: Nonfiction

Directions: Read the passage. Choose the best answer to the questions that follow.

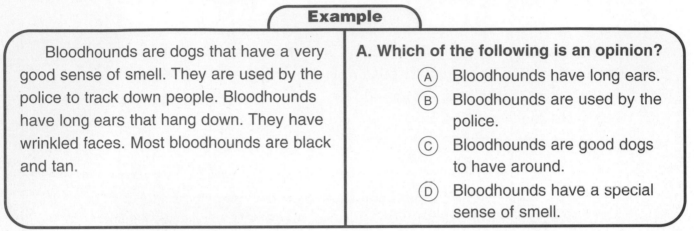

Example

Bloodhounds are dogs that have a very good sense of smell. They are used by the police to track down people. Bloodhounds have long ears that hang down. They have wrinkled faces. Most bloodhounds are black and tan.

A. Which of the following is an opinion?

- (A) Bloodhounds have long ears.
- (B) Bloodhounds are used by the police.
- (C) Bloodhounds are good dogs to have around.
- (D) Bloodhounds have a special sense of smell.

Clue — Read carefully. Make sure you look at all the answer choices before you choose the one you think is correct.

● Practice

Have you ever wondered how the Great Lakes came to be? The same elements came together to create Lake Superior, Lake Michigan, Lake Huron, Lake Erie, and Lake Ontario.

Thousands of years ago, *glaciers*—huge masses of slowly moving ice—covered the earth. More and more snow fell. Temperatures grew colder. Glaciers grew larger and larger.

The movement of glaciers pulled up huge amounts of soil and rocks. These were shoved ahead and to the sides of the glaciers.

Warming temperatures caused the glaciers to melt. The glaciers had taken up space. The soil and rocks that were pulled up and shoved along by the glaciers had taken up space. When the glaciers melted, there were huge holes.

Water from the melting glaciers and from rain filled these huge holes. They were no longer holes. They were lakes!

1. What is the best title for this passage?

- (A) Glaciers and Lakes
- (B) Glaciers Take Up Space
- (C) Melting Glaciers
- (D) How the Great Lakes Came to Be

2. What caused the glaciers to grow larger?

- (F) They pulled up huge amounts of soil and rocks.
- (G) More snow fell and temperatures got colder.
- (H) Temperatures grew warmer.
- (J) Melting water fell on them.

3. From where did the water come that filled up the glacier holes?

- (A) Native Americans filled up the holes to use them as lakes.
- (B) It rained a lot.
- (C) Rivers nearby flowed into the holes.
- (D) It came from the melting glaciers and rain.

STOP

GRADE 4

Name _____

READING: COMPREHENSION

● **Lesson 18: Nonfiction**

Directions: Read the passage. Choose the best answer to the questions that follow.

Example

How can a woodpecker bang its head into a tree all day without knocking itself out? Scientists have discovered that the bird's brain is packed inside thick, sponge-like bone. Around the bone are muscles that soften the shock of the constant pecking that the bird does with its bill.

A. Why does the woodpecker have a spongelike layer around its brain?

- Ⓐ to soak up extra liquid in the brain
- Ⓑ to transfer messages to the rest of the body
- Ⓒ to give its head a rounded shape
- Ⓓ to protect the brain from being hurt while the bird is pecking

Clue After you read, try to summarize the main points of the story in your head. Understanding the main points will help you recall the details.

● **Practice**

Forests and Animal Homes

Both rain forests and kelp forests are important to our ecology because they keep animals safe by providing animal homes. Rain forests keep land animals safe, while kelp forests keep sea creatures safe.

Like rain forests, kelp forests are homes for many types of animals. Crab, eel, lobster, and sea horses are just a few of the sea creatures that live in sea kelp. In California alone, kelp forests are home to more than 770 animal species. A sandy ocean bottom can make a home for some creatures, but a kelp forest can make a home for thousands more. Why? The animals can live on the many kinds of kelp surfaces—rocky and leafy ones, for example.

Like a rain forest, a kelp forest has layers. You will find three main layers in a kelp forest. They are the canopy, middle, and floor layers. The canopy is at the top, and the floor is at the bottom.

You will find different sea creatures and plants at different kelp forest levels. Herring and mackerel like to swim through the canopy, as do blue-rayed limpets. Sea slugs and snails feast on sea mats they find in the canopy.

Sea urchins look for food in the middle layer. Red seaweeds are often found in this layer of kelp forest as well, though they might be found at other levels.

Sea anemones, crabs, and lobsters live on the floor level. Older blue-rayed limpets feast here, too.

Like a rain forest, a kelp forest is a complex habitat for many sea creatures. It keeps them safe from predators and from people. And like a rain forest, to keep kelp forests an important part of our ecology, we must protect them from pollution and destruction.

GO ON

READING: COMPREHENSION

● Lesson 18: Nonfiction (cont.)

1. **Which sentence below best describes the main idea of this passage?**

    (A) A kelp forest has three levels.

    (B) Like rain forests, kelp forests help our ecology by providing homes for many animals.

    (C) Many sea creatures live in kelp forests and rain forests.

    (D) Kelp forests are like rain forests.

2. **Which of the following sea creatures live on the kelp forest floor?**

    (F) crabs

    (G) herring

    (H) mackerel

    (J) sea urchins

3. **Which of the following is a logical conclusion to make after reading this passage?**

    (A) Many of the animals in the kelp forests are enemies because they have to compete for food.

    (B) Kelp forests are dangerous places to visit.

    (C) Kelp forests provide many different kinds of food for sea creatures.

    (D) Kelp forests have not been studied very much by scientists.

4. **Why is a kelp forest a great home for so many animals?**

    (F) A kelp forest has many layers in which many different kinds of animals can live safely.

    (G) It is extremely large and can hold lots of animals.

    (H) The animals have been driven out of other parts of the ocean.

    (J) There is no other place for all the sea creatures to live.

5. **Which sentence below is most likely the topic sentence for this passage?**

    (A) In California alone, kelp forests are home to more than 770 animal species.

    (B) Like a rain forest, a kelp forest has layers.

    (C) Both rain forests and kelp forests are important as animal homes.

    (D) Like rain forests, kelp forests should be protected.

6. **How are rain forests and kelp forests different?**

    (F) Rain forests have animals, and kelp forests don't.

    (G) Rain forests are on land, and kelp forests are in the sea.

    (H) Kelp forests have many layers, and rain forests don't.

    (J) Rain forests are very important to our ecology, while kelp forests don't really affect it.

STOP

Name _____

READING: COMPREHENSION

● **Lesson 19: Nonfiction**

Directions: Read the passage. Choose the best answer to the questions that follow.

Example

The great auk once lived on islands in the Atlantic Ocean. This large black-and-white bird had a big bill. It was an excellent swimmer and diver but couldn't fly because of its very small wings. Sailors killed these birds by the thousands. The last great auk was seen in 1844.

A. **Which of the following about the great auk is true?**

Ⓐ It had a very small bill.

Ⓑ It was an excellent swimmer.

Ⓒ It had very large wings.

Ⓓ Thousands of these birds currently live on islands in the Atlantic.

Clue Pay close attention to the first sentences of each paragraph. These should tell you what you will read about in the rest of the paragraph.

● **Practice**

Alexander Graham Bell

Many believe that Alexander Graham Bell's greatest and most important personal goal was to invent the telephone, but this was not the case. Bell, who was born in 1847, called himself "a teacher of the deaf."

Bell's father was a well-known speech teacher. Bell also taught speech. He used what he had learned from his father to teach at a school for the deaf in England.

Bell went with his family to Canada in 1870. After two years, he opened a school for the deaf in Massachusetts.

The idea for the telephone came to Bell in 1874. At the same time Bell was experimenting with the telephone, he was working on equipment to help the deaf.

It was 1876 before Bell uttered the first sentence over the telephone, the well-known words: "Mr. Watson, come here; I want you." (Watson was Bell's assistant.) Bell received a patent for the telephone in the same year.

Hundreds of cases were filed against Bell in court. Many people claimed they had already thought of the telephone. But Bell did not lose his patent. He remains on record as its inventor.

The telephone was not Bell's only invention. He received 18 patents for other works and another 12 for work he had done with partners. Fourteen of the patents were for the telephone and telegraph. Others were for inventions such as the photophone, phonograph, and for different types of airplanes.

In 1888, Bell helped found the National Geographic Society. In 1890, he also began the Alexander Graham Bell Association for the Deaf. Bell passed away in August of 1922. Alexander Graham Bell is remembered as a man of many accomplishments.

GO ON

READING: COMPREHENSION

● Lesson 19: Nonfiction (cont.)

1. **What is the main idea of this passage?**

   (A) Alexander Graham Bell wanted to prove that he could think of many inventions.

   (B) Alexander Graham Bell invented the telephone.

   (C) Alexander Graham Bell was a man of many achievements.

   (D) Alexander Graham Bell received 30 patents in his lifetime.

2. **Which of the following did Bell also invent?**

   (F) automobile

   (G) light bulb

   (H) television

   (J) phonograph

3. **Which of the following subjects can you infer interested Bell more than others?**

   (A) electricity

   (B) sound

   (C) light

   (D) water

4. **Which of the following is not a fact about Alexander Graham Bell?**

   (F) Bell passed away in August of 1922.

   (G) The telephone was not Bell's only invention.

   (H) Bell's father was a well-known speech teacher.

   (J) Alexander Bell was a great man.

5. **Which sentence below is the concluding sentence of this passage?**

   (A) Bell passed away in August of 1922.

   (B) The telephone was not Bell's only invention.

   (C) In 1890, he also began the Alexander Graham Bell Association for the Deaf.

   (D) Alexander Graham Bell is remembered as a man of many accomplishments.

6. **What was the author's purpose in writing this article?**

   (F) to inform

   (G) to entertain

   (H) to persuade

   (J) to understand

GRADE 4

I. Reading
 A. Directions
 B. Sequencing
 C. Main Idea
II. Writing
 A. Capitalization
 B. Proofreading

Name _____

READING: COMPREHENSION
SAMPLE TEST

● **Directions:** Read the passage. Choose the best answer to the questions that follow.

Example

The saying "You don't know your own strength" must be true. Mildred Ludwick of Hawaii saw a little girl get struck by a car. The girl became pinned under a wheel. Ludwick used all her might and lifted the 3,000-pound car off the girl. Ludwick weighed only 105 pounds.

A. What is the main idea of this passage?

Ⓐ Extraordinary circumstances sometimes allow people to do amazing things.

Ⓑ Even small people can do really important things.

Ⓒ You should always know your own strength.

Ⓓ Always look before you cross the street.

Pig Race

"Welcome to the first annual Neighborhood Guinea Pig Race!" Emily announced.

Emily's guinea pig, Ruby, was entered in the first lane. Running in the second lane was Mark's guinea pig, named Woody. Amy entered her two guinea pigs. Otis was in lane three, and Macy was in lane four. While Amy and Mark got their pets ready to race, Emily was having trouble with Ruby. Ruby was sound asleep and wouldn't budge from under her wood shavings. "Come out, little piggie," Emily encouraged, but Ruby wouldn't budge.

"Why don't you try a carrot?" suggested Mark, holding out a small carrot. "That always works with Woody."

Emily poked on Ruby with the carrot and then stuck it under her nose. Sure enough, Ruby got up off her belly and followed the carrot.

"It worked!" exclaimed Emily. "Thanks, Mark!"

1. What is the main problem in this story?

Ⓐ Emily is impatient with Ruby.

Ⓑ Ruby is lazy.

Ⓒ Ruby won't come out of her cage for the race.

Ⓓ Ruby likes carrots too much.

2. What are the names of Amy's two guinea pigs?

Ⓕ Milo and Otis

Ⓖ Ruby and Woody

Ⓗ Woody and Otis

Ⓙ Otis and Macy

3. Why does Ruby finally budge?

Ⓐ Emily lures her out with a carrot.

Ⓑ The race is about to start.

Ⓒ She wakes up.

Ⓓ Mark uses Woody to get her to come out.

GO ON

Name _____

READING: COMPREHENSION
SAMPLE TEST (cont.)

● **Directions:** Read the passage. Choose the best answer to the questions that follow.

Comparing Earth and Venus

Earth and Venus are alike in many ways.

Earth and Venus are both planets that have volcanoes. Venus has more volcanoes than any other planet. Scientists have mapped more than 1,600 on Venus. Some scientists believe that there may be more than one million volcanoes on the planet.

Both planets look the same. They both have clouds and a thick atmosphere. The two are almost the same size and have almost the same mass. Venus's orbit around the sun is much like Earth's.

Though Earth and Venus are alike, there are also some differences. Water does not exist on Venus. The temperature on Venus is much hotter than on Earth.

On Earth, volcanoes erupt in a number of different ways. On Venus, however, almost all volcanoes erupt with flat lava flows. Scientists have not found information to show that any of Venus's volcanoes erupt and spew great amounts of ash into the sky.

4. **What is the topic sentence of this passage?**
   - (F) Both planets look the same.
   - (G) Though Earth and Venus are alike, there are also some differences.
   - (H) Earth and Venus are both planets that have volcanoes.
   - (J) Earth and Venus are alike in many ways.

5. **How is Venus's climate different than Earth's?**
   - (A) Venus gets more rain.
   - (B) Earth has more hot days during the year than Venus.
   - (C) The temperature on Venus is much hotter than on Earth.
   - (D) Venus has more cloudy days than Earth.

6. **Which of the following states a fact about Earth and/or Venus?**
   - (F) Water does not exist on Venus.
   - (G) It might be nice to visit Venus.
   - (H) Some people think Earth looks like Venus.
   - (J) It would be the same to live on Venus as it is here.

GO ON

GRADE
4

I. Reading
   A. Directions
   B. Sequencing
   C. Main Idea
II. Writing
   A. Capitalization
   B. Proofreading

Name _____

READING: COMPREHENSION
SAMPLE TEST (cont.)

● **Directions:** Read the passage. Choose the best answer to each question on the next page.

Missing Super-Cool

Lizzy loved to play with her Super-Cool dolls. She had Twirly-Curl Shirl, Beach Ball Belinda, and Can-Crushing Cal. Lizzy loved to dress them up and pretend they were driving the car or going to the ice-cream shop. They had a big plastic house they lived in, a purple car that really drove, and a beauty parlor where they could get their hair done.

Lizzy played make-believe all the time. Sometimes she would put all her Super-Cool dolls and their stuff in a suitcase and carry it across the driveway to her friend Tait's house. They would play with their dolls together for hours and hours. Sometimes they would even play with the dolls outside.

One day, Lizzy was getting out her dolls to play at home and noticed that some of Twirly-Curl Shirl's barrettes were missing. "That's funny," she thought. "I guess I must have lost them."

The next week, when Lizzy was playing at home again, she noticed that Beach Ball Belinda's sunglasses and flip-flops were missing. "Something's going on here," Lizzy thought.

The next day, Lizzy was playing at Tait's house again. When Tait left the room to go to the bathroom, Lizzy was picking through Tait's box of Super-Cool clothes. She was moving some clothes aside when she noticed her missing barrettes at the bottom of the box. She gasped and picked them out. She sorted through the box some more and found the missing sunglasses and flip-flops. "Oh, my gosh," she said.

Lizzy didn't know what to do. Should she ask Tait if she had taken them? But how else could they have gotten there? She didn't want to get in a fight with her best friend, but she didn't want Tait to steal from her again. She didn't know what she should do, so she decided to go and ask her mom.

That night when she was helping her mom set the table, Lizzy asked her mom about it. Her mom thought for a few seconds. "I think you should ask Tait if you left anything over there. Tell her that you found something there last time and wondered if you left anything again. That way you can give her the chance to confess if she wants."

The next day Lizzy did just as her mom had suggested.

"Well," said Tait, "My mom won't let me get those dolls, and their clothes are so cool. I took those things because I just love them. I'm sorry I did, but I just wanted to play with them."

"That's okay, Tait, I'll let you play with my stuff while I'm over here, but it has to go back home with me, okay?"

"Okay. Let's play right now."

READING: COMPREHENSION
SAMPLE TEST (cont.)

7. **What is the main message of this story?**

- (A) If you really want something, just take it.
- (B) You should always be honest with your friends.
- (C) Playing nicely is the only way to play.
- (D) Super-Cool dolls are better played with at your own house.

8. **To which Super-Cool doll do the missing barrettes belong?**

- (F) Can-Crushing Cal
- (G) Beach Ball Belinda
- (H) Twirly-Curl Shirl
- (J) All of the above

9. **How do you think Lizzy would have felt if Tait hadn't said anything about stealing the toys?**

- (A) Sad; she may have felt that she couldn't trust Tait.
- (B) Happy; she'd be grateful that she wouldn't have to talk about it.
- (C) Jealous; she would want to play at her house instead.
- (D) Calm; she would ask her mother to buy her another one.

10. **Because Tait couldn't have the toys she wanted —**

- (F) she took them from Lizzy.
- (G) she threw a temper tantrum.
- (H) she got other ones.
- (J) she played with her own.

11. **Who are the characters in this story?**

- (A) Shirl, Belinda, and Cal
- (B) Lizzy and Tait
- (C) Lizzy, Tait, and Mom
- (D) Lizzy, Tait, and Shirl

GO ON

READING: COMPREHENSION

SAMPLE TEST (cont.)

● **Directions:** Read the passage. Choose the best answer to each question on the next page.

The Underground Railroad

The Underground Railroad was a group of people who helped slaves escape to freedom. Those in charge of the escape effort were often called *conductors*, just like the conductors of a train. The people escaping were known as *passengers*, just like train passengers. And the places where the escaping slaves stopped for help were often called *stations*, just like the places trains stop.

Like a train ride, the Underground Railroad moved people along, but the way in which they moved was very different from a train ride. Those who escaped often followed routes that had been laid out by others before them. However, unlike a train ride, some routes went underground through dirt tunnels without any sort of tracks.

Similar to a train ride, those traveling the Underground Railroad often traveled great distances, but they had no train seats and no gentle rocking of the train car on the tracks. Instead, they had difficult trails to follow. They rarely traveled during the day, finding that it was safer to travel at night.

Escaping slaves had to be certain that they could find their way. They needed food and water to make the journey. Conductors often helped with this. One of the most famous Underground Railroad conductors was Harriet Tubman. She had escaped slavery herself. Another famous conductor was Levi Coffin.

Experts disagree about how well the Underground Railroad was organized. Still, it is believed that the system helped thousands of slaves reach freedom between 1830 and 1860.

GO ON

Name _____

READING: COMPREHENSION
SAMPLE TEST (cont.)

12. **What's is the author's purpose in writing this article?**

   (F) to quiz us on train vocabulary

   (G) to tell us about how the Underground Railroad worked

   (H) to tell a story about Harriet Tubman

   (J) to explain the meaning of the name *Underground Railroad*

13. **What were people called who were in charge of groups of escaping slaves?**

   (A) conductors

   (B) stations

   (C) passengers

   (D) masters

14. **What two emotions below best describe how slaves traveling on the Underground Railroad might have felt?**

   (F) frightened and excited

   (G) disappointed and mad

   (H) carefree and happy

   (J) silly and lighthearted

15. **Because of the Underground Railroad —**

   (A) other programs like it were set up.

   (B) many people had jobs.

   (C) conductors had to be found to run it.

   (D) thousands of slaves escaped.

16. **Which of the following is not a supporting detail for the article?**

   (F) The Underground Railroad was a group of people who helped slaves escape to freedom.

   (G) Still, it is believed that the system helped thousands of slaves reach freedom between 1830 and 1860.

   (H) The people escaping were known as *passengers*, just like train passengers.

   (J) The Underground Railroad offered free train rides to people.

17. **Which of the following is *not* a way in which the Underground Railroad and trains are alike?**

   (A) They have passengers.

   (B) They travel great distances.

   (C) They stop at stations.

   (D) They travel on tracks.

ANSWER SHEET

STUDENT'S NAME			SCHOOL
LAST	FIRST	MI	TEACHER

FEMALE ◯   MALE ◯

BIRTH DATE

MONTH	DAY	YEAR

JAN ◯
FEB ◯
MAR ◯
APR ◯
MAY ◯
JUN ◯
JUL ◯
AUG ◯
SEP ◯
OCT ◯
NOV ◯
DEC ◯

GRADE
③ ④ ⑤

Part 1: VOCABULARY

A	Ⓐ Ⓑ Ⓒ Ⓓ	6	Ⓕ Ⓖ Ⓗ Ⓙ	13	Ⓐ Ⓑ Ⓒ Ⓓ	20	Ⓕ Ⓖ Ⓗ Ⓙ	27	Ⓐ Ⓑ Ⓒ Ⓓ
B	Ⓕ Ⓖ Ⓗ Ⓙ	7	Ⓐ Ⓑ Ⓒ Ⓓ	14	Ⓕ Ⓖ Ⓗ Ⓙ	21	Ⓐ Ⓑ Ⓒ Ⓓ	28	Ⓕ Ⓖ Ⓗ Ⓙ
1	Ⓐ Ⓑ Ⓒ Ⓓ	8	Ⓕ Ⓖ Ⓗ Ⓙ	15	Ⓐ Ⓑ Ⓒ Ⓓ	22	Ⓕ Ⓖ Ⓗ Ⓙ	29	Ⓐ Ⓑ Ⓒ Ⓓ
2	Ⓕ Ⓖ Ⓗ Ⓙ	9	Ⓐ Ⓑ Ⓒ Ⓓ	16	Ⓕ Ⓖ Ⓗ Ⓙ	23	Ⓐ Ⓑ Ⓒ Ⓓ	30	Ⓕ Ⓖ Ⓗ Ⓙ
3	Ⓐ Ⓑ Ⓒ Ⓓ	10	Ⓕ Ⓖ Ⓗ Ⓙ	17	Ⓐ Ⓑ Ⓒ Ⓓ	24	Ⓕ Ⓖ Ⓗ Ⓙ	31	Ⓐ Ⓑ Ⓒ Ⓓ
4	Ⓕ Ⓖ Ⓗ Ⓙ	11	Ⓐ Ⓑ Ⓒ Ⓓ	18	Ⓕ Ⓖ Ⓗ Ⓙ	25	Ⓐ Ⓑ Ⓒ Ⓓ	32	Ⓕ Ⓖ Ⓗ Ⓙ
5	Ⓐ Ⓑ Ⓒ Ⓓ	12	Ⓕ Ⓖ Ⓗ Ⓙ	19	Ⓐ Ⓑ Ⓒ Ⓓ	26	Ⓕ Ⓖ Ⓗ Ⓙ	33	Ⓐ Ⓑ Ⓒ Ⓓ

Part 2: FICTION

A	Ⓐ Ⓑ Ⓒ Ⓓ	7	Ⓐ Ⓑ Ⓒ Ⓓ
1	Ⓐ Ⓑ Ⓒ Ⓓ	8	Ⓕ Ⓖ Ⓗ Ⓙ
2	Ⓕ Ⓖ Ⓗ Ⓙ	9	Ⓐ Ⓑ Ⓒ Ⓓ
3	Ⓐ Ⓑ Ⓒ Ⓓ	10	Ⓕ Ⓖ Ⓗ Ⓙ
4	Ⓕ Ⓖ Ⓗ Ⓙ	11	Ⓐ Ⓑ Ⓒ Ⓓ
5	Ⓐ Ⓑ Ⓒ Ⓓ	12	Ⓕ Ⓖ Ⓗ Ⓙ
6	Ⓕ Ⓖ Ⓗ Ⓙ		

Part 3: NONFICTION

A	Ⓐ Ⓑ Ⓒ Ⓓ	7	Ⓐ Ⓑ Ⓒ Ⓓ	14	Ⓕ Ⓖ Ⓗ Ⓙ
1	Ⓐ Ⓑ Ⓒ Ⓓ	8	Ⓕ Ⓖ Ⓗ Ⓙ	15	Ⓐ Ⓑ Ⓒ Ⓓ
2	Ⓕ Ⓖ Ⓗ Ⓙ	9	Ⓐ Ⓑ Ⓒ Ⓓ		
3	Ⓐ Ⓑ Ⓒ Ⓓ	10	Ⓕ Ⓖ Ⓗ Ⓙ		
4	Ⓕ Ⓖ Ⓗ Ⓙ	11	Ⓐ Ⓑ Ⓒ Ⓓ		
5	Ⓐ Ⓑ Ⓒ Ⓓ	12	Ⓕ Ⓖ Ⓗ Ⓙ		
6	Ⓕ Ⓖ Ⓗ Ⓙ	13	Ⓐ Ⓑ Ⓒ Ⓓ		

GRADE 4

I. Reading
A. Directions
B. Sequencing
C. Main Idea
II. Writing
A. Capitalization
B. Proofreading

Name _____

READING PRACTICE TEST

● **Part 1: Vocabulary**

Examples

For items A and 1–8, choose the word or words that mean the same or about the same as the underlined word.

A. **conceal a crime**

    (A) commit

    (B) cover up

    (C) know about

    (D) punish

For item B, read the question. Choose the answer you think is correct.

B. **Which tree was named for Pierre Magnol, the scientist who discovered it?**

    (F) pine

    (G) maple

    (H) magnolia

    (J) mahogany

1. **grab a cookie**

    (A) reach for

    (B) bake

    (C) eat

    (D) break

2. **give a signal**

    (F) radio

    (G) poster

    (H) gift

    (J) sign

3. **thorough cleaning**

    (A) quick

    (B) necessary

    (C) complete

    (D) house

4. **explore the island**

    (F) search

    (G) find

    (H) stalk

    (J) look for

5. **To consult someone is to —**

    (A) compliment

    (B) get advice

    (C) insult

    (D) give advice

6. **If someone is generous, he is —**

    (F) giving

    (G) guilty

    (H) selfish

    (J) greedy

7. **If something is spoiled it is —**

    (A) crusty

    (B) cooked

    (C) sunburned

    (D) ruined

8. **She put her cloak on.**

    (F) hat

    (G) cape

    (H) sweater

    (J) scarf

GO ON

Name _____

READING PRACTICE TEST
Part 1: Vocabulary (cont.)

For items 9–12, choose the word or words that mean the same or about the same as the underlined word.

9. The girls abandoned their brothers in the woods.
   Abandoned means —
   - (A) left alone intentionally
   - (B) played with
   - (C) amused
   - (D) walked with

10. To demonstrate, Janice made a circular motion with her hand.
    Circular means —
    - (F) circus
    - (G) in a circle
    - (H) waving
    - (J) slapping

11. Raschel wants to discontinue her magazine subscription.
    To discontinue is to —
    - (A) reorder
    - (B) order
    - (C) stop
    - (D) pay for

12. My older brother went on an expedition to Central America to study pyramids.
    An expedition is a —
    - (F) journey with a purpose
    - (G) vacation
    - (H) trip
    - (J) stroll

For items 13–17, choose the word that means the opposite of the underlined word.

13. weeping child
    - (A) young
    - (B) laughing
    - (C) skipping
    - (D) sad

14. dangerous snake
    - (F) slimy
    - (G) moist
    - (H) harmless
    - (J) long

15. friends and foes
    - (A) friends
    - (B) enemies
    - (C) pets
    - (D) parents

16. quality foods
    - (F) salty
    - (G) dessert
    - (H) well-made
    - (J) bad

17. coarse salt
    - (A) natural
    - (B) rough
    - (C) tough
    - (D) fine

GO ON

GRADE 4

Name _____

READING PRACTICE TEST
Part 1: Vocabulary (cont.)

For items 18–21, read the two sentences with blanks. Choose the word that fits best in both sentences.

18. My _____ is in the closet.
    Add a new _____ of paint.
    - (F) hat
    - (G) color
    - (H) shirt
    - (J) coat

19. The photography _____ meets today.
    The cave man carried a _____ .
    - (A) group
    - (B) club
    - (C) spear
    - (D) class

20. He will need new swimming _____ .
    Load those _____ in the van.
    - (F) goggles
    - (G) shoes
    - (H) boxes
    - (J) trunks

21. Our teacher tells us not to _____ anyone.
    The _____ at the party was tasty.
    - (A) food
    - (B) hit
    - (C) punch
    - (D) juice

For items 22–23, choose the answer in which the underlined word is used in the same way as the sentence in the box.

22. | The sky was clear. |
    - (F) Clear away those dinner dishes.
    - (G) The tower radioed that we were in the clear.
    - (H) He said it would be clear sailing from here on in.
    - (J) Clear skies and bright sun were forecast for today.

23. | Watch out for that falling limb. |
    - (A) Andrew checked his watch for the time.
    - (B) The captain asked him to take the first watch.
    - (C) Watch your step.
    - (D) We kept the watch fire burning all night.

For items 24–25, choose the answer that best defines the underlined part.

24. disbelieve   disorganized
    - (F) absence of
    - (G) more
    - (H) less than
    - (J) again

25. gentleness   kindness
    - (A) quality of
    - (B) less
    - (C) more
    - (D) opposite of

GO ON

Name _____

READING PRACTICE TEST
Part 1: Vocabulary (cont.)

26. **Which of these words probably comes from the Latin word *crimen*, meaning *accusation*?**

    (F) cringe

    (G) cry

    (H) criminal

    (J) crimp

27. **Which of these words probably comes from the Greek word *musterion*, meaning *secret rite*?**

    (A) musky

    (B) mystic

    (C) must

    (D) muster

28. **We hiked to a _____ campsite. Which word means the campsite was *far away*?**

    (F) remote

    (G) pleasant

    (H) crowded

    (J) level

29. **The girls were _____ to the show after they bought their tickets. Which word means that they were *allowed to enter*?**

    (A) going

    (B) cast

    (C) admitted

    (D) shown

Read the paragraph. Choose the word that fits best in each numbered blank.

Mountain gorillas live in the _____(30) in Rwanda, Uganda, and the Democratic Republic of the Congo. These _____,(31) beautiful animals are becoming very rare. They have lost much of their habitat as people move in and take over their land. Although there are _____(32) laws protecting gorillas, poachers continue to hunt them. Scientists and park rangers are working hard to _____(33) the mountain gorillas.

30. (F) deserts

    (G) forests

    (H) lakes

    (J) valleys

31. (A) large

    (B) small

    (C) skinny

    (D) violent

32. (F) loose

    (G) easy

    (H) stupid

    (J) strict

33. (A) chase away

    (B) hunt

    (C) protect

    (D) kill

STOP

READING PRACTICE TEST

● **Part 2: Fiction**

Directions: Read the passage. Choose the best answer to the questions that follow.

Example

"I can't find my baseball glove," complained Jane. "I left it in the closet, but it's not there. I must use my own glove if I'm going to play my best." That afternoon, just before her baseball game, Jane said, "I feel that I'm going to win for sure."

A. Why did Jane's attitude probably change just before the game?

(A) She found her glove.

(B) Her whole family was there.

(C) She had been promised ice cream after the game.

(D) Her coach had given a great pep talk.

The Babysitter

Cassie's mom has errands to run, so Cassie agrees to stay home to babysit for her little brother, who is asleep. Her mom also leaves Cassie a list of chores to do while she is gone. Cassie will be able to go to the mall with her friends when her chores are finished and her mom gets back.

As soon as Cassie's mom leaves, Cassie starts calling her friends on the phone. She talks to Kim for 20 minutes and to Beth for 15 minutes. She is supposed to call Maria when she finishes talking to Jackie.

After talking on the phone, Cassie decides to do her nails while she watches a movie on TV. After the movie, Cassie listens to the radio and reads a magazine.

Before Cassie realizes it, three and a half hours have passed and her mom is back home. Her mom walks in and finds the kitchen still a mess, crumbs all over the carpet, dusty furniture, and Cassie's little brother screaming in his room.

1. **Who was Cassie going to call after Beth?**

(A) Kim

(B) Maria

(C) Jackie

(D) her mom

2. **Which of the following is a chore Cassie probably wasn't supposed to do?**

(F) dust

(G) listen for her brother

(H) clean her room

(J) clean the kitchen

3. **What do you think the resolution to this problem will be?**

(A) Cassie's little brother will have to do all the chores.

(B) Cassie will be punished and will not go to the mall.

(C) Cassie's mom will drive her to the mall.

(D) Cassie, her mom, and her brother will watch a movie.

GO ON

GRADE
4

I. Reading
A. Directions
B. Sequencing
C. Main Idea
II. Writing
A. Capitalization
B. Proofreading

Name _____

READING PRACTICE TEST
Part 2: Fiction (cont.)

● **Directions:** Read the passage. Choose the best answer to each question.

David's Grandpa

David's grandpa is coming to visit for a week. David is really excited because he and his grandpa have always had a great time together. But, David is also nervous. His grandpa had a stroke a few months ago, and David's mom said his grandpa moves a little slower than he used to. "Oh, well," thinks David, "we'll still have fun."

On the day of Grandpa's arrival, David is up early. He is too excited to sleep. Finally, it is time to go to the airport. Off the plane comes Grandpa. But, he is using a cane! Mom never told David that. What about their long walks down to the creek? David gives his grandpa a big hug. His grandpa seems really old and tired.

On the way home, Grandpa keeps talking about how he doesn't want to be in anyone's way and if David's family gets tired of him, they can send him home early. David feels sorry for his grandpa. Then, David starts coming up with all kinds of new things they can do together, like build model airplanes, watch movies, put together his train set, and organize David's baseball card collection.

"No way are you going home one second early, Grandpa," says David. His grandpa looks very happy.

4. **Why is this visit different from others?**

   (F) David is excited about the visit.

   (G) Grandpa will not be staying as long this time.

   (H) Grandma is coming along with Grandpa.

   (J) Grandpa has had a stroke since the last time David saw him.

5. **How does David feel about his grandpa's visit?**

   (A) exhilarated

   (B) anxious

   (C) optimistic

   (D) depressed

6. **What is the turning point in this story?**

   (F) David sees his grandpa using a cane.

   (G) David's grandpa arrives.

   (H) David thinks of lots of new things he can do with his grandpa.

   (J) Grandpa looks very happy.

GO ON

READING PRACTICE TEST
Part 2: Fiction (cont.)

● **Directions:** Read the passage. Choose the best answer to each question on the next page.

Class President

Quinn was running for class president. He and his friend Zack hung colored posters up in the hallways. They declared, "QUINN SHOULD WIN!"

A fifth grader walked by them as they hung one on the door to the library. He read the poster and asked, "Why? Why should *you* win?" and then walked away.

Quinn had never thought about *why* before. He knew that he was popular and that a lot of people would vote for him.

"I suppose you should have some issues," Zack commented. "More recess time? Hey, how about that new gumball machine in the boys' bathroom you're always talking about?"

In the election meeting that afternoon, Mrs. Jacobs, the school principal, told them it was a great responsibility to be each class's president. All candidates running, she said, should be honest. "Let your   platform speak for itself," she said.

At home, Quinn and Zack made up new campaign posters that said, "VOTE QUINN: New gumball machine in the boys' room. Everyone will play soccer at lunch. Taco day is abolished!"

The next day at school, some of Quinn's regular friends avoided him, especially the girls. When he asked J.D. if he wanted to play soccer at lunch, J.D. responded, "Of course, Your Majesty."

"What's the matter with everyone?" Quinn muttered while standing in the lunch line.

"I'll tell you what's wrong," said a small girl in line behind him. "Nobody likes your campaign promises. The girls couldn't care less if you're going to get a gumball machine in the boys' room. A lot of people like taco day. And, nobody wants to be told they have to play soccer at recess. Some people like to play other games. You only made promises about what you like."

Quinn thought about what he could do. He decided that if he wanted to know what his classmates wanted, he should take a poll. So, he and Zack asked each fourth grader what they wanted most to change in their school. They made a bar graph so they could see what was most important to fourth graders. Then Quinn and Zack made up new campaign posters. Quinn's friends started talking to him again, and the next week he won the election. Quinn realized that listening to your classmates is the most important thing a class president can do.

GRADE 4

I. Reading
   A. Directions
   B. Sequencing
   C. Main Idea
II. Writing
   A. Capitalization
   B. Proofreading

Name _____

READING PRACTICE TEST
Part 2: Fiction (cont.)

7. **What is the main message of this story?**

   (A) Holding a public office is an important responsibility.

   (B) School elections are very complicated.

   (C) Popularity is more important than campaign promises.

   (D) Girls and boys don't always like the same things.

8. **What was Quinn's first campaign slogan?**

   (F) New gumball machine in the boys' room.

   (G) Everyone will play soccer at lunch.

   (H) Quinn should win!

   (J) Taco day is abolished!

9. **Which of the following probably would have happened if Quinn hadn't changed his slogans?**

   (A) He would have won anyway.

   (B) Mrs. Jacobs would have told him he couldn't run.

   (C) Zack would have refused to speak to him.

   (D) He would have lost the election.

10. **What causes Quinn's friends to stop speaking to him?**

    (F) He puts up his campaign posters.

    (G) He only makes promises for things he wants.

    (H) He decides to run for class president.

    (J) He changes his campaign promises.

11. **What is the turning point in this story?**

    (A) The girl in line tells him what is wrong with his promises.

    (B) Quinn decides to ask his classmates what they want.

    (C) Quinn wins the election.

    (D) Some of Quinn's friends refuse to talk to him.

12. **Which genre is this story?**

    (F) western

    (G) mystery

    (H) drama

    (J) nonfiction

STOP

GRADE
4

I. Reading
A. Directions
B. Sequencing
C. Main Idea
II. Writing
A. Capitalization
B. Proofreading

Name _____

READING PRACTICE TEST

● **Part 3: Nonfiction**

Directions: Read the passage. Choose the best answer to each question.

Example

Before the 1800s, people didn't have right or left shoes. They had shoes of just one shape that they used for both feet. When people first saw right and left shoes, they laughed. They called them *crooked shoes*.

A. Which of the following is an opinion?

Ⓐ Before the 1800s, people didn't have right or left shoes.

Ⓑ People called the new shoes *crooked shoes*.

Ⓒ People had only one shape of shoe.

Ⓓ The new shoes were funny-looking.

Bats

Perhaps you have heard that many types of bats have very small eyes and do not see well. Still, as they swoop through the night, they do not bump into objects and are able to find food, even though they can't see their prey. How is this possible? Echolocation!

You might recognize the beginning of the word *echolocation* as *echo*, and you might recognize the last part of the word as *location*. This gives you clues about how echolocation works. The bat sends out sounds. The sounds bounce off objects and return to the bat. Echolocation not only tells the bat that objects are nearby, it also tells the bat just how far away the objects are.

Bats are not the only creatures that use echolocation, Porpoises and some types of whales and birds use it as well. It is a very effective tool for the animals that use it.

1. **What is the main idea of this passage?**

Ⓐ Bats cannot see very well.

Ⓑ Many animals use echolocation.

Ⓒ Echolocation is an effective tool for bats and other animals.

Ⓓ Bats are not the only creatures that use echolocation.

2. **Which two words make up the word *echolocation*?**

Ⓕ *ech* and *olocation*

Ⓖ *echolocate* and *tion*

Ⓗ *echo* and *locate*

Ⓙ *echo* and *location*

3. **Bats have to use echolocation mainly because —**

Ⓐ they have no eyes.

Ⓑ they have poor eyesight.

Ⓒ they have big ears.

Ⓓ they fly past lots of obstacles.

GO ON

GRADE 4

I. Reading
  A. Directions
  B. Sequencing
  C. Main Idea
II. Writing
  A. Capitalization
  B. Proofreading

Name _____

READING PRACTICE TEST
Part 3: Nonfiction (cont.)

● **Directions:** Read the passage. Choose the best answer to each question on the next page.

The Origins of the Telegraph

Have you ever watched someone tap a key and send a code for S.O.S.? Perhaps you have seen an old film and seen a ship about to sink. Perhaps someone was tapping wildly on a device, trying to send for help.

From where did this system of tapping out dashes and dots come? Who invented this electronic device? Samuel Morse invented the telegraph and the electronic alphabet called Morse code.

When Morse was young, he was an artist. People in New York knew his work well and liked it a great deal. Being well known, Morse decided to run for office. He ran for the office of New York mayor and congressman, but he lost these political races.

In 1832, while Morse was sailing back to the United States from Europe, he thought of an electronic telegraph. This would help people communicate across great distances, even from ship to shore. He was anxious to put together his invention as quickly as possible. Interestingly, someone else had also thought of this same idea.

By 1835, he had put together his first telegraph, but it was only experimental. In 1844, he built a telegraph line from Baltimore to Washington, D.C. He later made his telegraph better, and in 1849, was granted a patent by the U.S. government. Within a few years, people communicated across 23,000 miles (37,007 km) of telegraph wire.

As a result of Samuel Morse's invention, trains ran more safely. Conductors could warn about dangers or problems across great distances and ask for help. People in business could communicate more easily, which made it easier to sell their goods and services. Morse had changed communication forever.

GO ON

GRADE
4

I. Reading
  A. Directions
  B. Sequencing
  C. Main Idea
II. Writing
  A. Capitalization
  B. Proofreading

Name _____

READING PRACTICE TEST
Part 3: Nonfiction (cont.)

4. **What is the main idea of this article?**

- (F) Trains run more safely because of the telegraph.
- (G) Telegraphs send electronic signals to communicate.
- (H) By the 1850s, people communicated effectively by telegraph.
- (J) Morse's invention of the telegraph changed communication forever.

5. **Before 1832, Morse had —**

- (A) run for office in New York.
- (B) improved his telegraph.
- (C) built his first telegraph.
- (D) come up with the idea for the telegraph.

6. **Which of the following can you infer about Samuel Morse's childhood?**

- (F) He was well educated.
- (G) He had to work at a young age to support his family.
- (H) He lived on a farm and was not able to go to school.
- (J) He was abandoned at a young age and forced to live on the streets.

7. **What can you infer about long-distance communication before Morse's invention?**

- (A) It was easy.
- (B) No one was interested in it.
- (C) It was difficult to do quickly.
- (D) There was no long-distance communication.

8. **Which of the following sentences from the article concludes this reading selection?**

- (F) As a result of Samuel Morse's invention, trains ran more safely.
- (G) People in business could communicate more easily, which made it easier to sell their goods and services.
- (H) Within a few years, people communicated across 23,000 miles (37,007 km) of telegraph wire.
- (J) Morse had changed communication forever.

9. **How is the telegraph not similar to the telephone?**

- (A) helps communicate over long distances
- (B) makes people safer
- (C) helps people sell goods and services
- (D) lets people hear their loved ones' voices

GO ON

READING PRACTICE TEST
Part 3: Nonfiction (cont.)

● **Directions:** Read the passage. Choose the best answer to each question on the next page.

Radio

Inventor Guglielmo Marconi came to the United States in 1899. Telegraph communication by wire was already in place, but Marconi wanted to show off his wireless communication—radio.

Marconi's invention could send Morse code without using any wires. He thought this would help with business communication. When introducing his work, he also planned to show how his invention could do things such as broadcasting a sporting event.

Other people had more and different ideas. These ideas led to programs that included spoken words and music being broadcast on the radio. Operas, comedy hours, and important speeches were now being heard in many homes throughout the country. Two famous radio broadcasts were the "War of the Worlds" presentation on October 31, 1938, a fictional story that told about invading aliens; and President Roosevelt's radio announcement of the Japanese attack on Pearl Harbor on December 8, 1941.

In 1922, there were 30 radio stations that sent broadcasts. By 1923, the number had grown to an amazing 556! There was a problem with so many stations broadcasting, however. There was no regular way to do things. Radio station owners organized their stations any way they saw fit.

Even though stations organized into networks, broadcasting still was not organized. The United States government passed laws to regulate radio. This let station owners know which airwaves they could use. The laws also addressed what was okay to say on the radio and what was not appropriate.

Even though television and the Internet are with us today, most homes and cars have radios. It looks as though this kind of communication is here to stay, thanks to Mr. Marconi and his invention.

GO ON

Name _____

READING PRACTICE TEST
Part 3: Nonfiction (cont.)

10. Which of the following would be an appropriate title for this article?

(F) Guglielmo Marconi

(G) Radio: How Did It Begin?

(H) Radio Is Here to Stay

(J) Wireless, Here We Go!

11. Which of the following came before there were 30 radio stations that sent broadcasts?

(A) There were an amazing 556 radio stations.

(B) The "War of the Worlds" program was broadcast.

(C) President Roosevelt announced the attack on Pearl Harbor.

(D) Guglielmo Marconi came to the United States.

12. What can you infer about people's reactions to radio?

(F) They didn't like it and preferred to watch events.

(G) It took a long time for them to get used to the idea.

(H) They immediately liked it and were excited about it.

(J) They shunned Marconi and thought his invention was too modern.

13. Which of the following is a fact?

(A) Radio was the most helpful invention ever created.

(B) Mr. Marconi was a genius.

(C) Radios send signals without wires.

(D) Radio will never go away.

14. Which of the following is not a supporting detail found in this article?

(F) The United States government passed laws to regulate radio.

(G) Marconi won the Nobel Prize in 1909.

(H) Marconi wanted to introduce his wireless communication.

(J) Marconi came to the United States in 1899.

15. Why did the author most likely write this article?

(A) to inform us about the introduction of radio in the United States

(B) to prove how successful a life Marconi had

(C) to inspire us to invent more communication devices

(D) to inform us about all the possible radio shows there are to make

READING: VOCABULARY
Lesson 1: Synonyms
• Page 262
- A. C
- B. G
- 1. C
- 2. F
- 3. C
- 4. G
- 5. D
- 6. F
- 7. A
- 8. H

READING: VOCABULARY
Lesson 2: Vocabulary Skills
• Page 263
- A. A
- B. J
- 1. B
- 2. H
- 3. A
- 4. H
- 5. A
- 6. F
- 7. B

READING: VOCABULARY
Lesson 3: Antonyms
• Page 264
- A. B
- B. F
- 1. B
- 2. G
- 3. C
- 4. F
- 5. C
- 6. F
- 7. A
- 8. F

READING: VOCABULARY
Lesson 4: Multi-Meaning Words
• Page 265
- A. D
- 1. D
- 2. H
- 3. A
- 4. H
- 5. D

READING: VOCABULARY
Lesson 5: Words in Context
• Page 266
- A. D
- B. F
- 1. B

- 2. H
- 3. D
- 4. H
- 5. D
- 6. G

READING: VOCABULARY
Lesson 6: Word Study
• Page 267
- A. B
- B. G
- 1. B
- 2. F
- 3. A
- 4. G
- 5. B
- 6. J

READING: VOCABULARY
SAMPLE TEST
• Pages 268–271
- A. B
- B. H
- 1. A
- 2. J
- 3. B
- 4. H
- 5. C
- 6. H
- 7. A
- 8. J
- 9. A
- 10. F
- 11. C
- 12. F
- 13. C
- 14. H
- 15. A
- 16. J
- 17. A
- 18. G
- 19. B
- 20. G
- 21. D
- 22. J
- 23. B
- 24. H
- 25. D
- 26. J
- 27. B
- 28. H
- 29. A
- 30. J
- 31. B
- 32. F
- 33. C
- 34. J

READING: COMPREHENSION
Lesson 7: Main Idea
• Page 272
- A. B
- 1. D
- 2. F

READING: COMPREHENSION
Lesson 8: Recalling Details/Sequencing
• Page 273
- A. D
- 1. D
- 2. H
- 3. A

READING: COMPREHENSION
Lesson 9: Making Inferences/Drawing Conclusions
• Page 274
- A. C
- 1. B
- 2. G

READING: COMPREHENSION
Lesson 10: Fact & Opinion/Cause & Effect
• Page 275
- A. D
- 1. D
- 2. F

READING: COMPREHENSION
Lesson 11: Parts of a Story
• Page 276
- A. B
- 1. A
- 2. F
- 3. D

READING: COMPREHENSION
Lesson 12: Fiction
• Page 277
- A. C
- 1. A
- 2. H
- 3. D

READING: C[O]
Lesson 13: Fi[c]
• Page 278
- A. C
- 1. A
- 2. G
- 3. C

Test Practice

309

Total Reading Grade

A. [P]
1. C
2. J
3. B

ANSWER KEY

READING: COMPREHENSION
Lesson 14: Fiction
• **Pages 279–280**
- **A.** A
- **1.** B
- **2.** H
- **3.** C
- **4.** J
- **5.** A
- **6.** H

READING: COMPREHENSION
Lesson 15: Fiction
• **Pages 281–282**
- **A.** B
- **1.** A
- **2.** H
- **3.** D
- **4.** H
- **5.** A
- **6.** G

READING: COMPREHENSION
Lesson 16: Nonfiction
• **Page 283**
- **A.** A
- **1.** C
- **2.** F
- **3.** A

READING: COMPREHENSION
Lesson 17: Nonfiction
• **Page 284**
- **A.** C
- **1.** D
- **2.** G
- **3.** D

READING: COMPREHENSION
Lesson 18: Nonfiction
• **Pages 285–286**
- **A.** D
- **1.** B
- **2.** F
- **3.** C
- **4.** F
- **5.** C
- **6.** G

READING: COMPREHENSION
Lesson 19: Nonfiction
Pages 287–288
B

- **4.** J
- **5.** D
- **6.** F

READING: COMPREHENSION
SAMPLE TEST
• **Pages 289–294**
- **A.** A
- **1.** C
- **2.** J
- **3.** A
- **4.** J
- **5.** C
- **6.** F
- **7.** B
- **8.** H
- **9.** A
- **10.** F
- **11.** C
- **12.** G
- **13.** A
- **14.** F
- **15.** D
- **16.** J
- **17.** D

READING: READING
PRACTICE TEST
Part 1: Vocabulary
• **Pages 296–299**
- **A.** B
- **B.** H
- **1.** A
- **2.** J
- **3.** C
- **4.** F
- **5.** B
- **6.** F
- **7.** D
- **8.** G
- **9.** A
- **10.** G
- **11.** C
- **12.** F
- **13.** B
- **14.** H
- **15.** A
- **16.** J
- **17.** D
- **18.** J
- **19.** B
- **20.** J
- **21.** C
- **22.** J
- **23.** C
- **24.** F
- **25.** A
- **26.** H
- **27.** B

- **28.** F
- **29.** C
- **30.** G
- **31.** A
- **32.** J
- **33.** C

Part 2: Fiction
• **Pages 300–303**
- **A.** A
- **1.** C
- **2.** H
- **3.** B
- **4.** J
- **5.** B
- **6.** H
- **7.** A
- **8.** H
- **9.** D
- **10.** G
- **11.** B
- **12.** H

Part 3: Nonfiction
• **Pages 304–308**
- **A.** D
- **1.** C
- **2.** J
- **3.** B
- **4.** J
- **5.** A
- **6.** F
- **7.** C
- **8.** J
- **9.** D
- **10.** G
- **11.** D
- **12.** H
- **13.** C
- **14.** G
- **15.** A

Answer Key

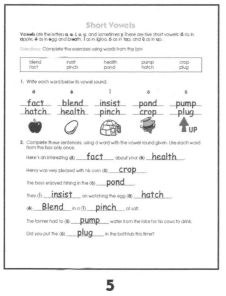

Short Vowels

Vowels are the letters a, e, i, o, u, and sometimes y. There are five short vowels: ă as in apple, ĕ as in egg and breath, ĭ as in igloo, ŏ as in top, and ŭ as in up.

Directions: Complete the exercises using words from the box.

| blend | insist | health | pump | crop |
| fact | pinch | pond | hatch | plug |

1. Write each word below its vowel sound.

ă	ĕ	ĭ	ŏ	ŭ
fact	blend	insist	pond	pump
hatch	health	pinch	crop	plug

2. Complete these sentences, using a word with the vowel sound given. Use each word from the box only once.

Here's an interesting (ă) **fact** about your (ĕ) **health**.

Henry was very pleased with his corn (ŏ) **crop**.

The boys enjoyed fishing in the (ŏ) **pond**.

They (ĭ) **insist** on watching the egg (ă) **hatch**.

(ĕ) **Blend** in a (ĭ) **pinch** of salt.

The farmer had to (ŭ) **pump** water from the lake for his cows to drink.

Did you put the (ŭ) **plug** in the bathtub this time?

5

Short Vowels

Directions: Read the words. After each, write the correct vowel sound. Underline the letter or letters that spell the sound in the word. The first one has been done for you.

Word	Vowel		Word	Vowel
1. struck	u		9. breath	e
2. scramble	a		10. edge	e
3. strong	o		11. kick	i
4. chill	i		12. stop	o
5. thud	u		13. quiz	i
6. dread	e		14. brush	u
7. plunge	u		15. crash	a
8. mask	a		16. dodge	o

Directions: List four words (nouns and verbs) with short vowel sounds. Then, write two sentences using the words.

Example: Ann, can, hand, Pam
Ann can give Pam a hand.

Answers will vary.

1. **Sentences will vary.**

2. _____

6

Listening for Vowels

Directions: Circle the word in each row with the same vowel sound as the first word. The first one has been done for you.

blend	twig	brand	(fed)	bleed
fact	first	shell	(bad)	bead
plug	card	steal	(stuff)	plan
pinch	(kiss)	reach	ripe	come
health	dear	bath	tap	(head)
crop	hope	(stock)	drip	strap

Directions: Write the words from the box that answer the questions.

| blend | insist | health | pump | crop | fact | pinch | fond | hatch | plug |

1. Which two words have the same vowel sound as the first vowel in **bundle**?
   pump **plug**

2. Which two words have the same vowel sound as the first vowel in **bottle**?
   crop **fond**

3. Which two words have the same vowel sound as the first vowel in **wilderness**?
   insist **pinch**

4. Which two words have the same vowel sound as the first vowel in **manner**?
   fact **hatch**

5. Which two words have the same vowel sound as the first vowel in **measure**?
   blend **health**

7

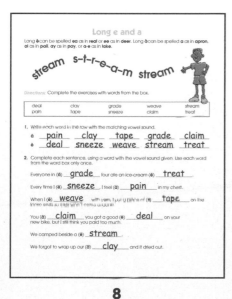

Long e and a

Long ē can be spelled ea as in real or ee as in deer. Long ā can be spelled a as in apron, ai as in pail, ay as in pay, or a-e as in lake.

stream s-t-r-e-a-m stream

Directions: Complete the exercises with words from the box.

| deal | clay | grade | weave | stream |
| pain | tape | sneeze | claim | treat |

1. Write each word in the row with the matching vowel sound.

| ā | pain | clay | tape | grade | claim |
| ē | deal | sneeze | weave | stream | treat |

2. Complete each sentence, using a word with the vowel sound given. Use each word from the word box only once.

Everyone in (ā) **grade** four ate an ice-cream (ē) **treat**.

Every time I (ē) **sneeze** I feel a **pain** in my chest.

When I (ē) **weave** with yarn, I put a piece of (ā) **tape** on the loose ends so they won't come undone.

You (ā) **claim** you got a good (ē) **deal** on your new bike, but I still think you paid too much.

We camped beside a (ē) **stream**.

We forgot to wrap up our (ā) **clay** and it dried out.

8

Long e and a

When a vowel is long, it sounds the same as its letter name.

Examples: Long ē as in treat, eel, complete.
Long ā as in ape, trail, say, apron.

Directions: Read the words. After each word, write the correct vowel sound. Underline the letter or letters that spell the sound in the word. The first one has been done for you.

Word	Vowel		Word	Vowel
1. speech	e		9. plate	a
2. grain	a		10. breeze	e
3. deal	e		11. whale	a
4. baste	a		12. clay	a
5. teach	e		13. veal	e
6. waiting	a		14. apron	a
7. cleaning	e		15. raining	a
8. crane	a		16. freeze	e

Directions: Choose one long vowel sound. On another sheet of paper, list six words (nouns and verbs) that have that sound. Below, write two sentences using the words.

Example: freeze, teaches, breeze, speech, keep, Eve

Eve teaches speech in the breeze.
Sentences will vary.

9

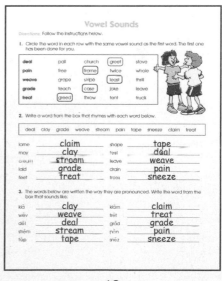

Vowel Sounds

Directions: Follow the instructions below.

1. Circle the word in each row with the same vowel sound as the first word. The first one has been done for you.

deal	pail	church	(greet)	stove
pain	free	(frame)	twice	whole
weave	grape	stripe	(least)	thrill
grade	teach	(face)	joke	leave
treat	(greed)	throw	tent	truck

2. Write a word from the box that rhymes with each word below.

| deal | clay | grade | weave | stream | pain | tape | sneeze | claim | treat |

lame	**claim**	shape	**tape**
may	**clay**	feel	**deal**
cream	**stream**	leave	**weave**
laid	**grade**	drain	**pain**
feet	**treat**	froze	**sneeze**

3. The words below are written the way they are pronounced. Write the word from the box that sounds like:

klā	**clay**	klām	**claim**
wēv	**weave**	trēt	**treat**
dēl	**deal**	grād	**grade**
strēm	**stream**	pān	**pain**
tāp	**tape**	snēz	**sneeze**

10

GRADE 4

I. Reading
  A. Directions
  B. Sequencing
  C. Main Idea
II. Writing
  A. Capitalization
  B. Proofreading

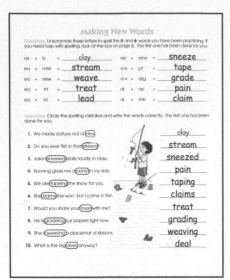

Making New Words

Directions: Unscramble these letters to spell the ā and ē words you have been practicing. If you need help with spelling, look at the box on page 8. The first one has been done for you.

ay + lc =	**clay**	ee + zsne =	**sneeze**	
ea + mtrs =	**stream**	a-e + pt =	**tape**	
ea + vew =	**weave**	a-e + drg =	**grade**	
ea + rtt =	**treat**	ai + np =	**pain**	
ea + ld =	**lead**	ai + mlc =	**claim**	

Directions: Circle the spelling mistakes and write the words correctly. The first one has been done for you.

1. We made statues out of clay. — clay
2. Do you ever fish in that stream? — stream
3. Jason sneezed really loudly in class. — sneezed
4. Running gives me a pane in my side. — pain
5. We are tapeing the show for you. — taping
6. She klaims she won, but I came in first. — claims
7. Would you share your treet with me? — treat
8. He is gradeing our papers right now. — grading
9. She is weeving a placemat of ribbons. — weaving
10. What is the big deel anyway? — deal

11

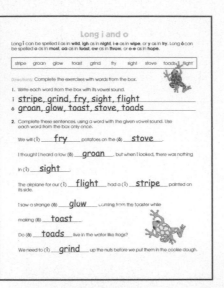

Long i and o

Long ī can be spelled **i** as in **wild**, **igh** as in **night**, **i-e** as in **wipe**, or **y** as in **try**. Long ō can be spelled **o** as in **most**, **oa** as in **toast**, **ow** as in **throw**, or **o-e** as in **hope**.

stripe	groan	glow	toast	grind	fry	sight	stove	toads	flight

Directions: Complete the exercises with words from the box.

1. Write each word from the box with its vowel sound.

ī   stripe, grind, fry, sight, flight
ō   groan, glow, toast, stove, toads

2. Complete these sentences, using a word with the given vowel sound. Use each word from the box only once.

We will (ī) **fry** potatoes on the (ō) **stove**.

I thought I heard a low (ō) **groan**, but when I looked, there was nothing in (ī) **sight**.

The airplane for our (ī) **flight** had a (ī) **stripe** painted on its side.

I saw a strange (ō) **glow** coming from the toaster while making (ō) **toast**.

Do (ō) **toads** live in the water like frogs?

We need to (ī) **grind** up the nuts before we put them in the cookie dough.

12

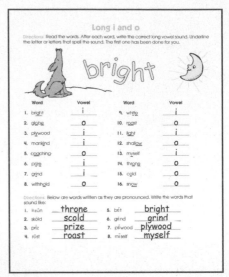

Long i and o

Directions: Read the words. After each word, write the correct long vowel sound. Underline the letter or letters that spell the sound. The first one has been done for you.

bright

	Word	Vowel		Word	Vowel
1.	bright	i	9.	white	i
2.	slight	o	10.	roast	o
3.	plywood	i	11.	light	o
4.	mankind	i	12.	shallow	o
5.	coaching	o	13.	myself	i
6.	prize	i	14.	throng	o
7.	grind	i	15.	cold	o
8.	withhold	o	16.	snow	o

Directions: Below are words written as they are pronounced. Write the words that sound like:

1. thrōn — **throne**   5. brīt — **bright**
2. skōld — **scold**   6. grīnd — **grind**
3. prīz — **prize**   7. plīwood — **plywood**
4. rōst — **roast**   8. mīself — **myself**

13

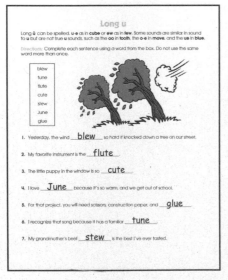

Long u

Long ū can be spelled **u-e** as in **cube** or **ew** as in **few**. Some sounds are similar in sound to **u** but are not true **u** sounds, such as the **oo** in **tooth**, the **o-e** in **move**, and the **ue** in **blue**.

Directions: Complete each sentence using a word from the box. Do not use the same word more than once.

| blew |
| tune |
| flute |
| cute |
| stew |
| June |
| glue |

1. Yesterday, the wind **blew** so hard it knocked down a tree on our street.
2. My favorite instrument is the **flute**.
3. The little puppy in the window is so **cute**.
4. I love **June** because it's so warm, and we get out of school.
5. For that project, you will need scissors, construction paper, and **glue**.
6. I recognize that song because it has a familiar **tune**.
7. My grandmother's beef **stew** is the best I've ever tasted.

14

The Long and Short of It

Directions: Fill in the circle next to the word that has the same vowel sound as the first word in the row.

1. shop	● lot	○ should	○ show	○ load
2. huge	○ bug	○ team	○ bib	● suit
3. seal	○ mice	● meet	○ whole	○ side
4. pin	○ pine	○ pan	● till	○ slide
5. lock	○ luck	● pot	○ cloak	○ load
6. peg	○ sale	○ bead	● bed	○ raid
7. ran	○ rain	○ sit	● pat	○ race
8. mile	○ bee	○ mean	○ moan	● mine
9. fox	● rock	○ duck	○ axe	○ toad
10. dime	○ dim	● tile	○ dip	○ deep
11. doe	○ wave	○ hot	○ low	● dot
12. us	● bun	○ use	○ fuse	○ box
13. ride	○ rain	○ road	● pie	○ rip
14. sit	○ map	○ find	○ ties	● fill
15. bone	○ time	● soap	○ band	○ bond
16. nuts	● bus	○ let	○ sand	○ tune
17. jet	○ jeans	● bean	○ red	○ jut
18. paid	○ pad	● main	○ lad	○ lied
19. bell	○ tall	○ ball	○ bead	● fell
20. ape	● pay	○ cap	○ tap	○ tie

15

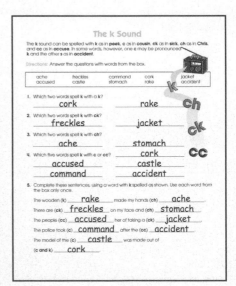

The k Sound

The **k** sound can be spelled with **k** as in **peek**, **c** as in **cousin**, **ck** as in **sick**, **ch** as in **Chris**, and **cc** as in **accuse**. In some words, however, one **c** may be pronounced **k** and the other **s** as in **accident**.

Directions: Answer the questions with words from the box.

ache	freckles	command	cork
accused	castle	stomach	rake
			jacket accident

1. Which two words spell k with a k?
cork   **rake**

2. Which two words spell k with ck?
freckles   **jacket**

3. Which two words spell k with ch?
ache   **stomach**

4. Which five words spell k with c or cc?
accused   **cork**
castle
command   **accident**

5. Complete these sentences, using a word with k spelled as shown. Use each word from the box only once.

The wooden (k) **rake** made my hands (ch) **ache**.

There are (ck) **freckles** on my face and (ch) **stomach**.

The people (cc) **accused** her of taking a (ck) **jacket**.

The police took (c) **command** after the (cc) **accident**.

The model of the (c) **castle** was made out of (c and k) **cork**.

16

The f Sound

The f sound can be spelled with **f** as in **fun**, **gh** as in **laugh**, or **ph** as in **phone**.

Directions: Answer the questions with words from the box.

| fuss | paragraph | phone | friendship | freedom |
| defend | flood | alphabet | rough | laughter |

1. Which three words spell f with **ph**?
   paragraph   phone   alphabet
2. Which two words spell f with **gh**?
   rough   laughter
3. Which five words spell f with an **f**?
   fuss   defend   flood
   friendship   freedom
4. Complete these sentences, using a word with f spelled as shown. Use each word from the box only once.

   I don't know why my teacher makes so much (f) **fuss** over writing a (ph) **paragraph**.

   A (f) **friendship** can help you through (gh) **rough** times.

   The soldiers will (f) **defend** our (f) **freedom**.

   Can you say the (ph) **alphabet** backwards?

   When I answered the (ph) **phone**, all I could hear was (gh) **laughter**.

   If it keeps raining, we'll have a (f) **flood**.

17

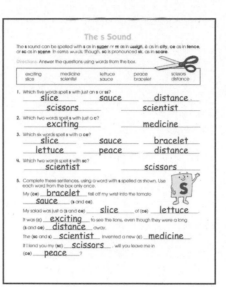

The s Sound

The s sound can be spelled with **s** as in **super**, **ss** as in **assign**, **c** as in **city**, **ce** as in **fence**, or **sc** as in **scene**. In some words, though, **sc** is pronounced **sk**, as in **scare**.

Directions: Answer the questions using words from the box.

| exciting | medicine | lettuce | peace | scissors |
| slice | scientist | sauce | bracelet | distance |

1. Which five words spell s with just an **s** or **ss**?
   slice   sauce   distance
   scissors   scientist
2. Which two words spell s with just a **c**?
   exciting   medicine
3. Which six words spell s with a **ce**?
   slice   sauce   bracelet
   lettuce   peace   distance
4. Which two words spell s with **sc**?
   scientist   scissors
5. Complete these sentences, using a word with s spelled as shown. Use each word from the box only once.

   My (ce) **bracelet** fell off my wrist into the tomato sauce **sauce**.

   My salad was just a (s and ce) **slice** of (ce) **lettuce**.

   It was (c) **exciting** to see the lions, even though they were a long (s and ce) **distance** away.

   The (sc and s) **scientist** invented a new (c) **medicine**.

   If I lend you my (sc) **scissors**, will you leave me in (ce) **peace**?

18

Syllables

A **syllable** is a word—or part of a word—with only one vowel sound. Some words have just one syllable, such as **cat**, **dog**, and **house**. Some words have two syllables, such as **in-sist** and **be-fore**. Some words have three syllables, such as **re-mem-ber**; four syllables, such as **un-der-stand-ing**; or more. Often words are easier to spell if you know how many syllables they have.

Syl-la-bles

Directions: Write the number of syllables in each word below.

	Word	Syllables		Word	Syllables
1.	amphibian	4	11.	want	1
2.	liter	2	12.	communication	5
3.	guild	1	13.	pedestrian	4
4.	chili	2	14.	kilo	2
5.	vegetarian	5	15.	autumn	2
6.	comedian	4	16.	dinosaur	3
7.	warm	1	17.	grammar	2
8.	piano	3	18.	dry	1
9.	barbarian	4	19.	solar	2
10.	chef	1	20.	wild	1

Directions: Next to each number, write words with the same number of syllables.

1 _____
2 _____
3 _____   Answers will vary.
4 _____
5 _____

19

Syllables

Directions: Write each word from the box next to the number that shows how many syllables it has.

| fuss | paragraph | phone | friendship | freedom |
| defend | flood | alphabet | rough | laughter |

One: fuss   flood   phone   rough
Two: defend   friendship   freedom   laughter
Three: paragraph   alphabet

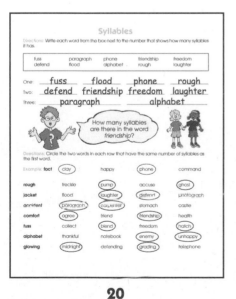

How many syllables are there in the word friendship?

Directions: Circle the two words in each row that have the same number of syllables as the first word.

Example: **fact**   (clay)   happy   (phone)   command

rough	freckle	(pump)	accuse	(ghost)
jacket	flood	(laughter)	(defent)	photograph
accident	(paragraph)	(carpenter)	stomach	castle
comfort	(agree)	friend	(friendship)	health
fuss	collect	(blend)	freedom	(hatch)
alphabet	thankful	notebook	(enemy)	(unhappy)
glowing	(midnight)	defending	(grading)	telephone

20

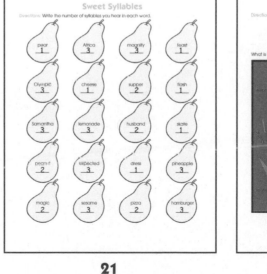

Sweet Syllables

Directions: Write the number of syllables you hear in each word.

pear 1	Africa 3	magnify 3	feast 1
Olympic 3	cheese 1	supper 2	flash 1
Samantha 3	lemonade 3	husband 2	skate 1
peanut 2	expected 3	dress 1	pineapple 3
magic 2	sesame 3	pizza 2	hamburger 3

21

Syllables

Directions: Color the spaces for each word:
green if the word has 4 syllables
blue if the word has 3 syllables
brown if the word has 2 syllables
red if the word has 1 syllable

What is it? _____

22

I. Reading
  A. Directions
  B. Sequencing
  C. Main Idea
II. Writing
  A. Capitalization
  B. Proofreading

Synonyms

Synonyms are words that mean the **same** thing.
Big and **huge** are **synonyms**.
Tiny and **small** are synonyms.

Directions: Circle the synonym for each word.

ugly	humbly	hasty	homely	hosiery
mean	vicious	vigorous	various	valiant
kind	generate	generous	genius	general
beautiful	eloquent	elevate	element	elegant

Write a paragraph using the four words you circled.

Answers will vary.

23

Synonyms

Directions: Write a synonym for each word from the word box.

yell	under	small
smile	sick	big
close	help	start
stay	shy	talk
stop	hurry	fix

1. timid — shy
2. large — big
3. rush — hurry
4. ill — sick
5. tiny — small
6. repair — fix
7. scream — yell
8. begin — start
9. grin — smile
10. aid — help
11. remain — stay
12. below — under
13. halt — stop
14. speak — talk
15. shut — close

24

Antonyms

Antonyms are words that mean the **opposite**.
Big and **small** are **antonyms**.
Hot and **cold** are **antonyms**.

Directions: Look at the picture and read the sentence. Circle the word that does **not** make sense. Then, write the word that would make the sentence true.

1. Pam is surprised because there is (something) in the box.
nothing — nothing everything

2. The plane will (leave) at one o'clock.
arrive — runway arrive

3. Tim doesn't know that there is a bee on the (front) of his shirt.
back — sleeve back

4. When you set the table, place the fork on the (right) side of the plate.
left — left same

5. Kim is (sad) because she found the missing bunny.
happy — tired happy

6. He stayed in bed because he was (well).
sick — sick young

25

Antonyms

Directions: Circle the pair of antonyms in each box. Complete each sentence with one of the circled words.

| sweet | (quiet) | (noisy) | fast |

1. The blowing horns were **noisy**
2. It was **quiet** in the library.

| (rough) | empty | (smooth) | straight |

3. The cat's fur felt **smooth**
4. The sandpaper was **rough**

| close | (wrong) | near | (right) |

5. Never drive the **wrong** way on a one-way street.
6. Jan has the **right** answer.

| (bought) | decorated | sent | (sold) |

7. I **sold** my old bike when I outgrew it.
8. Mom **bought** me a warmer jacket.

| laugh | sleepy | (lose) | (find) |

9. Did you **find** the key I lost?
10. In a strange place, it's easy to **lose** your way.

| (break) | own | hurt | (repair) |

11. A flying ball might **break** a window.
12. He needed tools to **repair** the car.

26

Homophones

Homophones are two words that sound the same, have different meanings, and are usually spelled differently.

Example: write and **right**

Directions: Write the correct homophone in each sentence below.

weight — how heavy something is
wait — to be patient

threw — tossed
through — passing between

steal — to take something that doesn't belong to you
steel — a heavy metal

1. The bands marched **through** the streets lined with many cheering people.
2. **Wait** for me by the flagpole.
3. One of our strict rules at school is: Never **steal** from another person.
4. Could you estimate the **weight** of this bowling ball?
5. The bleachers have **steel** rods on both ends and in the middle.
6. He walked in the door and **threw** his jacket down.

27

Homophones

Directions: Write the correct homophone in each sentence below.

cent — a coin having the value of one penny
scent — odor or aroma

chews — grinds with the teeth
choose — to select

course — the path along which something moves
coarse — rough in texture

heard — received sounds in the ear
herd — a group of animals

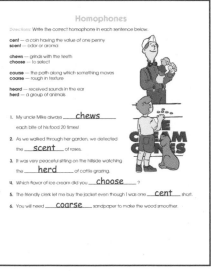

1. My uncle Mike always **chews** each bite of his food 20 times!
2. As we walked through her garden, we detected the **scent** of roses.
3. It was very peaceful sitting on the hillside watching the **herd** of cattle grazing.
4. Which flavor of ice cream did you **choose** ?
5. The friendly clerk let me buy the jacket even though I was one **cent** short.
6. You will need **coarse** sandpaper to make the wood smoother.

28

GRADE
4

I. Reading
  A. Directions
  B. Sequencing
  C. Main Idea
II. Writing
  A. Capitalization
  B. Proofreading

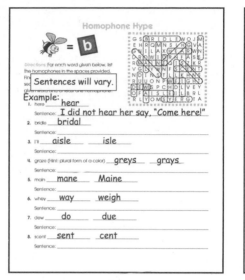

Homophone Hype

Directions: For each word given below, list the homophones in the spaces provided.

Sentences will vary.

Example:

1. here _____hear_____
   Sentence: _I did not hear her say, "Come here!"_

2. bridle _____bridal_____
   Sentence: _____

3. I'll _____aisle_____ _____isle_____
   Sentence: _____

4. graze (Hint: plural form of a color) _____greys_____ _____grays_____
   Sentence: _____

5. main _____mane_____ _____Maine_____
   Sentence: _____

6. whey _____way_____ _____weigh_____
   Sentence: _____

7. dew _____do_____ _____due_____
   Sentence: _____

8. scent _____sent_____ _____cent_____
   Sentence: _____

29

Stop for Directions

Directions: Follow the directions to draw a picture in the rectangle.

1. Draw a yellow house in the middle of the rectangle.
2. On the right side of the house, draw a tree.
3. Draw seven red apples growing on the tree.
4. Draw a big yellow sun shining in the upper right-hand corner.
5. Draw two red birds flying in the sky over the house.
6. Draw a black cat sitting in front of the house.
7. Underneath the apple tree, draw a patch of green grass and three purple tulips.
8. To the left of the house, draw a boy wearing a green baseball cap.

30

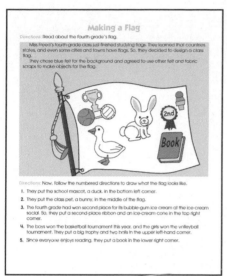

Making a Flag

Directions: Read about the fourth-grade's flag.

Miss Freed's fourth-grade class just finished studying flags. They learned that countries, states, and even some cities and towns have flags. So, they decided to design a class flag.

They chose blue felt for the background and agreed to use other felt and fabric scraps to make objects for the flag.

Directions: Now, follow the numbered directions to draw what the flag looks like.

1. They put the school mascot, a duck, in the bottom left corner.
2. They put the class pet, a bunny, in the middle of the flag.
3. The fourth grade had won second place for its bubble-gum ice cream at the ice-cream social. So, they put a second-place ribbon and an ice-cream cone in the top right corner.
4. The boys won the basketball tournament this year, and the girls won the volleyball tournament. They put a big trophy and two balls in the upper left-hand corner.
5. Since everyone enjoys reading, they put a book in the lower right corner.

31

GRADE 4

I. Reading
   A. Directions
   B. Sequencing
   C. Main Idea
II. Writing
   A. Capitalization
   B. Proofreading

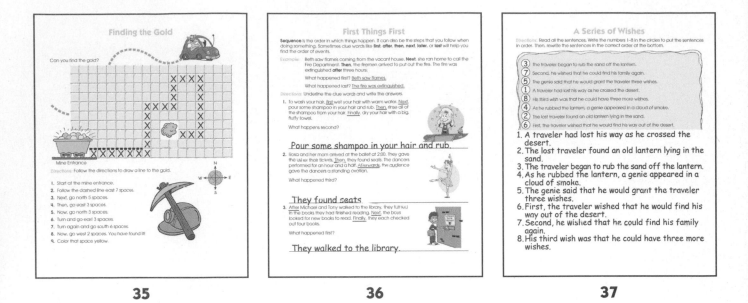

Finding the Gold

Can you find the gold?

Mine Entrance

Directions: Follow the directions to draw a line to the gold.

1. Start at the mine entrance.
2. Follow the dashed line east 7 spaces.
3. Next, go north 5 spaces.
4. Then, go east 3 spaces.
5. Now, go north 3 spaces.
6. Turn and go east 3 spaces.
7. Turn again and go south 6 spaces.
8. Now, go west 2 spaces. You have found it!
9. Color that space yellow.

35

First Things First

Sequence is the order in which things happen. It can also be the steps that you follow when doing something. Sometimes clue words like **first, after, then, next, later,** or **last** will help you find the order of events.

Example: Beth saw flames coming from the vacant house. **Next,** she ran home to call the Fire Department. **Then,** the firemen arrived to put out the fire. The fire was extinguished **after** three hours.

What happened first? Beth saw flames.

What happened last? The fire was extinguished.

Directions: Underline the clue words and write the answers.

1. To wash your hair, first wet your hair with warm water. Next, pour some shampoo in your hair and rub. Then, rinse all of the shampoo from your hair. Finally, dry your hair with a big, fluffy towel.

What happens second?

Pour some shampoo in your hair and rub.

2. Rosa and her mom arrived at the ballet at 2:00. They gave the usher their tickets. Then, they found seats. The dancers performed for an hour and a half. Afterwards, the audience gave the dancers a standing ovation.

What happened third?

They found seats

3. After Michael and Tony walked to the library, they turned in the books they had finished reading. Next, the boys looked for new books to read. Finally, they each checked out four books.

What happened first?

They walked to the library.

36

A Series of Wishes

Directions: Read all the sentences. Write the numbers 1–8 in the circles to put the sentences in order. Then, rewrite the sentences in the correct order at the bottom.

(3) The traveler began to rub the sand off the lantern.
(7) Second, he wished that he could find his family again.
(5) The genie said that he would grant the traveler three wishes.
(1) A traveler had lost his way as he crossed the desert.
(8) His third wish was that he could have three more wishes.
(4) As he rubbed the lantern, a genie appeared in a cloud of smoke.
(2) The lost traveler found an old lantern lying in the sand.
(6) First, the traveler wished that he would find his way out of the desert.

1. A traveler had lost his way as he crossed the desert.
2. The lost traveler found an old lantern lying in the sand.
3. The traveler began to rub the sand off the lantern.
4. As he rubbed the lantern, a genie appeared in a cloud of smoke.
5. The genie said that he would grant the traveler three wishes.
6. First, the traveler wished that he would find his way out of the desert.
7. Second, he wished that he could find his family again.
8. His third wish was that he could have three more wishes.

37

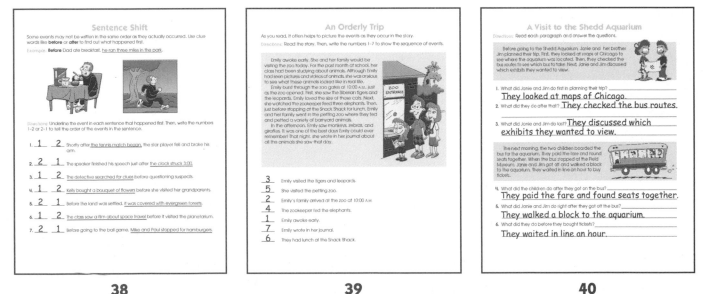

Sentence Shift

Some events may not be written in the same order as they actually occurred. Use clue words like **before** or **after** to find out what happened first.

Example: Before Dad ate breakfast, he ran three miles in the park.

Directions: Underline the event in each sentence that happened first. Then, write the numbers 1–2 or 2–1 to tell the order of the events in the sentence.

1. **1 2** Shortly after the tennis match began, the star player fell and broke his arm.
2. **2 1** The speaker finished his speech just after the clock struck 3:00.
3. **1 2** The detective searched for clues before questioning suspects.
4. **1 2** Kelly bought a bouquet of flowers before she visited her grandparents.
5. **2 1** Before the land was settled, it was covered with evergreen forests.
6. **1 2** The class saw a film about space travel before it visited the planetarium.
7. **2 1** Before going to the ball game, Mike and Paul stopped for hamburgers.

38

An Orderly Trip

As you read, it often helps to picture the events as they occur in the story.

Directions: Read the story. Then, write the numbers 1–7 to show the sequence of events.

Emily awoke early. She and her family would be visiting the zoo today. For the past month at school, her class had been studying about animals. Although Emily had seen pictures and videos of animals, she was anxious to see what these animals looked like in real life.

Emily burst through the zoo gates at 10:00 A.M. just as the zoo opened. First, she saw the Siberian tigers and the leopards. Emily loved the size of those cats. Next, she watched the zookeeper feed three elephants. Then, just before stopping at the Snack Shack for lunch, Emily and her family went to the petting zoo where they fed and petted a variety of barnyard animals.

In the afternoon, Emily saw monkeys, zebras, and giraffes. It was one of the best days Emily could ever remember! That night, she wrote in her journal about all the animals she saw that day.

3 Emily visited the tigers and leopards.
5 She visited the petting zoo.
2 Emily's family arrived at the zoo at 10:00 A.M.
4 The zookeeper fed the elephants.
1 Emily awoke early.
7 Emily wrote in her journal.
6 They had lunch at the Snack Shack.

39

A Visit to the Shedd Aquarium

Directions: Read each paragraph and answer the questions.

Before going to the Shedd Aquarium, Janie and her brother Jim planned their trip. First, they looked at maps of Chicago to see where the aquarium was located. Then, they checked the bus routes to see which bus to take. Next, Janie and Jim discussed which exhibits they wanted to view.

1. What did Janie and Jim do first in planning their trip?
They looked at maps of Chicago.

2. What did they do after that? They checked the bus routes.

3. What did Janie and Jim do last? They discussed which exhibits they wanted to view.

The next morning, the two children boarded the bus for the aquarium. They paid the fare and found seats together. When the bus stopped at the Field Museum, Janie and Jim got off and walked a block to the aquarium. They waited in line an hour to buy tickets.

4. What did the children do after they got on the bus?
They paid the fare and found seats together.

5. What did Janie and Jim do right after they got off the bus?
They walked a block to the aquarium.

6. What did they do before they bought tickets?
They waited in line an hour.

40

GRADE 4

I. Reading
   A. Directions
   B. Sequencing
   C. Main Idea
II. Writing
   A. Capitalization
   B. Proofreading

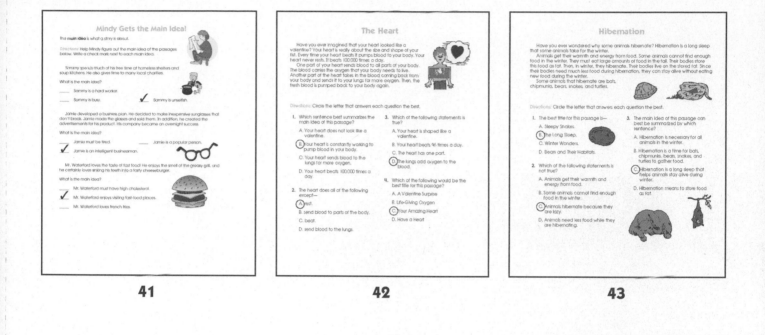

Mindy Gets the Main Idea!

The **main idea** is what a story is about.

Directions: Help Mindy figure out the main idea of the passages below. Write a check mark next to each main idea.

Sammy spends much of his free time at homeless shelters and soup kitchens. He also gives time to many local charities.

What is the main idea?

_____ Sammy is a hard worker.

_____ Sammy is busy.   ✓ Sammy is unselfish.

Jamie developed a business plan. He decided to make inexpensive sunglasses that don't break. Jamie made the glasses and sold them. In addition, he created the advertisements for his product. His company became an overnight success.

What is the main idea?

_____ Jamie must be tired.   _____ Jamie is a popular person.

✓ Jamie is an intelligent businessman.

Mr. Waterford loves the taste of fast food! He enjoys the smell of the greasy grill, and he certainly loves sinking his teeth into a tasty cheeseburger.

What is the main idea?

_____ Mr. Waterford must have high cholesterol.

✓ Mr. Waterford enjoys visiting fast-food places.

_____ Mr. Waterford loves french fries.

41

The Heart

Have you ever imagined that your heart looked like a valentine? Your heart is really about the size and shape of your fist. Every time your heart beats it pumps blood to your body. Your heart never rests. It beats 100,000 times a day.

One part of your heart sends blood to all parts of your body. The blood carries the oxygen that your body needs to live. Another part of the heart takes in the blood coming back from your body and sends it to your lungs for more oxygen. Then, the fresh blood is pumped back to your body again.

Directions: Circle the letter that answers each question the best.

1. Which sentence best summarizes the main idea of this passage?
   A. Your heart does not look like a valentine.
   B. Your heart is constantly working to pump blood in your body.
   C. Your heart sends blood to the lungs for more oxygen.
   D. Your heart beats 100,000 times a day.

2. The heart does all of the following except—
   A. rest.
   B. send blood to parts of the body.
   C. beat.
   D. send blood to the lungs.

3. Which of the following statements is true?
   A. Your heart is shaped like a valentine.
   B. Your heart beats 96 times a day.
   C. The heart has one part.
   D. The lungs add oxygen to the blood.

4. Which of the following would be the best title for this passage?
   A. A Valentine Surprise
   B. Life-Giving Oxygen
   C. Your Amazing Heart
   D. Have a Heart

42

Hibernation

Have you ever wondered why some animals hibernate? Hibernation is a long sleep that some animals take for the winter.

Animals get their warmth and energy from food. Some animals cannot find enough food in the winter. They must eat large amounts of food in the fall. Their bodies store this food as fat. Then, in winter, they hibernate. Their bodies live on the stored fat. Since their bodies need much less food during hibernation, they can stay alive without eating new food during the winter.

Some animals that hibernate are bats, chipmunks, bears, snakes, and turtles.

Directions: Circle the letter that answers each question the best.

1. The best title for this passage is—
   A. Sleepy Snakes.
   B. The Long Sleep.
   C. Winter Wonders.
   D. Bears and Their Habitats.

2. Which of the following statements is not true?
   A. Animals get their warmth and energy from food.
   B. Some animals cannot find enough food in the winter.
   C. Animals hibernate because they are lazy.
   D. Animals need less food while they are hibernating.

3. The main idea of this passage can best be summarized by which sentence?
   A. Hibernation is necessary for all animals in the winter.
   B. Hibernation is a time for bats, chipmunks, bears, snakes, and turtles to gather food.
   C. Hibernation is a long sleep that helps animals stay alive during winter.
   D. Hibernation means to store food as fat.

43

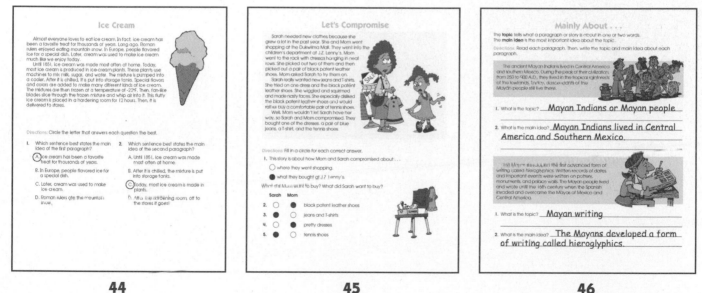

Ice Cream

Almost everyone loves to eat ice cream. In fact, ice cream has been a favorite treat for thousands of years. Long ago, Roman rulers enjoyed eating mountain snow. In Europe, people flavored ice for a special dish. Later, cream was used to make ice cream much like we enjoy today.

Until 1851, ice cream was made most often at home. Today, most ice cream is produced in ice-cream plants. These plants use machines to mix milk, sugar, and water. The mixture is pumped into a cooler. After it is chilled, it is put into storage tanks. Special flavors and colors are added to make many different kinds of ice cream. The mixtures are then frozen at a temperature of -22F. Then, fan-like blades slice through the frozen mixture and whip air into it. This fluffy ice cream is placed in a hardening room for 12 hours. Then, it is delivered to stores.

Directions: Circle the letter that answers each question the best.

1. Which sentence best states the main idea of the first paragraph?
   A. Ice cream has been a favorite treat for thousands of years.
   B. In Europe, people flavored ice for a special dish.
   C. Later, cream was used to make ice cream.
   D. Roman rulers ate the mountain snow.

2. Which sentence best states the main idea of the second paragraph?
   A. Until 1851, ice cream was made most often at home.
   B. After it is chilled, the mixture is put into storage tanks.
   C. Today, most ice cream is made in plants.
   D. After the hardening room, off to the stores it goes!

44

Let's Compromise

Sarah needed new clothes because she grew a lot in the past year. She and Mom went shopping at the Oakwind Mall. They went into the children's department at J.Z. Lenny's. Mom went to the rack with dresses hanging in neat rows. She picked out two of them and then picked out a pair of black patent leather shoes. Mom asked Sarah to try them on.

Sarah really wanted new jeans and T-shirts. She tried on one dress and the black patent leather shoes. She wiggled and squirmed and made nasty faces. She especially disliked the black patent leather shoes and would rather buy a comfortable pair of tennis shoes.

Well, Mom wouldn't let Sarah have her way, so Sarah and Mom compromised. They bought one of the dresses, a pair of blue jeans, a T-shirt, and the tennis shoes.

Directions: Fill in a circle for each correct answer.

1. This story is about how Mom and Sarah compromised about . . .
   ○ where they went shopping.
   ● what they bought at J.Z. Lenny's.

What did Mom want to buy? What did Sarah want to buy?

	Sarah	Mom
2.	○	● black patent leather shoes
3.	●	○ jeans and T-shirts
4.	○	● pretty dresses
5.	●	○ tennis shoes

45

Mainly About . . .

The **topic** tells what a paragraph or story is about in one or two words. The **main idea** is the most important idea about the topic.

Directions: Read each paragraph. Then, write the topic and main idea about each paragraph.

The ancient Mayan Indians lived in Central America and southern Mexico. During the peak of their civilization, from 250 to 900 A.D., they lived in the tropical rainforests of the lowlands. Today, descendants of the Mayan people still live there.

1. What is the topic? **Mayan Indians or Mayan people**

2. What is the main idea? **Mayan Indians lived in Central America and Southern Mexico.**

The Mayan developed the first advanced form of writing called hieroglyphics. Written records of dates and important events were written on pottery, monuments, and palace walls. The Mayan people lived and wrote until the 16th century when the Spanish invaded and overcame the Mayas of Mexico and Central America.

1. What is the topic? **Mayan writing**

2. What is the main idea? **The Mayans developed a form of writing called hieroglyphics.**

46

GRADE 4

I. Reading
  A. Directions
  B. Sequencing
  C. Main Idea
II. Writing
  A. Capitalization
  B. Proofreading

Moon Facts

Directions: Write a word from "Origin of the Moon" on page 47 that matches each given detail.

1. **capture** — A theory that says the Moon originally had an orbit that was much like Earth's orbit.
2. **formation** — A theory that says Earth and the Moon were formed from gas and dust left by the Sun.
3. **escape** — A theory that says the Moon was pulled out of Earth by the pull from the Sun's gravity.
4. **collision** — A theory that says a piece of Earth broke off when a body from space smashed into it.
5. **bulge** — The escape theory explains that the Sun's gravity created this on one side of Earth.
6. **impact** — This word for a collision may have caused pieces of Earth to break off.
7. **formation** — Earth and the Moon were double planets in this theory.
8. **satellite** — This word describes what the Moon became after it was captured by Earth.

48

Recognizing Details: Blind Bats

Directions: Read about bats. Then, answer the questions.

Bats sleep all day because they cannot see well in the bright sunlight. They hang upside down in dark places such as barns, caves, or hollow trees. As soon as darkness begins to fall, bats wake up. They fly around easily and quickly at night.

Bats make sounds that help them fly, since they cannot see well. People cannot hear these sounds. When bats make sounds, the sounds hit objects in front of them and bounce back at them. Bats can tell if something is in their way because there is an echo. Some people say this is like a radar system!

There are many different kinds of bats. Some bats fly all night, while others fly only in the evening or the early morning.

Most bats eat mosquitoes and moths, but there are some bats that will catch fish swimming in water and eat them. Still other kinds of bats eat birds or mice. Bats that live in very hot areas eat only some parts of flowers.

Bats that live in cold areas of the country sometimes sleep all winter. That means they hibernate. Other bats that live in cold areas fly to warmer places for the winter. We call this migration.

1. Who cannot hear the sounds bats make? **people**
2. Why do bats sleep all day? **They cannot see well in bright sunlight.**
3. When do bats eat? **at night**
4. Where do bats eat only parts of flowers live? **in very hot areas**
5. Why do bats make sounds? **to tell if something is in their way**
6. What does hibernate mean? **to sleep all winter**
7. What is the main idea of this selection? **Bats are active at night because they cannot see well in bright sunlight.**
8. Do you think a bat would make a good pet? Why or why not? **Answers will vary.**

49

Recognizing Details: "Why Bear Has a Short Tail"

Some stories try to explain the reasons why certain things occur in nature.

Directions: Read the legend "Why Bear Has a Short Tail." Then, answer the questions.

Long ago, Bear had a long tail like Fox. One winter day, Bear met Fox coming out of the woods. Fox was carrying a long string of fish. He had stolen the fish, but that is not what he told Bear.

"Where did you get those fish?" asked Bear, rubbing his paws together. Bear loved fish. It was his favorite food.

"I was out fishing and caught them," replied Fox.

Bear did not know how to fish. He had only tasted fish that others gave him. He was eager to learn to catch his own.

"Please Fox, will you tell me how to fish?" asked Bear.

So, the mean old Fox said to Bear, "Cut a hole in the ice and stick your tail in the hole. It will get cold, but soon the fish will begin to bite. When you can stand it no longer, pull your tail out. It will be covered with fish!"

"Will it hurt?" asked Bear, patting his tail.

"It will hurt some," admitted Fox. "But the longer you leave your tail in the water, the more fish you will catch."

Bear did as Fox told him. He loved fish, so he left his tail in the icy water a very, very long time. The ice froze around Bear's tail. When he pulled free, his tail remained stuck in the ice. That is why bears today have short tails.

1. How does Fox get his string of fish? **He stole it.**
2. What does he tell Bear to do? **to put his tail in a hole in the ice to catch fish**
3. Why does Bear do as Fox told him? **He loves to eat fish but doesn't know how to catch them.**
4. How many fish does Bear catch? **none**
5. What happens when Bear tries to pull his tail out? **His tail remains stuck in the ice.**

50

Recognizing Details: "Why Bear Has a Short Tail"

Directions: Review the legend "Why Bear Has a Short Tail." Then, answer the questions.

1. When Bear asks Fox where he got his fish, is Fox truthful in his response? Why or why not? **No. Fox lies to trick Bear.**
2. Why does Bear want to know how to fish? **He loves to eat fish. It is his favorite food.**
3. In reality, are bears able to catch their own fish? How? **Yes, with their paws.**
4. Is Bear very smart to believe Fox? Why or why not? **No. Bear should have known Fox was sly and tricky.**
5. How would you have told Bear to catch his own fish? **Answers will vary.**
6. What is one word you would use to describe Fox? **sly, tricky, crafty** Explain your answer. **Answers will vary.**
7. What is one word you would use to describe Bear? **silly, trusting** Explain your answer. **Answers will vary.**
8. Is this story realistic? **No**
9. Could it have really happened? Explain your answer. **Answers will vary.**

51

Conclusions About Precycling

Directions: Read each sentence. Write **true** or **false** on the line.

1. Precycling is something you do before riding a bicycle. **false**
2. You have to think ahead to precycle. **true**
3. Buying in bulk means buying fattening food. **false**
4. Packaging materials can be wasteful. **true**

Answers will vary but may include:

1. What does the phrase "cleverly designed garbage" mean? **Cleverly designed is excess packaging.**
2. List some ways you can precycle. **I can buy paper that has a recycle label or buy drinks in packages I can reuse.**
3. Explain why using cloth shopping bags is a way to help save the earth. **It reduces the amount of disposable shopping bags that are used.**
4. "Precycle." is a made-up word. Tell why you think it is a good word to use. **The prefix "pre" means "before." We should think about recycling before we buy.**
5. Tell how you think precycling will help save the earth. **It will help reduce the amount of trash that goes into our landfills.**

53

A Picture Is Worth . . .

Directions: Look at the first picture. Put a check mark in the box by each sentence which seems sensible. Look at the second picture. Write six sentences that tell your conclusions about the picture.

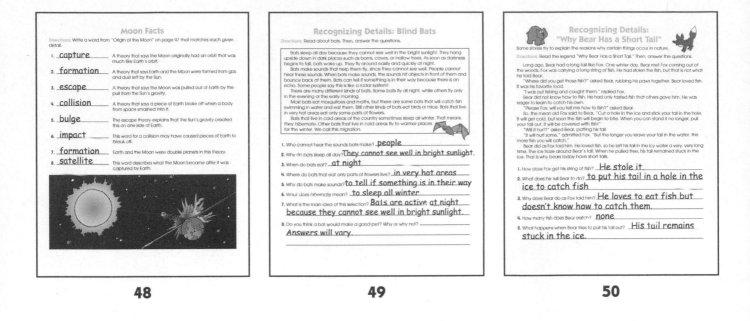

- ☑ It is a very hot day.
- ☑ The beach is a popular place to go.
- ☐ The beach is a quiet place to study.
- ☑ Some people picnic at the beach.
- ☑ A lifeguard helps protect swimmers.
- ☐ It is hard to nap on a noisy beach.
- ☐ Sailing is just for kids.
- ☑ Sailing and swimming are fun water sports.
- ☐ Every town has a beach.

Write your own conclusions: **Examples:**

1. **It is fall.**
2. **The yard needs to be raked.**
3.
4.
5.
6.

Answers will vary.

54

GRADE 4

I. Reading
 A. Directions
 B. Sequencing
 C. Main Idea
II. Writing
 A. Capitalization
 B. Proofreading

Reading Skills: Bus Schedules

Schedules are important to our daily lives. Your parents' jobs, school, even watching television—all are based on schedules. When you travel, you probably follow a schedule, too. Most forms of public transportation, such as subways, buses, and trains, run on schedules. These "timetables" tell passengers when they will leave each stop or station.

Directions: Use the following city bus schedule to answer the questions.

No. 2 Cross-Town Bus Schedule

State St. at Park Way	Oak St. at Green Ave.	Fourth St. at Ninth Ave.	Buyall Shopping Center
5:00 A.M.	5:14 A.M.	5:23 A.M.	5:30 A.M.
6:38	6:52	7:01	7:08
7:50	8:05	8:14	8:21
9:04	9:18	9:27	9:34
10:15	10:29	10:38	10:47
12:20 P.M.	12:34 P.M.	12:43 P.M.	12:50 P.M.
1:46	2:00	2:09	2:16
3:30	3:44	3:53	4:00
5:20	5:34	5:43	5:50
6:02	6:16	6:25	6:32

1. The first bus of the day leaves the State St./Park Way stop at 5 A.M. What time does the last bus of the day leave this stop? **6:02 p.m.**

2. The bus that leaves the Oak St./Green Ave. stop at 8:05 A.M. leaves the Buyall Shopping Center at what time? **8:21 a.m.**

3. What time does the first afternoon bus leave the Fourth St./Ninth Ave. stop? **12:43 p.m.**

4. How many buses each day run between the State St./Park Way stop and the Buyall Shopping Center? **10**

55

Reading Skills: Labels

Directions: You should never take any medicine without your parents' permission, but it is good to know how to read the label of a medicine bottle. Read the label to answer the questions.

Children's Cold Relief Sneezing and Runny Nose Formula

For relief of runny nose and sneezing due to common colds, hay fever, or other allergies.

Dosage:
Children under 2 years, only as directed by a physician.
Children 2 to 5 years old, 1 teaspoon.
Children 6 to 11 years old, 2 teaspoons.

All doses may be repeated every 4 to 6 hours, but not more than four doses every 24 hours.

Warning: May cause drowsiness or sleepiness. Do not give to children with heart disease. Keep this and all medicines out of reach of children.

1. How much medicine should a 5-year-old take? **1 teaspoon**
2. How often can this medicine be taken? **every 4 to 6 hours**
3. How do you know how much medicine to give a 1-year-old? **ask a physician**
4. Who should not take this medicine? **children with heart disease**

56

A Class of Its Own

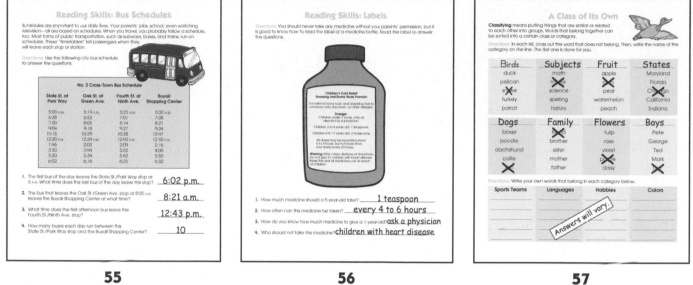

Classifying means putting things that are similar or related to each other into groups. Words that belong together can be sorted into a certain class or category.

Directions: In each list, cross out the word that does not belong. Then, write the name of the category on the line. The first one is done for you.

Birds	Subjects	Fruit	States
duck	math	apple	Maryland
pelican	~~nose~~	pear	Florida
~~snake~~	science	~~pear~~	~~Chicago~~
turkey	spelling	watermelon	California
parrot	history	peach	Indiana

Dogs	Family	Flowers	Boys
boxer	~~fox~~	tulip	Pete
poodle	brother	rose	George
dachshund	sister	violet	Ted
collie	mother	~~pine~~	Mark
	father	daisy	~~X~~

Directions: Write your own words that belong in each category below.

Sports Teams	Languages	Hobbies	Colors

Answers will vary.

57

Categorizing Books

Directions: Write the letter of the shelf on which each book belongs.

Shelf A—Mystery   Shelf B—Sports
Shelf C—Science   Shelf D—Cooking
Shelf E—Riddles and Jokes   Shelf F—Famous People

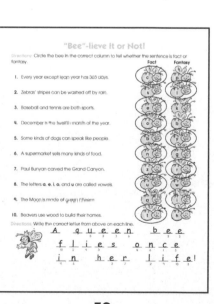

1. Planets and Their Moons — **C**
2. Great Baseball Moments — **B**
3. A Laugh a Minute — **E**
4. Great Pasta Dishes — **D**
5. Young Abe Lincoln — **F**
6. The Clue of the Broken Lock — **A**
7. How to Collect Rocks — **C**
8. Tennis Tips — **B**

Little Bonus: Write the letter of the shelf where you might find this information.

1. **D** How do you prepare a spaghetti dinner?
2. **C** How long does the Moon take to orbit Earth?
3. **E** Where does a five-hundred pound angry elephant sit?
4. **F** Which presidents once served as members of Congress?

58

"Bee"-lieve It or Not!

Directions: Circle the bee in the correct column to tell whether the sentence is fact or fantasy.

	Fact	Fantasy

1. Every year except leap year has 365 days.
2. Zebras' stripes can be washed off by rain.
3. Baseball and tennis are both sports.
4. December is the twelfth month of the year.
5. Some kinds of dogs can speak like people.
6. A supermarket sells many kinds of food.
7. Paul Bunyan carved the Grand Canyon.
8. The letters a, e, i, o, and u are called vowels.
9. The Moon is made of green cheese.
10. Beavers use wood to build their homes.

Directions: Write the correct letter from above on each line.

A q u e e n   b e e
f l i e s   o n c e
i n   h e r   l i f e!

59

Person to Person

Directions: Write a category heading for each list. Then, add an appropriate third word to each list.

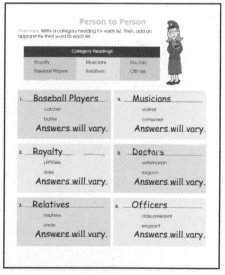

Category Headings

Royalty	Musicians	Doctors
Baseball Players	Relatives	Officers

1. **Baseball Players**
catcher
batter
Answers will vary.

4. **Musicians**
violinist
composer
Answers will vary.

2. **Royalty**
prince
duke
Answers will vary.

5. **Doctors**
veterinarian
surgeon
Answers will vary.

3. **Relatives**
nephew
uncle
Answers will vary.

6. **Officers**
class president
sergeant
Answers will vary.

60

GRADE 4

I. Reading
  A. Directions
  B. Sequencing
  C. Main Idea
II. Writing
  A. Capitalization
  B. Proofreading

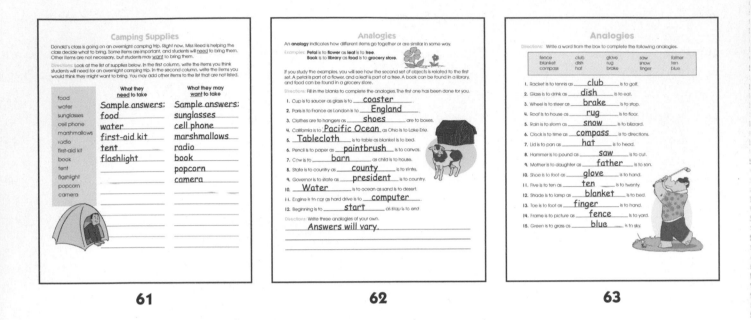

Camping Supplies (page 61)

Donald's class is going on an overnight camping trip. Right now, Miss Reed is helping the class decide what to bring. Some items are important, and students will **need** to bring them. Other items are not necessary, but students may **want** to bring them.

Directions: Look at the list of supplies below. In the first column, write the items you think students will need for an overnight camping trip. In the second column, write the items you would think they might want to bring. You may add other items to the list that are not listed.

	What they **need** to take	What they **may** want to take
food	Sample answers:	Sample answers:
water	food	sunglasses
sunglasses	water	cell phone
cell phone	first-aid kit	marshmallows
marshmallows	tent	radio
radio	flashlight	book
first-aid kit		popcorn
book		camera
tent		
flashlight		
popcorn		
camera		

Analogies (page 62)

An **analogy** indicates how different items go together or are similar in some way.

Examples: Petal is to **flower** as leaf is to **tree**.
Book is to **library** as food is to **grocery store**.

If you study the examples, you will see how the second set of objects is related to the first set. A petal is part of a flower, and a leaf is part of a tree. A book can be found in a library, and food can be found in a grocery store.

Directions: Fill in the blanks to complete the analogies. The first one has been done for you.

1. Cup is to saucer as glass is to **coaster**
2. Paris is to France as London is to **England**
3. Clothes are to hangers as **shoes** are to boxes.
4. California is to **Pacific Ocean** as Ohio is to Lake Erie.
5. **Tablecloth** is to table as blanket is to bed.
6. Pencil is to paper as **paintbrush** is to canvas.
7. Cow is to **barn** as child is to house.
8. State is to country as **county** is to states.
9. Governor is to state as **president** is to country.
10. **Water** is to ocean as sand is to desert.
11. Engine is to car as hard drive is to **computer**
12. Beginning is to **start** as stop is to end.

Directions: Write three analogies of your own.
Answers will vary.

Analogies (page 63)

Directions: Write a word from the box to complete the following analogies.

fence	club	glove	saw	father
blanket	dish	rug	snow	ten
compass	hat	brake	finger	blue

1. Racket is to tennis as **club** is to golf.
2. Glass is to drink as **dish** is to eat.
3. Wheel is to steer as **brake** is to stop.
4. Roof is to house as **rug** is to floor.
5. Rain is to storm as **snow** is to blizzard.
6. Clock is to time as **compass** is to directions.
7. Lid is to pan as **hat** is to head.
8. Hammer is to pound as **saw** is to cut.
9. Mother is to daughter as **father** is to son.
10. Shoe is to foot as **glove** is to hand.
11. Five is to ten as **ten** is to twenty.
12. Shade is to lamp as **blanket** is to bed.
13. Toe is to foot as **finger** is to hand.
14. Frame is to picture as **fence** is to yard.
15. Green is to grass as **blue** is to sky.

Figures of Speech (page 64)

A **figure of speech** can make a sentence more interesting. Here are four popular kinds of figures of speech:

Personification—gives human characteristics to things.
Example: The Sun touched us with its warm fingers.
Hyperbole—a great exaggeration.
Example: She's the happiest person in the universe.
Simile—compares two unlike things, using like or as.
Example: He is hungry as a horse.
Metaphor—suggests a comparison of two unlike things.
Example: The vacant field was a desert.

Directions: Underline each figure of speech. Write the type on each line.

1. The wind howled as the storm grew closer. — **Personification**
2. The little lady nibbled at her lunch like a bird. — **Simile**
3. Sarah's little sister is a doll in her new clothes. — **Metaphor**
4. The camp leader said he would never sleep again. — **Hyperbole**
5. The banana cream pie was heaven. — **Metaphor**
6. We were as busy as bees all day long. — **Simile**
7. His patience just flew out the window. — **Personification**
8. He said that his life was an open book. — **Metaphor**
9. The heavy fog crept slowly into shore. — **Personification**
10. The champion wrestler is as strong as an ox. — **Simile**
11. I am so full that I never want to eat again. — **Hyperbole**
12. Sometimes my memory is a blank tape. — **Metaphor**

Directions: Write four sentences that contain a figure of speech.
1. (personification)
2. (hyperbole)
3. (simile)
4. (metaphor)
Answers will vary.

Like . . . a Simile (page 65)

Directions: In the sentences below, underline the two things or persons being compared. In the blank, write **simile** or **metaphor**. Remember, a simile uses **like** or **as**; metaphors do not.

1. Angel was as mean as a wild bull. — **simile**
2. Toni and Mattie were like toast and jam. — **simile**
3. Mr. Ashby expected the students to be as busy as beavers. — **simile**
4. The pin was a masterpiece in Mattie's mind. — **metaphor**
5. The park's peacefulness was a friend to Mattie. — **metaphor**
6. The words came as slow as molasses into Mattie's mind. — **simile**
7. Mrs. Stamp's apartment was like a museum. — **simile**
8. Mrs. Benson was as happy as a lark when Mattie won the contest. — **simile**
9. Mr. Phillip's smile was a glowing beam to Mattie and Mrs. Benson. — **metaphor**
10. Mattie ran as fast as the wind to get her money. — **simile**
11. Angel's mean words cut through Charlene like glass. — **simile**
12. Mr. Bacon was a fairy godmother to Mattie. — **metaphor**
13. The gingko tree's leaves were shaped like fans. — **simile**

Directions: Complete the following sentences using similes.
1. Matt was as artistic as — **Example: Picasso**
2. Hannibal's teeth were like
3. Toni's mind
4. Mattie was
5. Mrs. Stamp
Answers will vary.

Knight in Training (page 67)

Remember that a **statement of fact** can be proven true or false. An **opinion** is what you believe or think. Use the information in the letter on page 66 to help you complete this activity.

Directions: Write **F** if the sentence is a statement of fact or **O** if it is an opinion.

F 1. Pages are young boys who serve knights.
O 2. Being a page is a hard job.
F 3. Some knights hunt with falcons.
F 4. A squire is a young man sixteen or older.
O 5. Being a squire is better than being a page.
F 6. A squire goes to battle with his knight.
O 7. Jousting is cruel to horses.
O 8. Jousting is the best kind of contest.
F 9. In jousting, a knight uses a lance to knock another knight off his horse.
O 10. All suits of armor are hot and ugly.
F 11. A knight wears armor to protect his body.
O 12. A knight's coat of arms is very beautiful.
F 13. A coat of arms helps spectators recognize the knights in armor.
F 14. Pages learn to hunt with falcons.
O 15. All squires are brave.

GRADE 4

I. Reading
  A. Directions
  B. Sequencing
  C. Main Idea
II. Writing
  A. Capitalization
  B. Proofreading

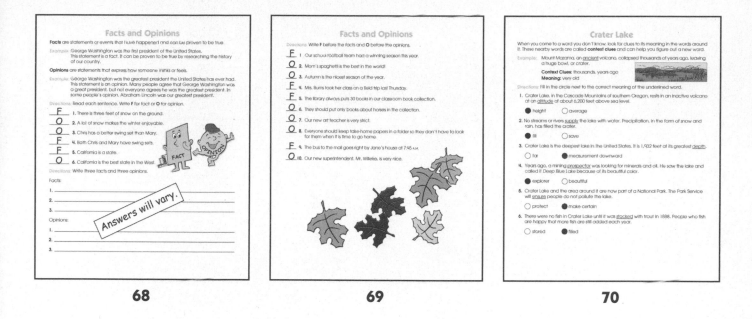

Facts and Opinions (page 68)

Facts are statements or events that have happened and can be proven to be true.

Example: George Washington was the first president of the United States. This statement is a fact. It can be proven to be true by researching the history of our country.

Opinions are statements that express how someone thinks or feels.

Example: George Washington was the greatest president the United States has ever had. This statement is an opinion. Many people agree that George Washington was a great president, but not everyone agrees he was the greatest president. In some people's opinion, Abraham Lincoln was our greatest president.

Directions: Read each sentence. Write **F** for fact or **O** for opinion.

F 1. There is three feet of snow on the ground.
O 2. A lot of snow makes the winter enjoyable.
O 3. Chris has a better swing set than Mary.
F 4. Both Chris and Mary have swing sets.
F 5. California is a state.
O 6. California is the best state in the West.

Directions: Write three facts and three opinions.

Facts:
1.
2.
3.
Opinions:
1.
2.
3.

Answers will vary.

68

Facts and Opinions (page 69)

Directions: Write **F** before the facts and **O** before the opinions.

F 1. Our school football team had a winning season this year.
O 2. Mom's spaghetti is the best in the world!
O 3. Autumn is the nicest season of the year.
F 4. Mrs. Burns took her class on a field trip last Thursday.
F 5. The library always puts 30 books in our classroom book collection.
O 6. They should put only books about horses in the collection.
O 7. Our new art teacher is very strict.
O 8. Everyone should keep take-home papers in a folder so they don't have to look for them when it is time to go home.
F 9. The bus to the mall goes right by Jane's house at 7:45 A.M.
O 10. Our new superintendent, Mr. Willeke, is very nice.

69

Crater Lake (page 70)

When you come to a word you don't know, look for clues to its meaning in the words around it. These nearby words are called **context clues** and can help you figure out a new word.

Example: Mount Mazama, an underlined(ancient) volcano, collapsed thousands of years ago, leaving a huge bowl, or crater.

Context Clues: thousands, years ago
Meaning: very old

Directions: Fill in the circle next to the correct meaning of the underlined word.

1. Crater Lake, in the Cascade Mountains of southern Oregon, rests in an inactive volcano at an altitude of about 6,200 feet above sea level.
  ● height ○ average
2. No streams or rivers supply the lake with water. Precipitation, in the form of snow and rain, has filled the crater.
  ● fill ○ save
3. Crater Lake is the deepest lake in the United States. It is 1,932 feet at its greatest depth.
  ○ far ● measurement downward
4. Years ago, a mining prospector was looking for minerals and oil. He saw the lake and called it *Deep Blue Lake* because of its beautiful color.
  ● explorer ○ beautiful
5. Crater Lake and the area around it are now part of a National Park. The Park Service will ensure people do not pollute the lake.
  ○ protect ● make certain
6. There were no fish in Crater Lake until it was stocked with trout in 1888. People who fish are happy that more fish are still added each year.
  ○ stored ● filled

70

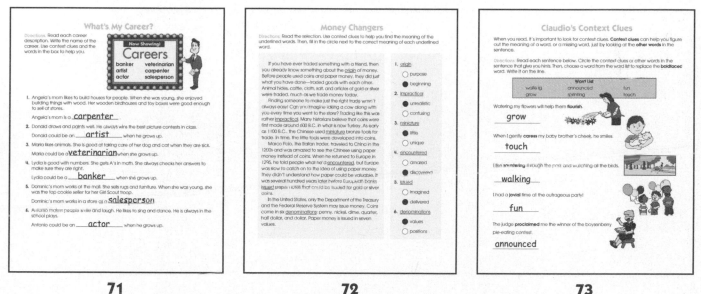

What's My Career? (page 71)

Directions: Read each career description. Write the name of the career. Use context clues and the words in the box to help you.

Now Showing!
Careers
banker veterinarian
artist carpenter
actor salesperson

1. Angela's mom likes to build houses for people. When she was young, she enjoyed building things with wood. Her wooden birdhouses and toy boxes were good enough to sell at stores.
Angela's mom is a **carpenter**.
2. Donald draws and paints well. He always wins the best picture contests in class.
Donald could be an **artist** when he grows up.
3. Maria likes animals. She is good at taking care of her dog and cat when they are sick.
Maria could be a **veterinarian** when she grows up.
4. Lydia is good with numbers. She gets A's in math. She always checks her answers to make sure they are right.
Lydia could be a **banker** when she grows up.
5. Dominic's mom works at the mall. She sells rugs and furniture. When she was young, she was the top cookie seller for her Girl Scout troop.
Dominic's mom works in a store as a **salesperson**.
6. Antonio makes people smile and laugh. He likes to sing and dance. He is always in the school plays.
Antonio could be an **actor** when he grows up.

71

Money Changers (page 72)

Directions: Read the selection. Use context clues to help you find the meaning of the underlined words. Then, fill in the circle next to the correct meaning of each underlined word.

If you have ever traded something with a friend, then you already know something about the origin of money. Before people used coins and paper money, they did just what you have done—traded goods with each other. Animal hides, cattle, cloth, salt, and articles of gold or silver were traded, much as we trade money today.

Finding someone to make just the right trade wasn't always easy! Can you imagine taking a cow along with you every time you went to the store? Trading like this was rather impractical. Many historians believe that coins were first made around 600 B.C. in what is now Turkey. As early as 1100 B.C., the Chinese used miniature bronze tools for trade. In time, the little tools were developed into coins.

Marco Polo, the Italian trader, traveled to China in the 1200s and was amazed to see the Chinese using paper money instead of coins. When he returned to Europe in 1295, he told people what he'd encountered, but Europe was slow to catch on to the idea of using paper money. They didn't understand how paper could be valuable. It was several hundred years later before European banks issued paper notes that could be traded for gold or silver coins.

In the United States, only the Department of the Treasury and the Federal Reserve System may issue money. Coins come in six denominations: penny, nickel, dime, quarter, half dollar, and dollar. Paper money is issued in seven values.

1. origin
  ○ purpose
  ● beginning
2. impractical
  ● unrealistic
  ○ confusing
3. miniature
  ● little
  ○ unique
4. encountered
  ○ amazed
  ● discovered
5. issued
  ○ imagined
  ● delivered
6. denominations
  ● values
  ○ positions

72

Claudio's Context Clues (page 73)

When you read, it's important to look for context clues. **Context clues** can help you figure out the meaning of a word, or a missing word, just by looking at the **other words** in the sentence.

Directions: Read each sentence below. Circle the context clues or other words in the sentence that give you hints. Then, choose a word from the word list to replace the **boldfaced** word. Write it on the line.

Word List
walking announced fun
grow sprinting touch

Watering my flowers will help them **flourish**.
grow

When I gently **caress** my baby brother's cheek, he smiles.
touch

I like **sauntering** through the park and watching all the birds.
walking

I had a **jovial** time at the outrageous party!
fun

The judge **proclaimed** me the winner of the boysenberry pie-eating contest.
announced

73

GRADE 4

I. Reading
  A. Directions
  B. Sequencing
  C. Main Idea
II. Writing
  A. Capitalization
  B. Proofreading

What Do You Mean?

Directions: Choose a word from the word list to replace the **boldfaced** word in each sentence. Write the word on the line. Use a dictionary to help you with any new words.

Word List		
fat	awful	strutting
shouting	skinny	empty

The **obese** elephant must have weighed 10 tons!

__fat__

The **clamor** from the lion's den frightened me.

__shouting__

The skunk emitted a **repugnant** odor when a predator drew near him.

__awful__

Swaggering off the stage and holding a trophy, the boy smirked at everybody and shouted, "I am the best!"

__strutting__

The island remained **desolate** for 100 years.

__empty__

74

Pick Another Word!

Directions: Choose a word from the word list to replace the **boldfaced** word in each sentence. Write it on the line. Use a dictionary to help you with any new words. One word may be used more than once.

Word List		
improve	limped	escape
douse	serious	

The wounded soldier **staggered** back from the battlefield.

__limped__

The special effects will **enhance** the quality of the movie and make it even more exciting to watch.

__improve__

The firefighter prepared to **extinguish** the fire by getting the hose ready.

__douse__

In order to **hone** my jumpshot, I need to practice on the basketball court every day.

__improve__

The robbers tried to **flee** from the police, but they were caught.

__escape__

A funeral is a **solemn** event.

__serious__

75

Cause and Effect

Cause: An action or act that makes something happen.

Effect: Something that happens because of an action or cause.

Look at the following example of cause and effect.

Cause: We left our hot dogs on the grill too long.

Effect: Our hot dogs were burnt!

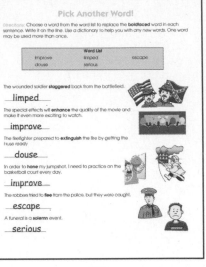

Directions: Read the story below. Then, write the missing effect.

Walter went to the art gallery to see the Picasso exhibit. He examined many of the paintings and felt inspired to paint himself. He visited the library and read about Picasso. He found out that many of Picasso's paintings had been influenced by African art and masks. Walter was now extremely excited to learn more about Picasso's art.

Cause: Walter did research about African art.

Effect: Walter was extremely excited to learn more about Picasso's art.

76

How Did It Happen?

Directions: Read the stories below. Then, write the missing cause or effect.

James traveled on a long plane ride. When he arrived at his destination, he had to change his watch back 6 hours. When his friend asked him to go to dinner at 6P.M., James said, "I am sorry, but not now."

Cause: James set his watch back 6 hours.

Effect: James could not make it to dinner.

Kevin's back ached because he had lifted heavy boxes all day long. Kevin set up an appointment at the yoga studio to work on stretching his muscles. Kevin learned new techniques and practiced them every day.

Kevin's back ached because he had lifted

Cause: heavy boxes all day long.

Effect: Kevin learned yoga.

77

Bonnie Blair

Speed skater Bonnie Blair is the only American woman to have won five Olympic gold medals. She is known as one of the best speed skaters in the world.

Born on March 18, 1964, Bonnie was the youngest in a speed skating family. Her five older brothers and sisters were champion skaters who encouraged her. They put a pair of skates over Bonnie's shoes when she was two years old because there weren't any skates small enough for her tiny feet.

As Bonnie grew, she trained hard six days a week, always pushing to improve her time. Bonnie kept this up until she was the world's best female speed skater. She won her first Olympic gold medal in the 500-meter race in 1988. In 1992, she won both the 500-meter and the 1,000-meter Olympic races in Albertville, France. She repeated her victories in 1994 in Lillehammer, Norway.

Bonnie's Olympic successes made her famous all over the world. Bonnie retired from speed skating in 1995 to focus on other competitions.

Directions: Answer the questions in complete sentences.

1. What was the effect of Bonnie being born into a speed skating family?

   She began skating at a young age and her family supported her.

2. What caused Bonnie's brothers and sisters to place skates over her shoes?

   There were no skates small enough for Bonnie's small feet.

3. What was the effect of Bonnie's practice and hard work?

   Bonnie won five Olympic gold medals.

78

Who Invented the Ice-Cream Cone? cont.

to solve the ice-cream vendor's problem. He then rolled one of his waffle Zalabia into a cone. When the cone cooled, the ice-cream vendor filled it with ice cream. The rest is ice-cream history!"

Use the information from the story to fill in the missing cause or effect below.

Cause	Effect
People kept walking off with Italo's ice-cream bowls.	Italo invented the ice-cream cone in 1896.
Italo wanted to protect his ice-cream cone idea.	Italo was granted a patent in 1903.
The ice-cream vendor ran out of bowls to serve his ice cream.	
The ice-cream vendor looked at the booth next to him.	Mr. Hamwi had an idea to solve the ice-cream vendor's problem.
Mr. Hamwi rolled one of his waffle-like pastries into a cone and let it cool.	The rest is ice-cream history!

80

GRADE
4

I. Reading
  A. Directions
  B. Sequencing
  C. Main Idea
II. Writing
  A. Capitalization
  B. Proofreading

Seashell Driveway! cont.

Directions: Use the information from the story to fill in the missing cause or effect below.

Cause	Effect
The winter snow washed away the shell driveway.	Kari and her family need a new driveway for the summer.
Kari and Kristin will collect shells for the driveway.	Kari's mom would pay them with candy.
Kari's driveway was long.	They would need at least 8 huge buckets of shells to cover the driveway.
The ocean washed the shells towards the shore.	Beautiful white-and-pink scalloped shells glistened under the clear-blue water.
The girls could not swim with the heavy buckets.	They lined up 8 large buckets on the beach.
The girls did a great job collecting the shells.	Kari's mom thinks she might double her candy offer.
Some of the shells were too smooth and shapely for the driveway.	The girls saved 12 shells for themselves.
Kari's mom drove the car over the shells.	The shells broke into tiny pieces.

83

500 Apples

Directions: Read the story below. Then, answer the question.

One day, a rickety old pickup truck stopped outside of my house. It was full of hundreds of red apples. The driver of the truck waved and called out the window. "Good morning, folks! You are the lucky winners of 500 red apples! Where would you like them?"

Use your imagination and tell what you think happens next in the story.

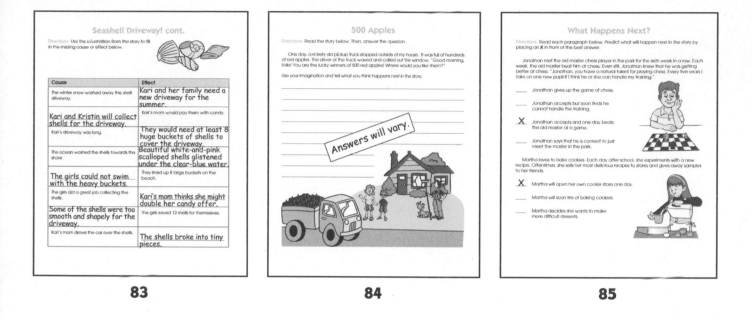

Answers will vary.

84

What Happens Next?

Directions: Read each paragraph below. Predict what will happen next in the story by placing an **X** in front of the best answer.

Jonathan met the old master chess player in the park for the sixth week in a row. Each week, the old master beat him at chess. Even still, Jonathan knew that he was getting better at chess. "Jonathan, you have a natural talent for playing chess. Every five years I take on one new pupil if I think he or she can handle my training."

____   Jonathan gives up the game of chess.

____   Jonathan accepts but soon finds he cannot handle the training.

X   Jonathan accepts and one day beats the old master at a game.

____   Jonathan says that he is content to just meet the master in the park.

Martha loves to bake cookies. Each day after school, she experiments with a new recipe. Oftentimes, she sells her most delicious recipes to stores and gives away samples to her friends.

X   Martha will open her own cookie store one day.

____   Martha will soon tire of baking cookies.

____   Martha decides she wants to make more difficult desserts.

85

A New Technique

Directions: Read the story on pages 87 and 88. Then, underline the best answers.

1. What statement best summarizes the story?
   Two best friends talk about video games while Megan's dad shops.
   <u>While playing video games, the friends talk about Jim's sister.</u>
   Two 4th-grade video game players can't wait to become older.

2. Why does Megan feel proud?
   <u>Jim played well using the technique she had taught him.</u>
   Megan's technique helped her hit with accuracy.
   They could play two more games with money Jim found.

3. What makes the new technique different from other playing methods?
   It is hard to learn.
   <u>It is played with the left hand.</u>
   It gave Megan confidence.

4. What statement best summarizes Jim and Megan's discussion?
   It will be fun to work on a summer work crew.
   <u>Jim's sister will do something unusual this summer.</u>
   Jim's dad lost his cool.

5. Why does Jim's dad lose his cool about the summer plans?
   <u>He is surprised and worried.</u>
   He is jealous and angry.
   He is delighted and happy.

6. How does Jim feel in the end about his sister's summer plans?
   He is proud.   He is frustrated.   <u>He understands.</u>

86

More About the Recycler

First, authors must decide who the main character is going to be in their story. Then, they reveal the character's personality by:

what the character does
what the character says
what other people say about the character

Directions: Answer the following questions about character.

Give two examples of what Sasha **does** to show that she is passionate about recycling.

1. _____

2. _____

Give an example of what Sa... ...passionate about recycling.

Answers will vary.

Give an example of what **other people say** about Sasha and her recycling efforts.

If Sasha drank a soda at a park and there was no recycling bin for the can, what do you think she would do? What would you do? Write your answers on the lines below.

_____

90

Conducting an Interview

An **interview** occurs between two people, usually a reporter and another person. The interviewer asks questions for the other person to answer.

Directions: Pretend that you are a reporter. Choose a character from a book that you have read. If you could ask the character anything you wanted to, what questions would you ask?

Make a **list of questions** you would like to ask your character.

1. _____
2. _____
3. _____
4. _____

Answers will vary.

Now, pretend that your character has come to life and could **answer your questions**. Write what you think your character would say.

1. _____
2. _____
3. _____
4. _____

91

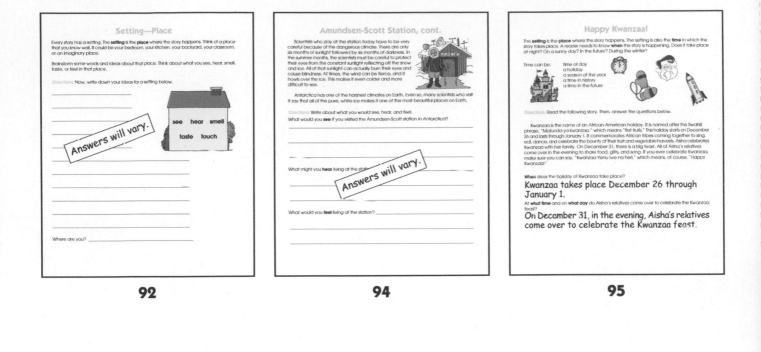

Setting—Place

Every story has a setting. The **setting** is the **place** where the story happens. Think of a place that you know well. It could be your bedroom, your kitchen, your backyard, your classroom, or an imaginary place.

Brainstorm some words and ideas about that place. Think about what you see, hear, smell, taste, or feel in that place.

Directions: Now, write down your ideas for a setting below.

Answers will vary.

see hear smell
taste touch

Where are you?

92

Amundsen-Scott Station, cont.

Scientists who stay at the station today have to be very careful because of the dangerous climate. There are only six months of sunlight followed by six months of darkness. In the summer months, the scientists must be careful to protect their eyes from the constant sunlight reflecting off the snow and ice. All of that sunlight can actually burn their eyes and cause blindness. At times, the wind can be fierce, and it howls over the ice. This makes it even colder and more difficult to see.

Antarctica has one of the harshest climates on Earth. Even so, many scientists who visit it say that all of the pure, white ice makes it one of the most beautiful places on Earth.

Directions: Write about what you would see, hear, and feel.
What would you **see** if you visited the Amundsen-Scott station in Antarctica?

What might you **hear** living at the station?

Answers will vary.

What would you **feel** living at the station?

94

Happy Kwanzaa!

The **setting** is the **place** where the story happens. The setting is also the **time** in which the story takes place. A reader needs to know **when** the story is happening. Does it take place at night? On a sunny day? In the future? During the winter?

Time can be: time of day
                 a holiday
                 a season of the year
                 a time in history
                 a time in the future

Directions: Read the following story. Then, answer the questions below.

Kwanzaa is the name of an African-American holiday. It is named after the Swahili phrase, "Matunda ya kwanzaa," which means "first fruits." This holiday starts on December 26 and lasts through January 1. It commemorates African tribes coming together to sing, eat, dance, and celebrate the bounty of their fruit and vegetable harvests. Aisha celebrates Kwanzaa with her family. On December 31, there is a big feast. All of Aisha's relatives come over in the evening to share food, gifts, and song. If you ever celebrate Kwanzaa, make sure you can say, "Kwanzaa Yenu iwe na heri," which means, of course, "Happy Kwanzaa!"

When does the holiday of Kwanzaa take place?
**Kwanzaa takes place December 26 through
January 1.**
At **what time** and on **what day** do Aisha's relatives come over to celebrate the Kwanzaa feast?
**On December 31, in the evening, Aisha's relatives
come over to celebrate the Kwanzaa feast.**

95

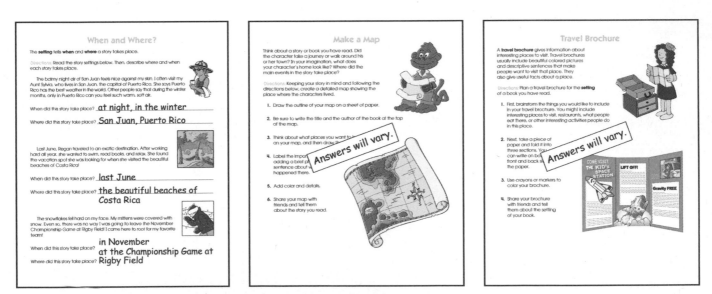

When and Where?

The **setting** tells **when** and **where** a story takes place.

Directions: Read the story settings below. Then, describe where and when each story takes place.

The balmy night air of San Juan feels nice against my skin. I often visit my Aunt Sylvia, who lives in San Juan, the capital of Puerto Rico. She says Puerto Rico has the best weather in the world. Other people say that during the winter months, only in Puerto Rico can you feel such warm, soft air.

When did this story take place? **at night, in the winter**

Where did this story take place? **San Juan, Puerto Rico**

Last June, Regan traveled to an exotic destination. After working hard all year, she wanted to swim, read books, and relax. She found the vacation spot she was looking for when she visited the beautiful beaches of Costa Rica!

When did this story take place? **last June**

Where did this story take place? **the beautiful beaches of
Costa Rica**

The snowflakes fell hard on my face. My mittens were covered with snow. Even so, there was no way I was going to leave the November Championship Game at Rigby Field! I came here to root for my favorite team!

When did this story take place? **in November**

Where did this story take place? **at the Championship Game at
Rigby Field**

96

Make a Map

Think about a story or book you have read. Did the character take a journey or walk around his or her town? In your imagination, what does your character's home look like? Where did the main events in the story take place?

Directions: Keeping your story in mind and following the directions below, create a detailed map showing the place where the characters lived.

1. Draw the outline of your map on a sheet of paper.

2. Be sure to write the title and the author of the book at the top of the map.

3. Think about what places you want to [put] on your map, and then draw [them].

4. Label the important [places] adding a brief [descriptive] sentence about w[hat] happened there.

5. Add color and details.

6. Share your map with friends and tell them about the story you read.

Answers will vary.

97

Travel Brochure

A **travel brochure** gives information about interesting places to visit. Travel brochures usually include beautiful colored pictures and descriptive sentences that make people want to visit that place. They also give useful facts about a place.

Directions: Plan a travel brochure for the **setting** of a book you have read.

1. First, brainstorm the things you would like to include in your travel brochure. You might include interesting places to visit, restaurants, what people eat there, or other interesting activities people do in this place.

2. Next, take a piece of paper and fold it into three sections. You can write on bo[th] front and back s[ides of] the paper.

3. Use crayons or markers to color your brochure.

4. Share your brochure with friends and tell them about the setting of your book.

Answers will vary.

COME VISIT
THE KID'S SPACE STATION
LIFT OFF!
Gravity FREE

98

GRADE
4

I. Reading
A. Directions
B. Sequencing
C. Main Idea
II. Writing
A. Capitalization
B. Proofreading

The Princess and the Pea

Fairy tales are short stories written for children involving magical characters.

Directions: Read the story "The Princess and the Pea." Then, answer the questions.

Once there was a prince who wanted to get married. The catch was, he had to marry a real princess. The Prince knew that real princesses were few and far between. When they heard he was looking for a bride, many young women came to the palace. All claimed to be real princesses.

"Hmmm," thought the Prince. "I must think of a way to sort out the real princesses from the fake ones. I will ask the Queen for advice."

Luckily, since he was a prince, the Queen was also his mother. So of course he had her son's best interests at heart. "A real princess is very delicate," said the Queen. "She must sleep on a mattress as soft as a cloud. If there is even a small lump, she will not be able to sleep."

"Why not?" asked the Prince. He was a nice man but not as smart as his mother.

"Because she is so delicate!" said the Queen impatiently. "Let's figure out a way to test her. Better still, let me figure out a test. You go down and pick a girl to try out my plan."

The Prince went down to the lobby of the castle. A very pretty but humble-looking girl caught his eye. He brought her back to his mother, who welcomed her.

"Please be our guest at the castle tonight," said the Queen. "Tomorrow, we will talk with you about whether you are a real princess."

The pretty but humble-looking girl was shown to her room. In it was a pile of five mattresses, all fluffy and clean. "A princess is delicate," said the Queen. "Sweet dreams!"

The girl climbed to the top of the pile and laid down, but she could not sleep. She tossed and turned and was quite cross the next morning.

"I found this under the fourth mattress when I got up this morning," she said. She handed a small green pea to the Queen. "No wonder I couldn't sleep!"

The Queen clapped her hands. The Prince looked confused. "A real princess is delicate. If this pea I put under the mattress kept you awake, you are definitely a princess."

"Of course I am," said the Princess. "Now, may I please take a nap?"

1. Why does the Prince worry about finding a bride? **His bride must be a real princess and real princesses are hard to find.**

2. According to the Queen, how can the Prince tell who is a real princess? **A real princess is very delicate.**

3. Who hides something under the girl's mattress? **the Queen**

99

Reviewing "The Princess and the Pea"

Directions: Review the story "The Princess and the Pea." Then, answer the questions.

1. Why does the Prince need a test to see who is a real princess? **Many young women wanted to marry him, but the Prince could only marry a "real" princess.**

2. Why does the Princess have trouble sleeping? **There was a pea under her mattress.**

3. In this story, the Queen puts a small pea under a pile of mattresses to see if the girl is delicate. What else could be done to test a princess for delicacy? **Answers will vary.**

The story does not tell whether the Prince and Princess got married and live happily ever after, only that the Princess wants to take a nap.

Directions: Write a new ending to the story.

What do you think happens after the Princess wakes up?

100

The Frog Prince

Directions: Read the story "The Frog Prince." Then, answer the questions.

Once upon a time, there lived a beautiful princess who liked to play alone in the woods. One day, as she was playing with her golden ball, it rolled into a lake. The water was so deep she could not see the ball. The Princess was very sad. She cried out. "I would give anything to have my golden ball back!"

Suddenly, a large ugly frog popped out of the water. "Anything?" he croaked. The Princess looked at him with distaste. "Yes," she said. "I would give anything."

"I will get your golden ball," said the frog. "In return, you must take me back to the castle. You must let me live with you and eat from your golden plate."

"Whatever you want," said the Princess. She thought the frog was very ugly, but she wanted her golden ball.

The frog dove down and brought the ball to the Princess. She put the frog in her pocket and took him home. "He is ugly," the Princess said. "But a promise is a promise. And a princess always keeps her word."

The Princess changed her clothes and forgot all about the frog. That evening, she heard a tapping at her door. She ran to the door to open it and a handsome prince stepped in.

"Who are you?" asked the Princess, already half in love.

"I am the prince you rescued at the lake," said the handsome Prince. "I was turned into a frog one hundred years ago today by a wicked lady. Because she always keeps her promises, only a beautiful princess could break the spell. You are a little forgetful, but you did keep your word!"

Can you guess what happened next? Of course, they were married and lived happily ever after.

1. What does the frog ask the Princess to promise? **to take him back to the castle, let him live with her and eat from her golden plate**

2. Where does the Princess put the frog when she leaves the lake? **in her pocket**

3. Why could only a princess break the spell? **Because they always keep their promises.**

101

Reviewing "The Frog Prince"

Directions: Review the story "The Frog Prince." Then, answer the questions.

1. What does the Princess lose in the lake? **a golden ball**

2. How does she get it back? **A frog dove to the bottom of the lake and got it for her in return for a promise from the Princess.**

3. How does the frog turn back into a prince? **The spell is broken when the Princess keeps her word.**

4. What phrases are used to begin and end this story? **"once upon a time" and "happily ever after"**

5. Are these words used frequently to begin and end fairy tales? **yes**

There is more than one version of most fairy tales. In another version of this story, the Princess has to kiss the frog in order for him to change back into a prince.

Directions: Write your answers.

1. What do you think would happen in a story where the Princess kisses the frog, but he remains a frog? **Answers will vary.**

2. What kinds of problems would a princess have living with a frog in the castle? Brainstorm ideas and write them here.

3. Rewrite the ending to "The Frog Prince" so that the frog remains a frog and does not turn into a handsome prince. Continue your story on another sheet of paper.

102

Fairy Tales

Directions: Think of fairy tales you know from books or videos, like "Cinderella," "Snow White," "Sleeping Beauty," "Rapunzel," and "Beauty and the Beast." Then, answer the questions.

1. What are some common elements in all fairy tales? **Answers may include: a hero or heroine, a villain, a problem, a happy ending**

2. How do fairy tales usually begin? **"Once upon a time"**

3. How do fairy tales usually end? **with a happy ending**

Directions: Locate and read several different versions of the same fairy tale. For example, "Princess Furball," "Cinderlad," and "Yeh Shen." Then, answer the questions.

1. How are the stories alike? **Answers will vary.**

2. How are they different?

3. Which story is best developed by the author?

4. Which story did you like best? Why?

103

The Hare and the Tortoise

"The Hare and the Tortoise" is called a **fable**. Fables are usually short stories. As you read this story and the other fables on the next few pages, look for two characteristics the fables have in common.

Directions: Read the fable "The Hare and the Tortoise." Then, answer the questions.

One day, the hare and the tortoise were talking. Or rather, the hare was bragging and the tortoise was listening.

"I am faster than the wind," bragged the hare. "I feel sorry for you because you are so slow! Why, you are the slowest fellow I have ever seen."

"Do you think so?" asked the tortoise with a smile. "I will race you to that big tree across the field."

"Ha!" scoffed the hare. "You must be kidding! You will most certainly be the loser! But, if you insist, we will race."

The tortoise nodded politely. "I'll be off," he said. Slowly and steadily, the tortoise moved across the field.

The hare stood back and laughed. "How sad that he should compete with me!" he said. His chest puffed up with pride. "I will take a little nap while the poor old tortoise lumbers along. When I wake up, he will still be only halfway across the field."

The tortoise kept on, slow and steady, across the field. Some time later, the hare awoke. He discovered that while he slept, the tortoise had won the race.

1. What is the main idea? (Check one.)

___ Tortoises are faster than hares.

___ Hares need more sleep than tortoises.

_✓_ Slow and steady wins the race.

2. The hare brags that he is faster than what? (Check one.)

___ a bullet

___ a greyhound

_✓_ the wind

3. Who is modest, the tortoise or the hare? **the tortoise**

104

GRADE 4

I. Reading
A. Directions
B. Sequencing
C. Main Idea
II. Writing
A. Capitalization
B. Proofreading

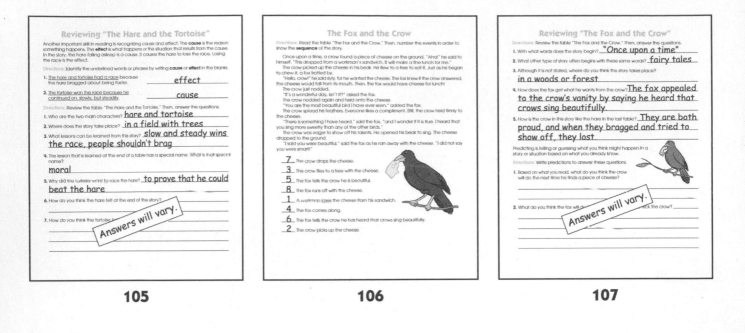

Reviewing "The Hare and the Tortoise"

Another important skill in reading is recognizing cause and effect. The **cause** is the reason something happens. The **effect** is what happens or the situation that results from the cause. In the story, the hare falling asleep is a cause. It causes the hare to lose the race. Losing the race is the effect.

Directions: Identify the underlined words or phrases by writing **cause** or **effect** in the blanks.

1. The hare and tortoise had a race because the hare bragged about being faster. **effect**

2. The tortoise won the race because he continued on slowly, but steadily. **cause**

Directions: Review the fable "The Hare and the Tortoise." Then, answer the questions.

1. Who are the two main characters? **hare and tortoise**

2. Where does the story take place? **in a field with trees**

3. What lessons can be learned from this story? **slow and steady wins the race, people shouldn't brag**

4. The lesson that is learned at the end of a fable has a special name. What is that special name? **moral**

5. Why did the tortoise want to race the hare? **to prove that he could beat the hare**

6. How do you think the hare felt at the end of the story?

7. How do you think the tortoise f...

Answers will vary.

105

The Fox and the Crow

Directions: Read the fable "The Fox and the Crow." Then, number the events in order to show the **sequence** of the story.

Once upon a time, a crow found a piece of cheese on the ground. "Aha!" he said to himself. "This dropped from a workman's sandwich. It will make a fine lunch for me."
The crow picked up the cheese in his beak. He flew to a tree to eat it. Just as he began to chew it, a fox trotted by.
"Hello, crow!" he said slyly, for he wanted the cheese. The fox knew if the crow answered, the cheese would fall from his mouth. Then, the fox would have cheese for lunch!
The crow just nodded.
"It's a wonderful day, isn't it?" asked the fox.
The crow nodded again and held onto the cheese.
"You are the most beautiful bird I have ever seen," added the fox.
The crow spread his feathers. Everyone likes a compliment. Still, the crow held firmly to the cheese.
"There is something I have heard," said the fox, "and I wonder if it is true. I heard that you sing more sweetly than any of the other birds."
The crow was eager to show off his talents. He opened his beak to sing. The cheese dropped to the ground.
"I said you were beautiful," said the fox as he ran away with the cheese. "I did not say you were smart!"

7 The crow drops the cheese.

3 The crow flies to a tree with the cheese.

5 The fox tells the crow he is beautiful.

8 The fox runs off with the cheese.

1 A workman loses the cheese from his sandwich.

4 The fox comes along.

6 The fox tells the crow he has heard that crows sing beautifully.

2 The crow picks up the cheese.

106

Reviewing "The Fox and the Crow"

Directions: Review the fable "The Fox and the Crow." Then, answer the questions.

1. With what words does the story begin? **"Once upon a time"**

2. What other type of story often begins with these same words? **fairy tales**

3. Although it is not stated, where do you think the story takes place? **in a woods or forest**

4. How does the fox get what he wants from the crow? **The fox appealed to the crow's vanity by saying he heard that crows sing beautifully.**

5. How is the crow in this story like the hare in the last fable? **They are both proud, and when they bragged and tried to show off, they lost.**

Predicting is telling or guessing what you think might happen in a story or situation based on what you already know.

Directions: Write predictions to answer these questions.

1. Based on what you read, what do you think the crow will do the next time he finds a piece of cheese?

2. What do you think the fox will d...ck the crow?

Answers will vary.

107

The Boy Who Cried Wolf

Directions: Read the fable "The Boy Who Cried Wolf." Then, complete the puzzle.

Once, there was a shepherd boy who tended his sheep alone. The sheep were gentle animals. They were easy to take care of. The boy grew bored.
"I can't stand another minute alone with these sheep," he said crossly. He knew only one thing would bring people quickly to him. If he cried, "Wolf!" the men in the village would run up the mountain. They would come to help save the sheep from the wolf.
"Wolf!" he yelled loudly, and he blew on his horn.
Quick as a wink, a dozen men came running. When they realized it was a joke, they were very angry. The boy promised never to do it again. But a week later, he grew bored and cried, "Wolf!" again. Again, the men ran to him. This time they were very, very angry.
Soon afterwards, a wolf really came. The boy was scared. "Wolf!" he cried. "Wolf! Wolf! Wolf!"
He blew his horn, but no one came, and the wolf ate all his sheep.

```
        V I L L A G E
  M O U N T A I N     S
    E                 C
                      A
          G E N T L E D
```

Across:
2. This is where the boy tends sheep.
4. When no one came, the wolf _____ all the sheep.
5. Sheep are _____ and easy to take care of.

Down:
1. The people who come are from here.
2. At first, when the boy cries, "Wolf!" the _____ come running.
3. When a wolf really comes, this is how the boy feels.

108

Reviewing "The Boy Who Cried Wolf"

Directions: Identify the underlined words as a **cause** or an **effect**.

1. The boy cries wolf because he is bored. **effect**

2. The boy blows his horn and the men come running. **cause**

3. No one comes, and the wolf eats all the sheep. **effect**

Directions: Answer the questions.

1. What lesson can be learned from this story? **Sample answer: Always tell the truth.**

2. How is this story like the two other fables you read?

3. Is the boy in the story l...of the hare? How so?

Answers will vary.

109

The City Mouse and the Country Mouse

Directions: Read the fable "The City Mouse and the Country Mouse." Then, answer the questions.

Once there were two mice, a city mouse and a country mouse. They were cousins. The country mouse was always begging his cousin to visit him. Finally, the city mouse agreed.
When he arrived, the city mouse was not very polite. "How do you stand it here?" he asked, wrinkling his nose. "All you have to eat is corn and barley. All you have to wear is old, tattered work clothes. And all you have to listen to are the other animals. Why don't you come and visit me? Then, you will see what it's like to really live!"
The country mouse liked corn and barley. He liked the sounds of the other animals. And he liked his old work clothes fine. Secretly, he thought his cousin was silly to wear fancy clothes. Still, the city sounded exciting. Why not give it a try?
Since he had no clothes to pack, the country mouse was ready in no time. His cousin told him stories about the city as they traveled. The buildings were so high! The food was so good! The girl mice were so beautiful!
The home of the city mouse was nice. He lived in a hole in the wall in an old castle. "It is only a hole in the wall," said the city mouse, "but it is a very nice wall, indeed!"
That night, the mice crept out of the wall. Everyone had eaten, but the maid had not cleaned up. The table was still loaded with good food. The mice ate and ate. The country mouse was not used to rich food. He began to feel sick to his stomach.
Just then, they heard loud barking. Two huge dogs ran into the room. They nearly bit off the country mouse's tail! He barely made it to the hole in the wall in time. That did it!
"Thank you for showing me the city," said the country mouse, "but it is too exciting for me. I am going home where it is peaceful. I can't wait to settle my stomach with some corn and barley."

1. What are three things the city mouse says are wrong with the country? **no good food, old clothes to wear, animal noises**

2. Why doesn't it take the country mouse long to get ready to leave with the city mouse? **He has no clothes to pack.**

3. Why does the country mouse secretly think his cousin is silly? **because he wears fancy clothes**

110

Total Reading Grade 4   **326**   Answer Key

GRADE 4

I. Reading
A. Directions
B. Sequencing
C. Main Idea
II. Writing
A. Capitalization
B. Proofreading

Reviewing "The City Mouse and the Country Mouse"

Directions: Review the fable "The City Mouse and the Country Mouse." Use the Venn diagram to compare and contrast the lifestyles of the city mouse and the country mouse.

City Mouse   Both   Country Mouse

Answers will vary.

Directions: Write five m_____ order.

Directions: Answer these questions about the fable.

1. How do the two mice feel about each other? **They do not understand each other's way of life.**

2. Which mouse do you think is most like the hare? Why? **Answers will vary.**

111

Paul Bunyan

There is a certain kind of fable called a **tall tale**. In these stories, each storyteller tries to "top" the other. The stories get more and more unbelievable. A popular hero of American tall tales is Paul Bunyan, a giant of a man. Here are some of the stories that have been told about him.

Even as a baby, Paul was very big. One night, he rolled over in his sleep and knocked down a mile of trees. Of course, Paul's father wanted to find some way to keep Paul from getting hurt in his sleep and to keep him from knocking down all the forests. So, he cut down some tall trees and made a boat for Paul to use as a cradle. He tied a long rope to the boat and let it drift out a little way into the sea to rock Paul to sleep.

One night, Paul had trouble sleeping. He kept turning over in his bed. Each time he turned, the cradle rocked. And each time the cradle rocked, it sent up waves as big as buildings. The waves got bigger and bigger until the people on the land were afraid they would all be drowned. They told Paul's parents that Paul was a danger to the whole state! So, Paul and his parents had to move away.

After that, Paul didn't get into much trouble when he was growing up. His father taught him some very important lessons, such as, "If there are any towns or farms in your way, be sure to step around them!"

Directions: Answer these questions about Paul Bunyan.

1. What kind of fable is the story of Paul Bunyan? **tall tale**

2. What did Paul's father make for Paul to use as a cradle? **boat**

3. What happened when Paul rolled over in his cradle? **He made waves as big as buildings.**

4. What did Paul's father tell Paul to do to towns and farms that were in his way? **Step around them!**

112

More Paul Bunyan

When Paul Bunyan grew up, he was taller than other men—by about 50 feet or so! Because of his size, he could do almost anything. One of the things he did best was to cut down trees and turn them into lumber. With only four strokes of his axe, he could cut off all the branches and bark. After he turned all the trees for miles into these tall square posts, he tied a long rope to an axe head. Then, he yelled, "T-I-M-B-E-R-R-R!" and swung the rope around in a huge circle. With every swing, 100 trees fell to the ground.

One cold winter day, Paul found a huge blue ox stuck in the snow. It was nearly frozen. Although it was only a baby, even Paul could hardly lift it. Paul took the ox home and cared for it. He named it Babe, and they became best friends. Babe was a big help to Paul when he was cutting down trees.

When Babe was full grown, it was hard to tell how big he was. There were no scales big enough to weigh him. Paul once measured the distance between Babe's eyes. It was the length of 42 axe handles!

Once, Paul and Babe were working with other men to cut lumber. The job was very hard because the road was so long and winding. It was said that the road was so crooked that men starting home for camp would meet themselves coming back! Well, Paul hitched Babe to the end of that crooked road. Babe pulled and pulled. He pulled so hard that his eyes nearly turned pink. There was a loud snap. The first curve came out of the road and Babe pulled harder. Finally, the whole road started to move. Babe pulled it completely straight!

Directions: Answer these questions about Paul Bunyan and Babe.

1. What was Paul Bunyan particularly good at doing? **cutting down trees**

2. What did Paul find in the snow? **a huge blue ox**

3. How big was the distance between Babe's eyes? **42 axe handles**

4. What did Babe do to the crooked road? **He pulled it completely straight.**

113

Mr. Nobody

Directions: After reading the poem "Mr. Nobody," number in order the things people blame him for.

I know a funny little man
As quiet as a mouse,
Who does the mischief that is done
In everybody's house!
No one ever sees his face,
And yet we all agree
That every plate we break was cracked
By Mr. Nobody.

It's he who always tears out books,
Who leaves the door ajar,
He pulls the buttons from our shirts,
And scatters pins afar;
That squeaking door will always squeak,
The reason is, you see,
We leave the oiling to be done
By Mr. Nobody.

The finger marks upon the wall
By none of us are made;
We never leave the blinds unclosed,
To let the carpet fade.
The bowl of soup we do not spill,
It's not our fault, you see
These mishaps—every one is caused
By Mr. Nobody.

7 Putting finger marks on walls

3 Leaving the door ajar

9 Spilling soup

2 Tearing out books

8 Leaving the blinds open

5 Scattering pins

1 Breaking plates

4 Pulling buttons off shirts

6 Squeaking doors

114

The Chickens

Directions: Read the poem "The Chickens." Then, answer the questions.

Said the first little chicken
With a queer little squirm,
"I wish I could find
A fat little worm."

Said the next little chicken
With an odd little shrug,
"I wish I could find
A fat little bug."

Said the third little chicken
With a small sigh of grief,
"I wish I could find
A green little leaf."

Said the fourth little chicken
With a faint little moan,
"I wish I could find
A small gravel stone."

"See here!" said the mother
From the green garden patch,
"If you want any breakfast,
Just come here and scratch!"

1. What does the second little chicken want? **a fat little bug**

2. Which meal are all the chickens wishing for? **breakfast**

3. Where is the mother hen? **in the garden**

4. Which of the following do the chickens not want?

_____ leaf ✓ corn _____ worm _____ bug _____ stone

5. What does the mother hen tell her chicks to do if they want breakfast? **"Come and scratch in the garden."**

115

I'm Glad

Directions: Read the poem "I'm Glad." Then, work the puzzle.

I'm glad the sky is painted blue
And the Earth is painted green,
With such a lot of nice fresh air
All sandwiched in between.

Crossword puzzle:
G R E E N (down/across)
B L U E
S A N D W I C H E D
S K Y
A I R
E A R T H
G A

Across:
3. The sky is painted this color.
4. How what we breathe is placed between the Earth and sky.
6. This is what we breathe, and it's between the Earth and sky.

Down:
1. The color of the Earth in the poem.
2. How the speaker feels.
4. Painted blue.
5. Painted green.

116

GRADE 4

I. Reading
 A. Directions
 B. Sequencing
 C. Main Idea
II. Writing
 A. Capitalization
 B. Proofreading

Over the Hills and Far Away (117)

Directions: Read the poem "Over the Hills and Far Away." Then, answer the questions.

Tom, Tom the piper's son.
Learned to play when he was one.
But the only tune that he could play
Was "Over the Hills and Far Away."

Now Tom with his pipe made such a noise
That he pleased the girls and he pleased the boys,
And they all danced when they heard him play
"Over the Hills and Far Away."

Tom played his pipe with such great skill,
Even pigs and dogs could not keep still.
The dogs would wag their tails and prance.
The pigs would oink and grunt and prance.

Yes, Tom could play, his music soared—
But soon the pigs and dogs got bored.
The children, too, thought it was wrong,
For Tom to play just one dull song.

1. How old is Tom when he learns to play? **one**
2. What tune does Tom play? **"Over the Hills and Far Away"**
3. What do the dogs do when Tom plays? **wag their tails and dance**
4. Why does everyone get tired of Tom's music? **He only knows how to play one song.**
5. What do the pigs do when Tom plays? **oink, grunt, and prance**
6. What instrument does Tom play? **pipe**

The Spider and the Fly (118)

Directions: Read the poem "The Spider and the Fly." Then, number the events in order.

"Won't you come into my parlor?" said the spider to the fly.
"It's the nicest little parlor that you will ever spy.
The way into my parlor is up a winding stair.
I have so many pretty things to show you inside there."

The little fly said, "No! No! No! To do so is not sane.
For those who travel up your stair do not come down again."

The spider turned himself around and went back in his den—
He knew for sure the silly fly would visit him again.
The spider wove a tiny web, for he was very sly.
He was making preparations to trap the silly fly.

Then out his door the spider came and merrily did sing,
"Oh, fly, oh lovely, lovely fly with pearl and silver wings."

Alas! How quickly did the fly come buzzing back to hear
The spider's words of flattery, which drew the fly quite near.

The fly was trapped within the web, the spider's winding stair,
Then the spider jumped upon him, and ate the fly right there!

4 The spider sings a song about how beautiful the fly is.
7 The spider jumps on the fly.
1 The spider invites the fly into his parlor.
3 The spider spins a tiny new web to catch the fly.
6 The fly becomes caught in the spider's web.
2 The fly says he knows it's dangerous to go into the spider's parlor.
8 The spider eats the fly.
5 The fly comes near the web to hear the song.

Grasshopper Green (119)

Directions: Read the poem "Grasshopper Green." Then, answer the questions.

Grasshopper Green is a comical guy,
He lives on the best of fare.
Bright little trousers, jacket, and cap,
These are his summer wear.

Out in the meadow he loves to go,
Playing away in the sun.
It's hoppertly, skippertly, high and low.
Summer's the time for fun.

Grasshopper Green has a cute little house.
He stays near it every day.
It's under the hedge where he is safe,
Out of the gardener's way.

Gladly he's calling the children to play
Out in the beautiful sun.
It's hoppertly, skippertly, high and low.
Summer's the time for fun.

1. What does **comical** mean in this poem? **amusing or jolly**
2. What are three things Grasshopper Green wears in the summer? **trousers, jacket, and cap**
3. Where does he love to go and play? **out in the meadow**
4. Whom does Grasshopper Green call to play? **the children**
5. What is summer the time for? **fun**
6. Use a dictionary. What does **fare** mean in this poem? **food**
7. You won't find the words **hoppertly** and **skippertly** in a dictionary. Based on the poem, write your own definitions of these words. **Answers will vary.**

Little Robin Redbreast (120)

Directions: Read the poem "Little Robin Redbreast." Then, answer the questions.

Little Robin Redbreast
Sat up in a tree.
Up went the kitty cat
Down went he.

Down came the kitty cat—
Away Robin ran.
Said little Robin Redbreast,
"Catch me if you can."

Then Little Robin Redbreast
Hopped upon a wall,
Kitty cat jumped after him,
And almost had a fall.

Little Robin chirped and sang,
And what did kitty say?
Kitty cat said, "Meow!" quite loud.
And Robin flew away.

1. What is the main idea? (Check one.)
 ✓ The robin is smarter than the cat and a lot faster, too.
 ___ When people see a robin, it means spring is near.
 ___ The robin is scared away.
2. What nearly happens when the cat jumps on the wall? **He almost falls off.**
3. Where is the robin when the cat first goes after him? **up in a tree**
4. Where does the robin go after the cat climbs the tree? **down**
5. What does the robin say to the cat? **"Catch me if you can."**

Hickory, Dickory, Dock (121)

Directions: Read the poem "Hickory, Dickory, Dock." Then, answer the questions.

Hickory, dickory, dock.
The mouse ran up the clock.
The clock struck one,
And down he run.
Hickory, dickory, dock.

Dickory, dickory, dare.
The pig flew in the air.
The man in brown
Soon brought him down.
Dickory, dickory, dare.

Hickory Dickory Dock

1. What is the main idea? (Check one.)
 ___ Mice and pigs can cause a lot of problems to clocks and men in brown suits.
 ✓ There is no main idea. This poem is just for fun.
 ___ Beware of mice in your clocks and flying pigs.
2. Why do you think the mouse runs down the clock? **Answers will vary**

Directions: Number these events in order.

2 The clock strikes one.
3 The mouse runs back down the clock.
1 The mouse runs up the clock.
5 The man in brown brings the pig down.
4 The pig flies in the air.

Camp Rules (122)

Directions: Read the story and answer the questions that follow.
A made-up story is called **fiction**.

Donald, Arnold, and Jack are at Camp Explore-It All this week. They think camp is a lot of fun. They have also learned from their instructors that there are some very important rules all campers must obey so that everyone has a good time.

All campers must take swimming tests to see what depth of water they can swim in safely. Donald and Jack pass the advanced test and can swim in the deep water. Arnold, however, only passes the intermediate test. He is supposed to stay in the area where the water is waist deep. When it is time to swim, Arnold decides to sneak into the advanced area with Donald and Jack. After all, he has been swimming in deep water for three years. No way is he going to stay in the shallow water with the babies.

Donald and Jack don't think Arnold should come into the deep water, but they can't tell him anything. So the boys jump into the water and start swimming and playing. Fifteen minutes later, Arnold is yelling, "Help!" He swims out too far and is too tired to make it back in. The lifeguard jumps in and pulls him out. Everyone stops to see what is happening. Arnold feels very foolish.

Check:
The main idea of this story is
☐ Arnold ends up feeling foolish.
☐ All campers take swimming tests.
☐ You can learn a lot from instructors.
☐ Camp is fun.
☑ Rules are made for good reasons.
☐ Rules are made to be broken.

Underline:
Arnold got himself into a(n) **dangerous** situation.
amusing funny **dangerous** ambiguous

Circle:
Arnold thought the guys in the shallow area were (bullies (babies)). However, he should have ((stayed with them) gone to the advanced area).

Write:
What lesson do you think Arnold learned? **Answers will vary.**
Example: Stay within your limits.

What do you think the other campers learned? **Answers will vary.**
Example: Don't disobey rules or you could get hurt.

GRADE 4

I. Reading
  A. Directions
  B. Sequencing
  C. Main Idea
II. Writing
  A. Capitalization
  B. Proofreading

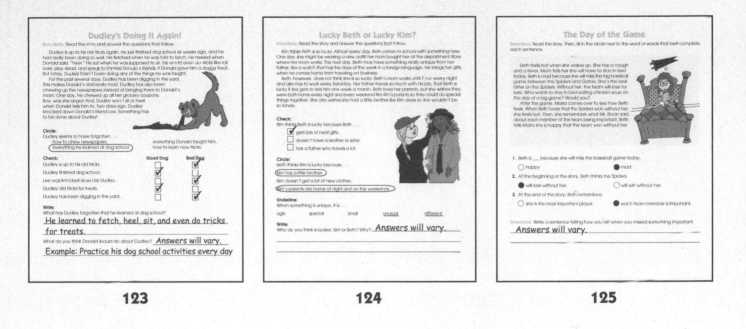

Dudley's Doing It Again!

Directions: Read the story and answer the questions that follow.

Dudley is up to his old tricks again. He just finished dog school six weeks ago, and he had really been doing so well. He fetched when he was told to fetch. He heeled when Donald said, "heel." He sat when he was supposed to sit. He worked even ou tricks like roll over, play dead, and speak to impress Donald's friends. If Donald gave him a doggy treat. But lately, Dudley hasn't been doing any of the things he was taught.

For the past several days, Dudley has been digging in the yard. This makes Donald's dad really mad. Dudley has also been chewing up the newspapers instead of bringing them to Donald's mom. One day, he chewed up all her grocery coupons. Boy, was she angry! And, Dudley won't sit or heel when Donald tells him to. Two days ago, Dudley knocked down Donald's friend Lee. Something has to be done about Dudley!

Circle:
Dudley seems to have forgotten . . .
how to chew newspapers.   everything Donald taught him.
(everything he learned at dog school.)   how to learn new tricks.

Check:
	Good Dog	Bad Dog
Dudley is up to his old tricks.		✓
Dudley finished dog school.	✓	
Lee was knocked down by Dudley.		✓
Dudley did tricks for treats.	✓	
Dudley has been digging in the yard.		✓

Write:
What has Dudley forgotten that he learned at dog school?
He learned to fetch, heel, sit, and even do tricks for treats.
What do you think Donald should do about Dudley? Answers will vary.
Example: Practice his dog school activities every day

123

Lucky Beth or Lucky Kim?

Directions: Read the story and answer the questions that follow.

Kim thinks Beth is so lucky. Almost every day, Beth comes to school with something new. One day, she might be wearing a new outfit her mom bought her at the department store where her mom works. The next day, Beth may have something really unique from her father, like a watch that has the days of the week in a foreign language. He brings her gifts when he comes home from traveling on business.

Beth, however, does not think she is so lucky. Beth's mom works until 7 P.M. every night and also has to work every Saturday. Her father travels so much with his job, that Beth is lucky if she gets to see him one week a month. Beth loves her parents, but she wishes they were both home every night and every weekend like Kim's parents so they could do special things together. She also wishes she had a little brother like Kim does so she wouldn't be so lonely.

Check:
Kim thinks Beth is lucky because Beth . . .
☑ gets lots of neat gifts.
☐ doesn't have a brother or sister.
☐ has a father who travels a lot.

Circle:
Beth thinks Kim is lucky because . . .
(Kim has a little brother.)
Kim doesn't get a lot of new clothes.
(Kim's parents are home at night and on the weekends.)

Underline:
When something is unique, it is . . .
ugly   special   small   unusual   different

Write:
Who do you think is luckier, Kim or Beth? Why? Answers will vary.

124

The Day of the Game

Directions: Read the story. Then, fill in the circle next to the word or words that best complete each sentence.

Beth feels hot when she wakes up. She has a cough and a fever. Mom tells her she will have to stay in bed today. Beth is mad because she will miss the big baseball game between the Spiders and Gators. She's the best hitter on the Spiders. Without her, the team will lose for sure. Who wants to stay in bed eating chicken soup on the day of a big game? Would you?

After the game, Maria comes over to see how Beth feels. When Beth hears that the Spiders won without her, she feels hurt. Then, she remembers what Mr. Bryan said about each member of the team being important. Beth tells Maria she is happy that the team won without her.

1. Beth is ___ because she will miss the baseball game today.
   ○ happy   ● mad
2. At the beginning of the story, Beth thinks the Spiders
   ● will lose without her.   ○ will win without her.
3. At the end of the story, Beth remembers
   ○ she is the most important player.   ● each team member is important.

Directions: Write a sentence telling how you felt when you missed something important.
Answers will vary.

125

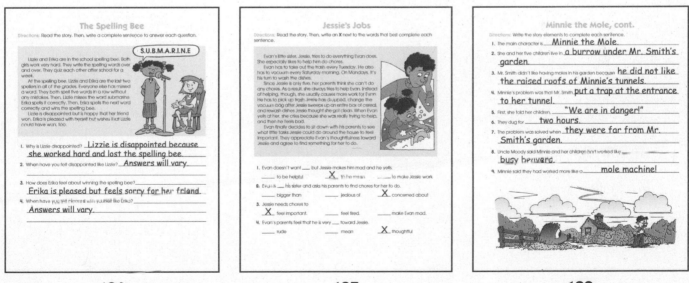

The Spelling Bee

Directions: Read the story. Then, write a complete sentence to answer each question.

Lizzie and Erika are in the school spelling bee. Both girls work very hard. They write the spelling words over and over. They quiz each other after school for a week.

At the spelling bee, Lizzie and Erika are the last two spellers in all of the grades. Everyone else has missed a word. They both spell five words in a row without any mistakes. Then, Lizzie misses the word submarine. Erika spells it correctly. Then, Erika spells the next word correctly and wins the spelling bee.

Lizzie is disappointed but is happy that her friend won. Erika is pleased with herself but wishes that Lizzie could have won, too.

1. Why is Lizzie disappointed? Lizzie is disappointed because she worked hard and lost the spelling bee.
2. When have you felt disappointed like Lizzie? Answers will vary.
3. How does Erika feel about winning the spelling bee? Erika is pleased but feels sorry for her friend.
4. When have you felt pleased with yourself like Erika? Answers will vary.

126

Jessie's Jobs

Directions: Read the story. Then, write an **X** next to the words that best complete each sentence.

Evan's little sister, Jessie, tries to do everything Evan does. She especially likes to help him do chores.

Evan has to take out the trash every Tuesday. He also has to vacuum every Saturday morning. On Mondays, it's his turn to wash the dishes.

Since Jessie is only five, her parents think she can't do any chores. As a result, she always tries to help Evan. Instead of helping, though, she usually causes mom more work for Evan. He has to pick up trash Jessie has dropped, change the vacuum bag after Jessie sweeps up an entire box of cereal, and rewash dishes Jessie thought she got clean. When Evan yells at her, she cries because she was really trying to help, and then he feels bad.

Evan finally decides to sit down with his parents to see what little tasks Jessie could do around the house to feel important. They appreciate Evan's thoughtfulness toward Jessie and agree to find something for her to do.

1. Evan doesn't want ___ but Jessie makes him mad and he yells.
   ___ to be helpful   _X_ to be mean   ___ to make Jessie work
2. Evan is ___ his sister and asks his parents to find chores for her to do.
   ___ bigger than   ___ jealous of   _X_ concerned about
3. Jessie needs chores to
   _X_ feel important.   ___ feel tired.   ___ make Evan mad.
4. Evan's parents feel that he is very ___ toward Jessie.
   ___ rude   ___ mean   _X_ thoughtful

127

Minnie the Mole, cont.

Directions: Write the story elements to complete each sentence.

1. The main character is Minnie the Mole.
2. She and her five children live in a burrow under Mr. Smith's garden.
3. Mr. Smith didn't like having moles in his garden because he did not like the raised roofs of Minnie's tunnels.
4. Minnie's problem was that Mr. Smith put a trap at the entrance to her tunnel.
5. First, she told her children, "We are in danger!"
6. They dug for two hours.
7. The problem was solved when they were far from Mr. Smith's garden.
8. Uncle Moody said Minnie and her children had worked like busy beavers.
9. Minnie said they had worked more like a mole machine!

129

GRADE
4

I. Reading
  A. Directions
  B. Sequencing
  C. Main Idea
II. Writing
  A. Capitalization
  B. Proofreading

Magic Alphabet

Directions: Write the letter of the phrase that completes each statement about the magic trick below.

Hannah can make any letter of the alphabet appear on Rachel's hand. First, she asks Rachel to pick her favorite letter of the alphabet. Then, Hannah writes that letter on a sugar cube with a pencil. Next, she drops the sugar cube into a cup of water. Then, she asks Rachel to hold her hand over the glass and says, "Hocus-Pocus." The letter floats up onto Rachel's hand by magic!

What is Hannah's secret? After she writes the letter on the sugar cube, she presses her finger on it, and the letter rubs off. When Rachel holds her hand over the glass, Hannah touches it with her finger and the letter rubs off.

A. pressing hard on the sugar cube.

C. she can transfer the letter to her own hand.

B. she thinks it happens by magic.

D. the letter rubs off on Rachel's hand.

1. Hannah writes the letter on the sugar cube so that . . . **C**
2. Hannah transfers the letter to her finger by . . . **A**
3. When Hannah touches Rachel's hand with her finger, . . . **D**
4. Since the letter appears to float onto Rachel's hand, . . . **B**

130

Salt and Pepper

Directions: Read the story. Then, write a complete sentence to answer each question.

Salt and Pepper lived in the window at Peterson's Pet Shop. Salt was a little white kitten, whose cage sat in the front window beside a black dog named Pepper. As neighbors, the two became best friends.

One day, Manuel and his father came into the pet shop for a kitten. Manuel chose Salt because she was so playful. When Mr. Peterson lifted Salt out of her cage, Salt meowed sadly at Pepper who said bravely, "I'm sure we'll meet again someday."

Several days later, Lorinda and her mother stopped by the pet shop to look at the puppies. "Oh, Mama," said Lorinda. "This little black dog has such beautiful eyes."

"He seems to be just what we've been looking for," said her mother. "I hope he gets along with our neighbor Manuel's new white kitten."

"Oh, I think they'll be best friends," Lorinda replied. "Won't they be cute together? Just like salt and pepper!"

1. What was the effect of Salt and Pepper living near each other in the pet shop window? **They became best friends.**
2. What caused Manuel to come to the pet shop? **He wanted a kitten.**
3. What caused Salt to feel sad? **Salt didn't want to leave Pepper.**
4. What caused Lorinda and her mother to pick out Pepper? **They liked his beautiful eyes.**

131

Arnold and Annie

Directions: Write an **X** next to each item that answers the question. You could have more than one answer for each question.

Arnold's sister Annie is watching TV. Arnold walks in and changes the channel to watch his favorite show, *Super Hero*. Annie says it's not fair because she was watching her movie first. Arnold tells Annie that she knows *Super Hero* is his favorite show and that she should just have expected him to turn the channel when it came on. He says she shouldn't have even started watching the movie.

Annie and Arnold continue to argue and fight over the TV. Finally, their mom comes in to see what's going on. When they tell her, she tells Arnold that Annie was there first and that he'll only miss one half of *Super Hero* because the movie will be over when the second half starts. But Arnold insists that he should get to watch all of his favorite show. He throws down the remote control and storms out of the room calling his sister a brat. Arnold's mom decides Arnold's TV watching is over for the rest of the day.

1. How would you describe Arnold's behavior?
   ☐ sympathetic ☒ mean ☒ rude
   ☐ understanding ☒ caring

2. What rude behavior did Arnold show?
   ☐ pulled his sister's hair ☒ called Annie a brat
   ☒ threw down the remote control ☐ kicked the TV
   ☒ insisted on having his way ☐ yelled at his mom

3. What might be Arnold's reasons for wanting to switch to *Super Hero*?
   ☒ his favorite show ☐ dislikes movies ☒ his daily habit
   ☒ enjoys fighting ☒ loves the heroes

Directions: On another sheet of paper, answer the following question.

Do you think Arnold's mom was unfair to him? Why or why not?
Answers will vary.

132

Kim's New Baby Brother

Directions: Write a word from the box to complete each sentence.

Kim is disappointed about her new baby brother. He screams and yells too much! Mom spends all of her time taking care of him. Kim is tired of being ignored.

Kim stuffs her backpack with her favorite toys and a peanut butter sandwich. She'll spend the day at a friend's house. She has had enough!

At her friend's house, Kim talks to Mrs. Sweetly. Mrs. Sweetly says that she understands how Kim feels, but that Kim should tell her mother.

When they talk, Mom tells Kim that she loves her just as much as ever and that baby brother loves her, too. Mom teaches Kim how to comfort the baby. Then, she takes Kim out for lunch, just the two of them. Now, Kim likes her baby brother and isn't jealous anymore.

| angry | wise | love | jealous | better |

1. Kim is **jealous** of her new baby brother.
2. Kim feels **angry** while she is packing her backpack.
3. Mrs. Sweetly gives Kim **wise** advice.
4. Kim feels **better** about the baby after talking to her mom.
5. Kim's mom gives her the **love** and attention she needs.

133

A Black Hole

Directions: A story about something true is called **nonfiction**. Read about the black hole and answer the questions that follow.

Have you ever heard of a mysterious black hole? Some scientists believe that a black hole is an invisible object somewhere in space. Scientists believe that it has such a strong pull toward it, called gravity, that nothing can escape from it.

These scientists believe that a black hole is a star that has collapsed. The collapse made its pull even stronger. It seems invisible because even its own starlight cannot escape! It is believed that anything in space that comes near the black hole will be pulled into it forever. Some scientists believe there are many black holes in our galaxy.

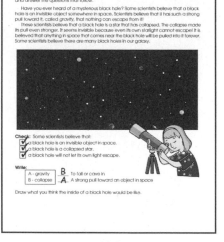

Check: Some scientists believe that:
☒ a black hole is an invisible object in space.
☒ a black hole is a collapsed star.
☒ a black hole will not let its own light escape.

Write:
A - gravity **B** To fall or cave in
B - collapse **A** A strong pull toward an object in space

Draw what you think the inside of a black hole would be like.

134

A Funnel Cloud—Danger!

Directions: Read about tornados and answer the questions that follow.

Did you know that a tornado is the most violent windstorm on Earth? A tornado is a whirling, twisting storm that is shaped like a funnel.

A tornado usually occurs in the spring on a hot day. It begins with thunderclouds and thunder. A cloud becomes very dark. The bottom of the cloud begins to twist and form a funnel. Rain and lightning begin. The funnel cloud drops from the dark storm clouds. It moves down toward the ground.

A tornado is very dangerous. It can destroy almost everything in its path.

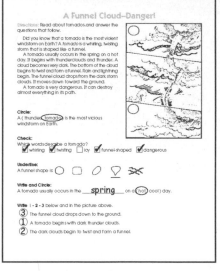

Circle:
A (thunder / ⟨tornado⟩) is the most vicious windstorm on Earth.

Check:
Which words describe a tornado?
☒ whirling ☒ twisting ☐ icy ☒ funnel-shaped ☒ dangerous

Underline:
A funnel shape is ○ □ ⬭ ▽ ✖

Write and Circle:
A tornado usually occurs in the **spring** on a (⟨hot⟩/ cool) day.

Write 1 - 2 - 3 below and in the picture above.
③ The funnel cloud drops down to the ground.
① A tornado begins with dark thunder clouds.
② The dark clouds begin to twist and form a funnel.

135

Hummingbirds

Hummingbirds are very small birds. This tiny bird is quite an acrobat. Only a few birds, such as kingfishers and sunbirds, can hover, which means to stay in one place in the air. But no other bird can match the flying skills of the hummingbird. The hummingbird can hover, fly backward, and fly upside down!

Hummingbirds got their name because their wings move very quickly when they fly. This causes a humming sound. Their wings move so fast that you can't see them at all. This takes a lot of energy. These little birds must have food about every 20 minutes to have enough strength to fly. Their favorite foods are insects and nectar. Nectar is the sweet water deep inside a flower. Hummingbirds use their long, thin bills to drink from flowers. When a hummingbird sips nectar, it hovers in front of a flower. It never touches the flower with its wings or feet.

Besides being the best at flying, the hummingbird is also one of the prettiest birds. Of all the birds in the world, the hummingbird's colors are among the brightest. Some are bright green with red and white markings. Some are purple. One kind of hummingbird can change its color from reddish-brown to purple to red!

The hummingbird's nest is special, too. It looks like a tiny cup. The inside of the nest is very soft. This is because one of the things the mother bird uses to build the nest is the silk from a spider's web.

Directions: Answer these questions about hummingbirds.

1. How did hummingbirds get their name? **Because their wings move very quickly when they fly, and it causes a humming sound.**
2. What does hover mean? **to hang in the air**
3. How often do hummingbirds need to eat? **every 20 minutes**
4. Name two things that hummingbirds eat. **insects and nectar**
5. What is one of the things a mother hummingbird uses to build her nest? **silk from a spider's web**

136

Bats

Bats are the only mammals that can fly. They have wings made of thin skin stretched between long fingers. Bats can fly amazing distances. Some small bats have been known to fly more than 25 miles in one night.

Most bats eat insects or fruit. But some eat only fish, others only blood, and still others the nectar and pollen of flowers that bloom at night. Bats are active only at night. They sleep during the day in caves or other dark places. At rest, they always hang with their heads down.

You may have heard the expression "blind as a bat." But bats are not blind. They don't, however, use their eyes to guide their flight or to find the insects they eat. A bat makes a high-pitched squeak, then waits for the echo to return to it. This echo tells it how far away an object is. This is often called the bat's sonar system. Using this system, a bat can fly through a dark cave without bumping into anything. Hundreds of bats can fly around in the dark without ever running into each other. They do not get confused by the squeaks of the other bats. They always recognize their own echoes.

Directions: Answer these questions about bats.

1. Bats are the only mammals that
   □ eat insects. ☑ fly. □ live in caves.
2. Most bats eat
   □ plants. □ other animals. ☑ fruits and insects.
3. Bats always sleep
   ☑ with their heads down. □ lying down. □ during the night.
4. Bats are blind. True **False**
5. Bats use a built-in sonar system to guide them. **True** False
6. Bats are confused by the squeaks of other bats. True **False**

137

Oceans

If you looked at Earth from up in space, you would see a planet that is mostly blue. This is because more than two-thirds of Earth is covered with water. You already know that this is what makes our planet different from the others, and what makes life on Earth possible. Most of this water is in the four great oceans: Pacific, Atlantic, Indian, and Arctic. The Pacific is by far the largest and the deepest. It is more than twice as big as the Atlantic, the second largest ocean.

The water in the ocean is salty. This is because rivers are always pouring water into the oceans. Some of this water picks up salt from the rocks it flows over. It is not enough salt to make the rivers taste salty. But the salt in the oceans has been building up over millions of years. The oceans get more and more salty every century.

The ocean provides us with huge amounts of food, especially fish. There are many other things we get from the ocean, including sponges and pearls. The oceans are also great "highways" of the world. Ships are always crossing the oceans, transporting many goods from country to country.

The science of studying the ocean is called oceanography. Today, oceanographers have special equipment to help them learn about the oceans and seas. Electronic instruments can be sent deep below the surface to make measurements. The newest equipment uses sonar or echo-sounding systems that bounce sound waves off the sea bed and use the echoes to make pictures of the ocean floor.

Directions: Answer these questions about the oceans.

1. How much of the Earth is covered by water? **two-thirds**
2. Which is the largest and deepest ocean? **Pacific**
3. What is the science of studying the ocean? **oceanography**
4. What new equipment do oceanographers use? **sonar or echo sounding systems**

138

Deep-Sea Diving

One part of the world is still largely unexplored. It is the deep sea. Over the years, many people have explored the sea. But the first deep-sea divers wanted to find sunken treasure. They weren't interested in studying the creatures or life there. Only recently have they begun to learn some of the mysteries of the sea.

It's not easy to explore the deep sea. Divers must have a way of breathing under water. They must be able to protect themselves from the terrific pressure. The pressure of air is about 15 pounds on every square inch. But the pressure of water is about 1,300 pounds on every square inch!

The first diving suits were made of rubber. They had a helmet of brass with windows in it. The shoes were made of lead and weighed 20 pounds each! These suits let divers go down a few hundred feet, but they were no good for exploring very deep water. With a metal diving suit, a diver could go down 700 feet. Metal suits were first used in the 1930s.

In 1987, a diver named William Beebe wanted to explore deeper than anyone had ever gone before. He was not interested in finding treasure. He wanted to study deep-sea creatures and plants. He invented a hollow metal ball called the bathysphere. It weighed more than 5,000 pounds, but in it Beebe went down 3,028 feet. He saw many things that had never been seen by humans before.

Directions: Answer these questions about early deep-sea diving.

1. What were the first deep-sea divers interested in? **sunken treasure**
2. What are two problems that must be overcome in deep-sea diving?
   a. **the terrific water pressure**
   b. **breathing under water**
3. How deep could a diver go wearing a metal suit? **700 feet**
4. Who was the deep-sea explorer who invented the bathysphere? **William Beebe**

139

Space Pioneer

Neil Armstrong is one of the great pioneers of space. On July 20, 1969, Armstrong was commander of Apollo 11, the first manned American spacecraft to land on the Moon. He was the first person to walk on the Moon.

Armstrong was born in Ohio in 1930. He took his first airplane ride when he was 6 years old. As he grew older, he did jobs to earn money to learn to fly. On his 16th birthday, he received his student pilot's license.

Armstrong served as a Navy fighter pilot during the Korean War. He received three medals. Later, he was a test pilot. He was known as one of the best pilots in the world. He was also an engineer. He contributed much to the development of new methods of flying. In 1962, he was accepted into an astronaut training program.

Armstrong had much experience when he was named to command the historic flight to the Moon. It took four days to fly to the Moon. As he climbed down the ladder to be the first person to step onto the Moon, he said these now-famous words: "That's one small step for man, one giant leap for mankind."

Directions: Answer these questions about Neil Armstrong.

1. What did Neil Armstrong do before any other person in the world? **He walked on the Moon.**
2. How old was Neil Armstrong when he got his student pilot's license? **16 years old**
3. What did Armstrong do during the Korean War? **served as a Navy fighter pilot**
4. On what date did a person first walk on the Moon? **July 20, 1969**

140

Sally Ride, First Woman in Space

Directions: Read about Sally Ride. Then, answer the questions.

Sally Ride was the first American woman in space. She was only 31 years old when she went into space in 1982. Besides being the first American woman, she was also the youngest person ever to go into space!

Many people wanted to be astronauts. When Sally Ride was chosen, there were 8,000 people who wanted to be in the class. Only 35 were selected. Six of those people were women. Sally Ride rode in the spaceship Challenger. She was called a mission specialist. Like an astronaut, Sally Ride had to study for several years before she went into space. She spent 6 days on her journey. She has even written a book for children about her adventure! It is called To Space and Back.

1. What was significant about Sally Ride's journey into space? **She was the first American woman and youngest person in space.**
2. How old was Sally Ride when she went into space? **31**
3. What was the name of her spaceship? **Challenger**
4. What was her title on the trip into space? **mission specialist**
5. How long did Sally Ride's journey last? **6 days**
6. What was the name of the book she wrote? **To Space and Back**
7. Why do you think many people want to be astronauts? **Answers will vary.**

141

GRADE 4

I. Reading
   A. Directions
   B. Sequencing
   C. Main Idea
II. Writing
   A. Capitalization
   B. Proofreading

Clouds

Directions: Read about clouds. Then, answer the questions.

Have you ever wondered where clouds come from? Clouds are made from billions and billions of tiny water droplets in the air. The water droplets form into clouds when warm, moist air rises and is cooled.

Have you ever seen your breath when you were outside on a very cold day? Your breath is warm and moist. When it hits the cold air, it is cooled. A kind of small cloud is formed by your breath!

Clouds come in many sizes and shapes. On some days, clouds blanket the whole sky. Other times, clouds look like wispy puffs of smoke. There are other types of clouds as well.

Weather experts have named clouds. Big, fluffy clouds that look flat on the bottom are called cumulus clouds. Stratocumulus is the name for rounded clouds that are packed very close together. You can still see patches of sky, but stratocumulus clouds are thicker than cumulus ones.

If you spot cumulonimbus clouds, go inside. These clouds are wide at the bottom and have thin tops. The tops of these clouds are filled with ice crystals. On hot summer days, you may even have seen cumulonimbus clouds growing. They seem to boil and grow as though they are coming from a big pot. A violent thunderstorm usually occurs after you see these clouds. Often, there is hail.

Cumulus, stratocumulus, and cumulonimbus are only three of many types of clouds. If you listen closely, you will hear television weather forecasters talk about them and other clouds. Why? Because clouds are good indicators of weather.

1. How are clouds formed? **Water droplets in the air form clouds when warm, moist air rises and cools.**

2. How can you make your own cloud? **by breathing outside on a cold day**

3. What should you do when you spot cumulonimbus clouds? **go inside**

4. What often happens after you see cumulonimbus clouds? **violent thunderstorms, sometimes hail**

5. What kind of big fluffy clouds look flat on the bottom? **cumulus**

142

Thunderstorms

Directions: Read about thunderstorms. Then, answer the questions.

Thunderstorms can be scary! The sky darkens. The air feels heavy. Then, the thunder begins. Sometimes, the thunder sounds like a low rumble. Other times, thunder is very loud. Loud thunder can be heard 15 miles away.

Thunderstorms begin inside big cumulonimbus clouds. Remember, cumulonimbus are the summer clouds that seem to boil and grow. It is as though there is a big pot under the clouds.

Thunder is heard after lightning flashes across the sky. The noise of thunder happens when lightning heats the air as it cuts through it. Some people call this quick, sharp sound a thunderclap. Sometimes thunder sounds "rumbly." This rumble is the thunder's sound wave bouncing off hills and mountains.

Weather experts say there is an easy way to figure out how far away a storm is. First, look at your watch. Count the number of seconds between the flash of lightning and the sound of thunder. To find how far away the storm is, divide the number of seconds by five. This will give the number of miles the storm is from you.

How far away is the storm if you count 20 seconds between the flash of lightning and the sound of thunder? Twenty divided by five is four miles. What if you count only five seconds? One mile! Get inside quickly. The air is charged with electricity. You could be struck by lightning. It is not safe to be outside in a thunderstorm.

1. Where do thunderstorms begin? **inside cumulonimbus clouds**

2. When is thunder heard? **after lightning flashes**

3. What causes thunder to sound "rumbly"? **the sound wave bounces off hills and mountains**

4. To find how far away a storm is, count the seconds between the thunder and lightning and divide by what number? **5**

5. If you count 40 seconds between the lightning and thunder, how far away is the storm? **8 miles**

6. What comes first, thunder or lightning? **lightning**

143

Your Five Senses

Your senses are very important to you. You depend on them every day. They tell you where you are and what is going on around you. Your senses are sight, hearing, touch, smell, and taste.

Try to imagine for a minute that you were suddenly unable to use your senses. Imagine, for instance, that you are in a cave and your only source of light is a candle. Without warning, a gust of wind blows out the flame.

Your senses are always at work. Your eyes let you read this book. Your nose brings the scent of dinner cooking. Your tongue helps you taste dinner later. Your hand feels the softness as you stroke a puppy. Your ears tell you if a storm is approaching.

Your senses also help keep you from harm. They warn you if you touch something that will burn you. They keep you from looking at a light that is too bright, and they tell you if a car is coming up behind you. Each of your senses collects information and sends it as a message to your brain. The brain is like the control center for your body. It sorts out the messages sent by your senses and acts on them.

Directions: Answer these questions about the five senses.

1. Circle the main idea:

   Your senses keep you from harm.

   (Your senses are important to you in many ways.)

2. Name the five senses.
   a. **sight**
   b. **hearing**
   c. **touch**
   d. **smell**
   e. **taste**

3. Which part of your body acts as the "control center"? **your brain**

144

Touch

Unlike the other senses, which are located only in your head, your sense of touch is all over your body. Throughout your life, you receive an endless flow of information about the world and yourself from your sense of touch. It tells you if something is hot or cold, hard or soft. It sends messages of pain, such as a headache or sore throat, if there is a problem.

There are thousands of tiny sensors all over your body. They are all linked together. These sensors are also linked to your spinal cord and your brain to make up your central nervous system. Through this system, the various parts of your body can send messages to your brain. It is then the brain's job to decide what it is you are actually feeling. All this happens in just a split second.

Not all parts of your body have the same amount of feeling. Areas that have the most nerves, or sensors, have the greatest amount of feeling. For instance, the tips of your fingers have more feeling than parts of your arm.

Some sensors get used to the feeling of an object after a period of time. When you first put your shirt on in the morning, you can feel its pressure on your skin. However, some of the sensors stop responding during the day.

One feeling you cannot get used to is the feeling of pain. Pain is an important message, because it tells your brain that something harmful is happening to you. Your brain reacts by doing something right away to protect you.

Directions: Answer these questions about the sense of touch.

1. Circle the main idea:

   (The sense of touch is all over your body.)

   You cannot get used to the sense of pain.

2. The nerves, spinal cord, and brain are linked together to make the **central nervous system**

3. One feeling you can never get used to is **pain**

4. All parts of your body have the same amount of feeling.   True   (False)

5. It is the brain's job to receive messages from the sensors on your body and decide what you are actually feeling.   (True)   False

145

Smell

Your nose is your sense organ for smelling. Smells are mixed into the air around you. They enter your nose when you breathe.

In the upper part of your nose, there are special smell sensors. They pick up smells and send messages to your brain. The brain then decides what it is you are smelling.

Smelling can be a pleasant sense. Sometimes, smells can remind you of a person or place. For instance, have you ever smelled a particular scent and then suddenly thought about your grandmother's house? Smell also can make you feel hungry. In fact, your sense of smell is linked very closely to your sense of taste. Without your sense of smell, you would not taste food as strongly.

Smelling also can be quite unpleasant. But this, too, is important. By smelling food, you can tell if it is spoiled and not fit to eat. Your sense of smell also can sometimes warn you of danger, such as a fire.

The sense of smell tires out more quickly than your other senses. This is why you get used to some everyday smells and no longer notice them after a while.

Directions: Answer these questions about the sense of smell.

1. Smells are mixed in **the air around you**

2. The sense of smell is linked closely to the sense of **taste**

3. Give an example of why smelling bad smells can be important to you.

   You can smell spoiled food or be warned of danger like a fire.

146

Taste

The senses of taste and smell work very closely together. If you can't smell your food, it is difficult to recognize the taste. You may have noticed this when you've had a bad cold with a stuffed-up nose.

Tasting is the work of your tongue. All over your tongue are tiny taste sensors called taste buds. If you look at your tongue in a mirror, you can see small groups of taste buds. They are what give your tongue its rough appearance. Each taste bud has a small opening in it. Tiny pieces of food and drink enter this opening. There taste sensors gather information about the taste and send messages to your brain. Your brain decides what the taste is.

Taste buds located in different areas of your tongue recognize different tastes. There are only four tastes your tongue can recognize: sweet, sour, bitter, and salty. All other flavors are a mixture of taste and smell.

Directions: Answer these questions about the sense of taste.

1. It is difficult to taste your food if you can't **smell**

2. The tiny taste sensors on your tongue are called **taste buds**

3. The four tastes that your tongue can recognize are **sweet, sour, bitter, and salty**

4. All other flavors are a mixture of **taste and smell**

147

GRADE 4

I. Reading
A. Directions
B. Sequencing
C. Main Idea
II. Writing
A. Capitalization
B. Proofreading

Sight

You can see this page because of light. Without light, there would be no sight. In a dark room, you might see only a few large shapes. If it is pitch black, you can't see anything at all.

Light reflects, or bounces off, things and then travels to your eyes. The light enters your eye through the pupil. The pupil is the black circle in the middle of your eye. It gets bigger in low light to let in as much light as possible. In bright light, it shrinks so that too much light doesn't get in.

Light enters through the pupil and then passes through the lens. The lens bends the light so that it falls on the back of your eye on the retina. The retina has millions of tiny cells that are very sensitive to light. When an image is formed in the eye, it is upside down. This image is sent to your brain. The brain receives the message and turns the picture right side up again.

Some people are far-sighted. This means they can clearly see things that are far away, but things close by may be blurred. People who are near-sighted can clearly see things better if they are close by. Glasses or contact lenses can help correct these problems.

Some people can see only a little bit or perhaps not at all. This is called being blind. Blind people rely on their sense of touch to learn more about the world. They can even use their sense of touch to read. Some blind people read with a special printing system called Braille. The system is named for the man who invented it. Braille has small raised dots, instead of letters, on a page.

Directions: Answer these questions about the sense of sight.

1. Without ___light___, there would be no sight.
2. Reflect means ___to bounce off of___
3. The part of the eye that controls the amount of light entering your eye by getting bigger and smaller is called the ___pupil___
4. To correct near-sightedness or far-sightedness, you can wear ___glasses or contact lenses___
5. What is the name of the special printing system for blind people? ___Braille___

148

Sorting Nouns

Nouns are words that name a person, place, or thing.

Directions: Write each noun in the correct box.

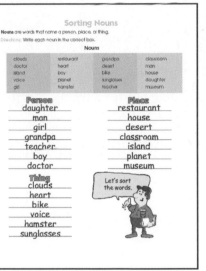

Nouns			
clouds	restaurant	grandpa	classroom
doctor	heart	desert	man
island	boy	bike	house
voice	planet	sunglasses	daughter
girl	hamster	teacher	museum

Person
daughter
man
girl
grandpa
teacher
boy
doctor

Place
restaurant
house
desert
classroom
island
planet
museum

Thing
clouds
heart
bike
voice
hamster
sunglasses

Let's sort the words.

149

Common and Proper Nouns

A **common noun** names a person, place, or thing. A common noun begins with a small, or lowercase, letter.

Examples: nurse   store   book

A **proper noun** names a particular person, place, or thing. Proper nouns begin with a capital, or uppercase, letter.

Examples: George Washington   Niagara Falls   Plymouth Rock

Directions: Write each noun on a jersey for the correct team. Remember to capitalize proper nouns.

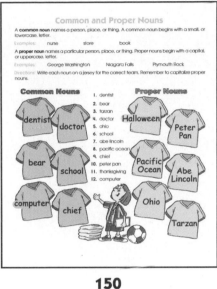

Common Nouns
dentist, doctor, bear, school, computer, chief

Proper Nouns
Halloween, Peter Pan, Pacific Ocean, Abe Lincoln, Ohio, Tarzan

1. dentist
2. bear
3. tarzan
4. doctor
5. ohio
6. school
7. abe lincoln
8. pacific ocean
9. chief
10. peter pan
11. thanksgiving
12. computer

150

All American

Directions: Color the spaces **red** that contain a common noun. Color the spaces **blue** that contain a proper noun.

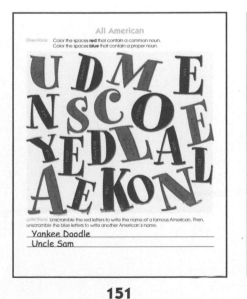

Directions: Unscramble the red letters to write the name of a famous American. Then, unscramble the blue letters to write another American's name.

Yankee Doodle
Uncle Sam

151

All in a Name

Directions: Write a proper noun next to each common noun.

1. girl   Susie
2. boy
3. teacher
4. pet
5. store
6. continent
7. state
8. lake
9. river
10. book

Answers will vary.

Directions: Write a common noun next to each proper noun.

1. the Chicago Bears   team
2. Andover Middle School   school
3. Newsweek   magazine
4. April   month
5. holiday   day
6. Thanksgiving   holiday
7. Sue's Diner   restaurant
8. Thomas Jefferson   president
9. San Francisco   city
10. Mt. Everest   mountain

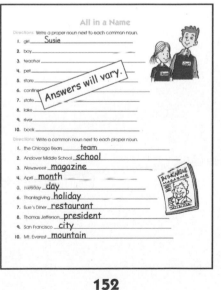

152

Common and Proper Nouns

Remember, a **common noun** names any person, place, or thing.
A **proper noun** names a specific person, place, or thing.
A proper noun always begins with a capital letter.

Example: boy, state (common nouns)
Peter, Georgia (proper nouns)

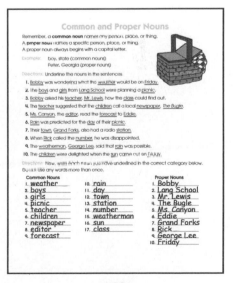

Directions: Underline the nouns in the sentences.

1. Bobby was wondering what the weather would be on Friday.
2. The boys and girls from Lang School were planning a picnic.
3. Bobby asked his teacher, Mr. Lewis, how the class could find out.
4. The teacher suggested that the children call a local newspaper, The Bugle.
5. Ms. Canyon, the editor, read the forecast to Eddie.
6. Rain was predicted for the day of their picnic.
7. Their town, Grand Forks, also had a radio station.
8. When Rick called the number, he was disappointed.
9. The weatherman, George Lee, said that rain was possible.
10. The children were delighted when the sun came out on Friday.

Directions: Now, write each noun you have underlined in the correct category below. But do not use any words more than once.

Common Nouns
1. weather
2. boys
3. girls
4. picnic
5. teacher
6. children
7. newspaper
8. editor
9. forecast
10. rain
11. day
12. town
13. station
14. number
15. weatherman
16. sun
17. class

Proper Nouns
1. Bobby
2. Lang School
3. Mr. Lewis
4. The Bugle
5. Ms. Canyon
6. Eddie
7. Grand Forks
8. Rick
9. George Lee
10. Friday

153

GRADE
4

I. Reading
A. Directions
B. Sequencing
C. Main Idea
II. Writing
A. Capitalization
B. Proofreading

Room for One More

A **singular noun** names one person, place, or thing. A **plural noun** names more than one person, place, or thing. Usually, to form the plural you just add **s**. Words that end in **s**, **sh**, **ch**, or **x** need **es** to form the plural.

Examples:
Singular Nouns	Plural Nouns
car	cars
bus	buses
lunch	lunches
fox	foxes

Directions: Write the correct singular or plural noun in parentheses to complete each sentence.

1. Mike was packing two (suitcase, suitcases) for a trip. **suitcases**
2. One (suitcase, suitcases) is a carry-on bag. **suitcase**
3. He decided to take three (shirt, shirts) along. **shirts**
4. Mike will wear his favorite blue (shirt, shirts) on the plane. **shirt**
5. He will leave the two tennis (shoe, shoes) at home. **shoes**
6. Mike can't seem to find the one missing black (shoe, shoes)! **shoe**
7. It's with the big (bunch, bunches) hiding under the bed. **bunch**
8. Why do shoes hide in (bunch, bunches) like that? **bunches**
9. Would one (sweater, sweaters) be enough? **sweater**
10. (Sweater, Sweaters) seem to take up too much room. **Sweaters**
11. Mike packs six (box, boxes) of candy for his friends. **boxes**
12. He will try to squeeze in one more (box, boxes). **box**

154

Forming Plural Nouns

Most **singular nouns** can be made into **plural nouns** by following one of these rules.

Rules	Examples
1. Add **s** to most nouns.	elephant, elephants
2. If the noun ends in **s**, **sh**, **ch**, or **x**, add **es**.	box, boxes
3. If the noun ends in **y** with a consonant before it, change the **y** to **i** and add **es**.	fly, flies
4. If the noun ends in **y** with a vowel before it, add **s**.	monkey, monkeys
5. To some nouns ending in **f**, add **s**.	chief, chiefs
6. To some nouns ending in **f** or **fe**, change the **f** to **v** and add **es**.	knife, knives thief, thieves
7. Some nouns stay the same for singular and plural.	sheep, sheep
8. Some nouns have an irregular plural.	goose, geese

Directions: Change each singular noun to plural. Write the number of the rule you used. Use a dictionary when needed.

Singular	Plural	Rule #	Singular	Plural	Rule #
1. chimney	chimneys	4	11. woman	women	8
2. class	classes	2	12. bus	buses	2
3. wolf	wolves	6	13. judge	judges	1
4. deer	deer	7	14. shelf	shelves	6
5. story	stories	3	15. chair	chairs	1
6. elf	elves	6	16. beach	beaches	2
7. tooth	teeth	8	17. tax	taxes	2
8. brush	brushes	2	18. lady	ladies	3
9. attorney	attorneys	4	19. roof	roofs	1
10. mouse	mice	8	20. penny	pennies	3

155

Totally Irregular!

Irregular nouns do not form the plural by adding **s** or **es**. You must memorize them. These nouns look the same whether singular or plural.

deer	salmon	trout	sheep	moose
tuna	cod	pike	bass	elk

These irregular nouns form their plurals using special spellings.

goose	geese
man	men
woman	women
tooth	teeth
ox	oxen
foot	feet
child	children
mouse	mice

Directions: Write singular or plural to identify the form of the underlined noun.

1. Many men, women, and children like fishing. **plural**
2. A child can easily catch a bass using live bait. **singular**
3. A salmon or a cod are not as easy for a child to catch. **singular**
4. Fly fishers can catch many trout without bait. **plural**
5. A fly rod can be six feet long. **plural**
6. Either a man or a woman can fish with a fly rod. **singular**
7. You might see an elk or a deer while fishing. **singular**
8. Moose are often found along the river also. **plural**
9. The cold river water can make your teeth chatter. **plural**

156

I, We; Me, Us

I and **we** are **subject pronouns**. **Me** and **us** are **object pronouns**.

Examples:
Mark and I are on our way to the park. (subject pronoun)
We just love to launch rockets! (subject pronoun)
Will Sara come with **me**? (object pronoun)
Please feel welcome to join **us**. (object pronoun)

Directions: Choose the correct pronoun for each sentence from those in parentheses. Write it in the blank.

1. **We** plan to launch rockets at the park on Saturday. (We, us)
2. Monica bought **me** a two-stage rocket. (I, me)
3. Bill and **I** both brought fresh batteries for the rocket launcher. (I, me)
4. Curt plans to build **us** a rocket. (we, us)
5. Gwen wants **me** to attend the rocket safety course. (I, me)
6. **I** always like to paint the fins a bright color. (I, me)
7. Tom wants Michele and **me** to chase after his rocket when it lands. (I, me)
8. Heather wants **us** to go to the launching site. (we, us)
9. Carolyn and **I** just bought a model rocket with a payload section. (I, me)
10. Jim will be showing **us** his model rocket. (we, us)
11. David taught **me** all the safety rules. (I, me)

157

Pronoun Party

Pronouns are words that take the place of singular or plural nouns.

Singular	Plural	When Used
I, me	we, us	to talk about yourself
you	you	to talk to a person
he, she, it, him, her	they, them	to talk about other persons or things

Example: **Jeremy** brought a gift to the party.
He brought a gift to the party.

Directions: Write the pronoun that takes the place of the underlined noun or nouns.

1. Nancy planned a party for Pam. **her**
2. Is Mom going to take us? **she**
3. Tommy is taking Pam a present. **He**
4. Todd and Neil bought her a CD. **They**
5. Dad gave the boys the money. **them**
6. Pam will like the music. **it**
7. Pam saw Todd and me yesterday. **us**
8. Todd and I didn't talk about the party. **We**

158

Pick the Right Pronoun

Use **I**, **we**, **he**, or **she** when the pronoun is a subject.

Examples: **Craig** plays the violin.
He plays the violin.
Mindy plays the piano.
She plays the piano.

Use **me**, **us**, **her**, **him**, or **them** when the pronoun is not a subject.

Examples: Mom took **Connie** shopping.
Mom took **her** shopping.
Dad went fishing with **Alex**.
Dad went fishing with **him**.

Use **it** and **you** in any part of a sentence.

Examples: The **bicycle** is new.
It is new.
I waited for the **bus**.
I waited for **it**.

I	he	me	her
we	she	us	him
			them

Directions: Write the correct pronoun that completes each sentence.

1. Danny and (me, I) went camping. **I**
2. (We, Us) went to the baseball game. **We**
3. The teacher took (we, us) to the library. **us**
4. (Him, He) was a famous American. **He**
5. Aunt Mary gave a dollar to (them, we). **them**
6. (Her, You) and Greg are my best friends. **You**
7. Please take this note to (he, him). **him**
8. Charlie took Alan and (me, I) to the party. **me**

159

GRADE 4

I. Reading
  A. Directions
  B. Sequencing
  C. Main Idea
II. Writing
  A. Capitalization
  B. Proofreading

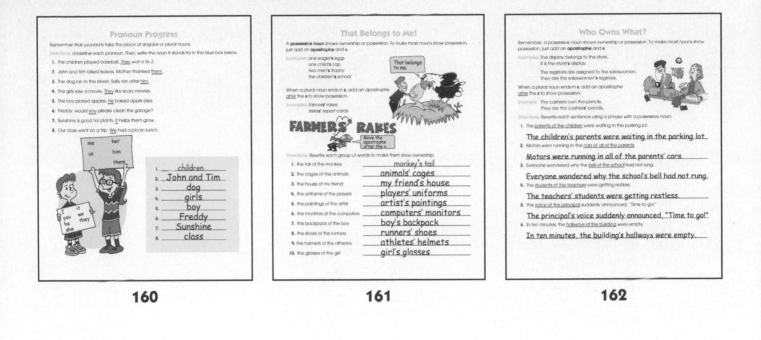

Pronoun Progress

Remember that pronouns take the place of singular or plural nouns.

Directions: Underline each pronoun. Then, write the noun it stands for in the blue box below.

1. The children played baseball. They won 6 to 2.
2. John and Tim raked leaves. Mother thanked them.
3. The dog ran in the street. Sally ran after him.
4. The girls saw a movie. They like scary movies.
5. The boy picked apples. He baked apple pies.
6. Freddy, would you please clean the garage?
7. Sunshine is good for plants. It helps them grow.
8. Our class went on a trip. We had a picnic lunch.

me	her
us	him
	them

I	it
you	we they
he	
she	

1. _children_
2. _John and Tim_
3. _dog_
4. _girls_
5. _boy_
6. _Freddy_
7. _Sunshine_
8. _class_

160

That Belongs to Me!

A **possessive noun** shows ownership or possession. To make most nouns show possession, just add an **apostrophe** and an **s**.

Examples: one eagle's eggs
one child's cap
two men's trophy
the children's school

That belongs to me.

When a plural noun ends in **s**, add an apostrophe *after* the **s** to show possession.

Examples: farmers' rakes
sisters' report cards

FARMERS' RAKES

Move the apostrophe after the s.

Directions: Rewrite each group of words to make them show ownership.

1. the tail of the monkey — monkey's tail
2. the cages of the animals — animals' cages
3. the house of my friend — my friend's house
4. the uniforms of the players — players' uniforms
5. the paintings of the artist — artist's paintings
6. the monitors of the computers — computers' monitors
7. the backpack of the boy — boy's backpack
8. the shoes of the runners — runners' shoes
9. the helmets of the athletes — athletes' helmets
10. the glasses of the girl — girl's glasses

161

Who Owns What?

Remember, a possessive noun shows ownership or possession. To make most nouns show possession, just add an **apostrophe** and an **s**.

Examples: The display belongs to the store.
It is the store's display.

The registers are assigned to the saleswomen.
They are the saleswomen's registers.

When a plural noun ends in **s**, add an apostrophe *after* the **s** to show possession.

Example: The cashiers own the pencils.
They are the cashiers' pencils.

Directions: Rewrite each sentence using a phrase with a possessive noun.

1. The parents of the children were waiting in the parking lot.
   The children's parents were waiting in the parking lot.
2. Motors were running in the cars of all of the parents.
   Motors were running in all of the parents' cars.
3. Everyone wondered why the bell of the school had not rung.
   Everyone wondered why the school's bell had not rung.
4. The students of the teachers were getting restless.
   The teachers' students were getting restless.
5. The voice of the principal suddenly announced, "Time to go!"
   The principal's voice suddenly announced, "Time to go!"
6. In ten minutes, the hallways of the building were empty.
   In ten minutes, the building's hallways were empty.

162

Possessive Nouns Review

Directions: Write the correct possessive form of the underlined noun.

1. The balloon string is long. — balloon's
2. Mary pencil was broken. — Mary's
3. Both boys grades were good. — boys'
4. This house is Cliff house. — Cliff's
5. Tony aunt came to visit. — Tony's
6. Some flowers leaves were large. — flowers'
7. We saw two bears tracks. — bears'
8. The children room was messy. — children's
9. My sister birthday is today. — sister's
10. The clowns acts made us laugh. — clowns'
11. Jonah filled Pete dish. — Pete's
12. Mark joined the two boys game. — boys'
13. The baseball players uniforms are clean. — players'
14. The dog dish was empty. — dog's
15. The three cats paws were wet. — cats'

It's Mine!

163

Possessive Pronouns

Possessive pronouns are pronouns that show ownership without using an apostrophe. Some possessive pronouns are used with nouns.

Examples:

Pronouns Used With a Noun	
my house	its paws
your shoes	our pets
his dog	their names
her car	

Directions: Write a possessive pronoun that completes the second sentence.

1. Chad, this book belongs to you. It is __your__ book.
2. It came from the library we belong to. It came from __our__ library.
3. I found it in the car that belongs to me. I found it in __my__ car.
4. The cover of the book looked familiar. __Its__ cover looked familiar.
5. I thought it was Mary's book. I thought it was __her__ book.
6. She said it was Jim Long's book. She said it was __his__ book.
7. I went to the Long family's house. I went to __their__ house.
8. Luckily, you were there to claim the book. You claimed __your__ book.
9. I stayed to play with Jim's dog. I played with __his__ dog.
10. The dog's collar is new. __Its__ collar is new.

164

Yours, Mine, and Ours

Possessive pronouns can show ownership with or without using the noun.

Examples:

The jacket is **my** jacket.
The jacket is **mine.**

The cap is **your** cap.
The cap is **yours.**

The shoes are **his** shoes.
The shoes are **his.**

The glove is **her** glove.
The glove is **hers.**

We have **our** jackets.
The jackets are **ours.**

The children have **their** bats.
The bats are **theirs.**

This jacket is mine.

And this cap is yours.

Directions: Write a possessive pronoun on the line that means the same as the words in parentheses.

1. The comb is __yours__. (your comb)
2. The bottle is __hers__. (the baby girl's bottle)
3. The books were __his__. (Mark's books)
4. The computers are __theirs__. (the sisters' computers)
5. The mailman brought __ours__. (our mail)
6. __Mine__ are in bloom. (My flowers)
7. The blue bicycle is __yours__. (your bicycle)
8. __Hers__ is today. (Sara's piano lesson)

165

GRADE
4

I. Reading
  A. Directions
  B. Sequencing
  C. Main Idea
II. Writing
  A. Capitalization
  B. Proofreading

Pronoun Pro!

Remember, pronouns are words that take the place of singular or plural nouns. Possessive pronouns are a type of pronoun that shows ownership.

Directions: Write a pronoun from the box that can take the place of the underlined word or words.

we	she
he	his
yours	they
them	their
mine	ours

1. I forgot to bring my lunch today. **mine**
2. Lisa will share her lunch with me. **She**
3. Steve has a soccer game on Friday. **He**
4. My game is on Saturday. **Mine**
5. My friend and I will ride bicycles to the game. **We**
6. Sam's bicycle is a mountain bike. **His**
7. What is Sam's chance of scoring a goal? **his**
8. We plan to congratulate the best players. **them**
9. Is the Martin's house on Main Street? **their**
10. Their house looks just like your house. **yours**
11. Purple and yellow pansies grow in the flower bed. **They**
12. I think our pansies are prettier than their pansies. **ours**
13. Gina and Max went grocery shopping. **They**
14. Beth asked to go along with Gina and Max. **them**

166

Verbs

A **verb** is a word that can show action. A verb can also tell what someone or something is or is like.

Examples: The boats **sail** on Lake Michigan.
We **eat** dinner at 6:00.
I **am** ten years old.
The clowns **were** funny.

Directions: Circle the verb in each sentence.

1. John (sips) milk.
2. They (throw) the football.
3. We (hiked) in the woods.
4. I (enjoy) music.
5. My friend (smiles) often.
6. A lion (hunts) for food.
7. We (ate) lunch at noon.
8. Fish (swim) in the ocean.
9. My team (won) the game.
10. They (were) last in line.
11. The wind (howled) during the night.
12. Kangaroos (live) in Australia.
13. The plane (flew) into the clouds.
14. We (recorded) the song.
15. They (forgot) the directions.

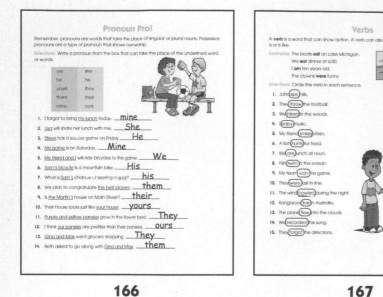

A verb is a word that can show action.

A verb can also tell what someone or something is or is like.

167

What's the Action?

Verbs that tell what people or things do are called **action verbs.**

Examples: Birds **fly** over the water.
Laura **rakes** leaves.

Directions: Circle **yes** if the sentence tells about an action that could happen. Circle **no** if it tells about something that could not happen. Then, write the verb from each sentence on a line below.

1. Kevin threw a ball. — (yes) / no
2. An elephant sews clothes. — yes / (no)
3. My dog learned to read. — yes / (no)
4. Mom filled the tank with gas. — (yes) / no
5. Seatbelts protect passengers. — (yes) / no
6. Juanita searched for her necklace. — (yes) / no
7. Monkeys travel to Mars each year. — yes / (no)
8. It rained cats and dogs. — yes / (no)
9. Pedro read ten books in one month. — (yes) / no
10. Camels flew across the desert. — yes / (no)
11. We caught ten fish on Saturday. — (yes) / no
12. Apples grew on the cherry tree. — yes / (no)

threw	protect	read
sews	searched	flew
learned	travel	caught
filled	rained	grew

168

Helping Verbs

A **verb phrase** is a verb that has more than one word. It is made up of a **main verb** plus one or more **helping verbs.**

Example:
verb phrase
Tim **has practiced** hard.
  ↑   ↑
helping verb main verb

These words are often used as helping verbs with the main verb.

am, is, are, was, were, have, has

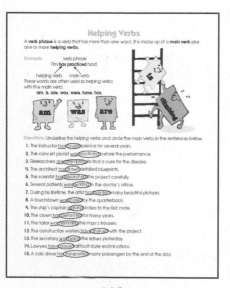

am **was** **are**

Directions: Underline the helping verbs and circle the main verbs in the sentences below.

1. The instructor has (taught) science for several years.
2. The concert pianist was (practicing) before the performance.
3. Researchers are (attempting) to find a cure for the disease.
4. The architect has (drawn) detailed blueprints.
5. The scientist has (researched) the project carefully.
6. Several patients were (waiting) in the doctor's office.
7. During his lifetime, the artist has (painted) many beautiful pictures.
8. A touchdown was (scored) by the quarterback.
9. The ship's captain is (giving) orders to the first mate.
10. The clown has (performed) for many years.
11. The tailor was (hemming) the man's trousers.
12. The construction workers have (finished) with the project.
13. The secretary was (typing) the letters yesterday.
14. Lawyers have (passed) difficult state examinations.
15. A cab driver has (transported) many passengers by the end of the day.

169

Verb Tenses

A **present-tense** verb shows action that is happening now. A **past-tense** verb shows action that happened earlier. A **future-tense** verb shows action that will take place in the future.

Examples: The clockmaker **repairs** the clock. (present)
The clockmaker **repaired** the clock. (past)
The clockmaker **will repair** the clock. (future)

Directions: Write these verbs using the tenses shown in parentheses.

	try	walk	work
(present)	Tom **tries**	Karen **walks**	They **work**
(past)	Tom **tried**	Karen **walked**	They **worked**
(future)	Tom **will try**	Karen **will walk**	They **will work**

Directions: Write the correct verb in each blank below.

1. time (future)
2. chart (present)
3. trickle (past)
4. use (past)
5. fell (present)
6. reset (future)
7. dine (present)
8. move (future)
9. help (past)
10. invent (past)
11. operate (future)

1. John **will time** the runners in the race.
2. A calendar **charts** the days of each month.
3. Sand **trickled** through the hourglass.
4. People **used** the hourglass before clocks were invented.
5. A pendulum **tells** time by Earth's rotation.
6. John **will reset** his watch when changing time zones.
7. He **dines** at 8:00 every evening during the week.
8. Martha **will move** the hands of the clock.
9. In the distant past, the Sun and the Moon **helped** man tell time.
10. The Egyptians **invented** the solar calendar.
11. Timepieces 100 years from now **will operate** differently.

170

Irregular Verbs

Verbs that do not add **ed** to form the past tense are called **irregular verbs.** The spelling of these verbs changes.

Examples:

present	past	present	past
begin, begins	began	do, does	did
break, breaks	broke	eat, eats	ate

Directions: Write the past tense of each irregular verb below.

1. Samuel almost **fell** (fall) when he licked a rock in the path.
2. Diana made sure she **took** (take) a canteen on her hike.
3. David **ran** (run) over to a shady tree for a quick break.
4. Jimmy **broke** (break) off a long piece of grass to put in his mouth while he was walking.
5. Eva **knew** (know) the path along the river very well.
6. The clouds **began** (begin) to sprinkle raindrops on the hikers.
7. Kathy **threw** (throw) a small piece of bread to the birds.
8. Everyone **ate** (eat) a very nutritious meal after a long adventure.
9. We all **slept** (sleep) very well that night.

Many irregular verbs have a different past-tense ending when the helping verbs **have** and **has** are used.

Examples: Steven **has worn** special hiking shoes today.
Marlene and I **have known** about this trail for years.

Directions: Circle the correct irregular verb below.

1. Peter has (flew / (flown)) down to join us for the adventure.
2. Mark has (saw / (seen)) a lot of animals on the hike today.
3. Andy and Mike have (went / (gone)) on this trail before.
4. Bill has (took / (taken)) extra precautions to make sure no cacti prick his legs.
5. Heather has (ate / (eaten)) all the snacks her mom packed for her.

171

GRADE 4

I. Reading
  A. Directions
  B. Sequencing
  C. Main Idea
II. Writing
  A. Capitalization
  B. Proofreading

Verb Search

Sometimes endings are added to verbs to tell about a past action. The **base word** is the verb without the ending.

Examples: Dad **washed** his new van.
(The base word is **wash**.)

We **walked** to the store.
(The base word is **walk**.)

Directions: Underline the verb in each sentence, and write the base word on the line.

1. She planned a trip to Colorado. — plan
2. Nancy's dog followed her to the park. — follow
3. My friends need help with their homework. — need
4. Can you carry the books for me? — carry
5. Ethan explored the attic. — explore
6. We painted our house white and green. — paint
7. The whole class laughed at my jokes. — laugh
8. The chef baked delicious pies and cakes. — bake
9. Judy slipped on the ice and broke her arm. — slip
10. His family owns a large house. — own
11. Please read the second chapter by tomorrow. — read
12. We looked through the microscope. — look
13. She dreamed about sunny beaches. — dream
14. Don't forget your socks! — forget

172

Helping Verbs

A verb may be a single word or a group of words. A verb with more than one word has a **main verb** and one or more **helping verbs**. A helping verb comes before the main verb.

Example:

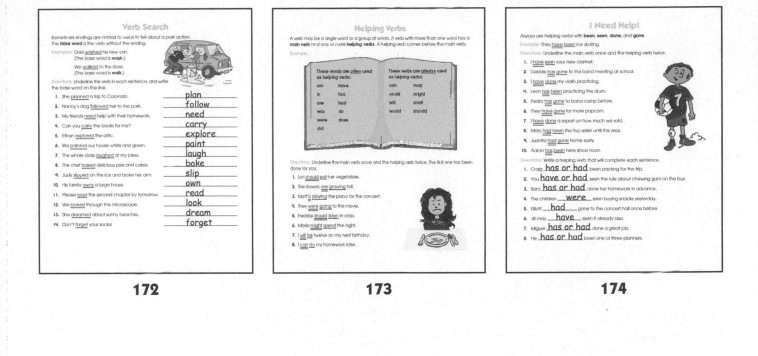

These words are often used as helping verbs:		These verbs are always used as helping verbs:	
am	have	can	may
is	has	could	might
are	had	will	shall
was	do	would	should
were	does		
did			

Directions: Underline the main verb once and the helping verb twice. The first one has been done for you.

1. Lori should eat her vegetables.
2. The flowers are growing tall.
3. Matt is playing the piano for the concert.
4. They were going to the movie.
5. Freddie should listen in class.
6. Maria might spend the night.
7. I will be twelve on my next birthday.
8. I can do my homework later.

173

I Need Help!

Always use helping verbs with **been**, **seen**, **done**, and **gone**.

Example: They have been ice skating.

Directions: Underline the main verb once and the helping verb twice.

1. I have seen your new clarinet.
2. Debbie has gone to the band meeting at school.
3. I have done my violin practicing.
4. Leon has been practicing the drum.
5. Pedro has gone to band camp before.
6. They have gone for more popcorn.
7. I have done a report on how much we sold.
8. Mary had been the top seller until this year.
9. Juanita had gone home early.
10. Aaron has been here since noon.

Directions: Write a helping verb that will complete each sentence.

1. Craig **has or had** been packing for the trip.
2. You **have or had** seen the rule about chewing gum on the bus.
3. Sara **has or had** done her homework in advance.
4. The children **were** seen buying snacks yesterday.
5. Elliott **had** gone to the concert hall once before.
6. Jill may **have** seen it already also.
7. Miguel **has or had** done a great job.
8. He **has or had** been one of three planners.

174

Let's Split!

Sometimes helping verbs and main verbs are separated by words that are not verbs.

Example: Jeff can usually win at word games.

Directions: Underline the main verb once and the helping verbs twice.

1. Carlos did not tell anyone his secret.
2. I am usually working on Saturday.
3. Frank will not get a new locker.
4. I might not finish the large pizza.
5. Does the basketball game start at noon?
6. Tim will not play baseball today.
7. Was your mother angry about the window?
8. I am often able to babysit on weekends.
9. Teaching school has always been my ambition.
10. Do not play the music loudly.

Directions: Write the correct helping verb to complete the sentence.

1. Joanie (are, is) going to the zoo. — is
2. The policemen (is, are) directing traffic. — are
3. I (was, is) eating pizza. — was
4. I (is, am) doing a puzzle for my project. — am
5. The birds (was, were) singing outside my window. — were
6. The frogs (was, were) croaking loudly. — were
7. Max (is, are) sprinkling the lawn. — is
8. We (was, were) jogging on the track. — were

175

Right Now

A verb is in the **present tense** when it tells what a noun does or is doing now. Generally, if the noun doing the action is singular, the present-tense verb will end in s.

Examples: Allison **walks** to school.
The girls **walk** to school.

Directions: Underline the correct present-tense verb in each sentence.

1. Stray dogs sometimes (bite, bites) strangers.
2. The warden (catch, catches) stray dogs.
3. She (tempt, tempts) them with dog treats.
4. My dog (knows, know) about this trick.
5. Other dogs (runs, run) away to safety.

Directions: Write the correct form of the present-tense verb to complete each sentence.

1. My father (shave, shaves) every day. — shaves
2. The chorus (sing, sings) beautifully. — sings
3. The ice-cream cones (taste, tastes) delicious. — taste
4. My neighbor (teach, teaches) French. — teaches
5. Meg (dash, dashes) to school every July. — dashes
6. The birds (fly, flies) from tree to tree. — fly
7. Elm Street (cross, crosses) Main Street. — crosses
8. Michael and Keith (play, plays) tennis. — play
9. They (wait, waits) for the bus at the corner. — wait
10. The clowns (make, makes) us laugh. — make

176

Done Deal

A verb is in the **past tense** when it tells what a noun already did or has done. Most verbs form their past tense by adding ed to the base word.

Example: walk — walked

Sometimes you must make spelling changes to form the past-tense verb. When the verb ends in a silent e, drop the e, and add ed.

Example: hope — hoped

When the verb ends in y after a consonant, change the y to i and add ed.

Example: hurry — hurried

When the verb ends in a single consonant after a single short vowel, double the final consonant, then add ed.

Example: trap — trapped

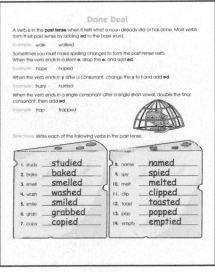

Directions: Write each of the following verbs in the past tense.

1. study — studied
2. bake — baked
3. smell — smelled
4. wash — washed
5. smile — smiled
6. grab — grabbed
7. copy — copied
8. name — named
9. spy — spied
10. melt — melted
11. clip — clipped
12. toast — toasted
13. pop — popped
14. empty — emptied

177

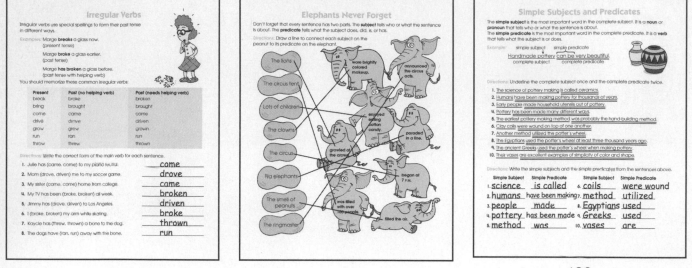

178

Irregular Verbs

Irregular verbs use special spellings to form their past tense in different ways.

Examples: Marge **breaks** a glass now.
(present tense)

Marge **broke** a glass earlier.
(past tense)

Marge **has broken** a glass before.
(past tense with helping verb)

You should memorize these common irregular verbs:

Present	Past (no helping verb)	Past (needs helping verb)
break	broke	broken
bring	brought	brought
come	came	come
drive	drove	driven
grow	grew	grown
run	ran	run
throw	threw	thrown

Directions: Write the correct form of the main verb for each sentence.

1. Julie has (came, come) to my piano recital. — **come**
2. Mom (drove, driven) me to my soccer game. — **drove**
3. My sister (came, come) home from college. — **came**
4. My TV has been (broke, broken) all week. — **broken**
5. Jimmy has (drove, driven) to Los Angeles. — **driven**
6. I (broke, broken) my arm while skating. — **broke**
7. Kayla has (threw, thrown) a bone to the dog. — **thrown**
8. The dogs have (ran, run) away with the bone. — **run**

179

Elephants Never Forget

Don't forget that every sentence has two parts. The **subject** tells who or what the sentence is about. The **predicate** tells what the subject does, did, is, or has.

Directions: Draw a line to connect each subject on the peanut to its predicate on the elephant.

The lions — wore brightly colored makeup.
The circus tent — announced the circus acts.
Lots of children — enjoyed eating cotton candy.
The clowns — paraded in a line.
The circus — growled at the crowd.
Big elephants — began at 7 P.M.
The smell of peanuts — was filled with over 100 people.
The ringmaster — filled the air.

180

Simple Subjects and Predicates

The **simple subject** is the most important word in the complete subject. It is a **noun** or **pronoun** that tells who or what the sentence is about.
The **simple predicate** is the most important word in the complete predicate. It is a **verb** that tells what the subject is or does.

Example: simple subject   simple predicate
Handmade pottery Can be very beautiful.
complete subject   complete predicate

Directions: Underline the complete subject once and the complete predicate twice.

1. The science of pottery making is called ceramics.
2. Humans have been making pottery for thousands of years.
3. Early people made household utensils out of pottery.
4. Pottery has been made many different ways.
5. The earliest pottery making method was probably the hand-building method.
6. Clay coils were wound on top of one another.
7. Another method utilized the potter's wheel.
8. The Egyptians used the potter's wheel at least three thousand years ago.
9. The ancient Greeks used the potter's wheel when making pottery.
10. Their vases are excellent examples of simplicity of color and shape.

Directions: Write the simple subjects and the simple predicates from the sentences above.

Simple Subject	Simple Predicate	Simple Subject	Simple Predicate
1. science	is called	6. coils	were wound
2. humans	have been making	7. method	utilized
3. people	made	8. Egyptians	used
4. pottery	has been made	9. Greeks	used
5. method	was	10. vases	are

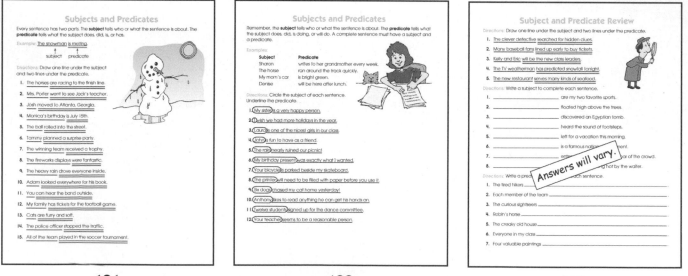

181

Subjects and Predicates

Every sentence has two parts. The **subject** tells who or what the sentence is about. The **predicate** tells what the subject does, did, is, or has.

Example: The snowman is melting.
subject   predicate

Directions: Draw one line under the subject and two lines under the predicate.

1. The horses are racing to the finish line.
2. Mrs. Porter went to see Jack's teacher.
3. Josh moved to Atlanta, Georgia.
4. Monica's birthday is July 15th.
5. The ball rolled into the street.
6. Tammy planned a surprise party.
7. The winning team received a trophy.
8. The fireworks displays were fantastic.
9. The heavy rain drove everyone inside.
10. Adam looked everywhere for his book.
11. You can hear the band outside.
12. My family has tickets for the football game.
13. Cats are furry and soft.
14. The police officer stopped the traffic.
15. All of the team played in the soccer tournament.

182

Subjects and Predicates

Remember, the **subject** tells who or what the sentence is about. The **predicate** tells what the subject does, did, is doing, or will do. A complete sentence must have a subject and a predicate.

Examples:

Subject	Predicate
Sharon	writes to her grandmother every week.
The horse	ran around the track quickly.
My mom's car	is bright green.
Denise	will be here after lunch.

Directions: Circle the subject of each sentence. Underline the predicate.

1. My sister is a very happy person.
2. I wish we had more holidays in the year.
3. Laura is one of the nicest girls in our class.
4. John is fun to have as a friend.
5. The rain nearly ruined our picnic!
6. My birthday present was exactly what I wanted.
7. Your bicycle is parked beside my skateboard.
8. The printer will need to be filled with paper before you use it.
9. Six dogs chased my cat home yesterday!
10. Anthony likes to read anything he can get his hands on.
11. Twelve students signed up for the dance committee.
12. Your teacher seems to be a reasonable person.

183

Subject and Predicate Review

Directions: Draw one line under the subject and two lines under the predicate.

1. The clever detective searched for hidden clues.
2. Many baseball fans lined up early to buy tickets.
3. Kelly and Eric will be the new class leaders.
4. The TV weatherman has predicted snowfall tonight.
5. The new restaurant serves many kinds of seafood.

Directions: Write a subject to complete each sentence.

1. _____ are my two favorite sports.
2. _____ floated high above the trees.
3. _____ discovered an Egyptian tomb.
4. _____ heard the sound of footsteps.
5. _____ left for a vacation this morning.
6. _____ is a famous national monument.
7. _____ entered the roar of the crowd.
8. _____ by the waiter.

Answers will vary.

Directions: Write a predicate to complete each sentence.

1. The tired hikers _____
2. Each member of the team _____
3. The curious sightseers _____
4. Robin's horse _____
5. The creaky old house _____
6. Everyone in my class _____
7. Four valuable paintings _____

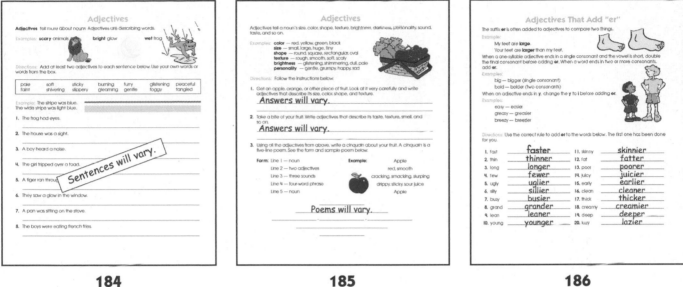

184

Adjectives

Adjectives tell more about nouns. Adjectives are describing words.

Examples: **scary** animals   **bright** glow   **wet** frog

Directions: Add at least two adjectives to each sentence below. Use your own words or words from the box.

pale	soft	sticky	burning	furry	glistening	peaceful
faint	shivering	slippery	gleaming	gentle	foggy	tangled

Example: The stripe was blue. The wide stripe was light blue.

1. The frog had eyes.

2. The house was a sight.

3. A boy heard a noise.

4. The girl tripped over a toad.

5. A tiger ran through.

6. They saw a glow in the window.

7. A pan was sitting on the stove.

8. The boys were eating french fries.

Sentences will vary.

185

Adjectives

Adjectives tell a noun's size, color, shape, texture, brightness, darkness, personality, sound, taste, and so on.

Examples: **color** — red, yellow, green, black
size — small, large, huge, tiny
shape — round, square, rectangular, oval
texture — tough, smooth, soft, scaly
brightness — glistening, shimmering, dull, pale
personality — gentle, grumpy, happy, sad

Directions: Follow the instructions below.

1. Get an apple, orange, or other piece of fruit. Look at it very carefully and write adjectives that describe its size, color, shape, and texture.

    Answers will vary.

2. Take a bite of your fruit. Write adjectives that describe its taste, texture, smell, and so on.

    Answers will vary.

3. Using all the adjectives from above, write a cinquain about your fruit. A cinquain is a five-line poem. See the form and sample poem below.

Form:	Line 1 — noun	Example:	Apple
	Line 2 — two adjectives		red, smooth
	Line 3 — three sounds		cracking, smacking, slurping
	Line 4 — four-word phrase		drippy, sticky, sour juice
	Line 5 — noun		Apple

    Poems will vary.

186

Adjectives That Add "er"

The suffix **er** is often added to adjectives to compare two things.

Example:
My feet are **large**.
Your feet are **larger** than my feet.

When a one-syllable adjective ends in a single consonant and the vowel is short, double the final consonant before adding **er**. When a word ends in two or more consonants, add **er**.

Examples:
big — bigger (single consonant)
bold — bolder (two consonants)

When an adjective ends in y, change the y to i before adding **er**.

Examples:
easy — easier
greasy — greasier
breezy — breezier

Directions: Use the correct rule to add **er** to the words below. The first one has been done for you.

1. fast	faster	11. skinny	skinnier
2. thin	thinner	12. fat	fatter
3. long	longer	13. poor	poorer
4. few	fewer	14. juicy	juicier
5. ugly	uglier	15. early	earlier
6. silly	sillier	16. clean	cleaner
7. busy	busier	17. thick	thicker
8. grand	grander	18. creamy	creamier
9. lean	leaner	19. deep	deeper
10. young	younger	20. lazy	lazier

187

Adjectives That Add "est"

The suffix **est** is often added to adjectives to compare more than two things.

Example:
My glass is **full**.
Your glass is **fuller**.
His glass is **fullest**.

When a one-syllable adjective ends in a single consonant and the vowel sound is short, you usually double the final consonant before adding **est**.

Examples:
big — biggest (short vowel)
steep — steepest (long vowel)

When an adjective ends in y, change the y to i before adding **est**.

Example:
easy — easiest

Directions: Use the correct rule to add **est** to the words below. The first one has been done for you.

1. thin	thinnest	11. quick	quickest
2. skinny	skinniest	12. trim	trimmest
3. cheap	cheapest	13. silly	silliest
4. busy	busiest	14. tall	tallest
5. loud	loudest	15. glum	glummest
6. kind	kindest	16. red	reddest
7. dreamy	dreamiest	17. happy	happiest
8. ugly	ugliest	18. high	highest
9. pretty	prettiest	19. wet	wettest
10. early	earliest	20. clean	cleanest

188

How Adjectives Compare

There are certain spelling rules to follow when **adjectives** are used to compare people, places, or things.

1. To many adjectives, simply add **er** or **est** to the end.
  fast faster fastest

2. When an adjective ends with a single vowel, double the final consonant and add **er** or **est**.
  fat fatter fattest

3. When an adjective ends in an **e**, drop the final **e** and add **er** or **est**.
  brave braver bravest

4. If an adjective ends in a y preceded by a consonant, change the y to i and add **er** or **est**.
  heavy heavier heaviest

Directions: Complete the chart below using the spelling rules you have learned. Write the number of the rule you used.

Adjective	Add er	Add est	Rule
1. weak	weaker	weakest	
2. kind	kinder	kindest	1
3. easy	easier	easiest	4
4. clear	clearer	clearest	1
5. close	closer	closest	3
6. noisy	noisier	noisiest	4
7. large	larger	largest	3
8. red	redder	reddest	2
9. pretty	prettier	prettiest	4
10. hungry	hungrier	hungriest	4
11. big	bigger	biggest	2
12. happy	happier	happiest	4
13. wet	wetter	wettest	2
14. cute	cuter	cutest	3
15. plain	plainer	plainest	1
16. busy	busier	busiest	4
17. loud	louder	loudest	1
18. strong	stronger	strongest	1
19. fresh	fresher	freshest	1
20. hot	hotter	hottest	2

189

Adjectives Preceded by "More"

Most adjectives of two or more syllables are preceded by the word **more** as a way to show comparison between two things.

Examples:

Correct: intelligent, more intelligent
Incorrect: intelligenter

Correct: famous, more famous
Incorrect: famouser

Directions: Write **more** before the adjectives that fit the rule. Draw an **X** in the blanks of the adjectives that do not fit the rule. To test yourself, say the words aloud using **more** and adding **er** to hear which way sounds correct. The first two have been done for you.

X	1. cheap	more	11. awful
more	2. beautiful	more	12. delicious
X	3. quick	more	13. embarrassing
more	4. terrible	X	14. nice
more	5. difficult	more	15. often
more	6. interesting	X	16. hard
X	7. polite	more	17. valuable
X	8. cute	X	18. close
X	9. dark	X	19. fast
X	10. sad	more	20. important

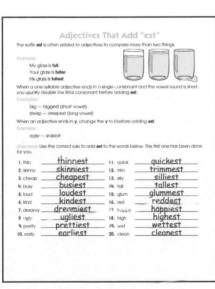

GRADE 4

I. Reading
  A. Directions
  B. Sequencing
  C. Main Idea
II. Writing
  A. Capitalization
  B. Proofreading

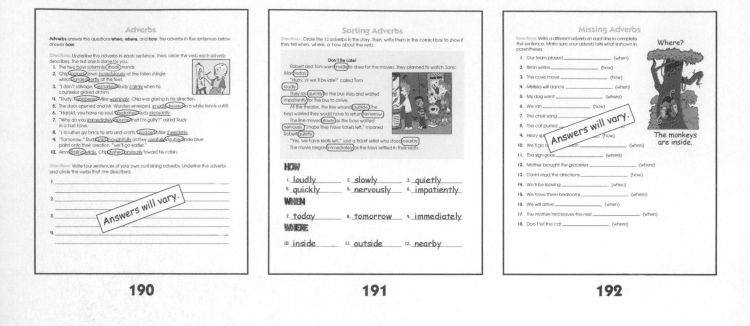

190

Adverbs

Adverbs answer the questions **when**, **where**, and **how**. The adverbs in the sentences below answer **how**.

Directions: Underline the adverbs in each sentence. Then, circle the verb each adverb describes. The first one is done for you.

1. The two boys solemnly shook hands.
2. Chip looked down incredulously at the fallen shingle which landed softly at his feet.
3. "I don't salvage," remarked Rudy calmly when his counselor glared at him.
4. "Rudy," whispered Mike warningly. Chip was glaring in his direction.
5. The door opened and Mr. Warden emerged, smartly dressed, in a white tennis outfit.
6. "Harold, you have no soul," explained Rudy pleasantly.
7. "Why do you immediately assume that I'm guilty?" asked Rudy in a hurt tone.
8. "I'd rather go back to arts and crafts," nodded Mike sheepishly.
9. "Tomorrow," Rudy said thoughtfully as they carefully daubed pale blue paint onto their creation, "we'll go earlier."
10. Arms flailing wildly, Chip rushed anxiously toward his cabin.

Directions: Write four sentences of your own containing adverbs. Underline the adverbs and circle the verbs that are described.

1. _____
2. _____
3. _____ Answers will vary.
4. _____

191

Sorting Adverbs

Directions: Circle the 12 adverbs in the story. Then, write them in the correct box to show if they tell when, where, or how about the verb.

Don't Be Late!
Robert and Tom went inside to dress for the movies. They planned to watch Sonic Mania today.
"Hurry, or we'll be late!" called Tom loudly.
They ran quickly to the bus stop and waited impatiently for the bus to arrive.
At the theater, the line wound outside. The boys worried they would have to return tomorrow.
The line moved slowly as the boys waited nervously. "I hope they have tickets left," moaned Robert quietly.
"Yes, we have seats left," said a ticket seller who stood nearby.
The movie began immediately as the boys settled in their seats.

HOW
1. loudly   2. slowly   3. quietly
4. quickly   5. nervously 6. impatiently

WHEN
7. today   8. tomorrow   9. immediately

WHERE
10. inside   11. outside   12. nearby

192

Missing Adverbs

Directions: Write a different adverb on each line to complete the sentence. Make sure your adverb tells what is shown in parentheses.

1. Our team played _____ (when)
2. Brian writes _____ (how)
3. The cows move _____ (how)
4. Melissa will dance _____ (when)
5. My dog went _____ (where)
6. We ran _____ (how)
7. The choir sang _____
8. The cat purred _____
9. Hilary sp_____ (how)
10. We'll go _____ (when)
11. The sign goes _____ (where)
12. Mother brought the groceries _____ (where)
13. David read the directions _____ (how)
14. We'll be leaving _____ (when)
15. We have three bedrooms _____ (where)
16. We will arrive _____ (when)
17. The mother bird leaves the nest _____ (when)
18. Don't let the cat _____ (where)

Answers will vary.

Where?

The monkeys are inside.

193

Adverbs

Adverbs are words that tell when, where, or how.

Adverbs of time tell when.
Example:
  The train left yesterday.
  Yesterday is an adverb of time. It tells when the train left.

Adverbs of place tell where.
Example:
  The girl walked away.
  Away is an adverb of place. It tells where the girl walked.

Adverbs of manner tell how.
Example:
  The boy walked quickly.
  Quickly is an adverb of manner. It tells how the boy walked.

Directions: Write the adverb for each sentence in the first blank. In the second blank, write whether it is an adverb of time, place, or manner. The first one has been done for you.

1. The family ate downstairs. | downstairs | place
2. The relatives laughed loudly. | loudly | manner
3. We will finish tomorrow. | tomorrow | time
4. The snowstorm will stop soon. | soon | time
5. She sings beautifully. | beautifully | manner
6. The baby slept soundly. | soundly | manner
7. The elevator stopped suddenly. | suddenly | manner
8. Does the plane leave today? | today | time
9. The phone call came yesterday. | yesterday | time
10. She ran outside. | outside | place

194

Adverb Review

Remember, adverbs tell when, where, or how about the verb in a sentence.

Directions: Circle the verb and underline the adverb in each sentence. Then, write the verb and adverb in the correct column. The first one has been done for you.

I run faster.

Verb	Adverb
bought	recently
rides	often
walked	cautiously
started	suddenly
took	outside
went	early
slid	safely
visited	again
helped	earlier
fought	bravely
finished	quickly
baked	yesterday
takes	upstairs
gets	monthly
threw	everywhere
crept	quietly

1. Jason bought his bicycle recently.
2. Lucy often rides her horse.
3. We walked cautiously on the ice.
4. Suddenly, it started to snow.
5. Derek took his wagon outside.
6. Jackie went home early.
7. Bill slid safely into second base.
8. My cousin visited us again.
9. Earlier, I helped the principal.
10. The soldiers fought bravely.
11. We quickly finished the puzzle.
12. Yesterday, I baked brownies.
13. Susie takes her shower upstairs.
14. My dad gets a paycheck monthly.
15. The baby threw toys everywhere.
16. The mouse crept out quietly.

195

Misused Words

Sometimes, people have difficulty using **good**, **well**, **sure**, **surely**, **real**, and **really** correctly. This chart may help you.

Adjectives	Adverbs
Good is an adjective when it describes a noun. That was a **good** dinner.	**Good** is never used as an adverb.
Well is an adjective when it means in good health or having a good appearance. She looks **well**.	**Well** is an adverb when it is used to tell that something is done capably or effectively. She writes **well**.
Sure is an adjective when it modifies a noun. A robin is a **sure** sign of spring.	**Surely** is an adverb. He **surely** wants a job.
Real is an adjective that means genuine or true. That was a **real** diamond.	**Really** is an adverb. Mary **really** played a good game.

Directions: Use the chart to help you choose the correct word from those in parentheses. Write it in the blank.

1. You did a very **good** job of writing your book report. (good, well)
2. The detective in the story used his skills **well**. (good, well)
3. He **surely** solved the case before anyone else did. (sure, surely)
4. I **really** want to read that book now. (real, really)
5. Did it take you long to decide who the **real** criminal was? (real, really)
6. Although the butler looked **well** and healthy, he died. (well, good)
7. Detective Rains read the clues **well** as he worked on the case. (good, well)
8. You **surely** get a good grade on that report. (surely, sure)
9. You had to **really** work hard to get those good grades. (real, really)

GRADE 4

I. Reading
  A. Directions
  B. Sequencing
  C. Main Idea
II. Writing
  A. Capitalization
  B. Proofreading

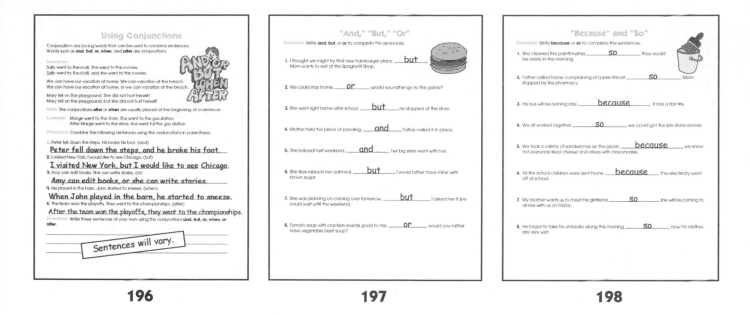

Using Conjunctions

Conjunctions are joining words that can be used to combine sentences. Words such as **and, but, or, when,** and **after** are conjunctions.

Examples:
Sally went to the mall. She went to the movies.
Sally went to the mall and she went to the movies.

We can have our vacation at home. We can vacation at the beach.
We can have our vacation at home, or we can vacation at the beach.

Mary fell on the playground. She did not hurt herself.
Mary fell on the playground, but she did not hurt herself.

Note: The conjunctions **after** or **when** are usually placed at the beginning of a sentence.

Example: Marge went to the store. She went to the gas station.
After Marge went to the store, she went to the gas station.

Directions: Combine the following sentences using the conjunctions in parenthesis.

1. Peter fell down the steps. He broke his foot. (and)
Peter fell down the steps, and he broke his foot.
2. I visited New York. I would like to see Chicago. (but)
I visited New York, but I would like to see Chicago.
3. Amy can edit books. She can write stories. (or)
Amy can edit books, or she can write stories.
4. He played in the barn. John started to sneeze. (when)
When John played in the barn, he started to sneeze.
5. The team won the playoffs. They went to the championships. (after)
After the team won the playoffs, they went to the championships.

Directions: Write three sentences of your own using the conjunctions **and, but, or, when,** or **after.**

Sentences will vary.

196

"And," "But," "Or"

Directions: Write **and, but,** or **or** to complete the sentences.

1. I thought we might try that new hamburger place. **but** Mom wants to eat at the Spaghetti Shop.

2. We could stay home, **or** would you rather go to the game?

3. She went right home after school, **but** he stopped at the store.

4. Mother held the piece of paneling, **and** Father nailed it in place.

5. She babysat last weekend, **and** her big sister went with her.

6. She likes raisins in her oatmeal, **but** I would rather have mine with brown sugar.

7. She was planning on coming over tomorrow, **but** I asked her if she could wait until the weekend.

8. Tomato soup with crackers sounds good to me, **or** would you rather have vegetable beef soup?

197

"Because" and "So"

Directions: Write **because** or **so** to complete the sentences.

1. She cleaned the paintbrushes **so** they would be ready in the morning.

2. Father called home complaining of a sore throat **so** Mom stopped by the pharmacy.

3. His bus will be running late **because** it has a flat tire.

4. We all worked together **so** we could get the job done sooner.

5. We took a variety of sandwiches on the picnic **because** we knew not everyone liked cheese and olives with mayonnaise.

6. All the school children were sent home **because** the electricity went off at school.

7. My brother wants us to meet his girlfriend **so** she will be coming to dinner with us on Friday.

8. He forgot to take his umbrella along this morning **so** now his clothes are very wet.

198

"When" and "After"

Directions: Write **when** or **after** to complete the sentences.

Answers may vary.

1. I knew we were in trouble **when** I heard the thunder in the distance.

2. We carried the baskets of cherries to the car **after** we were finished picking them.

3. Mother took off her apron **after** I reminded her that our dinner guests would be here any minute.

4. I wondered if we would have school tomorrow **after** I noticed the snow begin to fall.

5. The boys and girls all clapped **when** the magician pulled the colored scarves out of his sleeve.

6. I was startled **when** the phone rang so late last night.

7. You will need to get the film developed **after** you have taken all the pictures.

8. The children began to run **when** the snake started to move!

199

Conjunctions

Directions: Choose the best conjunction from the box to combine the pairs of sentences. Then, rewrite the sentences.

and   but   or   because   when   after   so

Answers may vary:

1. I like Leah. I like Ben.
I like Leah and Ben.

2. Should I eat the orange? Should I eat the apple?
Should I eat the orange or the apple?

3. You will get a reward. You turned in the lost item.
You will get a reward because you turned in the lost item.

4. I really mean what I say! You had better listen!
I really mean what I say, and you had better listen!

5. I like you. You're nice, friendly, helpful, and kind.
I like you because you're nice, friendly, helpful, and kind.

6. You can have dessert. You ate all your peas.
You can have dessert because you ate all your peas.

7. I like your shirt better. You should decide for yourself.
I like your shirt better, but you should decide for yourself.

8. We walked out of the building. We heard the fire alarm.
We walked out of the building after we heard the fire alarm.

9. I like to sing folk songs. I like to play the guitar.
I like to sing folk songs, and I like to play the guitar.

200

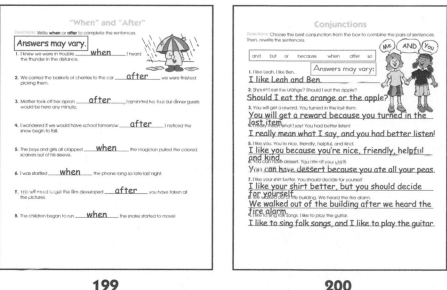

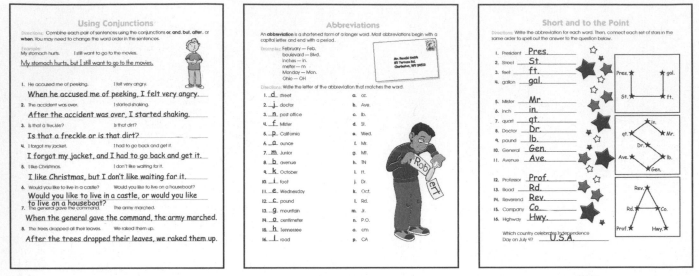

201

Using Conjunctions

Directions: Combine each pair of sentences using the conjunctions **or**, **and**, **but**, **after**, or **when**. You may need to change the word order in the sentences.

Example:
My stomach hurts.   I still want to go to the movies.
My stomach hurts, but I still want to go to the movies.

1. He accused me of peeking.   I felt very angry.
When he accused me of peeking, I felt very angry.
2. The accident was over.   I started shaking.
After the accident was over, I started shaking.
3. Is that a freckle?   Is that dirt?
Is that a freckle or is that dirt?
4. I forgot my jacket.   I had to go back and get it.
I forgot my jacket, and I had to go back and get it.
5. I like Christmas.   I don't like waiting for it.
I like Christmas, but I don't like waiting for it.
6. Would you like to live in a castle?   Would you like to live on a houseboat?
Would you like to live in a castle, or would you like to live on a houseboat?
7. The general gave the command.   The army marched.
When the general gave the command, the army marched.
8. The trees dropped all their leaves.   We raked them up.
After the trees dropped their leaves, we raked them up.

Abbreviations

An **abbreviation** is a shortened form of a longer word. Most abbreviations begin with a capital letter and end with a period.

Examples: February — Feb.
boulevard — Blvd.
inches — in.
meter — m
Monday — Mon.
Ohio — OH

Directions: Write the letter of the abbreviation that matches the word.

1. _d_ street   a. oz.
2. _j_ doctor   b. Ave.
3. _n_ post office   c. lb.
4. _f_ Mister   d. St.
5. _p_ California   e. Wed.
6. _a_ ounce   f. Mr.
7. _m_ Junior   g. Mt.
8. _b_ avenue   h. TN
9. _k_ October   i. ft.
10. _i_ foot   j. Dr.
11. _e_ Wednesday   k. Oct.
12. _c_ pound   l. Rd.
13. _g_ mountain   m. Jr.
14. _o_ centimeter   n. P.O.
15. _h_ Tennessee   o. cm
16. _l_ road   p. CA

202

Short and to the Point

Directions: Write the abbreviation for each word. Then, connect each set of stars in the same order to spell out the answer to the question below.

1. President   Pres.
2. Street   St.
3. feet   ft.
4. gallon   gal.
5. Mister   Mr.
6. Inch   in.
7. quart   qt.
8. Doctor   Dr.
9. pound   lb.
10. General   Gen.
11. Avenue   Ave.
12. Professor   Prof.
13. Road   Rd.
14. Reverend   Rev.
15. Company   Co.
16. Highway   Hwy.

Which country celebrates Independence Day on July 4?   U.S.A.

203

Capital Letters and Periods

The first letter of a person's first, last and middle name is always capitalized.

Example: Elizabeth Jane Marks is my best friend.

The first letter of a person's title is always capitalized. If the title is abbreviated, the title is followed by a period.

Example: Her mother is Dr. Susan Jones Marks.
Ms. Jessica Joseph was a visitor.

Directions: Write **C** if the sentence is punctuated and capitalized correctly. Draw an **X** if the sentence is not punctuated and capitalized correctly. The first one has been done for you.

_X_ 1. I asked Elizabeth if I should call her mother Mrs. marks or dr. Marks.
_C_ 2. Mr. and Mrs. Francesco were friends of the DeVuonos.
_X_ 3. Dr. Daniel Long and Dr Holly Barrows both spoke with the patient.
_C_ 4. Did you get Mr. MacMillan for English next year?
_C_ 5. Mr. Sweet and Ms. Ellison were both at the concert.
_X_ 6. When did the doctor. tell you about this illness?
_C_ 7. Dr. Donovan is the doctor that Mr. Winham trusted.
_X_ 8. Why don't you ask Doctor. Williams her opinion?
_C_ 9. All three of the doctors diagnosed Ms. Twelp.
_X_ 10. Will Ms. Davis and Ms Simpson be at school today?
_X_ 11. Did Dr Samuels see your father last week?
_C_ 12. Is Judy a medical doctor or another kind of specialist?
_X_ 13. We are pleased to introduce Ms King and Mr. Graham.

204

Capitalize I, Names, and Initials

The pronoun **I** is always capitalized. Each part of a person's or pet's name begins with a capital letter.

Examples: I, Mary Ann Smith, Lassie

An initial (the first letter of a name) is always capitalized and is followed by a period.

Example: M. A. Smith

Directions: Rewrite each sentence using capital letters correctly.

1. Where did molly parsons get her dog, laddie?
Where did Molly Parsons get her dog, Laddie?
2. Her grandmother, louella cane, bought it for the family.
Her grandmother, Louella Cane, bought it for the family.
3. The most unusual pet is tom simpson's parrot named showboat.
The most unusual pet is Tom Simpson's parrot named Showboat.
4. I have heard showboat say words quite clearly.
I have heard Showboat say words quite clearly.
5. Tom says his parrot's full name is a. h. showboat.
Tom says his parrot's full name is A.H. Showboat.
6. What do the initials a. h. stand for?
What do the initials A.H. stand for?
7. tom told me that his parrot's first name is always and his middle name is hungry.
Tom told me that his parrot's first name is Always and his middle name is Hungry.
8. I call my dog "m. m." instead of megan mae.
I call my dog "M.M." instead of Megan Mae.

Directions: Follow each direction carefully.

1. Write your full name.
Answers will vary.
2. Write the full name and initials of one of your parents.
Answers will vary.
3. Use the pronoun "I" to tell what you like to eat best.
Answers will vary.

205

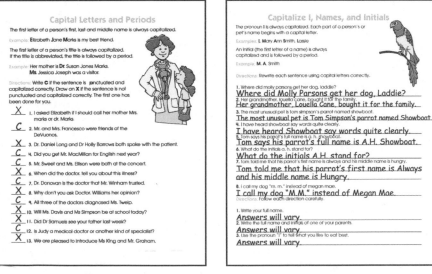

GRADE 4

I. Reading
  A. Directions
  B. Sequencing
  C. Main Idea
II. Writing
  A. Capitalization
  B. Proofreading

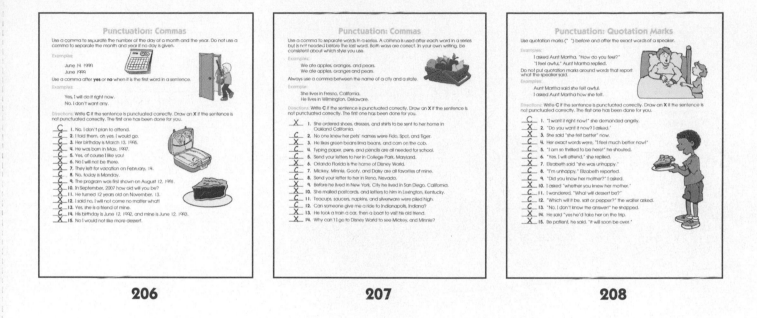

Punctuation: Commas

Use a comma to separate the number of the day of a month and the year. Do not use a comma to separate the month and year if no day is given.

Examples:

June 14, 1991
June 1991

Use a comma after **yes** or **no** when it is the first word in a sentence.

Examples:

Yes, I will do it right now.
No, I don't want any.

Directions: Write **C** if the sentence is punctuated correctly. Draw an **X** if the sentence is not punctuated correctly. The first one has been done for you.

C 1. No, I don't plan to attend.
C 2. I told them, oh yes, I would go.
C 3. Her birthday is March 13, 1985.
C 4. He was born in May, 1997.
C 5. Yes, of course I like you!
C 6. No I will not be there.
X 7. They left for vacation on February, 14.
C 8. No, today is Monday.
C 9. The program was first shown on August 12, 1991.
X 10. In September, 2007 how old will you be?
X 11. He turned 12 years old on November, 13.
X 12. I said no, I will not come no matter what!
C 13. Yes, she is a friend of mine.
C 14. His birthday is June 12, 1992, and mine is June 12, 1993.
X 15. No I would not like more dessert.

206

Punctuation: Commas

Use a comma to separate words in a series. A comma is used after each word in a series but is not needed before the last word. Both ways are correct. In your own writing, be consistent about which style you use.

Examples:

We ate apples, oranges, and pears.
We ate apples, oranges and pears.

Always use a comma between the name of a city and a state.

Example:

She lives in Fresno, California.
He lives in Wilmington, Delaware.

Directions: Write **C** if the sentence is punctuated correctly. Draw an **X** if the sentence is not punctuated correctly. The first one has been done for you.

X 1. She ordered shoes, dresses, and shirts to be sent to her home in Oakland California.
C 2. No one knew her pets' names were Fido, Spot, and Tiger.
X 3. He likes green beans lima beans, and corn on the cob.
C 4. Typing paper, pens, and pencils are all needed for school.
C 5. Send your letters to her in College Park, Maryland.
C 6. Orlando Florida is the home of Disney World.
C 7. Mickey, Minnie, Goofy, and Daisy are all favorites of mine.
C 8. Send your letter to her in Reno, Nevada.
X 9. Before he lived in New York, City he lived in San Diego, California.
C 10. She mailed postcards, and letters to him in Lexington, Kentucky.
C 11. Teacups, saucers, napkins, and silverware were piled high.
C 12. Can someone give me a ride to Indianapolis, Indiana?
X 13. He took a train a car, then a boat to visit his old friend.
X 14. Why can't I go to Disney World to see Mickey, and Minnie?

207

Punctuation: Quotation Marks

Use quotation marks (" ") before and after the exact words of a speaker.

Examples:

I asked Aunt Martha, "How do you feel?"
"I feel awful," Aunt Martha replied.

Do not put quotation marks around words that report what the speaker said.

Examples:

Aunt Martha said she felt awful.
I asked Aunt Martha how she felt.

Directions: Write **C** if the sentence is punctuated correctly. Draw an **X** if the sentence is not punctuated correctly. The first one has been done for you.

C 1. "I want it right now!" she demanded angrily.
X 2. "Do you want it now? I asked."
X 3. She said "she felt better" now.
C 4. Her exact words were, "I feel much better now!"
C 5. "I am so thrilled to be here!" he shouted.
C 6. "Yes, I will attend," she replied.
X 7. Elizabeth said "she was unhappy."
C 8. "I'm unhappy," Elizabeth reported.
C 9. "Did you know her mother?" I asked.
X 10. I asked "whether you knew her mother."
C 11. I wondered, "What will dessert be?"
C 12. "Which will it be, salt or pepper?" the waiter asked.
C 13. "No, I don't know the answer!" he snapped.
X 14. He said "yes he'd take her on the trip."
X 15. Be patient, he said, "it will soon be over."

208

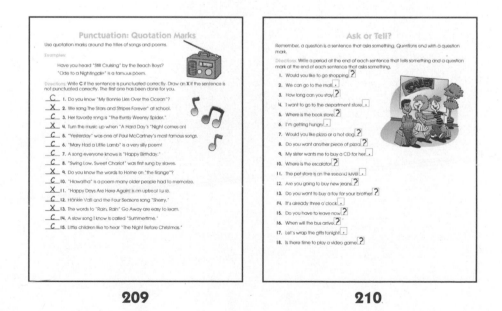

Punctuation: Quotation Marks

Use quotation marks around the titles of songs and poems.

Examples:

Have you heard "Still Cruising" by the Beach Boys?
"Ode to a Nightingale" is a famous poem.

Directions: Write **C** if the sentence is punctuated correctly. Draw an **X** if the sentence is not punctuated correctly. The first one has been done for you.

C 1. Do you know "My Bonnie Lies Over the Ocean"?
X 2. We sang The Stars and Stripes Forever" at school.
C 3. Her favorite song is "The Eensty Weensy Spider."
X 4. Turn the music up when "A Hard Day's "Night comes on!
C 5. "Yesterday" was one of Paul McCartney's most famous songs.
C 6. "Mary Had a Little Lamb" is a very silly poem!
C 7. A song everyone knows is "Happy Birthday."
C 8. "Swing Low, Sweet Chariot" was first sung by slaves.
X 9. Do you know the words to Home on "the Range"?
C 10. "Hiawatha" is a poem many older people had to memorize.
X 11. "Happy Days Are Here Again! is an upbeat tune.
C 12. Frankie Valli and the Four Seasons sang "Sherry."
X 13. The words to "Rain, Rain" Go Away are easy to learn.
C 14. A slow song I know is called "Summertime."
C 15. Little children like to hear "The Night Before Christmas."

209

Ask or Tell?

Remember, a question is a sentence that asks something. Questions end with a question mark.

Directions: Write a period at the end of each sentence that tells something and a question mark at the end of each sentence that asks something.

1. Would you like to go shopping **?**
2. We can go to the mall **.**
3. How long can you stay **?**
4. I want to go to the department store **.**
5. Where is the book store **?**
6. I'm getting hungry **.**
7. Would you like pizza or a hot dog **?**
8. Do you want another piece of pizza **?**
9. My sister wants me to buy a CD for her **.**
10. Where is the escalator **?**
11. The pet store is on the second level **.**
12. Are you going to buy new jeans **?**
13. Do you want to buy a toy for your brother **?**
14. It's already three o'clock **.**
15. Do you have to leave now **?**
16. When will the bus arrive **?**
17. Let's wrap the gifts tonight **.**
18. Is there time to play a video game **?**

210

GRADE 4

I. Reading
  A. Directions
  B. Sequencing
  C. Main Idea
II. Writing
  A. Capitalization
  B. Proofreading

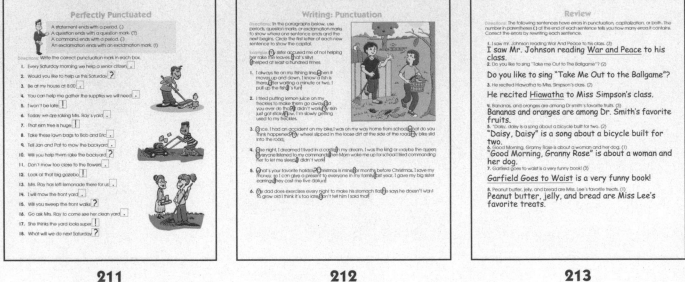

Perfectly Punctuated

A statement ends with a period. (.)
A question ends with a question mark. (?)
A command ends with a period. (.)
An exclamation ends with an exclamation mark. (!)

Directions: Write the correct punctuation mark in each box.

1. Every Saturday morning we help a senior citizen .
2. Would you like to help us this Saturday ?
3. Be at my house at 8:00 .
4. You can help me gather the supplies we will need .
5. I won't be late !
6. Today we are raking Mrs. Ray's yard .
7. That elm tree is huge !
8. Take these lawn bags to Bob and Eric .
9. Tell Jan and Pat to mow the backyard .
10. Will you help them rake the backyard ?
11. Don't mow too close to the flowers .
12. Look at that big gazebo !
13. Mrs. Ray has left lemonade there for us .
14. I will mow the front yard .
15. Will you sweep the front walks ?
16. Go ask Mrs. Ray to come see her clean yard .
17. She thinks the yard looks super !
18. What will we do next Saturday ?

211

Writing: Punctuation

Directions: In the paragraphs below, use periods, question marks, or exclamation marks to show where one sentence ends and the next begins. Circle the first letter of each new sentence to show the capital.

212

Review

Directions: The following sentences have errors in punctuation, capitalization, or both. The number in parentheses ( ) at the end of each sentence tells you how many errors it contains. Correct the errors by rewriting each sentence.

1. I saw mr. Johnson reading War And Peace to his class. (3)
I saw Mr. Johnson reading <u>War and Peace</u> to his class.

2. Do you like to sing "Take me Out to The Ballgame"? (2)
Do you like to sing "Take Me Out to the Ballgame"?

3. He recited Hiawatha to Miss Simpson's class. (2)
He recited <u>Hiawatha</u> to Miss Simpson's class.

4. Bananas, and oranges are among Dr smith's favorite fruits. (3)
Bananas and oranges are among Dr. Smith's favorite fruits.

5. "Daisy, daisy is a song about a bicycle built for two. (2)
"Daisy, Daisy" is a song about a bicycle built for two.

6. Good Morning, Granny Rose is about a woman and her dog. (1)
"Good Morning, Granny Rose" is about a woman and her dog.

7. Garfield goes to waist is a very funny book! (3)
<u>Garfield Goes to Waist</u> is a very funny book!

8. Peanut butter, jelly, and bread are Miss Lee's favorite treats. (1)
Peanut butter, jelly, and bread are Miss Lee's favorite treats.

213

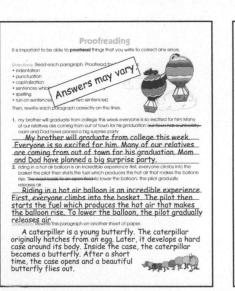

Proofreading

It is important to be able to **proofread** things that you write to correct any errors.

Directions: Read each paragraph. Proofread for
- indentation
- punctuation
- capitalization
- sentences which
- spelling
- run-on sentences

Answers may vary.

Then, rewrite each paragraph correctly on the lines.

1. My brother will graduate from college this week. Everyone is so excited for him. Many of our relatives are coming from out of town for his graduation. Mom and Dad have planned a big surprise party.

2. Riding in a hot air balloon is an incredible experience. First, everyone climbs into the basket. The pilot then starts the fuel which produces the hot air that makes the balloon rise. To lower the balloon, the pilot gradually releases air.

Directions: Rewrite this paragraph on another sheet of paper.

A caterpillar is a young butterfly. The caterpillar originally hatches from an egg. Later, it develops a hard case around its body. Inside the case, the caterpillar becomes a butterfly. After a short time, the case opens and a beautiful butterfly flies out.

214

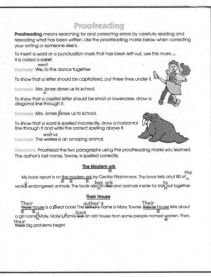

Proofreading

Proofreading means searching for and correcting errors by carefully reading and rereading what has been written. Use the proofreading marks below when correcting your writing or someone else's.

To insert a word or a punctuation mark that has been left out, use this mark. It is called a **caret**.
Example: We went to the dance together.

To show that a letter should be capitalized, put three lines under it.
Example: Mrs. Jones drove us to school.

To show that a capital letter should be small or lowercase, draw a diagonal line through it.
Example: Mrs. Jones drove us to school.

To show that a word is spelled incorrectly, draw a horizontal line through it and write the correct spelling above it.
Example: The walrus is an amazing animal.

Directions: Proofread the two paragraphs using the proofreading marks you learned. The author's last name, Towne, is spelled correctly.

The Modern Ark

My book report is on the modern ark by Cecilia Fitzsimmons. The book tells about 80 of the world's endangered animals. The book also has an ark and animals inside for kids to put together.

Their House

Their House is a great book! The author's name is Mary Towne. Their house tells about a girl named Molly. Molly's family buys an old house from some people named Warren. Then, their big problems begin!

215

I. Reading
A. Directions
B. Sequencing
C. Main Idea
II. Writing
A. Capitalization
B. Proofreading

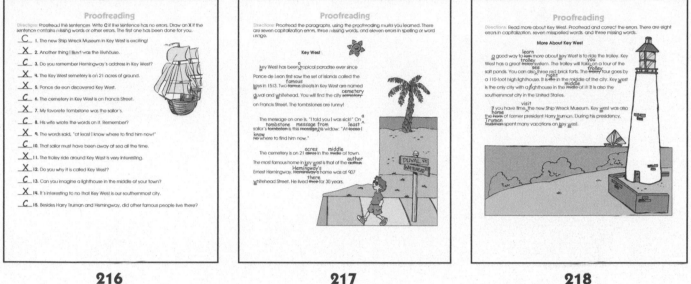

Proofreading

Directions: Proofread the sentences. Write **C** if the sentence has no errors. Draw an **X** if the sentence contains missing words or other errors. The first one has been done for you.

C 1. The new Ship Wreck Museum in Key West is exciting!
X 2. Another thing I liked was the lighthouse.
C 3. Do you remember Hemingway's address in Key West?
X 4. The Key West cemetery is on 21 acres of ground.
X 5. Ponce de eon discovered Key West.
C 6. The cemetery in Key West is on Francis Street.
X 7. My favorete tombstone was the sailor's.
C 8. His wife wrote the words on it. Remember?
X 9. The words said, "at least I know where to find him now!"
C 10. That sailor must have been away at sea all the time.
X 11. The troley ride around Key West is very interesting.
X 12. Do you why it is called Key West?
C 13. Can you imagine a lighthouse in the middle of your town?
X 14. It's interesting to no that Key West is our southernmost city.
C 15. Besides Harry Truman and Hemingway, did other famous people live there?

216

Proofreading

Directions: Proofread the paragraphs, using the proofreading marks you learned. There are seven capitalization errors, three missing words, and eleven errors in spelling or word usage.

Key West

Key West has been a tropical paradise ever since Ponce de Leon first saw the set of islands called the keys in 1513. Two famous streets in Key West are named duval and whitehead. You will find the city cemetery on Francis Street. The tombstones are funny!

The message on one is: "I told you I was sick!" On a tombstone message from least sailor's tombstone is this message his widow: "At least I know where to find him now."

The cemetery is on 21 acres in the middle of town. The most famous home in key west is that of the author Ernest Hemingway. Hemingway's home was at 907 whitehead Street. He lived there for 30 years.

217

Proofreading

Directions: Read more about Key West. Proofread and correct the errors. There are eight errors in capitalization, seven misspelled words, and three missing words.

More About Key West

A good way to learn more about Key West is to ride the trolley. Key West has a great trolley system. The trolley will take you on a tour of the salt ponds. You can also see three red brick forts. The trolley tour goes by a 110-foot high lighthouse. It is right in the middle of the city. Key west is the only city with a lighthouse in the middle of it! It is also the southernmost city in the United States.

If you have time, visit the new Ship Wreck Museum. Key west was also the home of former president Harry Truman. During his presidency, Truman spent many vacations on key west.

218

Run-On Sentences

A **run-on sentence** occurs when two or more sentences are joined together without punctuation.

Examples:

Run-on sentence: I lost my way once did you?
Two sentences with correct punctuation: I lost my way once. Did you?
Run-on sentence: I found the recipe it was not hard to follow.
Two sentences with correct punctuation: I found the recipe. It was not hard to follow.

Directions: Rewrite the run-on sentences correctly with periods, exclamation points, and question marks. The first one has been done for you.

1. Did you take my umbrella I can't find it anywhere!
Did you take my umbrella? I can't find it anywhere!

2. How can you stand that noise I can't!
How can you stand that noise? I can't!

3. The cookies are gone I see only crumbs.
The cookies are gone. I see only crumbs.

4. The dogs were barking they were hungry.
The dogs were barking. They were hungry.

5. She is quite ill please call a doctor immediately!
She is quite ill. Please call a doctor immediately!

6. The clouds came up we knew the storm would hit soon.
The clouds came up. We knew the storm would hit soon.

7. You weren't home he stopped by this morning.
You weren't home. He stopped by this morning.

219

Two for One

You can combine two subjects with the word **and** to form one longer sentence. The new sentence will have a **compound subject**.

Example: **Dennis** painted the fence.
Chuck painted the fence.
Dennis and Chuck painted the fence.

Directions: Combine the subjects to write one longer sentence.

1. The quarter rolled under the sofa.
The dime rolled under the sofa.
The quarter and dime rolled under the sofa.

2. The sandwiches are in our picnic basket.
The chips are in our picnic basket.
The sandwiches and chips are in our picnic basket.

You can also combine two predicates with the word **and** to form one longer sentence. The new sentence will have a **compound predicate**.

Example: Our team won the tournament.
Our team received a trophy.
Our team won the tournament and received a trophy.

Directions: Combine the predicates to write one longer sentence.

1. The kids went to the library.
The kids checked out books.
The kids went to the library and checked out books.

2. Katy folded her camp clothes.
Katy packed them in her luggage.
Katy folded her camp clothes and packed them in her luggage.

220

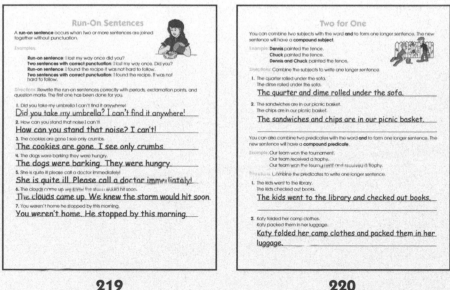

GRADE
4

I. Reading
  A. Directions
  B. Sequencing
  C. Main Idea
II. Writing
  A. Capitalization
  B. Proofreading

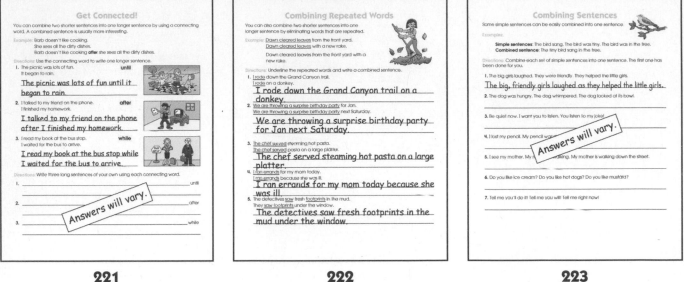

Get Connected!

You can combine two shorter sentences into one longer sentence by using a connecting word. A combined sentence is usually more interesting.

Example: Barb doesn't like cooking.
She sees all the dirty dishes.
Barb doesn't like cooking **after** she sees all the dirty dishes.

Directions: Use the connecting word to write one longer sentence.

1. The picnic was lots of fun.   **until**
It began to rain.
The picnic was lots of fun until it began to rain.

2. I talked to my friend on the phone.   **after**
I finished my homework.
I talked to my friend on the phone after I finished my homework.

3. I read my book at the bus stop.   **while**
I waited for the bus to arrive.
I read my book at the bus stop while I waited for the bus to arrive.

Directions: Write three long sentences of your own using each connecting word.

1. _____ until
2. _____ after
3. _____ while

Answers will vary.

221

Combining Repeated Words

You can also combine two shorter sentences into one longer sentence by eliminating words that are repeated.

Example: Dawn cleared leaves from the front yard.
Dawn cleared leaves with a new rake.
Dawn cleared leaves from the front yard with a new rake.

Directions: Underline the repeated words and write a combined sentence.

1. I rode down the Grand Canyon trail.
I rode on a donkey.
I rode down the Grand Canyon trail on a donkey.

2. We are throwing a surprise birthday party for Jan.
We are throwing a surprise birthday party next Saturday.
We are throwing a surprise birthday party for Jan next Saturday.

3. The chef served steaming hot pasta.
The chef served pasta on a large platter.
The chef served steaming hot pasta on a large platter.

4. I ran errands for my mom today.
I ran errands because she was ill.
I ran errands for my mom today because she was ill.

5. The detectives saw fresh footprints in the mud.
They saw footprints under the window.
The detectives saw fresh footprints in the mud under the window.

222

Combining Sentences

Some simple sentences can be easily combined into one sentence.

Examples:

Simple sentences: The bird sang. The bird was tiny. The bird was in the tree.
Combined sentence: The tiny bird sang in the tree.

Directions: Combine each set of simple sentences into one sentence. The first one has been done for you.

1. The big girls laughed. They were friendly. They helped the little girls.
The big, friendly girls laughed as they helped the little girls.

2. The dog was hungry. The dog whimpered. The dog looked at its bowl.

3. Be quiet now. I want you to listen. You listen to my joke!

4. I lost my pencil. My pencil was ...

5. I see my mother. My ... walking. My mother is walking down the street.

6. Do you like ice cream? Do you like hot dogs? Do you like mustard?

7. Tell me you'll do it! Tell me you will! Tell me right now!

Answers will vary.

223

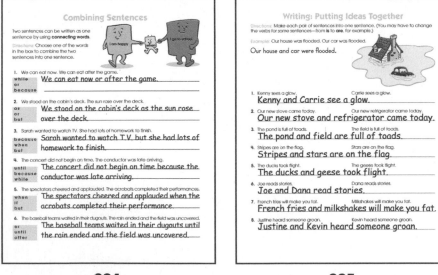

Combining Sentences

Two sentences can be written as one sentence by using **connecting words**.

Directions: Choose one of the words in the box to combine the two sentences into one sentence.

1. We can eat now. We can eat after the game.
while / or / because
We can eat now or after the game.

2. We stood on the cabin's deck. The sun rose over the deck.
as / or / but
We stood on the cabin's deck as the sun rose over the deck.

3. Sarah wanted to watch TV. She had lots of homework to finish.
because / when / but
Sarah wanted to watch T.V. but she had lots of homework to finish.

4. The concert did not begin on time. The conductor was late arriving.
until / because / while
The concert did not begin on time because the conductor was late arriving.

5. The spectators cheered and applauded. The acrobats completed their performances.
when / if / but
The spectators cheered and applauded when the acrobats completed their performance.

6. The baseball teams waited in their dugouts. The rain ended and the field was uncovered.
or / until / after
The baseball teams waited in their dugouts until the rain ended and the field was uncovered.

224

Writing: Putting Ideas Together

Directions: Make each pair of sentences into one sentence. (You may have to change the verbs for some sentences—from **is** to **are**, for example.)

Example: Our house was flooded. Our car was flooded.
Our house and car were flooded.

1. Kenny sees a glow.   Carrie sees a glow.
Kenny and Carrie see a glow.

2. Our new stove came today.   Our new refrigerator came today.
Our new stove and refrigerator came today.

3. The pond is full of toads.   The field is full of toads.
The pond and field are full of toads.

4. Stripes are on the flag.   Stars are on the flag.
Stripes and stars are on the flag.

5. The ducks took flight.   The geese took flight.
The ducks and geese took flight.

6. Joe reads stories.   Dana reads stories.
Joe and Dana read stories.

7. French fries will make you fat.   Milkshakes will make you fat.
French fries and milkshakes will make you fat.

8. Justine heard someone groan.   Kevin heard someone groan.
Justine and Kevin heard someone groan.

225

GRADE 4

I. Reading
   A. Directions
   B. Sequencing
   C. Main Idea
II. Writing
   A. Capitalization
   B. Proofreading

Writing: Putting Ideas Together

Directions: Write each pair of sentences as one sentence.

Example: Jim will deal the cards one at a time. Jim will give four cards to everyone.

Jim will deal the cards one at a time and give four cards to everyone.

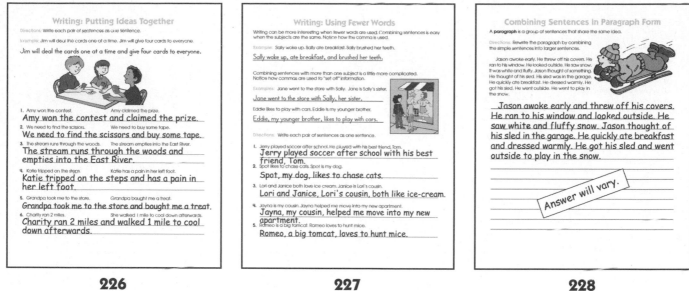

1. Amy won the contest.   Amy claimed the prize.
   Amy won the contest and claimed the prize.

2. We need to find the scissors.   We need to buy some tape.
   We need to find the scissors and buy some tape.

3. The stream runs through the woods.   The stream empties into the East River.
   The stream runs through the woods and empties into the East River.

4. Katie tripped on the steps.   Katie has a pain in her left foot.
   Katie tripped on the steps and has a pain in her left foot.

5. Grandpa took me to the store.   Grandpa bought me a treat.
   Grandpa took me to the store and bought me a treat.

6. Charity ran 2 miles.   She walked 1 mile to cool down afterwards.
   Charity ran 2 miles and walked 1 mile to cool down afterwards.

226

Writing: Using Fewer Words

Writing can be more interesting when fewer words are used. Combining sentences is easy when the subjects are the same. Notice how the comma is used.

Example: Sally woke up. Sally ate breakfast. Sally brushed her teeth.
Sally woke up, ate breakfast, and brushed her teeth.

Combining sentences with more than one subject is a little more complicated. Notice how commas are used to "set off" information.

Examples: Jane went to the store with Sally. Jane is Sally's sister.
Jane went to the store with Sally, her sister.

Eddie likes to play with cars. Eddie is my younger brother.
Eddie, my younger brother, likes to play with cars.

Directions: Write each pair of sentences as one sentence.

1. Jerry played soccer after school. He played with his best friend, Tom.
   Jerry played soccer after school with his best friend, Tom.

2. Spot likes to chase cats. Spot is my dog.
   Spot, my dog, likes to chase cats.

3. Lori and Janice both love ice cream. Janice is Lori's cousin.
   Lori and Janice, Lori's cousin, both like ice-cream.

4. Jayna is my cousin. Jayna helped me move into my new apartment.
   Jayna, my cousin, helped me move into my new apartment.

5. Romeo is a big tomcat. Romeo loves to hunt mice.
   Romeo, a big tomcat, loves to hunt mice.

227

Combining Sentences in Paragraph Form

A **paragraph** is a group of sentences that share the same idea.

Directions: Rewrite the paragraph by combining the simple sentences into larger sentences.

Jason awoke early. He threw off his covers. He ran to his window. He looked outside. He saw snow. It was white and fluffy. Jason thought of something. He thought of his sled. His sled was in the garage. He quickly ate breakfast. He dressed warmly. He got his sled. He went outside. He went to play in the snow.

Jason awoke early and threw off his covers. He ran to his window and looked outside. He saw white and fluffy snow. Jason thought of his sled in the garage. He quickly ate breakfast and dressed warmly. He got his sled and went outside to play in the snow.

Answer will vary.

228

Paragraph Form

A **paragraph** is a group of sentences about one main idea.

When writing a paragraph:
1. **Indent** the first line.
2. **Capitalize** the first word of each sentence.
3. **Punctuate** each sentence.

There are many reasons to write a paragraph. A paragraph can describe something or tell a story. It can tell how something is made or give an opinion. Do you know other reasons to write a paragraph?

Directions: Read the ... the paragraphs correctly on the lines ...
1. Indent 2. Cap...

Answers will vary.

the number of teeth you have depends on your age a baby has no teeth at all gradually milk teeth, or baby teeth, begin to grow later, these teeth fall out and permanent teeth appear by the age of twenty-five, you should have thirty-two permanent teeth

The number of teeth you have depends on your age. A baby has no teeth at all. Gradually, milk teeth, or baby teeth begin to grow. Later, these teeth fall out and permanent teeth appear. By the age of twenty-five, you should have thirty-two permanent teeth.

my family is going to Disneyland tomorrow we plan to arrive early my dad will take my little sister to Fantasyland first meanwhile, my brother and I will visit Frontierland and Adventureland after lunch we will all meet to go to Tomorrowland

My family is going to Disneyland tomorrow. We plan to arrive early. My dad will take my little sister to Fantasyland first. Meanwhile, my brother and I will visit Frontierland and Adventureland. After lunch we will all meet to go to Tomorrowland.

229

Topic Sentences—Paragraphs

Directions: Read each topic listed below. Write a topic sentence for each topic.
Example: Topic: Seasons
Topic Sentence: There are four seasons in every year.
or: Of all the seasons, my favorite is summer.

1. Topic: Winter
   Topic Sentence:
2. Topic: Skateboards
   Topic Sentence:
3. Topic: America
   Topic Sentence:
4. Topic: Horses
   Topic Sentence:
5. Topic: Books
   Topic Sentence:

Directions: Choose two of your ... above.
Write each as the beginning ... paragraphs below.
Write at least four supp... with each topic sentence to make two complete par...

Answers will vary.

1.

2.

230

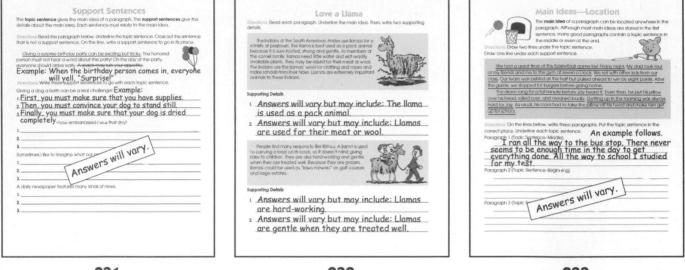

Support Sentences

The **topic sentence** gives the main idea of a paragraph. The **support sentences** give the details about the main idea. Each sentence must relate to the main idea.

Directions: Read the paragraph below. Underline the topic sentence. Cross out the sentence that is not a support sentence. On the line, write a support sentence to go in its place.

<u>Giving a surprise birthday party can be exciting but tricky.</u> The honored person must not hear a word about the party! On the day of the party, everyone should arrive early. A snack must fill your appetite.

Example: When the birthday person comes in, everyone will yell "Surprise!"

Directions: Write three support sentences to go with each topic sentence.

Giving a dog a bath can be a real challenge! **Example:**

1. First, you must make sure that you have supplies.
2. Then, you must convince your dog to stand still.
3. Finally, you must make sure that your dog is dried completely. how embarrassed I was that day!

1. _____
2. _____
3. _____

Sometimes I like to imagine what our...

1. _____
2. _____
3. _____

A daily newspaper features many kinds of news.

1. _____
2. _____
3. _____

Answers will vary.

231

Love a Llama

Directions: Read each paragraph. Underline the main idea. Then, write two supporting details.

The Indians at the South American Andes use llamas for a variety of purposes. The llama is best used as a pack animal because it is sure-footed, strong and gentle. As members of the camel family, llamas need little water and eat readily available plants. They may be raised for their meat or wool. The Indians use the llamas' wool for clothing and ropes and make sandals from their hides. Llamas are extremely important animals to these Indians.

Supporting Details

1. Answers will vary but may include: The llama is used as a pack animal.
2. Answers will vary but may include: Llamas are used for their meat or wool.

People find many reasons to like llamas. A llama is used to carrying a load on its back, so it doesn't mind giving rides to children. They are also hard-working and gentle when they are treated well. Because they are grazers, llamas could be used as "lawn mowers" on golf courses and large estates.

Supporting Details

1. Answers will vary but may include: Llamas are hard-working.
2. Answers will vary but may include: Llamas are gentle when they are treated well.

232

Main Ideas—Location

The **main idea** of a paragraph can be located anywhere in the paragraph. Although most main ideas are stated in the first sentence, many good paragraphs contain a topic sentence in the middle or even at the end.

Directions: Draw two lines under the topic sentence. Draw one line under each support sentence.

We had a great time at the basketball game last Friday night. My dad took four of my friends and me to the gym at seven o'clock. We sat with other kids from our class. Our team was behind at the half but pulled ahead to win by eight points. After the game, we stopped for burgers before going home.

The alarm rang for a full minute before Jay heard it. Even then, he put his pillow over his head, rolled over, and moaned loudly. Getting up in the morning was always hard for Jay. As usual, his mom had to take the pillow off his head and make him get up for school.

Directions: On the lines below, write three paragraphs. Put the topic sentence in the correct place. Underline each topic sentence. **An example follows.**

Paragraph 1 (Topic Sentence–Middle)

I ran all the way to the bus stop. There never seems to be enough time in the day to get everything done. All the way to school I studied for my test.

Paragraph 2 (Topic Sentence–Beginning)

_____

Paragraph 3 (Topic S...

Answers will vary.

233

That's a Mouthful!

Directions: Circle the word in each row that is first in A-B-C, or alphabetical order. Then, write it on the lines.

1. hot (hen) the — h e n
2. swell (stick) watch — s t i c k
3. watch (taste) twist — t a s t e
4. stand (clock) glass — c l o c k
5. spider monkey (babies) — b a b i e s
6. (knife) plate match — k n i f e
7. start (scarf) sharp — s c a r f
8. (bat) box bed — b a t
9. tub (tap) ten — t a p
10. under shelf (scrub) — s c r u b

Directions: Write the boxed letters with the same numbers below.

What is the world's biggest word?

r u b b e r ,
b e c a u s e   i t
s t r e t c h e s !

234

Johnny Appleseed

John Chapman, born in 1774, was better known as Johnny Appleseed. He planted a large number of apple trees along the early frontier.

Directions: Number the apple words in alphabetical order. Then, write the word on the line with the matching number to finish a ballad.

2 blossoms	14 nature	15 near	
1 apple seeds	4 crunchy	9 Jonathan	
5 day	3 brush	13 name	
18 Winesap	11 loved	12 mother	
7 fame	16 tasted	17 wasted	
10 king	8 fruit	6 eat	

Johnny, Johnny Appleseed was his _name_

Planting **apple seeds** awarded him _fame_

The apple seeds once were _wasted_

'Til Johnny's apples were _tasted_

Then far and _near_, through the land he _loved_ so dear.

Apple _blossoms_ were everywhere,

Apples, apples, the _king_ of _fruit_ they say.

Apples, apples _eat_ one every _day_

They're _mother_ _nature_'s toothbrush,

So eat one if you can't _brush_

A _Jonathan_ _Winesap_ or McIntosh,

They're a _crunchy_ snack, by gosh!

235

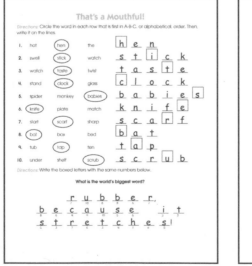

GRADE 4

I. Reading
  A. Directions
  B. Sequencing
  C. Main Idea
II. Writing
  A. Capitalization
  B. Proofreading

In Your Kitchen Cupboard

Directions: Write the names of the spices in alphabetical order.

paprika	chili pepper	black pepper	cardamom
cocoa	cinnamon	cloves	ginger
vanilla	allspice	tumeric	nutmeg
mace	cayenne		

1. allspice
2. black pepper
3. cardamom
4. cayenne
5. chili pepper
6. cinnamon
7. cloves
8. cocoa
9. ginger
10. mace
11. nutmeg
12. paprika
13. turmeric
14. vanilla

Respellings in the dictionary can help you learn how to say a word correctly.

Directions: Draw a line to match the word to its pronunciation.

ki en'   pe'per   kär'də mem   pe pre' ke   ter'mər ik

cardamom cayenne pepper tumeric paprika

236

A Word From Your Dictionary

A dictionary entry usually shows the following information:

Respelling — to help you say the word correctly
Part of speech — to help you use the word correctly
Syllables — to help you divide the word
Definition — to tell the meaning of the word
Sample sentence — to show how the word is used in context

rack•et¹ (rak' ət) n. also rac•quet, a light bat made of a frame laced with strong strings.
rack•et² (rak'ət) n. 1. a loud noise: The fourth graders made a racket until the teacher asked them to work quietly. 2. a fraudulent or dishonest business.

Directions: Use the dictionary entries above to help you write each answer.

1. Name the part of speech given for racket in both entries. **noun**
2. Write the sample sentence given for one definition. **The fourth graders made a racket until the teacher asked them to work quietly**
3. How many syllables are in racket? **two**
4. Which syllable is accented, the first or the second? **first**

Directions: Write the definition from above for each underlined word.

1. Who is making that terrible racket upstairs? **a loud noise**

2. Police officers arrested the men involved in a gambling racket.
a fraudulent or dishonest business

237

Guide-Worthy Words

Directions: Use a pencil to write ten vocabulary words from the box under each of the guide words. Remember to put them in alphabetical order.

reflection	syllable	abrupt	authority
reindeer	scowl	accidently	ammunition
resolute	stance	accustom	ancient
retort	stealth	additional	appoint
salute	subside	allow	ashamed
schoolmaster	surpass	almanac	assign

babyhood	crest	defense	exult
barometer	commerce	defiant	earthenware
barracks	commotion	demoralize	enormous
beneficial	consternation	discard	entirely
burrow	cordial	disposition	epidemic
calamity	corporal	disturbance	explosive

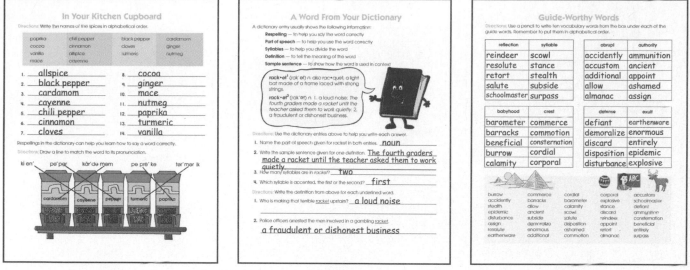

burrow commerce cordial corporal accustom
accidently barracks barometer explosive schoolmaster
stealth allow calamity stance defiant
epidemic ancient scowl discard ammunition
disturbance subside salute reindeer consternation
assign demoralize disposition appoint beneficial
resolute enormous ashamed retort entirely
earthenware additional commotion almanac surpass

238

Weird Words

Directions: Use a dictionary to help you answer the questions using complete sentences.

1. Which would you use to treat a sore throat: a **gargoyle** or a **gargle**?
I would use a gargle to treat a sore throat.

2. Which might be used on a gravestone: an **epiphyte** or an **epitaph**?
An epitaph might be used on a gravestone.

3. Which is an instrument: **calligraphy** or a **calliope**?
A calliope is an instrument.

4. Would a building have a **gargoyle** or an **argyle** on it?
A building would have a gargoyle.

5. If you trick someone, do you **bamboozle** him or **barcarole** him?
If you trick someone you bamboozle him.

6. If you studied handwriting, would you learn **calligraphy** or **cajolery**?
If you studied handwriting, you would learn calligraphy.

7. What would a gondolier sing: a **barcarole** or an **argyle**?
A gondolier would sing a barcarole.

8. If you tried to coax someone, would you be using **cajolery** or **calamity**?
If you tried to coax someone, you might use cajolery.

9. Which might you wear: **argyles** or **calliopes**?
You might wear argyles.

10. In Venice, Italy, would you travel in a **gondola** or a **calamity**?
In Venice, Italy, you would travel in a gondola.

239

Library Skills: Using the Library Catalog

Every book in a library is listed in the library's catalog. Videos, CD's, and other materials may also be included. Some library catalogs are drawers filled with file cards; some are computerized. Here is an example of a card from a card catalog:

970.2
Gridley Indians
   Gridley, Marion E.
   American Indian Women
   Hawthorn Books, Inc., 1974

The catalog helps you find books and other materials. Library catalogs list items by titles, authors, and subjects. All three of these listings are in alphabetical order.

To find a book titled Great Explorer: Christopher Columbus, you would look under G in the card catalog. To find other books about Columbus, you would look under C. If you knew the name of an author who had written a book about Columbus, you could look in the card catalog under the author's last name.

Many libraries use computer catalogs instead of card catalogs. The computer catalog is also organized by titles, authors, and subjects. To find a book, type in the title, subject, or author's name.

Directions: Answer the questions about using a library catalog.

1. To find the book American Indian Women, would you look under the author, title, or subject? **title**
2. To find a book about the Cherokee people, would you look under the author, title, or subject? **subject**
3. To find a book called Animals of Long Ago, would you look under the author, title, or subject? **title**
4. Marion E. Gridley has written books about Native Americans. To find one of her books, would you look under the author, title, or subject? **author (or subject)**
5. To find books about the Moon, would you look under the author, title, or subject? **subject**
6. To find the book Easy Microwave Cooking for Kids, would you look under the author, title, or subject? **title**
7. Diana Reische has written a book about the Pilgrims. Would you look under the author, title, or subject to find it? **author or subject**

240

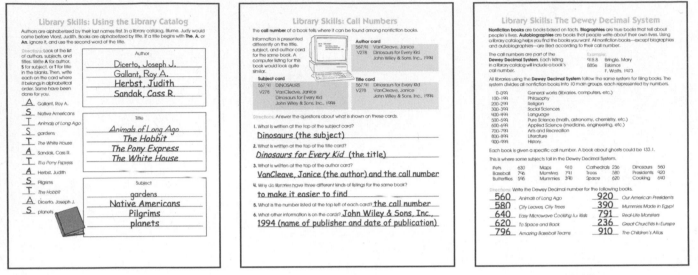

Library Skills: Using the Library Catalog

Authors are alphabetized by their last names first. In a library catalog, Blume, Judy would come before Viorst, Judith. Books are alphabetized by title. If a title begins with **The**, **A**, or **An**, ignore it, and use the second word of the title.

Directions: Look at the list of authors, subjects, and titles. Write **A** for author, **S** for subject, or **T** for title in the blanks. Then, write each one on the card where it belongs in alphabetical order. Some have been done for you.

Author
Dicerto, Joseph J.
Gallant, Roy A.
Herbst, Judith
Sandak, Cass R.

A — Gallant, Roy A.
S — Native Americans
T — Animals of Long Ago
S — gardens
T — The White House
A — Sandak, Cass R.
T — The Pony Express
A — Herbst, Judith
S — Pilgrims
T — The Hobbit
A — Dicerto, Joseph J.
S — planets

Title
Animals of Long Ago
The Hobbit
The Pony Express
The White House

Subject
gardens
Native Americans
Pilgrims
planets

241

Library Skills: Call Numbers

The **call number** of a book tells where it can be found among nonfiction books.

Information is presented differently on the title, subject, and author card for the same book. A computer listing for this book would look quite similar.

Author card
567.91 VanCleave, Janice
V278   Dinosaurs for Every Kid
        John Wiley & Sons, Inc., 1991

Subject card
567.91 DINOSAURS
V278   VanCleave, Janice
        Dinosaurs for Every Kid
        John Wiley & Sons, Inc., 1991

Title card
567.91 Dinosaurs for Every Kid
V278   VanCleave, Janice
        John Wiley & Sons, Inc., 1991

Directions: Answer the questions about what is shown on these cards.

1. What is written at the top of the subject card?
   Dinosaurs (the subject)

2. What is written at the top of the title card?
   Dinosaurs for Every Kid (the title)

3. What is written at the top of the author card?
   VanCleave, Janice (the author) and the call number

4. Why do libraries have three different kinds of listings for the same book?
   to make it easier to find

5. What is the number listed at the top left of each card? **the call number**

6. What other information is on the cards? **John Wiley & Sons, Inc., 1994 (name of publisher and date of publication)**

242

Library Skills: The Dewey Decimal System

Nonfiction books are books based on fact. **Biographies** are true books that tell about people's lives. **Autobiographies** are books that people write about their own lives. Using a library catalog helps you find the books you want. All nonfiction books—except biographies and autobiographies—are filed according to their call number.

The call numbers are part of the **Dewey Decimal System**. Each listing in a library catalog will include a book's call number.

Example:
918.8 Bringle, Mary
B85e   Eskimos
       F. Watts, 1973

All libraries using the **Dewey Decimal System** follow the same system for filing books. The system divides all nonfiction books into 10 main groups, each represented by numbers.

0-099	General works (libraries, computers, etc.)
100-199	Philosophy
200-299	Religion
300-399	Social Sciences
400-499	Language
500-599	Pure Science (math, astronomy, chemistry, etc.)
600-699	Applied Science (medicine, engineering, etc.)
700-799	Arts and Recreation
800-899	Literature
900-999	History

Each book is given a specific call number. A book about ghosts could be 133.1.

This is where some subjects fall in the Dewey Decimal System.

Pets	630	Maps	910	Cathedrals	236	Dinosaurs	560
Baseball	796	Monsters	791	Trees	580	Presidents	920
Butterflies	595	Mummies	390	Space	620	Cooking	640

Directions: Write the Dewey Decimal number for the following books.

560	Animals of Long Ago	**920**	Our American Presidents
580	City Leaves, City Trees	**390**	Mummies Made in Egypt
640	Easy Microwave Cooking for Kids	**791**	Real-Life Monsters
620	To Space and Back	**236**	Great Churches in Europe
796	Amazing Baseball Teams	**910**	The Children's Atlas

243

Library Skills: The Dewey Decimal System

All libraries that use the Dewey Decimal System follow the same order. All books between 500 and 599 are related to science. All books between 900 and 999 are history.

Each library divides its system even further. For example, one library may have kites at 796.15, while another library may have kites at 791.13.

Directions: Look at the number on each book. Then, use the Dewey Decimal System directory at the bottom of the page to find out what the book is about. Write the subject on the line.

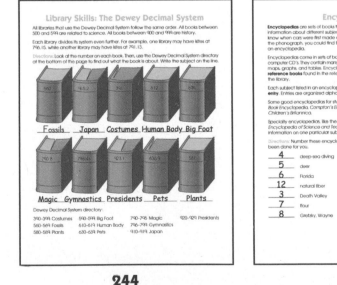

Fossils Japan Costumes Human Body Big Foot

Magic Gymnastics Presidents Pets Plants

Dewey Decimal System directory:

390-399 Costumes	590-599 Big Foot	790-795 Magic	920-929 Presidents
560-569 Fossils	610-619 Human Body	796-799 Gymnastics	
580-589 Plants	630-639 Pets	910-919 Japan	

244

Encyclopedia Skills

Encyclopedias are sets of books that provide information about different subjects. If you want to know when cars were first made or who invented the phonograph, you could find the information in an encyclopedia.

Encyclopedias come in sets of books and on computer CD's. They contain many facts, illustrations, maps, graphs, and tables. Encyclopedias are **reference books** found in the reference section of the library.

Each subject listed in an encyclopedia is called an **entry**. Entries are organized alphabetically.

Some good encyclopedias for students are *World Book Encyclopedia*, *Compton's Encyclopedia* and *Children's Britannica*.

Specialty encyclopedias, like the *McGraw-Hill Encyclopedia of Science and Technology*, contain information on one particular subject.

Directions: Number these encyclopedia entries in alphabetical order. The first one has been done for you.

4	deep-sea diving	9	Little League
5	deer	10	Little Rock
6	Florida	11	metric system
12	natural fiber	14	United Nations
3	Death Valley	13	poison oak
7	flour	1	Air Force
8	Gretsky, Wayne	2	Carter, Jimmy

245

Encyclopedia Skills: Using the Index

The **index** of an encyclopedia contains an alphabetical listing of all entries. To find information about a subject, decide on the best word to describe the subject. If you want to know about ducks, look up the word "duck" in the index. If you're really interested in learning about mallard ducks, then look under "mallard ducks." The index shows the page number and volume where the information is located.

Look at the index entry below about Neil Armstrong. Most index entries also tell you when a person lived and died and give a short description of the person.

> ARMSTRONG, NEIL   United States astronaut, b. 1930
>   Commander of *Gemini 8*, 1966; first man to walk on the Moon, July 1969
>   References in
>   Astronaut; illus. 2:56
>   Space travel 17:214

Neil Armstrong is listed under "Astronaut" and "Space travel." You can find information about him in both articles. The first entry shows there is an illustration (illus.) of Neil Armstrong in volume 2 on page 56 (2:56).

If Neil Armstrong were listed in a separate article in the encyclopedia, the index would look something like this:

> main article Armstrong, Neil
> 2:48

Directions: Answer these questions about using an encyclopedia index.

1. According to the index listing for Neil Armstrong, when was he born? __1930__

2. According to the index listing, who was Neil Armstrong? __commander of__ __Gemini 8 and first man to walk on the Moon__

3. When did he walk on the Moon? __July 1969__

4. What are the titles of the two articles containing information about Neil Armstrong?
__Astronaut__   __Space travel__

5. Where would you find the article on space travel?
Volume number __17__, page number __214__.

246

Encyclopedia Skills

Each book in a set of encyclopedias has a volume number and lists the range of subjects included. Volume 10 shown below includes all articles that would fall alphabetically between *insect* and *leaf*. Note that Volume 30 in this set is the Index.

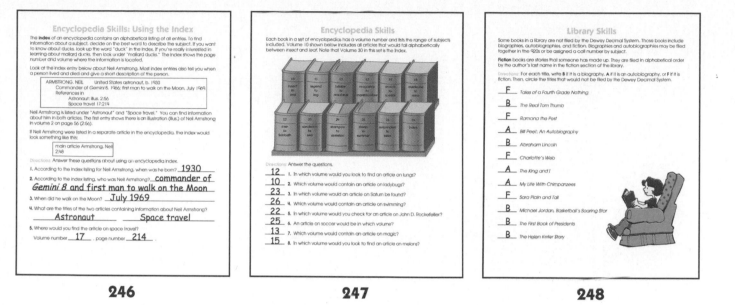

Directions: Answer the questions.

__12__ 1. In which volume would you look to find an article on lungs?

__10__ 2. Which volume would contain an article on ladybugs?

__23__ 3. In which volume would an article on Saturn be found?

__26__ 4. Which volume would contain an article on swimming?

__22__ 5. In which volume would you check for an article on John D. Rockefeller?

__25__ 6. An article on soccer would be in which volume?

__13__ 7. Which volume would contain an article on magic?

__15__ 8. In which volume would you look to find an article on melons?

247

Library Skills

Some books in a library are not filed by the Dewey Decimal System. Those books include biographies, autobiographies, and fiction. Biographies and autobiographies may be filed together in the 920s or be assigned a call number by subject.

Fiction books are stories that someone has made up. They are filed in alphabetical order by the author's last name in the fiction section of the library.

Directions: For each title, write **B** if it is a biography, **A** if it is an autobiography, or **F** if it is fiction. Then, circle the titles that would not be filed by the Dewey Decimal System.

__F__ Tales of a Fourth Grade Nothing

__B__ The Real Tom Thumb

__F__ Ramona the Pest

__A__ Bill Peet; An Autobiography

__B__ Abraham Lincoln

__F__ Charlotte's Web

__A__ The King and I

__A__ My Life With Chimpanzees

__F__ Sara Plain and Tall

__B__ Michael Jordan, Basketball's Soaring Star

__B__ The First Book of Presidents

__B__ The Helen Keller Story

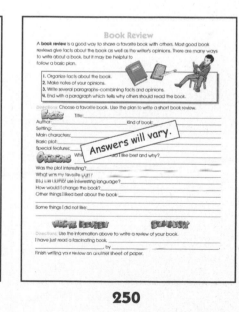

248

Is It Fiction or Nonfiction?

Directions: Write on the blank **fiction** or **nonfiction**.

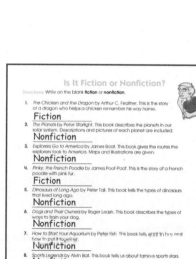

1. *The Chicken and the Dragon* by Arthur C. Feather. This is the story of a dragon who helps a chicken remember his way home.
Fiction

2. *The Planets* by Peter Starlight. This book describes the planets in our solar system. Descriptions and pictures of each planet are included.
Nonfiction

3. *Explorers Go to America* by James Boat. This book gives the routes the explorers took to America. Maps and illustrations are given.
Nonfiction

4. *Pinky, the French Poodle* by James Poof-Poof. This is the story of a French poodle with pink fur.
Fiction

5. *Dinosaurs of Long Ago* by Peter Tall. This book tells the types of dinosaurs that lived long ago.
Nonfiction

6. *Dogs and Their Owners* by Roger Leash. This book describes the types of ways to train your dog.
Nonfiction

7. *How to Start Your Aquarium* by Peter Fish. This book tells what to buy and how to put it together.
Nonfiction

8. *Sports Legends* by Alvin Bat. This book tells us about famous sports stars.
Nonfiction

9. *Flower Designs* by Hilda Vase. This book tells how to arrange flowers for special occasions.
Nonfiction

10. *Hamsters! Hamsters! Hamsters!* by Roger Pellet. This book tells how to train and care for your hamster.
Nonfiction

249

Book Review

A **book review** is a good way to share a favorite book with others. Most good book reviews give facts about the book as well as the writer's opinions. There are many ways to write about a book, but it may be helpful to follow a basic plan.

1. Organize facts about the book.
2. Make notes of your opinions.
3. Write several paragraphs—combining facts and opinions.
4. End with a paragraph which tells why others should read the book.

Directions: Choose a favorite book. Use the plan to write a short book review.

Title: _____
Author: _____ Kind of book: _____
Setting: _____
Main characters: _____
Basic plot: _____
Special features: _____

Answers will vary.

What I liked best and why? _____
Was the plot interesting? _____
What was my favorite part? _____
Did the author use interesting language? _____
How would I change the book? _____
Other things I liked best about the book: _____

Some things I did not like: _____

Directions: Use the information above to write a review of your book.
I have just read a fascinating book, _____
_____, by _____
Finish writing your review on another sheet of paper.

250

GRADE
4

I. Reading
 A. Directions
 B. Sequencing
 C. Main Idea
II. Writing
 A. Capitalization
 B. Proofreading

Answers to puzzles printed on cardboard in the back of this workbook:

Braille Busters **Winter**

Louis Braille was born on January 4, 1809. His invention of the Braille alphabet made it possible for blind people to read and write. Use the Braille alphabet below to decode these wintry riddles.

a b c d e f g h i j k l m

n o p q r s t u v w x y z

1. What is the jelly jar's favorite month?
jam-uary

2. What is Adam's favorite holiday?
new year's eve

3. What do Eskimos use to stick things together?
i-glue

4. How do you eat evergreen ice cream?
from pine cones

5. What is a liar's favorite month?
fib-ruary

6. What heavy snowstorm blanketed Emerald City?
the blizzard of oz

7. What do you get when your bike freezes?
ice-cycle

8. What do Eskimos eat for breakfast?
snowflakes

Seeing Double **Spring**

Bunny rabbits! Spring offers an array of double letters. Use the clues to write a word with double letters.

1. dustlike sparkles
gl**i**tter

2. light rain
dr**i**zzle

3. soft, airy
fl**u**ffy

4. textbook dictionary
gl**o**ssary

5. to help
a**s**sist

6. leaping
ho**pp**ing

7. brown, sticky syrup
mo**l**asses

8. every year
a**nn**ual

9. red and white striped candy
pe**pp**ermint

10. tells when guests arrive
do**o**rbell

11. pigskin sport
fo**o**tball

12. rapid repetitive talking
cha**tt**er

13. to eat quickly
go**bb**le

14. book pictures
illustrations

15. where you live
a**dd**ress

16. lines that never cross
pa**ll**el

"According to Hoyle" **Summer**

On August 29 we remember Edmond Hoyle. He lived in London during the early 1700s, and for many years gave instructions in the playing of games. Celebrate the day by solving this word search about fun and games.

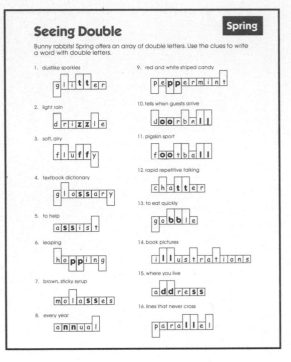

Word Box

chess	soccer	relax	video games	roller blading	competition
teams	baseball	fun	jump rope	swimming	computer
dice	volleyball	win	crazy eights	racing	games
luck	basketball	piece	go fish	tic-tac-toe	trivia
rules	biking	archery	mini golf	solitaire	marbles
sport	waterskiing	checkers	tennis	net	hockey
safety	challenge	skill	rally	board games	

Cool School Tools **Fall**

It's time to load your backpack and head back to school. Be sure you have all your school supplies. Decode to find out what you might need.

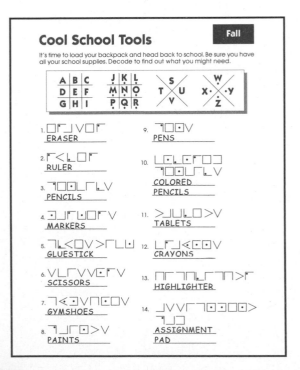

1. ERASER

2. RULER

3. PENCILS

4. MARKERS

5. GLUESTICK

6. SCISSORS

7. GYMSHOES

8. PAINTS

9. PENS

10. COLORED PENCILS

11. TABLETS

12. CRAYONS

13. HIGHLIGHTER

14. ASSIGNMENT PAD

Braille Busters

Louis Braille was born on January 4, 1809. His invention of the Braille alphabet made it possible for blind people to read and write. Use the Braille alphabet below to decode these wintry riddles.

a	b	c	d	e	f	g	h	i	j	k	l	m
⠁	⠃	⠉	⠙	⠑	⠋	⠛	⠓	⠊	⠚	⠅	⠇	⠍

n	o	p	q	r	s	t	u	v	w	x	y	z
⠝	⠕	⠏	⠟	⠗	⠎	⠞	⠥	⠧	⠺	⠭	⠽	⠵

1. What is the jelly jar's favorite month?

   _____

2. What is Adam's favorite holiday?

   _____

3. What do Eskimos use to stick things together?

   _____

4. How do you eat evergreen ice cream?

   _____

5. What is a liar's favorite month?

   _____

6. What heavy snowstorm blanketed Emerald City?

   _____

7. What do you get when your bike freezes?

   _____

8. What do Eskimos eat for breakfast?

   _____

Seeing Double

Bunny rabbits! Spring offers an array of double letters. Use the clues to write a word with double letters.

1. dustlike sparkles
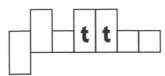

2. light rain
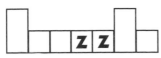

3. soft, airy
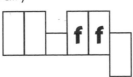

4. textbook dictionary
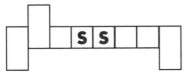

5. to help
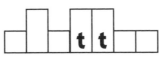

6. leaping
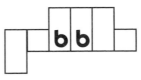

7. brown, sticky syrup
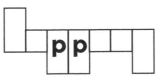

8. every year

9. red and white striped candy

10. tells when guests arrive
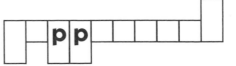

11. pigskin sport
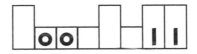

12. rapid repetitive talking

13. to eat quickly
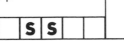

14. book pictures
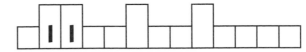

15. where you live
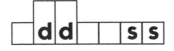

16. lines that never cross
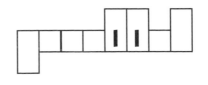

"According to Hoyle"

On August 29 we remember Edmond Hoyle. He lived in London during the early 1700s, and for many years gave instructions in the playing of games. Celebrate the day by solving this word search about fun and games.

```
C R A Z Y E I G H T S O C C E R C E B
O N R M I N I G O L F S H P X O O C O
M I C H E C K E R S S S O L A L M E A
P W H O C K E Y J E I R L T L L P I R
U T E A M S L K H F P A S F R E E P D
T R R S V O C C O M B G U B G R T V G
E I Y E O U M G U T K N T A N B I I A
R V L L L T X J E F M I R S I L T D M
G I L U L B I K I N G C C K M A I E E
A A A R E C S P O R T A O T M D O O S
M T R S Y A C W A T E R S K I I N G I
E S E L B R A M Y T E F A S W N J A N
S E L L A B E S A B L L I K S G C M N
C H A L L E N G E T I C T A C T O E E
O F X O L I D I C E R I A T I L O S T
```

Word Box

chess	soccer	relax	video games	roller blading	competition
teams	baseball	fun	jump rope	swimming	computer
dice	volleyball	win	crazy eights	racing	games
luck	basketball	piece	go fish	tic-tac-toe	trivia
rules	biking	archery	mini golf	solitaire	marbles
sport	waterskiing	checkers	tennis	net	hockey
safety	challenge	skill	rally	board games	

Cool School Tools

It's time to load your backpack and head back to school. Be sure you have all your school supplies. Decode to find out what you might need.

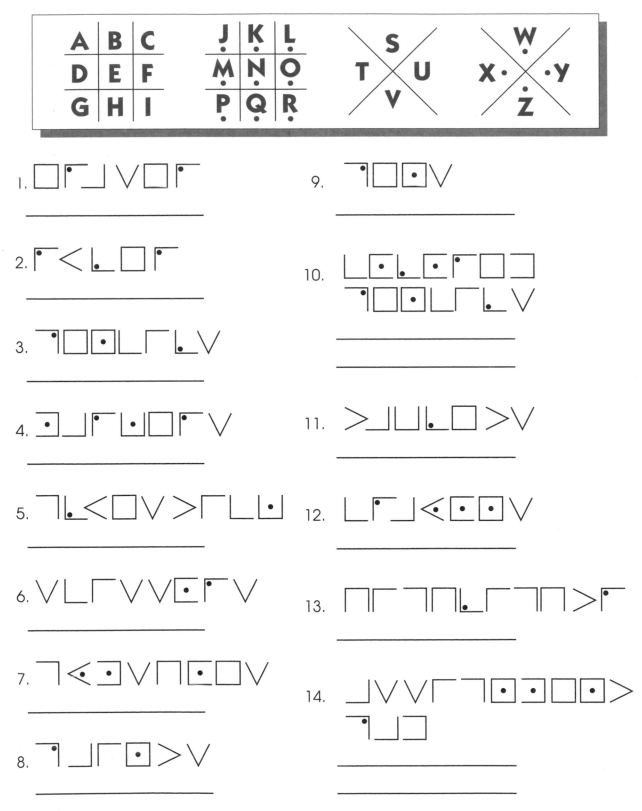